EcoJustice Education

EcoJustice Education offers a powerful model for cultural ecological analysis and a pedagogy of responsibility, providing teachers and teacher educators with the information and classroom practices they need to help develop citizens who are prepared to support and achieve diverse, democratic, and sustainable societies in an increasingly globalized world. Readers are asked to consider curricular strategies to bring these issues to life in their own classrooms across disciplines. Designed for introductory educational foundations and multicultural education courses, the text is written in a narrative, conversational style grounded in place and experience, but also pushes students to examine the larger ideological, social, historical, and political contexts of the crises humans and the planet we inhabit are facing.

Changes in the Second Edition: New chapter on Anthropocentrism; new material on Heterosexism; updated statistics and examples throughout; new and updated Companion Website content.

Rebecca A. Martusewicz is a teacher educator at Eastern Michigan University, where she developed a concentration in EcoJustice Education for the Master's in Social Foundations program.

Jeff Edmundson directs the teacher licensure program at the University of Oregon and teaches courses in EcoJustice at the undergraduate and graduate level.

John Lupinacci is an associate professor of Cultural Studies and Social Thought in Education in the Department of Teaching and Learning at Washington State University.

EcoJustice Education

Toward Diverse, Democratic, and Sustainable Communities

2nd Edition

Rebecca A. Martusewicz,
Jeff Edmundson, and
John Lupinacci

Routledge
Taylor & Francis Group

NEW YORK AND LONDON

Second Edition published 2015
by Routledge
711 Third Avenue, New York, NY 10017

and by Routledge
2 Park Square, Milton Park, Abingdon, Oxon OX14 4RN

First edition published 2011 by Routledge

Routledge is an imprint of the Taylor & Francis Group, an informa business

Library of Congress Cataloging-in-Publication Data
Martusewicz, Rebecca A.
  EcoJustice education : toward diverse, democratic,
  and sustainable communities / by Rebecca A. Martusewicz,
  Jeff Edmundson, and John Lupinacci.—Second edition.
  pages cm.—(Sociocultural, Political, and Historical Studies in Education)
  Includes bibliographical references and index.
  1. Social ecology—Study and teaching. 2. Environmental education.
  3. Environmental ethics. 4. Sustainability.
  5. Education—Social aspects.
  I. Edmundson, Jeff. II. Lupinacci, John. III. Title.
  HM861.M35 2015
  304.2—dc23
  2014010941

ISBN: 978–1–138–01883–9 (hbk)
ISBN: 978–1–138–01884–6 (pbk)
ISBN: 978–1–315–77949–2 (ebk)

Typeset in Sabon
by Swales & Willis Ltd, Exeter, Devon

To our students and their future students.

Contents in Brief

Detailed Contents

Preface

Why This Book?

This book is designed specifically for Social Foundations of Education and Multicultural Education courses in graduate and undergraduate teacher preparation programs. Traditional approaches to diversity and democracy in teacher education are focused on questions and problems within diverse human populations; inequalities related to race and ethnicity, gender, social class, sexuality, and ability are all common points of discussion in typical textbooks in the Social Foundations of Education. Such approaches, while important in their attempts to introduce students to social problems and the related role of education or purposes of schooling, are limited by an anthropocentric understanding that leaves out the wider context of biodiversity in our lives and its intimate connection to linguistic and cultural diversities.

Further, because they grow out of a culture that hyper-separates humans from the natural world, typical approaches to the teaching of diversity and democracy overlook how human diversity and social inequalities are intimately connected to ecological destruction via age-old and deeply-imbedded cultural assumptions and behaviors. Or, at best, such courses often tack on "environmental issues" to the end of their social justice-oriented, race-class-and-gender content, an approach that leaves in place this dualism between human communities and the more-than-human world. In this book, we ask you—prospective and practicing teachers and teacher educators—to think critically and ethically about the relationships that sustain life and the ways of thinking that undermine it. Thus, we approach racism, sexism, socio-economic injustice, poverty, and all other forms of violence as the consequence of the same sorts of ideological systems that lead to all forms of degradation of life. Our commitment to teach about these topics in this way falls directly in line with the necessity to not only understand a complex global context, but also to help respond to the world and our communities as teachers in ethical ways.

We wrote the first edition of this book to address this need in the education of teachers, and especially to respond to the call by many of our Social Foundations colleagues that such a book was needed. And, of course, as soon as it was published and we were using it, we realized what it was missing! The primary addition to this second edition is a new chapter on Learning Anthropocentrism, Chapter 4. This is a foundational chapter for understanding where the other forms of centric thinking get their power. Not that we did not realize that understanding anthropocentrism was important in the first edition; we just didn't take it on as a full chapter! Having a full discussion of anthropocentrism and human supremacy in this chapter helps to explain much more clearly how it is that we see social and ecological crises as intimately linked. Our hope is that it will help transform the way that typical Social Foundations and Multicultural Education courses are organized and taught so that teachers can begin the complicated work of EcoJustice Education in their own classes and communities.

Chapter Overview and Changes in the Second Edition

The Introduction looks at the interrelated ecological and social crises that call us to this work. Chapter 1, The Purposes of Education in an Age of Ecological Crises and Worldwide Insecurities, presents information on worldwide social movements that have been occurring since 2011, when we published the first edition. We address the crises to which these movements respond—especially worldwide economic problems causing poverty—along with an updated look at global climate change and other ecological crises. We discuss the purposes of education within this context as contrasted with what schools have been organized to do historically. Included in this discussion is a definition of EcoJustice Education as well as descriptions of several of the fields that have influenced this body of work.

Chapter 2, Rethinking Diversity and Democracy for Sustainable Communities, presents a critical discussion of what Diversity Education ought to mean when considering our nested, interdependent relationships as humans in larger life systems, and what democratic communities engaged in deep understanding of the importance of these systems to our survival would look like. Defining sustainable communities as those that do not interfere with the ability of natural systems to regenerate themselves, this discussion provides a framework for considering what diverse, democratic, and sustainable communities ought to look like, laying out some specific principles that will guide the rest of the book. Added to this chapter is a brief look at neoliberal policies and examples of corporate reform, as these interfere with democratic decision-making at the local level.

In Chapter 3, Cultural Foundations of the Crisis, we begin to look at the deeply-imbedded cultural assumptions that currently impede our abilities to envision and create the economic and political relationships necessary to just and sustainable communities. We look closely at modern Western cultures' discursive history as a means of introducing the over-arching mindset that is causing so much havoc in the world. As C. A. Bowers teaches, words have a history; the language we use reproduces important patterns of belief and behavior—moral codes that become deeply embedded in our day-to-day interactions. Thus, discourses developed and taken for granted over generations reinforce value hierarchies and patterns of centric thinking, which shape the industrial/consumer culture now sweeping the planet.

With this in mind, four chapters follow that extend this cultural ecological analysis to an examination of the ways centric thinking impacts our society, especially in schools. This examination begins with Chapter 4, Learning Anthropocentrism, where we explore how it is that modern industrial cultures come to view humans as superior to all other species, and what the effects of such a perspective are, both on the more-than-human world and on human communities. We look at the "animal industrial complex" and its influence on the organization of K-12 schools and universities.

The next three chapters look specifically at gender, class, and race inequalities in our society, especially as these play out in schools. Here, Social Foundations instructors will find the connection to the traditional content that they teach, but with an important twist. While they are presented in separate chapters here, we teach about these forms of human marginalization and exploitation as interrelated by the structures of value-hierarchized thought and the associated logic of domination in which they are grounded. We emphasize that these forms of unjust social experience are essentially interconnected and impossible to disconnect from our mistreatment of other life forms because they stem from the same fundamentally violent ways of thinking. Each of these forms has its own specificity that we will lay out carefully, especially in terms of how schooling contributes.

Chapter 5, Learning Androcentrism, examines the history of gendered schooling, placing women's experiences within this broad cultural framework. We trace the development of women's relation to public education and higher education, beginning in the 19th century and moving through changes in the 20th century that were brought about by the feminist movement. In the current context, we examine the psychological consequences of living within a system that defines women, non-hegemonic men, and members of the LGBTQQ community as inferior, focusing on achievement differences, sexuality, and citizenship, especially within the context of public schools. We have added additional information about experiences of LGBTQQ students to this second edition.

Chapter 6, Learning Our Place in the Social Hierarchy, takes this conceptual framework to the topic of class and offers an examination of socio-economic stratification, poverty, schooling, and the discourses that underlie these. After considering the evidence that class exists despite the ideology that says the contrary, we look at how class differences are reproduced in education. Value-hierarchized thinking leads to seeing many students as having deficits, which in turn justifies various forms of unequal education, particularly including the use of testing and the tracking of students. Hierarchy and deficit thinking also help create a culture within schooling that allows for the "pathologizing" of students as problems rather than victims of inequality.

Chapter 7, Learning Racism, takes a deep look at the historical construction of discourses on race and racism. Using an EcoJustice framework, as in Chapters 4, 5, and 6, this chapter introduces the historical construction of discourses on race and racism, especially as it is related to anthropocentrism and other forms of centric thinking. The chapter demonstrates the ways in which science contributed to the construction of race and the discourse of racism to rationalize the exploitation of people of color by white Europeans. After surveying the history of education for several cultures marginalized by racist discourses and policies, we consider how racism is institutionalized today. Along with ongoing direct discrimination, the discourse of race is reproduced and internalized in complex psychological ways. Among these are the taken-for-granted assumptions of white privilege that lead to "racial microaggressions." Racism is carried out in schooling imbedded in deficit explanations of academic achievement, the schoo-to-prison pipeline, and zero tolerance policies.

Chapter 8, Learning About Globalization, pushes the analysis of racism into the current context of globalization and enclosure of the cultural and environmental commons across so-called "undeveloped" or "developing" cultures. The commons are those aspects of the natural world—the land, the air, the water, the diverse species of living plants and animals— as well as the practices, beliefs, traditions, and skills once shared freely without the need for monetary exchange. Examining the development of economic policies since 1945 and the establishment of world markets as a priority of dominant industrialized countries, the chapter offers a series of case studies of the ways globalization is both impacting these cultures and being resisted.

Chapter 9, Learning From Indigenous Communities, returns to the notion of cultural diversity, looking specifically at what we can learn about ecological sustainability from the wisdom of Indigenous Peoples. We introduce our readers to the ways that cultural diversity intersects with both linguistic diversity and biodiversity as traditional Indigenous cultures have developed their languages, their patterns of belief and behavior, including spiritual traditions in close connection to the bio-regions that they have inhabited over time. We argue that it is in these ancient relationships that we find diverse ways of maintaining sustainable ways of living, ways that we would be wise to pay attention to, not in order to become like them, but rather in order to think through the problems we face.

Chapter 10, Teaching for the Commons, extends the earlier discussions of the cultural and environmental commons discussed in Chapters 8 and 9 into an examination of our own commons-based practices as they still get practiced in consumer cultures. While many of us can readily identify the environmental commons, it is increasingly difficult to understand how the cultural commons still play out among us in this hyper-consumer culture that we live in today. And yet, we do share practices and beliefs that are of mutual benefit to us, that do not cost us money, and that we use on a daily basis to survive. The cultural commons is as simple as the exchange of favors—borrowing sugar from a neighbor or trading child-care with a friend—or as complex as the doctrine of habeas corpus, or the other institutions and practices created by our Constitution. This final chapter is dedicated to introducing what it could mean to engage a pedagogy of responsibility that both uncovers the cultural and political processes we examine in this book and teaches how to revitalize the practices most important to living communities. We have updated the examples provided, especially those that look specifically at schools and teachers.

Semester after semester, our students respond to our analyses of the consequences of our hyper-consumer system saying, "Yeah, ok, but is there anywhere in the world where people aren't selfish, addicted consumers? Is there any culture that is really successfully resisting these processes of globalization?" Or, recognizing alternatives in far off places or earlier times, they say, "OK fine, that's cool, but is a change in thinking really possible in our culture? Can we live sustainably, here in the 21st century?" Our response is yes, but not without taking necessary steps: exploring other ways of knowing, and rethinking who we are as members of Western cultures. Drawing on real stories and experiences of both community organizations and of teachers who we know and have worked with, we explore what it means to introduce a cultural and ecological analysis in a variety of disciplines and across age groups. We introduce you to people doing this work in classrooms and communities just like those with which you are familiar.

How to Use This Book

We have included a number of features in this book to help you to understand and use the concepts that we are introducing to you. First, we try to write in a conversational tone, so you may "hear" us interacting with each other and with you in a conversational way that we try to use with our own students. This conversation will intertwine with the concepts that we introduce to you in order to open up "ways of seeing" that come when we apply a conceptual framework to analyze problems in the world. These concepts will be defined within the text as well as in a "Conceptual Toolbox" at the end of each chapter. We encourage you to become familiar with these as thinking tools. In addition, we include a number of pedagogical boxes and figures along the way to draw your attention to questions, statistics, or maybe even a story or two from our own lives that we think will enrich the theoretical explanations in the book. Sometimes, we even ask you to do some thinking, jot down some notes, and then, a bit further on, we come back and ask you what you were thinking about before we move on with the discussion. We hope that you'll take advantage of our invitations to think about those questions as we go. As with any pedagogical interaction, these questions are meant to spark your interpretive faculties, and engage you in the knowledge production process that is learning.

With the exception of Chapter 1, each chapter also includes a section called "What Schools and Teachers Can Do." Here we highlight specific activities and methods used by teachers in schools and communities across the country to help you, in your own practice, to begin to address the questions and issues we introduce in that chapter with your own students. We offer brief suggestions for age-appropriate activities and lessons across a broad range of disciplines in order to show you that it's possible to introduce EcoJustice to students of all ages.

These are not meant to be comprehensive, but rather exemplary. We realize that each of you works in very specific local contexts, and these contexts need to be taken into account as you figure out how to address the particular problems your community experiences. EcoJustice concepts and questions will help you to link those contexts to larger cultural and ecological analyses.

Finally, we offer suggestions for additional reading and other resources, especially those we share with our pre-service and practicing teachers. These suggestions have also been updated for this edition. We invite you to dig deeper into the ideas we lay out here using the authors we suggest. We also want students to become aware of who else is doing the sorts of work that we are calling for. Thus, the organizations and links that we suggest offer connections to the larger world of activism and education. We hope you'll find those sources useful as you orient yourself to an EcoJustice perspective. A companion website is also under development. The site includes guiding questions for students and a separate set for course instructors as well.

This is a book that works hard to demonstrate the urgency of changing how we think and why we need to teach others to change how they think.

Across the planet, living species—including humans—are facing a critical survival imperative. Solutions to these problems and our own survival hinge on a commitment from people—especially those of us in hyper-consuming Western industrial cultures—to rethink their lives and lifestyles and reconnect with living systems in response to the vast suffering limiting life on the planet. Whether focused on cultural life in the homogenous suburbs of energy-consuming communities in North America, in urban settings of economic abandonment, in rural communities where once thriving family farms are now turned to huge mono-crop factory farms, even in the "progressive" communities of college towns and "cool" cities, the effects of top-down decision-making and deep infatuations with accumulated material goods has infected the fabric of living relationships. It seems clear that epidemic symptoms of violent relationships are overtaking systems of local decision-making and viable alternatives to violence. It is impacting all of us, rich and poor, whether we're prepared to look at it or not. We want to prepare you to look at it, and to teach others to address these critical issues.

It is our hope that readers of this book, people from all sorts of educational backgrounds, will explore and even learn how to engage truly hopeful alternatives to the violent systems we are experiencing. We see this work as a primary responsibility of everyone, but particularly of teachers who can help others learn how to do it. Across the planet, responsible citizens in diverse cultures and bioregions actively and peacefully make decisions on a daily basis to support local efforts that strengthen life in their communities and resist the violence of "modern" industrial culture. So, along with some fairly difficult confrontations of how people mistreat each other and others in our living systems, we offer examples of uplifting stories—not as a romanticized love-fest with the environment—but with the intention of demonstrating holistic, just, and sustainable approaches to learning and teaching about how to live in our communities through strong relational experiences that include our interdependency with the natural world. So, turn the page! We invite you into this conversation as we explore what it means to teach for EcoJustice.

Acknowledgments

As we look back on the three years since the first edition of this book was published, we want to thank all those colleagues and students who have written to let us know that teaching and reading the book has been a useful endeavor. Knowing that these ideas and pedagogical practices are getting out to prospective and practicing teachers and others interested in the cultural roots of ecological and social crises means the world to us.

We have also been blessed by a strong community of students, colleagues, and friends in our own universities and across the country whose commitment to this work has helped to nurture us through the completion of this revision. Our colleague and friend P.K. Smith at Eastern Michigan University used the book with her undergraduate classes, a decision that helped her totally revise how she approached the Social Foundations course required of all teacher certification students. P.K. talked enthusiastically with Johnny and Rebecca about how the chapters worked and was very supportive of its revision.

We also thank Ethan Lowenstein, Linda Williams, Becca Nielsen, and Nancy Copeland of the Southeast Michigan Stewardship Coalition who have shared this book widely with the teachers and community partners in that organization. To Ethan, especially, we extend our thanks as we develop this framework and think about what a pedagogy of responsibility means for teachers struggling in our current context. Scott Morrison (now an Assistant Professor at Elon University) used the first edition as the basis of his dissertation research at the University of North Carolina at Chapel Hill, and has also contributed much to the conversation about how EcoJustice can and should be used with practicing educators.

Steven Mackie, of Northwest Oklahoma State University, wrote an early review in the *Midwestern Educational Researcher* (2011) and has been a strong supporter of the ideas in myriad ways, not to mention a close friend. Stephanie Daza and Jeong-eun Rhee (2013) also wrote a strong review for *Educational Studies*, which has helped tremendously in thinking about what this second edition needed. We are also grateful to the American Educational Studies Association for awarding this book the 2011 Critics' Choice Award. It is a great honor to be included in that group of outstanding educational researchers.

Other insights were offered by Audrey Dentith, Lesley University; Paul J. Ramsey, Eastern Michigan University; Teresa Shume, Minnesota State University Moorhead; Lucille Eckrich, Illinois State University; and Chloe Wilson, Eastern Michigan University. We are grateful for the close read these colleagues made of the book, and the time that they took to make suggestions for the second edition.

Gary Schnakenberg continues to be a major contributor to this book, not only in the chapter that he co-authored, but in his daily engagement in the primary ideas, his participation in many of our Skype conversations, and, most importantly to Rebecca, his continuing love and support of her in ways too rich to address here. There could be no better partner or friend. Rebecca also thanks Sweet Pea and Olive for their bombastic enthusiasm and insistence that she get away from her desk and go play ball with them!

For Jeff, Jerry Rosiek has been an essential intellectual mentor and colleague; his influence runs through this book in subtle ways. Ari Edmundson challenges Jeff to think precisely, never allowing him to get away with an inadequately thought-through idea. Eddy Shuldman has offered love and constant patience for the time away from family that the writing of this book has demanded.

For Johnny, the students and teachers mentioned throughout the book, especially those in the Southeast Michigan Stewardship Coalition, have been a great source of hope and inspiration. He would like to acknowledge all the students and colleagues at Washington State University, especially his new mentor and friend Pamela Bettis, who have all welcomed him into their scholarly community and support his teaching and researching from an EcoJustice perspective. He thanks his parents for providing a lifetime of love and support, as well as Brandon Skupski and Lizzy Haverkate who offered extensive patience and support through many conversations that contributed to his thoughts and commitments. Thanks to Lizzy, especially, for always reminding him where his heart is. A special acknowledgment goes to the city of Detroit and to the Great Lakes' diverse ecology for teaching him so much while writing this book, especially Lake Superior.

For all of us, Chet Bowers continues to hold a place of honor and respect as he continues to write and contribute powerfully to the field. This book would never have come into being without the mentorship that he offered us. Finally, we could not have done this work without the enduring critical feedback and friendship of Naomi Silverman and Joel Spring. Their enthusiastic support and patience has been a gift.

Chapter I

Introduction

The Purposes of Education in an Age of Ecological Crises and Worldwide Insecurities

Introduction

Each of us has had our "aha" moment when we realized the urgency of the ecological and social crises the planet faces. For Jeff, it was when he realized that our culture was about to burn up in a few hundred years the non-renewable fossil fuels that took millions of years to create—yet we were acting like they would never run out. For Rebecca, it was finally stopping her apologies for the enormous pain she experiences in the face of animal suffering, as she recognized that our culture relies on that shaming to keep a certain system of thinking in place. For Johnny, it was learning that difference is at the heart of all life, not just human life, so all kinds of exclusion will be violent. We have to do something about the unnecessary violence on the planet and it ought not be through violence to either humans or to non-humans. All three of us, as teacher educators, believe whole heartedly in the power of teachers and their collective potential to educate in ways that not only respond to the current conditions on the planet but also reclaim what it means to belong to each other, the land, the oceans, and to the multitude of living species with whom we share the planet.

The beginning of the 21st century has been an era in which many thousands of people have found themselves having to face survival as a species on Earth. While there is growing evidence that the ways in which industrialized consumer cultures currently live is not sustainable for human life on the planet, there is also the uplifting fact that more and more of the world's people are taking a stand to resist the spread of such unsustainable habits of living. We are without question entering the second decade of the 21st century immersed in diverse and interrelated social and political movements that say "no" to regimes of economic power and "yes" to each other and to sustainable and socially just ways of living. For example, in 2011 millions of people stood in solidarity against violent governments in North Africa and the Middle East; around the globe protests against similar tyrannical regimes spurred and inspired responses to unjust suffering. Furthermore, some of these regimes fell and continue to fall. The loud cries of "enough" were also heard right outside Wall Street. Occupy Wall Street, although staged in New York's Zuccotti Park, quickly spread to cities all over the United States, Canada, Europe, South America, and beyond. In local communities around the world, people are organizing to boycott genetically modified food and working to reclaim healthy, culturally relevant food systems. Students are standing up to a massive student loan debt burden, protesting and, in many cases, resisting the introduction of a federal student loan program in countries where post-secondary education does not yet require such heavy loans. Teachers are struggling too, being pushed to accept lower wages as unions are undermined by privatization efforts, but also resisting the corporate takeover of public schools. They join countless pockets of resistance framed in compassion and a belief that future generations can and will live sustainably and in peace here on Earth.

In this chapter and throughout this book we will take a look at how certain conditions of social suffering and environmental degradation came to be unquestioned aspects of everyday life. Additionally, we will look at how this is, without a doubt, one of the most exciting, inspiring, and difficult times to be a teacher. All over the globe, people are taking a stand in many capacities from simply changing their diets and daily routines to gathering in the streets and declaring that they have had enough. What comes next? Well, we believe what comes next in our communities hinges on what we as teachers commit to learning and teaching in our classrooms.

The Challenges We Face

As Al Gore's widely recognized and award-winning film *An Inconvenient Truth* (Guggenheim, 2006) so clearly demonstrates, there is now incontrovertible scientific evidence that our planet is experiencing changes in climate that are human-made and have serious effects on ecosystems and human communities across the planet. While there has been controversy over the last 20 years around whether such warming trends are in fact created by human activity, even politicians and corporate leaders who once dismissed Gore's warnings now agree with the overwhelming evidence presented by scientists across the world. The Intergovernmental Panel on Climate Change (IPCC) reports: "Human influence on the climate system is clear. This is evident from the increasing greenhouse gas concentrations in the atmosphere, positive radiative forcing, observed warming, and understanding of the climate system" (IPCC, 2013, p. 15).

Representing a wide range of institutions, scientists agree that increasing levels of CO_2, linked directly to dependence on fossil fuels as the primary energy source for industrializing economies, are causing massive melting of the polar icecaps and shifts in ocean currents leading to weather patterns wreaking havoc worldwide. Additionally, acidification of the world's oceans, also caused by the introduction of CO_2 via acid rain, now critically threatens the most basic levels of the world's food chain. It is now well established that 350 parts per million CO_2 is the maximum level allowable in the atmosphere without significant environmental damage. "To preserve our planet, scientists tell us we must reduce the amount of CO_2 in the atmosphere from its current levels of 400 parts per million to below 350 ppm. But 350 is more than a number—it's a symbol of where we need to head as a planet" (retrieved on November 8, 2013 from www.350.org). We are currently at approximately 400 parts per million and scientists estimate that CO_2 emissions have increased approximately 2% from the reported 2012 emissions levels, and since 1990 have increased nearly 61% (Le Quéré et al., 2013).

What Does Global Climate Change Look Like?

- Average temperatures have climbed 1.4 degrees Fahrenheit (0.8 degrees Celsius) around the world since 1880, much of this in recent decades.

- The 20th century's last two decades were the hottest in 400 years and possibly the warmest for several millennia, according to a number of climate studies. 11 of the past 12 years are among the dozen warmest since 1850.

- The Arctic is feeling the effects the most. Average temperatures in Alaska, western Canada, and eastern Russia have risen at twice the global average.

- Arctic ice is rapidly disappearing, and the region may have its first completely ice-free summer by 2040 or earlier. Polar bears and Indigenous cultures are already suffering from the sea-ice loss.

- Glaciers and mountain snows are rapidly melting—for example, Montana's Glacier National Park now has only 27 glaciers, versus 150 in 1910. In the northern hemisphere, thaws also come a week earlier in spring and freezes begin a week later.

- Coral reefs, which are highly sensitive to small changes in water temperature, suffered the worst bleaching—or die-off in response to stress—ever recorded in 1998, with some areas seeing bleach rates of 70%. Experts expect these sorts of events to increase in frequency and intensity in the next 50 years as sea temperatures rise.

(Global Warming Fast Facts National Geographic News. Updated June 14, 2007 http://news.nationalgeographic.com/ news/2004/12/1206_041206_global_warming.html)

For the most up-to-date information about global climate change and the effects of increasing CO_2 in our atmosphere go to CO_2 Now: http://co2now.org.

Tracing the origin of this increased CO_2, we are brought face to face with historical patterns of activity that clearly indicate just how inter-twined human communities are with the broader living systems on the planet. We see, for example, how the invention of the coal powered steam engine in 1712 irreversibly changed our approach to and understand-ing of energy, revolutionizing our economic and social system by speed-ing up production and, in turn, increasing both consumption and waste. The ability to quickly and efficiently extract coal and eventually oil and natural gas from the earth using a coal powered steam engine shifted our energy systems from the slower, more renewable forms based on solar produced inputs (grass-fed animal power, or animal and vegetable-fed human power, for example) to non-renewable but highly efficient fossil fuels. As Bill McKibben points out, this shift

> allowed for everything we consider normal and obvious about the modern world, from making fertilizer to making steel to making elec-tricity. These in turn fed all the subsidiary revolutions in transporta-tion and chemistry and communications, right down to the electron-based information age we now inhabit. Suddenly, 100% growth in the standard of living could be accomplished in a few decades, not in a few millennia.
>
> (McKibben, 2007, p. 6)

While global climate change continues to be on our radar screens as the primary challenge facing us in the 21st century, the use of fossil-fuel-based energy and the economic system it encouraged has actually had enormous impacts on all aspects of the life systems that we depend upon for survival—from soil to water, to air, to plant and animal species (see Figure 1.1).

As the 2010 British Petroleum oil-well disaster in the Gulf of Mexico clearly demonstrates, our addiction to fossil-fuel-based technologies has so much power that we are willing to destroy entire ecosystems, and the economic well-being of many human communities in order to take it out of the earth. And, what we are learning from ecologically aware cultural theorists is that these changes were made possible over time by important shifts in thinking that put individual gain above communities, human needs or wants above non-human, "progress" and growth above simple happiness and well-being.

Throughout the 20th century, "efficiency" was the clarion call revolu-tionizing nearly every aspect of social and economic life by promising a better life for all. Without necessarily understanding what it would mean for the life systems that we depend upon, modern societies, first in Europe and then in North America, spurred on by the discovery of how to use the Earth's resources to speed up production and therefore increase profits for the "captains of industry," developed industrialized economies and

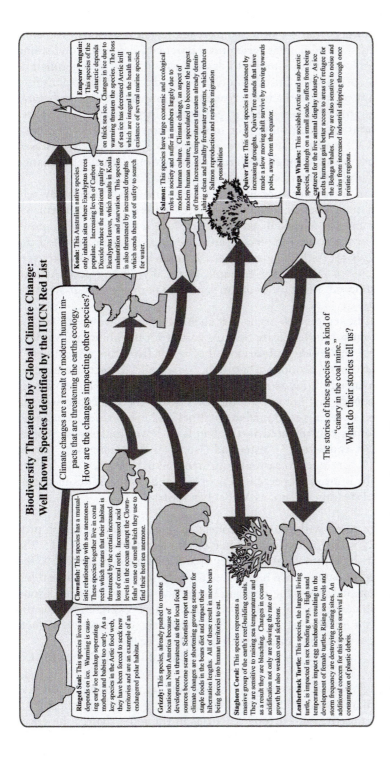

Biodiversity Threatened by Global Climate Change:
Well Known Species Identified by the IUCN Red List

Climate changes are a result of modern human impacts that are threatening the earths ecology.
How are the changes impacting other species?

Ringed Seal: This species lives and depends on ice. Warming is causing early ice breakup seperating mothers and babies too early. As a key species in the Artic food web, they have been forced to seek new territories and are an example of an endangered polar habitat.

Clownfish: This species has a mutualistic relationship with sea anemones. These species together live in coral reefs which means that their habitat is threatened by the certain increased loss of coral reefs. Increased acid levels in the ocean disrupt the Clownfishs' sense of smell which they use to find their host sea anemone.

Grizzy: This species, already pushed to remote locations in North America because of development, is threatened as their local food sources become scarce. Scientists report that climate changes are shortening growing seasons for staple foods in the bears diet and impact their hibernation lengths. All of these result in more bears being forced into human territories to eat.

Staghorn Coral: This species represents a massive group of the earth's reef-building corals. They are sensitive to raising sea temperatures and as a result they are bleaching. Changes in ocean acidification not only are slowing the rate of growth but also weaken coral skeletons.

Leatherback Turtle: This species, the largest living turtle, is impacted in sex bending ways. High sand temperatures impact egg incubation resulting in the development of female turtles. Rising sea levels and storm frequency are destroying nesting sites. An additional concern for this species survival is consumption of plastic debris.

Koala: This Australian native species only inhabit sites where Eucalyptus trees populate. Increasing levels of Carbon Dioxide reduce the nutritional quality of Eucalyptus leaves, which results in Koala malnutrition and starvation. This species is also threatened by increased droughts which sends them out of safety to search for water.

Emperor Penguin: This species of the Antarctic depends on thick sea ice. Changes in ice due to warming threaten the species. The loss of sea ice has decreased Arctic krill which are integral in the health and existence of several marine species.

Salmon: This species have large economic and ecological roles in society and suffer in numbers largely due to modern human culture. Climate change, an aspect of modern human culture, is speculated to become the largest of threats. Increased temperatures threaten already deminishing clean and healthy freshwater systems, which reduces Salmon reproduction and restricts migration possibilities

Quiver Tree: This desert species is threatened by increasing droughts. Quiver Tree stands that have made a slow moving shift survive by moving towards poles, away from the equator.

Beluga Whales: This sociable Arctic and sub-arctic species, although on a small scale, suffers from being captured for the live animal display industry. As ice melts humans gain better access to areas of refuge for the Beluga whales. They are also sensitive to noise and toxins from increased industrial shipping through once pristine regions.

The stories of these species are a kind of "canary in the coal mine." What do their stories tell us?

Figure 1.1 Biodiversity Threatened by Global Climate Change.

Source: IUCN. (2009). *Red list:S pecies and climate change: More than just the polar bear.* Gland, Switzerland: IUCN. (2009). IUCN. (2009). Dell'Amore, C. (2009). Ten climate change 'flagship' species named. *National Geographic News.*

consumer cultures that we now see have led to many serious problems: soil loss caused by damaging agricultural practices, deforestation leading to watershed loss and eventually to desertification, the endangerment of drinking water from the introduction of pesticides and other toxins into the environment, the extinction of plant and animal life due to habitat loss, and the loss of fisheries due to pollution of the oceans and careless modes of industrialized fishing. The Intergovernmental Panel on Climate Change (IPCC) reports that "on average 20% to 30% of species assessed are likely to be at increasingly high risk of extinction from climate change impacts possibly within this century" (IPCC, 2007, p. 242).

In addition to temperature increases, CO_2 and other toxins severely degrade air quality, especially in the poorer areas of urban settlements where economically marginalized people are forced to live near coal powered plants or toxin-belching incinerators, or huge trucking plazas of the shipping industry. Asthma rates are nearly three times the national average in the city of Detroit, for example, especially among poor African American children. Most other urban centers experience similar air quality problems.

We might be tempted to argue that such damage is "worth it" for the increased comfort and security that we gain from the ability to produce and purchase the goods and services that result from this system—isn't that the reason for economic "growth," after all? In fact, though we may be convinced of this as a reason to continue on as we have, there is growing evidence that human communities across the planet are actually experiencing widening economic inequalities and insecurities as material wealth becomes consolidated in the hands of fewer and fewer people. While "bigger and better," "faster and faster," and the mantra of "more, more, more" continues to saturate our lives, actual incomes and buying power for the bottom 90 percent of people in the United States has actually declined steadily. Again, as McKibben writes:

> Even for those with four-year college degrees, and even though productivity was growing faster than it has for decades, earning fell 5.2% between 2000 and 2004 when adjusted for inflation according to the most recent data from White House economists. Much the same thing has happened across the globe; in Latin America, for instance, despite a slavish devotion to growth economics, real per capita income is the same as a quarter century ago. More than eighty countries, in fact, have seen per capita incomes fall in the last decade.
> (McKibben, 2007, pp. 11–12)

Reports of global climate change, it turns out, are just the tip of the iceberg. Communities around the world are suffering, and while the fate of polar bears may be our current "canaries in the mine shaft," the crises that we face are much closer than those distant polar ice caps may indicate at first glance.

While many of the changes introduced by modern industrial societies have greatly improved the level of comfort in those societies, bringing us medicines and communication or transportation technologies, for example, many other changes have increased our relative *insecurity*. As we in the West take for granted our daily trips to Wal-Mart and Costco, filling ever-larger shopping carts with giant cans of baked beans, frozen pre-cooked jumbo shrimp, paper towels, and other bargains and consumer comforts, people around the world have been impoverished by an increasing interference with their ability to provide the food and water needed for survival. Many of these cultures have only been part of the world economy for a short time, prior to which many were self-sufficient, living on land now controlled by transnational corporations. While not "wealthy" by Western standards of material or political status, they were able to feed and shelter their families without external interference. According to the 2005 Human Development Report, a charter of the United Nations, "The richest 20% of the population hold three-quarters of world income . . . the poorest 40% hold 5% of the world's income and the poorest 20% hold just 1.5%. The poorest 40% roughly corresponds to the 2 billion people living on less than $2 a day" (United Nations, 2005, p. 36; see Figure 1.2).

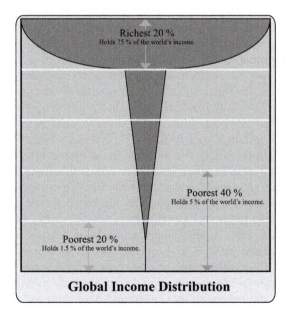

Figure 1.2 Global Income Distribution.

Source: UNDP (2005). *The state of human development.* New York, NY: United Nations.

To put such inequality into perspective, the 2013 Credit Suisse Global Wealth Report explains that "two-thirds of adults in the world have wealth below USD 10,000 and together account for merely 3% of global wealth, while the 32 million dollar millionaires own 41% of all assets" (Shorrocks & Davies, 2013, p. 20). Some would argue that the hunger and suffering that results from this critical gap is due to lack of economic development in those countries suffering most, and that if they'd just get on the world market bandwagon we could solve the world hunger problem.

But, even as more countries are brought under the auspices of global institutions such as the World Bank (see Chapter 8), the numbers of people joining slum communities in all urban areas is increasing, and more and more land needed to feed people is becoming unfit for cultivation. Globalized agribusiness, still touted as the most efficient way to feed the world, puts hundreds of acres of once fertile land under cultivation for the production of mono-crops grown for export. Such practice requires increasing amounts of chemical fertilizers and pesticides to be viable, and the use of huge machinery that wears out the soil that once produced the food and fed the animals that families depended upon for basic survival. Now those same families work producing commodity crops they cannot eat for wages that may not buy enough to feed themselves or their children. As economist Martin Khor (2009) and others are making increasingly clear, world hunger and poverty, including what has already occurred in the so-called "developed" world, is a result of the environmental degradation being caused by exploitation of natural systems and human life by an affluent minority. Hunger is not a result of ignorance or "underdevelopment"; it is a result of exploitation.

But it's not just the environment and economy that are declining. The same forces that create unsustainable agricultural practices and enlarge the wealth gap also undermine the glue that holds people and their communities together. Skyrocketing rates of divorce, child neglect, and mental illness bear witness to a society that can't maintain basic functions. Further, as Robert Putnam (2000) has shown most extensively, many forms of "social capital," from bowling leagues to political activity to even voting, have declined in the face of relentless individualism and privatization.

At the same time, and perhaps most importantly, the ability of still-existing local communities to make decisions about the issues that most impact the well-being of their members is being eroded by global economic interests and policies that increasingly seek to privatize what was once shared by all. For example, the takeover of local water supplies in the name of "efficiency" by transnational corporations such as Bechtel and Coca-Cola, or the patenting by Cargill and Monsanto of seeds that once served as the basis of many cultures' food supply, are severely undermining what Vandana Shiva (2005) calls "Earth Democracies" (see Chapter 2)—the decision-making power of local communities to protect the basic foundations of life, and the future of their children and ecosystems. Pressures to "modernize" the so-called less-developed world are leading to the loss of cultural, linguistic, and biological diversity linking ecological and social crisis to an increasing drive to industrialize the world. While globalizing economic interests gain more and more power to shape the fabric and fate of the planet's human and more-than-human lives, the world's "social majorities" experience ecological, economic, and political insecurities as never before (Shiva, 2005; Esteva & Prakash, 1998; Sachs, 1992).

Food Matters, 26 Countries with Bans on GMOs

Genetically modified organisms (GMOs) are plants or animals created through gene splicing techniques in the field of biotechnology also often referred to as genetic engineering. The Non-GMO Project, a non-profit 501(c)3 organization dedicates its work to third party verification of non-GMO food and products. According to its reports, there have been genetically modified potatoes, tomatoes, salmon, and pigs. They provide some scary facts about food ingredients in commercial production, reporting that 90% of the U.S. crop of canola is GMO and, in 2011, 88% of the corn crop, 90% of cotton, and 94% of the soy.

People around the world are saying no to GMOs and pushing their governments to do the same (this will come up again in Chapter 8). Walden Bello (2013), from The Nation, reports that in response to research showing the possible adverse effects of GMOs and to the dissent of health conscious consumers, several governments have declared "total or partial bans on their cultivation, importation, and field-testing" (para. 5). Bello (2013) reports: "A few years ago, there were sixteen countries that had total or partial bans on GMOs. Now there are at least twenty-six, including Switzerland, Australia, Austria, China, India, France, Germany, Hungary, Luxembourg, Greece, Bulgaria, Poland, Italy, Mexico and Russia. Significant restrictions on GMOs exist in about sixty other countries" (retrieved on December 5, 2013 from http://www.thenation.com/blog/176863/twenty-six-countries-ban-gmos-why-wont-us#).

So, while just a few years back this seemed like an impossible task, the past few years has seen great strides taken toward healthier and more sustainable food production. In the end this is about providing the safest and healthiest possible options for people. The question remains: So why isn't there a ban on GMOs everywhere? Why are we even battling for legislation in the U.S. to enforce labeling of food products?

Ah, but surely this is no way to start a textbook for teachers! It's so depressing! And isn't our work all about working with kids? What could increased CO_2 levels in our environment or unequal income distribution levels possibly have to do with schools in this country? And why should teachers, or students preparing to become teachers, care about these problems that seem to have little to do with life in the United States? It is our hope that by the end of this book, what begins here as depressing news about seemingly far-off problems will become matters that inspire a vision for responsible teaching toward healthy and viable communities for the 21st century.

The simplest answer is that nothing can be more important to teach about than the future of the planet and the lives that support it. Further, to recognize that we have a fundamentally unsustainable culture is to say that we have an obligation to try to change it. More deeply, we are calling for a rethinking of what it means to be educated: Rather than being educated to reproduce a culture that we know is doomed to failure, we must begin to educate ourselves and our students about what it means to live differently on the Earth.

Many teachers have learned that schools often reproduce the inequalities of race, class, and gender, and this book will offer some challenging insights into those issues. But this book will also help teachers understand how schools reproduce unsustainable ways of living, what that has to do with social inequalities like racism or sexism, and how to challenge those practices, policies, and the attending belief systems that keep them in place.

A Cultural Ecological Analysis

We begin from the basic idea that the purpose of public schools ought to be to help develop citizens who are prepared to support and achieve diverse, democratic, and sustainable societies because these are keys to our very survival. Further, these principles support ways of living with each other that are the most fair to all living beings. That means that we must help to prepare students at all levels to think critically and carefully—that is to say, *ethically*—about the patterns of belief and behavior in our culture that have led to destructive relationships and practices that have harmed the natural world, as well as human communities.

Thus, a primary premise guiding this book is that the ecological crisis is really a cultural crisis—that is, a crisis in the way people have learned to think and thus behave in relation to larger life systems and toward each other. It can be shifted if we learn to think differently about our relationships to each other and to the natural world, and if we help students to identify and revalue those critical practices of mutual support and interdependence that still exist in communities all over the world. You may be familiar with a popular image, often titled "Ego vs. Eco," that compares a human centered worldview to an ecological worldview. This image, which has made its way around through blogs, brochures, t-shirts, and posters, advocates for a paradigm shift and does a great job illustrating two fundamentally different worldviews. More specifically, in this book we will be examining how a human centered worldview undermines social justice and sustainability. We will advocate and suggest steps and strategies for educators to take an active role in recognizing that diverse ecological worldviews exist and that they play an important role in fostering such shift among students. Adapting the Internet meme "Ego vs. Eco," Figure 1.3 illustrates two such views.

Figure 1.3 Differing Worldviews.

Source: Adapted from the "Ego vs. Eco" figure credited on the internet to the creative commons, but can be traced to the Eco-Vision Sustainable Learning Center Non-Profit Organization in Delavan, Wisconsin, and to the organization Generation Alpha who use the original figure to accompany their tag line "Dismantle the EGOsystem. Embrace the ECOsytem."

We offer a model for what we call a cultural ecological analysis so that teachers and their students might begin to really examine *the cultural roots of the ecological crisis*. We argue that learning to recognize the ways of thinking and behaving that have a negative impact on our communities is part of developing "eco-ethical consciousness," a way of thinking and acting necessary to creating and protecting just and sustainable communities (Martusewicz & Edmundson, 2005).

EcoJustice Education

Teaching for EcoJustice is based on the recognition that "to be human is to live engaged in a vast and complex system of life, and human well-being depends on learning how to protect it" (Martusewicz & Edmundson, 2005, p. 71). As Wendell Berry (1995) wrote:

> In taking care of fellow creatures, we acknowledge that they belong to an order and a harmony of which we ourselves are parts. To answer to the perpetual crisis of our presence in this abounding and dangerous world, we have only the perpetual obligation to care.
> (Berry, 1995, p. 77)

Drawing on the work of C. A. Bowers (1997, 2001b) in particular, we offer the following six interrelated elements to define EcoJustice:

1. The recognition and analysis of the deep cultural assumptions underlying modern thinking that undermine local and global ecosystems essential to life.
2. The recognition and analysis of deeply entrenched patterns of domination that unjustly define people of color, women, the poor, and other groups of humans as well as the natural world as inferior and thus less worthy of life.
3. An analysis of the globalization of modernist thinking and the associated patterns of hyper-consumption and commodification that have led to the exploitation of the southern hemisphere by the north for natural and human resources.
4. The recognition and protection of diverse cultural and environmental commons—the necessary interdependent relationship of humans with the land, air, water, and other species with whom we share this planet, and the intergenerational practices and relationships among diverse groups of people that do not require the exchange of money as the primary motivation and generally result in mutual aid and support.
5. An emphasis on strong Earth democracies: the idea that decisions should be made by the people who are most affected by them, that

these decisions must include consideration of the right of the natural world to regenerate, and the well-being of future generations.

6. An approach to pedagogy and curriculum development that emphasizes both deep cultural analysis and community-based learning that encourages students to identify the causes, and remediate the effects, of social and ecological violence in the places in which they live.

Thus, the approach in this book differs sharply from what is usually called "environmental education," which, we believe, only touches the surface of the problems we face because it does not examine the ways our cultural behaviors and beliefs structure our taken-for-granted assumptions about our place in the world. While monitoring streams, studying forests, or monitoring habitat loss are certainly positive topics with which to engage students, they are little more than band-aids unless they are accompanied by an examination of the cultural mindsets creating pollution, deforestation, or species extinction. This approach also refuses the dichotomy between social justice and environmental concerns, arguing instead that they must be understood as grounded in the same cultural history. To look at the cultural roots of the ecological crisis is to ultimately argue that a fundamental cultural change needs to occur if we are to seriously challenge the various crises we face.

Other Related Approaches

We acknowledge a debt to other educational scholars for their groundbreaking work in bringing environmental questions into school and university curricula, including those working in environmental education; outdoor/experiential education; place-based education; education for sustainability; holistic education; ecoliteracy; environmental justice, critical animal studies, and ecopedagogy.

Environmental Education

Most ecologically-oriented education in the U.S., Europe, and Australia is in the category of "environmental education." The basic premises of environmental education include giving students basic knowledge of ecological systems, encouraging appreciation of the outdoors, and teaching awareness of ecological issues. These are all aspects of the work that we support. However, one of the problems in this approach is with the way that ecology is defined, for the most part, as the scientific study and management of natural systems assumed to be outside of human communities. Intersections among human social problems and ecological problems are generally ignored in the curriculum.

One branch of environmental education tends to come from the standpoint of the natural sciences, and so encourages students to understand how ecosystems function as interdependent systems. This approach has, for example, led to use of the metaphor of seeing an ecosystem as an interconnected "web of life," in which all the components are affected by a change to any part of the web: an important concept. However, the natural sciences approach has its limits. According to Fien (1995)

> Much of the dominant discourse in environmental education . . . has been based upon a technocentric approach to environmentalism which favors initiating young people into the concepts and skills needed for finding scientific and technological solutions to environmental problems without addressing their root social, political and economic causes.
>
> (Fien, 1995, p. 10)

When environmental education considers humans, it also tends to focus on the individual. This is demonstrated in the popular concept of "ecological footprint," whereby a person can estimate his or her individual impact on the environment (see, for example, www.myfootprint.org). With the recent attention on global warming, this concept has been extended into looking specifically at the individual "carbon footprint." While the footprint concept is indeed a helpful consciousness-raising tool, it looks only at individual behavior, rather than examining societal systems and the cultures that underlie them, and thus is rather limited.

Further, according to Sobel, "in recent years, environmental education [has] evolved into issues and catastrophe education—learning about rainforest destruction, ozone depletion, toxic waste and endangered species" (2004, pp. 8–9). While we cannot ignore the oncoming ecological disasters, neither can educators rely on "doom and gloom" approaches. For one, catastrophe education tends to create despair and apathy among students. More importantly, there's little evidence that it actually motivates anyone to change their thinking or behavior. Students also need to get outside, learn to see and hear and feel the beauty of the natural world, fall in love with forests, streams, and fields.

Experiential/Outdoor Education

One branch of environmental education emphasizes student experience in the outdoors as a path towards becoming more environmentally aware. People in this field try to encourage positive feelings towards the outdoors and tend to emphasize the value of learning by doing and the importance of learning specifics about how ecosystems work.

Many states have organized outdoor education programs for students. For example, in many areas of Oregon all sixth-graders spend up to a

week at an outdoor camp learning science concepts and nature appreciation. The science learning is integrated into the science curriculum for the
year. In Michigan, a state-wide movement called No Child Left Inside
seeks to support federal legislation being prepared that would require
schools to provide opportunities for students to go outside and engage
in learning that introduces them to meadows, forests, and streams. The
idea is that the joy of learning about living creatures and plant life will
also teach us a lot about ourselves and especially about the relationships
needed to live more sustainably (Louv, 2006).

Place-Based Education

Place-based education, on the other hand, is seen as both broader and
more specific. It is broader in that it looks at both natural and human
communities and their interaction with one another. It is more specific
because it involves students and community members in explorations and
projects in specific places in the local environment.

One definition of place-based education is "the process of using the
local community and environment as a starting point to teach concepts"
in many subjects across the curriculum (Sobel, 2004, p. 7). Students in
place-based education have, for example, both studied and helped rede-
sign a local river park, or done oral histories with long-time residents who
are farmers and artisans. According to Gruenewald and Smith (2008),

> place-based education can be understood as a community-based effort
> to reconnect the process of education, enculturation, and human
> development to the well-being of community life. Placed-based . . .
> education introduces children and youth to the skills and dispositions
> needed to regenerate and sustain communities.
> (Gruenewald & Smith, 2008, p. xvi)

This is an approach that attempts to make learning more relevant to students by getting them involved in their own communities, partnering with
other adults and organizations that care deeply about identifying and
solving real problems. When paired with the model of EcoJustice Education offered in this book, place-based education becomes a powerful
educational tool.

Education for Sustainability

Another commonly used approach is "education for sustainability." Keep
in mind that the word "sustainability" is used to mean many different
things. Colleges and businesses use it to refer to creating buildings that are
energy-efficient, or the development of more efficient recycling programs.

Businesses and some economists use the term "sustainable development" to mean the ability to grow (and thus consume more of the planet) in a manner that can be sustained indefinitely. Even "education for sustainability" is constrained, because, as Sterling (2001) points out:

> any "education for *something*", however worthy, such as for "the environment", or "citizenship", tends to become both accommodated and marginalized by the mainstream. So, while "education for sustainable development" has in recent years won a small niche [primarily in the UK], the overall educational paradigm otherwise remains unchanged.
>
> (Sterling, 2001, p. 14)

On the other hand, some use the concept of sustainability to mean a transformation to put environmental concerns at the center of a critical, participatory education. Sterling sees "sustainable education" as education that challenges the entire existing educational paradigm.

Holistic Education

Miller (1991) says that holistic education is concerned with "nurturing healthy, whole, curious persons who can learn whatever they need to know in any new context" (p. 7). On the Paths of Learning website, a good exemplar of the approach, it is stated that a

> holistic perspective asserts that education must start by nourishing the unique potentials of every child, within overlapping contexts of family, community, society, humanity, and the natural world. Holistic education is not a fixed ideology but an open-ended attempt to embrace the complexity and wholeness of human life . . . Holistic education is essentially a democratic education, concerned with both individual freedom and social responsibility. It is education for a culture of peace, for sustainability and ecological literacy, and for the development of humanity's inherent morality and spirituality.
> (Retrieved on December 20, 2009 from www.pathsoflearning.net)

As this quote indicates, holistic education highlights the importance of the individual's mental and physical health. This is also its limitation: by focusing primarily on the individual, it can hide the role of the culture in shaping who the individual is. This is sometimes called a "romantic" notion of the individual, after 19th century artists and philosophers who believed that the child had a wellspring of creativity and authenticity that was corrupted by culture.

Ecoliteracy

The Center for Ecoliteracy, located in San Francisco, California, was cofounded by Fritjof Capra, physicist and systems thinker; Peter Buckley, former CEO of Esprit International and environmental philanthropist; and Zenobia Barlow, now its executive director. The Center's work is a combination of sustainability education, holistic education, and place-based education. Their mission: "We believe that schools play a pivotal role in moving us beyond our growing environmental crises and toward a sustainable society. We recognize schooling for sustainability as a process that fosters abundant living on a finite planet and makes teaching and learning come alive" (www.ecoliteracy.org). Ecoliteracy is based on four main principles:

- nature is our teacher;
- sustainability is a community practice;
- the real world is the optimal learning environment;
- sustainable living is rooted in a deep knowledge of place.

This organization does great work in schools around food production and sustainability, encouraging school gardens and the use of local, sustainably-grown food in school lunchrooms, as well as instruction about food systems in the classroom. The Center also offers summer institutes for sustainable living and leadership academies. Their 2005 book *Ecological Literacy: Educating Our Children for a Sustainable World*, by Zenobia Barlow and Michael K. Stone, as well as *Ecoliterate: How Educators Are Cultivating Emotional, Social, and Ecological Intelligence* (2012), by Daniel Goleman, Lisa Bennett, and Zenobia Barlow, are great resources for teachers.

Environmental Justice

The EcoJustice approach is also influenced by, but differs from, the proponents of environmental justice. The basic point of the environmental justice movement is to highlight that environmental damage happens disproportionately in poor, working-class, and minority communities. For example, factories emitting dangerous gases or toxic disposal sites are often located in poor communities, highways divide up poor neighborhoods rather than affluent ones, and the availability of clean air and water is often less in low-income areas. This work will be discussed in detail in Chapter 7. The EcoJustice approach acknowledges the reality of environmental injustice, but sets it in a larger framework that includes the injustice to all life that is caused by a toxic disposal site.

Critical Animal Studies

Critical Animal Studies (CAS) is an approach that focuses on the cruel treatment of animals in modern society or discrimination by humans against other species. Defining CAS, the Institute for Critical Animal Studies (ICAS) explains:

> Rooted in animal liberation, CAS is an interdisciplinary field dedicated to establishing a holistic total liberation movement for humans, nonhuman animals, and the Earth. CAS is engaged in an intersectional, theory-to-action politics, in solidarity with movements to abolish all systems of domination.
>
> (Retrieved on November 3, 2013 from
> http://www.criticalanimalstudies.org/about/)

While many readers may find this an unusual point of view, it is important to see that once we accept the idea that one being is "better" than another, it is a fairly short step to discriminating against others. While EcoJustice Education takes a broader view by focusing on the cultural roots of these forms of domination and violence, Critical Animal Studies offers a deeper critique than many other perspectives and is a fast growing field (see Chapter 4 for a more detailed discussion of the work in this field).

Deep Green Resistance

Deep Green Resistance (DGR), called a movement of analysis and action, is best described by the statement that "the role of an activist is not to navigate systems of oppressive power with as much integrity as possible, but rather to confront and take down those systems" (Jensen, 2009). This sentiment is consistent throughout Jensen's work, and is further explored in the book co-written with activists and small-scale farmers Lierre Keith and Aric McBay titled *Deep Green Resistance: Strategy to Save the Planet* (2011). Keith describes Deep Green Resistance as a movement inspired by years of considering Jensen's question of whether the current culture will undergo a voluntary transformation to a sane and sustainable way of life. Deep Green Resistance is informed activism that moves from ethical inquiry about why things are the way they are to action aimed at changing the dominant culture. The movement identifies as being one for those who no longer have the patience to wait for change, based on the analysis that the planet will be destroyed beyond repair if action is not taken immediately. EcoJustice Education is a movement informed by Deep Green Resistance as its focus is not to work *with* systems of domination but rather to work in a multitude of local educational settings to dismantle the dominant discourses shaping modern culture. While some members of this shared interest take action by pulling up asphalt, sitting in trees, interrupting deforestation, freeing animals tortured in research labs, and dismantling dams—to name a few from a long list—EcoJustice educators take direct action to interrupt and destroy dominant discourses that rationalize the atrocities against which rethinking education is necessary.

Ecopedagogy

Growing out of the work of Paulo Freire, ecopedagogy is a growing scholarly field that applies basic principles of critical pedagogy to the study of intersecting social and ecological issues. Ecopedagogy includes "ecological ideas such as the intrinsic value of all species, the need to care for and live in harmony with the planet, as well as the emancipatory potential contained in human aesthetic experiences of nature" (Kahn, 2010, p. 19). EcoJustice thinking shares the critical attitude toward the so-called "free-market" system, whose single-minded focus on profit is devastating the planet faster than ever before. EcoJustice and the ecopedagogy movement agree that teachers and scholars must go deeper than traditional environmental education, pointing to a set of age-old cultural assumptions that lead us to believe that the planet is here primarily for humans and which results in the greed and destructiveness of the modern economy. EcoJustice Education, informed by and growing together with critical scholars in the ecopedagogy movement, insists that these cultural assumptions have resulted in both serious social injustices and serious environmental damage, and that these should be seen as intertwined and bound to the same belief system.

The above work that focuses primarily on the environment is very important, however, and conversations about our relationship to the planet should be seen as critical to the purpose of education. Unfortunately, schools have not taken up these approaches in any serious or systematic way. This book is about what teachers need to understand in order to help future citizens adequately address these problems. It is really about what we believe schools should be for: preparing our children to contribute to healthy, living, sustainable communities for the 21st century and beyond.

What Is Education For?

Our students report that they have heard few if any of these approaches in their school experiences. If that's true, it illuminates a key point: Schools have specific purposes, and these are most often not shared with students. Those purposes are sometimes determined by vigorous public debate, but often they are hidden in assumptions about who students are and about how the world works.

Historical Purposes of Schooling

You may have heard people talk about the "good old days" of schools, before they were subject to political struggles, when "all they taught was the 3 Rs—reading, (w)riting and (a)rithmetic." This makes a great slogan, but it has never been true. There have been many other goals for schools since they were created, and the goals for public schools in particular have been a topic of endless discussion.

Joel Spring, who has studied American schools for decades, divides the goals that have framed public schools into political, social, and economic goals (Spring, 2010). The major political goal, he suggests, is to educate people to be citizens and future leaders. Citizenship is often seen as teaching people to obey the law and those who are authorized to enforce it. This may appear to be unquestionable, but what if the law is that of Nazi Germany? In the U.S., there has been heavy emphasis on teaching patriotism through the Pledge of Allegiance, patriotic songs, and school spirit. But what if one comes from a community that has been mistreated by the U.S. government, such as Native Americans or Japanese Americans who were imprisoned during World War II—should they be required to express love for a country that has treated them with contempt? Philosopher Richard Brosio (1994) has argued that a primary, albeit conflicted and contradictory, imperative of public schooling has been to prepare future citizens for democracy—a goal that Thomas Jefferson argued for in the earliest days of our Republic—but that this goal has always taken a back seat to other economic purposes, as we shall see below.

Social goals have included "socializing" students to be good people. But whose values are considered to be the good ones? Schools are often asked to solve social problems ranging from poverty to AIDS to drunk driving. But, as Spring notes, "social reform through the school is a conservative approach to society's ills" (2002, p. 12) because it turns a problem caused by the very structure of the society into an individual problem. We'll see how this works in later chapters, especially when we examine "deficit" perspectives that essentially individualize the problems of poverty and see the resolutions in terms of remediating individual students seen as "lacking" certain cultural characteristics associated with success.

Finally, schools serve economic goals and increasingly continue to contribute to an economic system in which corporations and the "free market" have a stronger voice than "democratic" governments. We will take a closer look at this in Chapter 2, but for now it is important to note that schools have been expected to socialize students to be workers and, increasingly, to be hyper-consumers buying lots of stuff. In the 19th century, schools were asked to teach students to line up, obey orders, and not be tardy, as preparation for factory work. Further, schools are expected to prepare students for jobs, both through training and by finding ways to sort out which students are suited for college training. Most importantly, perhaps, it has been claimed that public schools for all meant that everyone could "have an equal place at the starting line." But, as labor activist and Chicago elementary teacher Margaret Haley argued in the late 19th century, such goals—learning to compete in the burgeoning industrial sphere—could only undermine the broad political goals of preparing students for democratic decision-making in their communities (Hoffman, 1981). Again, we'll look at this more closely in Chapter 2 as we examine the role of education in democratic decision-making.

All of these indicate that one key expectation for schools has been to teach students to continue society in pretty much the same way it has always been—to "reproduce" it. Although this book will suggest that responsible teaching should reproduce democratic and sustainable traditions, you should see the implication that schools are rarely the "great equalizer" they have been claimed to be. As you will see in Chapters 4, 5, 6, and 7 there are many ways that schools reproduce the marginalization of species, gender, class, and race even though none of this is done with conscious malicious intent. Teachers reproduce gender distinctions when they unconsciously interact differently with boys than girls. Schools reproduce class differences when they have "tracking" systems that offer different qualities of education to different students or offer totally different resources to schools serving the wealthy versus impoverished families. Racial divides are reproduced through cultural gaps between teachers and students and between students and the curriculum.

In summary, then, in describing and questioning the existing purposes of schools we hope to encourage you to consider a different vision of the goals of schooling, one that asks students to examine the traditions and practices of their society—and their schools—with an eye toward a different world.

Why We Teach for EcoJustice: A Pedagogy of Responsibility

The overall goal of this book is to provide teachers and teacher educators with the information and classroom practices they need to assume the responsibility for preparing citizens ready to create democratic and sustainable communities in an increasingly globalized world. EcoJustice Education is a movement of teachers, teacher educators, and community educators that is based largely on the foundational work of scholars like C. A. Bowers, Wendell Berry, Vandana Shiva, Gustavo Esteva and Madhu Suri Prakash, Val Plumwood, Carolyn Merchant, Helena Norberg-Hodge, Wolfgang Sachs and others—writers from a variety of fields who have written extensively on the cultural foundations of the ecological crisis. Bowers' work, in particular, has drawn together insights from philosophers, economists, social theories, ecologists, anthropologists, sociologists, and linguists from across the world to make specific analyses and recommendations for education (Bowers, 1997, 2012, 2013). These theoretical foundations, as well as the classroom practices and school reforms that result, are based on an understanding of the unavoidable and even crucial interrelationship among diverse human cultures and the more-than-human world

With these sources of inspiration, we suggest that the approach to teaching best suited to EcoJustice is a "pedagogy of responsibility" which first asks the question, "What are my just and ethical obligations to my communities?" This formulation asks teachers to focus on the obligations, practices, and wisdom—many of which already exist in both Indigenous cultures and present communities in industrial societies—that are necessary for a just and ecologically sustainable society (Edmundson & Martusewicz, 2013). Thus, a pedagogy of responsibility exists in the tension between two necessary ethical questions: What do we need to conserve, and what needs to be transformed? You will see that tension explored throughout this book.

The Purposes of Public Education From an EcoJustice Perspective

An EcoJustice approach calls for rethinking what citizenship means, what it means to be educated for citizenship, and what the purposes of public schooling ought to be. Today, and over the past several decades, those of us involved with U.S. public schooling have witnessed and experienced federal and state policies that define the purposes of schooling in terms of the preparation for work and the need for the U.S. to be economically dominant on a worldwide scale. Such interests have been in play since the beginnings of compensatory public education. Ironically, this demand that schools prepare people for work is made concurrent with an increasingly deregulated and globalized economic system that normalizes outsourcing, leaving hundreds of thousands of people out of work and without hope of employment as they watch their jobs leave the country—and an increasingly devastated ecological system, as well.

Schools currently help to reproduce a culture and economic system whose short-term profit motive and ideology of unlimited growth have created a society that dangerously overshoots the carrying capacity of the bio-systems depended upon for life. We argue, instead, that the purpose of public education must be to develop citizens who can actively work toward a democratic and sustainable society, one that values cultural diversity for what it offers to community problem solving and for the essential role that biodiversity plays in the very possibility of living systems. Such a citizenry requires a developed eco-ethical consciousness; people who recognize the importance of protecting their local community's health and welfare, while understanding the ways larger social, political, and economic systems function historically to degrade the social and ecological relationships necessary for life.

And, it requires teachers who can take on the responsible pedagogy necessary for confronting the deadly consequences of these current systems. Many teachers have learned that schools often reproduce the inequalities of race, class, gender, homophobia, and other oppressions, but they have little understanding of how these inequalities intertwine with the suffering of non-human creatures, the loss of habitat, and the degradation of soil, water, forests, or air.

The approach that we advocate throughout this book will help teachers understand how to interrupt the unsustainable and unjust ways of living that are too often reproduced in schools. We look closely at how social inequalities such as racism or sexism are connected to the harm being done to local and global ecosystems by the same underlying logic of domination. And, emphasizing our commitment to the local, to the power of diverse and democratic communities, we offer teachers approaches to pedagogy that challenge students to address those important connections in their own situated contexts, and to engage with the wisdom of elders in creating community-based solutions. In this way, we bring our hearts and minds to the protection of the places that we love by engaging democratic and sustainable ways of life, and we encourage you, as prospective and practicing teachers, to do the same.

In the chapters that follow, we offer you many activities and resources to help you begin to teach from an EcoJustice Education perspective. Beginning here, we provide a Conceptual Toolbox to help you review and begin to internalize and use some of the primary concepts that will shift the way you think about the world around you. We also provide you with suggested readings, films, and organizational resources. Please visit the Companion Website for this book at www.routledge.com/textbooks/9780415872515 for more resources, including lesson plans to help get you started.

Conceptual Toolbox

Cultural ecological analysis: The understanding that both ecological and social crises have intertwined cultural roots in the deep assumptions of modernity.

EcoJustice: The understanding that local and global ecosystems are essential to all life; challenging the deep cultural assumptions underlying modern thinking that undermine those systems; and the recognition of the need to restore the cultural and environmental commons.

Suggested Readings and Other Resources

Books and Essays

Bowers, C. A. (2001). *Educating for eco-justice and community.* Athens, GA: University of Georgia Press.

Edmundson, J., & Martusewicz, R. A. (2013). "Putting our lives in order": Wendell Berry, ecojustice, and a pedagogy of responsibility. In Andrejs Kulnieks, Kelly Young, & Dan Longboat (Eds.), *Contemporary studies in environmental and indigenous pedagogies: A curricula of stories and place* (pp. 171–184). Rotterdam, Netherlands: Sense Publishers.

Hansen, J. (2009). *Storms of my grandchildren: The truth about the coming climate catastrophe and our last chance to save humanity.* New York, NY: Bloomsbury.

McKibben, B. (2007). Introduction. *Deep economy: The wealth of communities and the durable future* (1st ed.). New York, NY: Times Books.

Films

Conners, N. (2008). *The 11th Hour.* United States: Warner Home Video.
A look at the state of the global environment including visionary and practical solutions for restoring the planet's ecosystems.

Guggenheim, D. (2006). *An Inconvenient Truth.* United States: Paramount Vantage.
Al Gore's film demonstrating the impacts of climate change.

Organizations and Links

350.Org (www.350.org)
International organization focusing on the changes needed to get us below the 350 parts per million of CO_2 that scientists say is necessary to avoid massive climate change.

EcoJustice Education (www.ecojusticeeducation.org)
An international networking and educational organization promoting diversity, democracy, and ecological justice.

Intergovernmental Panel on Climate Change (IPCC) (www.ipcc.ch)
This organization is a credible and world-recognized panel assembled by the UN to assess global climate change. They publish several reports that inform and influence policy by providing scientific views on current climate change and the impacts of climate change on environmental, social, and economic futures.

Chapter 2

Rethinking Diversity and Democracy for Sustainable Communities

Introduction

What do we mean when we use the concept, "community"? We start with this question because we believe that when we talk about education, or about becoming educators, we are aiming our selves, our relationships, our pedagogical practices, and our curricula at some vision of what it means to live well in a community.

Think About This: What Is a Community?

What definitions can you come up with as we start this conversation? Spend some time jotting down a few ideas, talk about those ideas with your peers and teacher, and then read on.

That is, as teachers, we are working through our teaching and our curricula to develop the sorts of people needed by a community. So, it is important that we try to be clear about the vision of community from which we are working, what it means, and whom our visions include or exclude.

In this book, we ask students to think specifically about three defining concepts when they consider what a healthy community is: diversity, democracy, and sustainability. We use these terms because the relationships and principles that they represent provide what we think communities need in order to be just and healthy places for future generations. Let's begin by talking about diversity, and we'll get back to a definition of community a little further on.

Linking Diversity, Democracy, and Sustainability

We begin from the premise that democracy and diversity (defined to include cultural, linguistic, and biological diversity) are absolutely necessary to the sustainability of our communities. We define democracy as any system that allows people real involvement in the decisions that affect their lives. We define sustainable communities as those that support the ability of natural systems to renew themselves. We emphasize sustainability as a very important concept for the future prospects of our children, and the life systems of the planet.

Thus, as the perspectives introduced to you in this book will emphasize, if we are to address the problems associated with social and ecological well-being, the processes of decision-making that we use in our communities must begin to include the impacts that we have on the living systems that we depend upon. This is what it means to link diversity, democracy, and sustainability. We will be discussing these concepts in further detail in this chapter, and throughout the book, as we help you to think about what it means to be an educator as our society faces the ecological and social crises of our time, and, importantly, how schools can help us to achieve the solutions that we need to live healthy, just, and sustainable lives.

Diversity as the Strength of All Communities

The idea that diversity is an important feature for teachers to pay attention to has been discussed by multicultural educators in quite a lot of depth and with good reason. But, before we begin talking about its relevance to people or communities, we need to get down to a basic definition of "diversity." As a starting point, we can define diversity as *the condition of difference necessary to all life and creativity*. Diversity is the condition of difference created when there is a relationship between one thing or idea and anything else. When there is a *relationship* there is also *a space of difference* between the two things. And that space is very important when it comes to defining what anything means or what its value is in comparison to anything else. We say, for example, "This is not that. It is different because . . ." In this sense, difference isn't really *a thing*, or an object, but rather a creative or *generative condition* created because of relationships among things. Indeed, we want to emphasize that relationships are key to both democracy and sustainability. And this is, in part, why diversity is so important.

So let's think about what this means when we're talking about human relationships. What is "cultural diversity"? In general, cultural diversity refers to all the myriad differences that we can discern among discrete groups of people, or among individuals. These groups may be defined as "different" from each other based on any number of categories or even combinations of categories. Most often, we tend to think of these differences in terms of race, ethnicity, nationality, gender, sexuality, class, or ability but there are many other experiences or situations that could cause cultural differences. Often in university and public school classes, these differences are examined as a matter of introducing how some groups are unfairly defined as less important, or inferior to others, and so suffer from economic, political, or educational exclusions. In fact, as many recent scholars have begun to demonstrate, people's very ways of identifying themselves are also often caught up in this politics of inclusion or exclusion. Whole communities of people may develop ways of seeing themselves and others based on these identity formations. This area of study and variations of it have been the purview of multicultural and social justice-oriented teacher education and have played a very important role in the study of education for democratic communities. We'll come back to this point in a moment when we discuss the importance of democracies.

Community and Diversity

But let's back up. What definitions of community did you come up with? At the start of this discussion, students in our classes generally come up with some rendition of the following answer: "A community is a group of people living and working together in relationships of mutual support." In addition, usually one or two, mostly biology majors, will offer a definition that includes a larger ecosystem, saying something like: "A community is a group of organisms living in mutually dependent relationships with each other." This response opens up a good opportunity to start a discussion about biodiversity, its importance to our human community, and its relationship to cultural diversity and even linguistic diversity.

Rebecca's Memory

When I think about my first experience recognizing diversity, a picture forms in my mind of myself as a young girl riding my horse through a meadow on a hot summer's day near my home in northern New York. I'm riding bareback (no saddle), feet dangling freely as the horse plods along, and I'm not paying much attention to her occasionally grabbing mouthfuls to eat, because the meadow itself has captured me. It is alive! All sorts of buzzing and peeping creatures—crickets and bees, horse flies and hummingbirds, finches, chickadees, and cicadas—are creating a cacophony for my ears while the Queen Anne's lace, vetch, daisies, grasses, black-eyed Susans, and oh so many more plants bob and sway in the breeze. A grass snake warming on the path slithers out of our way at the last minute, and my eye just catches the brown blur of a woodchuck scurrying into its hole. And all the smells! So earthy, rich, and pungent! All this living stuff, the same as I remember from last year and yet not the same! A bouquet of living diversity, and the horse and I are a part of it.

In his novel *Ishmael* (1992), Daniel Quinn's main character, a gorilla and teacher, explains to the narrator that "diversity is the strength of the community," going on to explain the important function that biodiversity plays in keeping living systems from collapsing. Biodiversity refers to all of the different species of plants and animals—from micro-organisms to large predators—living in a particular region, who are interdependent upon one another and thus combine to make a living system in a particular place or region (sometimes referred to as a bioregion). Quinn's novel teaches that the more different species an ecosystem has living in it, the more apt it is to survive the death of a particular species, whereas if there are few species living in one system, the death of one could mean the collapse of the system. *Biodiversity* is very important to maintaining the *interdependence* among all life. Each organism depends on a whole set of relationships with other organisms for survival. Nothing survives or even comes into existence outside its relationship to something else. Buddhists call this idea *dependent origination*.

So, all that stuff in the meadow that Rebecca described in her memory is absolutely dependent upon the microbes and nutrients in the soil that it grows in, to the plants that grew there in years past (which decomposed, contributed to the humus of the soil, and created the seeds that dropped into that soil), to the amount of rainfall we got that season, and a myriad of other factors. The bees and the birds and the snake and the woodchuck are dependent on the plants, and the plants are dependent upon them for pollination, for nutrients, and so on. The horse may also be considered an important part of the system, especially to the extent that she may be let out to pasture in that meadow. She may eat there, and her manure would certainly be an important contributor! And so is Rebecca, perhaps not directly for food in this particular meadow, but certainly for the sense of serenity she had on that sunny afternoon and many others like it. You get the idea. Everything that lives is dependent upon its relationship to a whole network of relationships for everything that makes life possible. All of these relationships produce all sorts of differences among the species that make up the living world. Biodiversity is the basis of all life, including human life. But what does this discussion about the diversity among all species have to do with our understanding of community?

Beginning from this understanding that human communities are nested in and absolutely dependent upon the well-being of a larger living system, the decisions that we make about how we live together ought to include an understanding of that dependence. We assume throughout this book and in our day-to-day work as educators and community members that, in order to live fully and make decisions that protect life for future generations, our understanding of community must be inclusive of the larger living world that we depend upon. The planet Earth is comprised of a complex system of integrated and interdependent life forms. If we exclude other species from our consideration when making decisions, is at our own peril because such exclusions will surely result in harm that will affect our own ability to live.

Johnny's Memory

I remember, as a young boy, standing in awe on the shore of Lake Superior. Overwhelmed by sight, smell, and sound, I recall being on a bit of a sensual overload. My mind was racing as I was hearing the sounds of the waves, the wind, the birds, the insects buzzing around, the leaves blowing, the cracking of the trees bending in the wind, and the pebbles being washed up on the flat rocks that lined the shore. This was so different from the noise of tires on pavement; sirens from ambulances, fire, and police vehicles; people yelling in a language I didn't speak or understand; dogs barking in the alley; and Motown records playing from the attic: the street sounds of an urban neighborhood. In awe of the complexity of that sunrise on Lake Superior, I remember the sight, the colors of the sky—the pinks, purples, blues, oranges, yellows, juxtaposed with the greens and browns of the forest and shore aside the spectrum of blues of the lake. Looking around, I realized that in this place I was not the dominant species. I had the realization that the world was a complex and incredibly diverse system. Everything was so alive. I was very young but somehow I knew then that whether it was the diversity of the urban landscape that was home, or the intensity of the shoreline of a Great Lake, diversity or the presence of difference made life enjoyable. It made life!

Exclusions and Value-Hierarchized Thinking

The question of who gets included in our conception of community has had important consequences in the history of our culture, as the exclusion of entire groups of people from the status of citizens, or even from identification as humans, will attest. Slavery; the genocide of Indigenous Peoples living on the North and South American continents; the internment of Japanese Americans after the bombing of Pearl Harbor; and the disenfranchisement of un-propertied white men, all male African Americans (until 1865), all women (until 1920 in the U.S.) and people considered "disabled" from full participation in political processes and the right to vote are just a few examples of such exclusions. What happens to people when they are excluded from consideration as decision-makers or citizens within a community? Clearly, as our students are quick to point out, these people are bound to suffer in ways that those included do not. First, they are degraded by the exclusion that defines them as less valuable than others, and second, because they are seen as less worthy, they will be prevented from contributing to decisions about what happens to them or others in the community. Their interests or needs will likely not be met, their knowledge and experience will not be considered important to the community, or, worse, they may be forced to live in situations in which they are exploited or controlled for someone else's benefit.

Thus, they will suffer. When women are excluded from decision-making and controlled by men by being defined as inferior, we call the ideology supporting their situation "sexism" and the system that supports and reproduces it "patriarchy." When we exclude an entire race of people from what they need to live well, or rationalize their exploitation based on the color of their skin or their ethnic background, we call these practices, "racism" or "ethnocentrism." And when we define the natural world as less important than human life, and thus as unworthy of our care, or claim it as a commodity or as property to do with as we please, we call that belief system "anthropocentrism." These are all examples of what eco-feminists have called *value-hierarchized ways of thinking* structured by a *logic of domination* that undermine community well-being and justice (Warren, 1998). A value hierarchy is a form of stratification, giving more value, status, or influence to some, and less to others. We will discuss these concepts in more depth in Chapter 3; here we are highlighting ways of thinking that rationalize behaviors that value some and devalue others, thus unjustly rationalizing their exclusion.

Further, sometimes cultural marginalization means that we disregard the knowledge that the people in a particular culture have about the natural world, and in so doing end up causing damage to an ecosystem that may have been kept in balance by that knowledge. Across the planet, Indigenous cultures—called "mature cultures" by Gary Snyder (1990) because of the centuries that they have been in existence—are being threatened by the globalization of Western economic, cultural, and linguistic systems. Many of these cultures have maintained complex knowledge about the land and the plant and animal species that live within a particular bioregion. Their ability to maintain a viable culture over many centuries depends upon the protection and passing on of this knowledge, and is accomplished via the languages that they share. The words and concepts used in any culture are created, shared, developed, and changed in relationship to the land and biological system that the people live within. This means that there is an important relationship among cultural diversity, linguistic diversity, and biodiversity, so that if one of these is threatened the others are as well. There are at present around 5,000 different languages across the world, but most of these are threatened as a handful of languages, most notably English, are exported globally. As we lose linguistic diversity, we also lose important cultural knowledge about how to live in specific bioregions, what species live there, what grows well, what rainfall levels demand, what nutrients naturally occur in the soil and what it needs and on and on. Such a loss threatens the biodiversity of a region that in turn damages the human community's survivability.

Social Justice and EcoJustice

Questions related to who gets valued and who does not, who gets to have authority to make decisions and who does not, or who gets to live and who does not, are always questions of justice. When we focus on justice related to human life, we use the term *social justice*, but when we see humans and the natural world as inexorably linked, we use the term *EcoJustice*, as defined in Chapter 1.

If our decision-making practices do not take account of a particular group's needs because they are excluded from our believed realm of responsibility, we not only commit injustice, we inevitably undermine the diversity that is the strength of the community. No matter if we're talking about cultural diversity or biodiversity, putting any of these groups in the margins or defining them as less deserving of care and reciprocity, is harmful to the whole community of life. While we in Western cultures may be quite accustomed to the idea that we should look out for ourselves first in order to succeed, this book will return again and again to the idea that members of ecological communities (including humans) depend upon one another, and that community well-being is essential to individual well-being. Such a position requires that we look carefully at the ways that we organize decision making in our communities or culture, and the sort of decision-making practices that could lead to a just and healthy society that is available for future generations.

Basic Principles of Democracy: How Should We Live Together?

If diversity is the strength of the community, and we know how that works to protect the natural world, how might it translate when talking about human decision-making practices and responsibilities? That is, how does diversity function in human communities?

First of all, we need to consider that human beings come together with any number of different ideas, ways of knowing, experiences, abilities, interests, and so on. As such, we often disagree with each other, which means there is bound to be conflict! Conflict is nothing more or less than the inevitable outcome of human interaction around these *differences*, and can be both a positive catalyst for all sorts of creative endeavors, or, on the other end of the continuum, a source of terrible violence. Again, diversity—or difference as a condition of life—is there playing in the spaces of our relationships all the time. It is how we deal with it that matters most. We can try to squelch it, asserting "the one right way" or some notion of universal truth, or we can acknowledge its power to create, and thus work for ways of using it toward the common good. In this sense, diversity is at the heart of democratic ways of thinking, and democracy as a way of life. Democracy, as a response to the conflict created by difference (of opinion, of beliefs, of personal or cultural history, for example), challenges us to think and communicate and take into account each other's ideas as a matter of trying to live well together in the absence of absolute answers about how to do that.

Imagine you are sitting in a group of people trying to solve a problem. If there are 25 people, but only one or two are allowed to put ideas on the table to solve the problem, what is the likelihood that the solution will be one that is good for all? On the other hand, what could happen if all 25 people get a turn at suggesting a solution, or have a full conversation about possibilities? In general, the more voices in community decision-making the more apt we are to come up with ideas and eventually decisions that work toward a healthy and just society. Moreover, it seems only fair that if the decision is going to affect a group of people, they should be given the opportunity to contribute ideas toward making the decision—they should be included. This basic idea—the right to participate in decision-making and to have one's voice heard—is one of the fundamental principles in a democracy. So, it follows, as our students soon point out, that diversity (even though it can cause conflict) is also the strength of human decision-making. And here we mean diversity very broadly: We should welcome as many diverse ideas from as many diverse groups of people who are most affected by a particular problem as possible, and do our best to discern together what the best solution will be given those diverse needs and possibilities.

So, what else defines a basic concept of democracy? We've already said that the more voices in decision-making the better. How would we translate that into a *principle*; that is, into a guiding idea that a group can use to be sure their decisions are fair to all concerned? Perhaps it would look something like this: Everyone has the right to voice his or her opinion. That's a simply put version of the notion of "equality": the equal right to participate in the decision-making processes necessary to any community. That guiding idea constitutes a first principle of democracy. Two more basic principles round out our beginning discussion of democracy (we'll complicate this some in a few moments!). The second principle suggests that while we have the right to voice our opinion as stated above, we also have the *responsibility* to participate. If the decision-making is to be fair, then we cannot just decide to opt out. Have you ever been involved in a group project where someone just decides that they don't want to contribute? They may or may not have what you would consider a good reason, but, in either case, the decision-making process will likely not be as strong without them there. And if a number of people opt out and leave it to one or two people, then the group could be in real trouble, to say nothing of the unfairness of leaving the burden of that responsibility to a few people, no matter how qualified they may be. The quality of any democratic decision-making is strengthened when those who are most affected by a particular issue or problem are involved in and responsible for its solution. Again, diversity is the strength of the community.

One more question leads to a third principle defining a basic concept of democracy: Who should benefit from these decisions? What should be our ultimate goal, or our bottom line, the criteria we most aim for when making these decisions? Is it fair to make a decision that only benefits a handful of people? In general, and ideally, a democratic decision should aim to benefit the whole community. Because of the history of how democracy is practiced at the local, state, and national levels in the U.S. and around the world, or even in our organizational interactions, we tend to think of democracy primarily in terms of representative processes, or "majority rule." But, as law scholar Lani Guinier (1995) has pointed out, often this practice amounts to the promotion of what she calls "a tyranny of the majority" whereby groups of people living in the community who may not be dominant in terms of numbers are effectively excluded from having a true voice in issues affecting their lives. Consider what "majority rule" by whites meant for African Americans for a hundred years after the Civil War, for example, or what it still means in highly segregated areas of the country. The idea and practice of "majority rule" is so common that sometimes our students use it as a stand-in for democracy itself, without really recognizing how it has been used to reproduce domination in our society. This is often a matter of confusing common procedures for the underlying or guiding principles. Procedures are how we decide to carry out the ideas in the principles, but sometimes these practices fall short of the principles themselves. So, it's very important to remind ourselves what the guiding ideas are that ground those practices and to ask whether they are actually being carried out to the best of our abilities.

Thus, as a starting principle, democracy is about making decisions and maintaining relationships that have the best interests of the whole community in mind. This entails a commitment among the members that all of those people—in fact, the whole living community—deserve to live well, and a recognition that all those diverse human voices have important contributions to make to the decisions about how to address the problems of living together on this planet. That said, this approach to decision-making begins from the recognition that no individual, and no group of individuals, no matter how brilliant, can ever be 100 percent certain that they know what is best.

This uncertainty exists as a common tension in this process both because nothing about our world is static—there's always something new to shift our situation—and because humans are fallible. The best we can do is make the best decisions we can given the context we're in and the particular contributions and information made available to us, allowing for as much diverse input as possible, with the willingness and expectation to return to the issues being discussed as new information arises.

In Johnny's Classroom: Centralized Versus Decentralized Decision-Making

For students in my teacher education classes, the fact that democracy has been taught in schools as, at best, an idealized model of representative decision-making (see below) creates conceptual difficulties when we try to discuss basic principles. Students try hard but seem to fall into a trap of believing that if it is to be practical, democracy must surrender decision-making to representatives of large groups of people. Rather than staying trapped, my students get further if we approach decision-making by asking not just who makes decisions but also where the decisions are made. I try to help students to differentiate between decentralized decision-making and centralized decision-making. Decentralized decision-making means that decisions are made by all those directly impacted. As decision-making rights are surrendered to representatives, decision-making moves toward a centralized and thus more authoritarian mode, and democracy is compromised. Think about a decision-making continuum with democracy or decentralized decision-making at one end and dictatorship or highly centralized forms of decision-making at the other. No matter the political framework, centralized forms of decision-making are faulty and by their very nature undemocratic. My students find that they are less likely to misrepresent democracy if they describe democratic decision-making as decentralized decision-making. This is important in an era in which decision-making has moved very far from citizens, to distances beyond even nations—in markets and corporate interests. When we look at democracy this way, students are able to articulate that decentralized decision-making goes hand in hand with strengthening local communities, rather than centralized distant decisions made that impact on local communities.

Yet, this approach to community decision-making or to a definition of democracy is probably not what most of us are accustomed to in our day-to-day lives, or in the way we understand and experience our system of governance in the United States. When the three authors of this text begin to work with our own students about the nature of democracy, we often don't name the process we're working out until we have all the principles named. They name:

1. the right to equal participation in the decision-making process;
2. the responsibility to participate fully in the decision-making process; and
3. the need to consider the well-being of the whole community as the bottom-line criterion for the decision made.

But, when we ask them to name this process, many stare blankly for quite some time before someone tentatively offers, "Democracy?" Then, in a rush of response, our students exclaim, "Wow, I've never thought about democracy like that before!" "That's not what our Political Science courses call democracy!" "Well, that could never work!"

How could it be that we live in what we call a democratic nation—the most powerful democratic nation in the world—and yet we do not experience its most fundamental principles? More importantly, what are the consequences of this gap between principles and practice for our communities, including their human and more-than-human members? And is there anything we can do as educators? This book will offer some answers.

Liberal/Representative Democracy, Strong Democracy, and Earth Democracy

First, it's important to understand that democracy is a human-made system of thought and practice that has been in existence, in one form or another, across the world for centuries, in many different cultures including Indigenous cultures. There is nothing given or natural or universal about it. It comes from regular people living together and trying to figure out what is the most fair and effective way to achieve a good life together. As such, there has been a good deal of historical disagreement—indeed, conflict—over what democracy means, how it should be defined, why, and what that could mean for how we actually practice it. Basic ideas about what it means to be human, and thus who has the perceived capacity to enter into decision-making, are at the heart of the debates about what democracy might mean, including those debates that founded our U.S. Constitution and the democratic framework on which it is based.

Think About This: "What Ought to Be?"

As we proceed into this discussion, be thinking about what you think about these different forms of democratic theory, how they compare to what you've been taught before, what forms make the most sense to you, and why. What do you think they mean both for what we ought to be doing in schools, and for what you know that we actually do? Here, we really want you to begin to develop a sense of what ought to be—that is, a vision of a good community and, thus, of a good educational process. This means that you may have to bracket out the temptation to throw up your hands and say, "Yes, but that could never happen!" You may be correct, but it is very important that we begin from a sense of what the best possible way of living ought to be, as a way of both measuring where we are currently as a society, and where we might need to go. This is an exercise in imagining how we should live together in the fullest way possible. Take some notes. We'll come back to this in a bit.

Liberal Democracy: Prioritizing the Needs of the Individual

For the most part, while the three principles that we've been talking about so far are representative of the old adage "of the people, by the people and for the people," our day-to-day understanding of democracy is not defined this way. Indeed, the history of our society is fraught with disagreement about who should and should not be allowed to make decisions for the community or nation. These debates have included strong beliefs about education and the need (or not) for public schooling. On the one hand, Thomas Jefferson believed that a strong community and nation would be built only if citizens (then defined as propertied white men!) could come to the table informed and ready to haggle over what was best for all concerned. For Jefferson, men come together to form communities by virtue of the "natural want of society," and they bring with them "faculties and qualities to effect its satisfaction by concurrence of others having the same want." He argued for a ward system in which communities would be divided up into neighborhood-sized political groups that would take on the decision-making most affecting the people in that particular ward. This system would divide:

> every county into hundreds [100 adult citizens or males], with a central school for all children, with a justice of the peace, a constable and a captain of militia. These officers, or some others within the hundred, should be a corporation to manage all its concerns, to take care of its roads, its poor and its police by patrols . . . Every hundred

should elect one or two jurors to serve where requisite, and all other elections should be made in the hundreds separately, and the votes of all the hundreds be brought together . . . These little republics would be the main strength of the great one.

(Jefferson, quoted in Crittendon, 2002, p. 20)

For Jefferson, politics is a part of everyday life affecting everyone. The ward system, organized at an appropriate scale, would operate to directly engage ordinary people in the local issues and problems that were most pertinent to them. Such a system of self-governance, he argued, would require that every citizen be able to read and to write and to deliberate. Thus, Jefferson was one of the first advocates for a strong and free public education as a requirement of a democratic society.

But others, most notably James Madison, criticized this form of participatory politics, arguing that a representative form of governance was preferable even at the local level because the common working man was not fit to rule; he would not be able to or interested in participating in such a process as Jefferson outlined. Only "the best men in the country" should be trusted with such a process. While it was agreed that "a collective unit of citizens were capable, at times, of 'cool and deliberate sense'" (Crittendon, 2002, p. 14), only the most virtuous men, argued Madison and the Federalists, "would offset 'the factious tempers . . . local prejudices, or . . . sinister designs' of many in the electorate" (Crittendon, 2002, p. 15). These men, he argued were those with the most "fit character" and also of the most means, who were not distracted by the day-to-day competition and challenges of economic dealings and thus could turn their attention fully on the political process. They would be elected representatives of the larger community of citizens and would take their concerns to a larger body that would make decisions for the community, or state, or nation.

To be clear, Jefferson also believed that only white propertied men should be considered citizens worthy of participation, but for Madison it was only the elite who were prepared to engage the democratic process and who should therefore represent others in the legislatures. Ordinary men of the "grazing multitude" (a phrase coined by George Washington) were selfish and oafish according to Madison and others, and as such were considered particularly unfit to govern at the national level. In short, the Federalists and others involved in the discussion of how our budding democracy should be organized based their decisions on the assumption of a natural hierarchy of morality, virtue, and capacity to rule among men, and thus on clear ideas of who was and was not prepared to participate in decision-making for this young nation. Only rational men of high moral character could promote the public good.

Thus, although many of those originally excluded from involvement have won the right to vote, our system has been based on debates around exclusion and inclusion from the start, and, indeed, has its roots in specific ideas about who is capable and worthy of deliberation and who is not. While Jefferson fought for a system based on the notion of popular rule (that is, rule by the people) via a decentralized system supported by education to develop the public's ability to deliberate, the Federalist vision of representation by those "above the fray" won out. The Federalist victory turned our country toward what is called "liberal democracy," a form based on the privileging of individual rights, interests, and choice.

Once we take the step of removing decision-making from the direct involvement of citizens, we open the possibility of politics and governing being experienced as the job of others, rather than the responsibility of all. With representative forms of governance comes the prioritization of the private, taking the business of public interests, ironically, out of the hands and, it turns out, out of the consciousness of the public. "Liberalism" is a political doctrine grounded in the rights of the individual as an autonomous, independent, and essentially self-interested being who is oriented toward accumulating material resources needed to survive. In this sense, as philosopher of education Richard Brosio (1994) has pointed out, liberalism serves the imperatives of capitalism far better than democracy, as we will see further on. Indeed, capitalism as a set of economic relationships depends on competition among individuals, whereas democracy is governed by principles of community well-being. Individualism is a central ideology now organizing our culture; it basically argues that human nature is essentially selfish and that society should be organized to capitalize on those tendencies first. These are beliefs organizing a set of political ideologies referred as "neoliberalism," currently in vogue and dominating both state-based and corporate decision-making. We'll take a closer look at neoliberalism later in this chapter, but the point here is that while the economic and political theory of neoliberalism is having very powerful effects on our lives currently, these ideas are not really new. Neoliberalism (neo means "new") is based on much older ideas born in the 16th through 18th centuries, ideas that were used to found the U.S. and organize our government. Understanding the historical roots of our current system is important to realizing that we need not accept its assumptions, especially when we can see the harms being perpetrated.

In the political philosophical theory of Enlightenment philosophers John Locke (1632–1704) and Jean Jacques Rousseau (1712–1778), the role of the state is primarily to protect individual freedom and to secure opportunities to satisfy personal goals and interests. Liberal democracy's approach to freedom is negative in the sense that it emphasizes "freedom from" interference, in particular from the state. It is an argument for the primacy of the individual over the state. Moreover, in this theory, society, as a collection of autonomous individuals, is best served by mobilizing these tendencies through competition. Protecting individual rights and private property is thus seen as a primary goal in liberal democracy.

This is why the Federalists believed strongly in the requirement for "virtuous men" who could rise above the business of "ordinary people" to govern. Of course, it is not difficult to see that historically, those men assigned highest moral virtue were also the biggest landowners, with the most success in accumulating resources within this very system. It is not by accident that we have seen politics within liberal democratic systems develop into competition among interest groups where those with the most economic power also have the most political influence.

It is also no accident that this form of governance developed hand in hand with the shift from agrarian, self-sufficient farming as a way of life, to an industrial economic system where, by the early 19th century, the goods and services required by members of the community to live were being produced in privately owned factories. Boosted by technological innovations (the steam engine) requiring the use of fossil fuels, this economic shift required ways of thinking that gave priority to autonomous individuals, assumed that selfish motivations were natural and dominant, and defined the human relation to the natural world as one of superiority and hyper-separation.

Basic Tenets of Liberal Democracy

1. Most humans are unable to govern themselves because they are essentially self-interested creatures and therefore unable to discern what is in the interest of the common good. They are more interested in the market place (private property and the accumulation of wealth) than politics.

2. Therefore, a representative democracy is best. The most virtuous/wise—that is, those interested in and able to discern the common good—should be elected by the people to govern.

3. Authority over well-being is therefore taken out of the hands of the people and located in government bureaucrats and political parties.

4. Since private property and the accumulation of resources are seen as a primary right, those who govern are also tightly allied with those who own the means of production.

5. Framers believed in the equal rights of all citizens. However, at the time of the founding of the Constitution, all people were not considered to be worthy or capable of citizenship. Thus, liberal democracy is founded upon the notion of a natural hierarchy among people.

(Adapted from Crittendon, J. (2002). *Democracy's Midwife: An Education in Deliberation.* Lanham, MD: Lexington Books)

Liberal Democracy and Hierarchized Thinking

The arguments about what it means to be human, and thus how democracy should be organized, that were made by the Federalists didn't just pop up out of nowhere. As we will be detailing in various chapters in this book, they were part of a cultural system of thought that Europeans brought with them to North America, a hierarchized way of thinking that privileged some people over others, the individual over the community, culture over nature, reason over emotion, mind over body, and so on. The notions of individualism that began to infiltrate and define democracy as the engagement of individual interest, choice, and rights, was necessary as well for the development of an industrialized economic system where competition, self-interested accumulation, and profit became naturalized as what an economy is. Moreover, this is a mindset in which various aspects of the natural world were defined not as an interdependent set of relationships among living things, but rather as so many commodities to be harvested and used in the pursuit of both imperial and individual profit (Cronon, 2003; Merchant, 1990).

On Neoliberalism: Social and Ecological Implications

We are the inheritors of the social and ecological consequences of this mindset today, in the form of policies and assumptions being referred to as neoliberalism. David Harvey (2005), giving a brief but thorough explanation of neoliberalism, explains:

> Neoliberalism is in the first instance a theory of political economic practices that proposes that human well-being can best be advanced by liberating individual entrepreneurial freedoms and skills within an institutional framework characterized by strong private property rights, free markets and free trade.
>
> (p. 2)

Furthermore, Harvey explains that such a theory of political economic practices is not possible without enforcement from governments. Harvey elaborates:

> The role of the state is to create and preserve an institutional framework appropriate to such practices. The state has to guarantee, for example, the quality and integrity of money. It must also set up those military, defence [sic], police, and legal structures and functions required to secure private property rights and to guarantee, by force if need be, the proper functioning of markets. Furthermore, if markets do not exist (in areas such as land, water, education, health care, social security, or environmental pollution) then they must be created, by state action if necessary.
>
> (Harvey, 2005, p. 2)

In other words, neoliberalism is both an economic and political restructuring of relationships through deregulation and privatization that works to reduce the role of government by shifting decision-making from the interest of communities toward the interests of profit for the elite few at the expense of all.

Undermining Democracy: "Model Legislation" and Neoliberal Corporate Reform

The American Legislative Exchange Council (ALEC) is an organization of corporate lobbyists and state legislators whose goal is to create "model bills" that member-legislators then take back to their states as legislation. Remember, our elected legislators are supposed to be representing the interests of their constituents. But whose interests are operating behind the scenes? As a neoliberal organization, ALEC explains their mission as advancing "the fundamental principles of free-market enterprise, limited government, and federalism at the state level through a nonpartisan public-private partnership of America's state legislators, members of the private sector and the general public" (retrieved on December 21, 2013 from http://www.alec.org/about-alec/). Currently, only one Democratic legislator is a member, and there is no evidence of "the general public" invited into their secret meetings. Corporations of this organization are not elected by citizens of the state to create this legislation; they buy their membership and then work to have their specific interests taken back to states and presented by the state representatives. ALEC boasts that the group has successfully created thousands of pro-corporate model bills, with one in five successfully passing into law. These model bills are aimed at gutting the Clean Air and Clean Water Acts, important environmental laws that they define as an "EPA regulatory trainwreck." They are also responsible for working to undermine worker pensions, helping to push voter suppression legislation, discouraging alternative energy use, promoting "Stand Your Ground" laws, and supporting a variety of bills that support the privatization of education (often in the name of addressing the needs of impoverished children). For more information on the specific legislative actions of ALEC, go to www.alecexposed.org/ or http://www.StandUpToALEC.org. We encourage you to read ALEC's self-promotional literature as well. Pay attention to the metaphors that they use to rationalize their work. Ask yourself, who does this legislation really benefit?

Market ideology and consumerism trump community, dominating our relationships and shaping the social and cultural organization of our lives. As Henderson and Hursh (2014) point out, this shift has had a negative impact on how we understand what democracy means, and what education has to do with it:

> [N]eoliberalism transforms not only the role of the state and the purpose of the economy, but also how decisions are made and the nature of democracy. No longer is democracy defined as citizens deliberating the nature of the social/ common/ecological good and how to achieve it, but rather democracy is defined as choosing between the existing products with education no different than any other product. . . . While most individuals are left with choosing between what is on offer, increasingly education and environmental policies are decided at national, federal, and international levels where corporate, philanthropic, and political elite have disproportionate monetary and cultural resources to negotiate and implement policies.
>
> (Henderson & Hursh, 2014, p. 170)

Schooling is implicated in the way knowledge is organized via curriculum, texts, and testing to support this economic system, and transmitted to define humans, "civilized" society, and the larger living world. Contemporary school reform movements are being strongly influenced by those who believe that privatizing the control of schools is more efficient. In this model, formerly publically controlled and funded schools are being sold off to private chartering companies who are no longer accountable to publically elected boards of education. Yet, per pupil funding still comes from public monies. Thus, we are seeing the ways that neoliberal ideas are being used to undermine one of the last publically controlled institutions in favor of for-profit schooling (Hursh, 2007, 2008; Henderson & Hursh, 2014).

But is this mindset or the political and economic systems born of it inevitable? For some, the political and economic systems that dominate the Western industrial world are the "natural outcome" of human "evolution," insinuating that non-Western cultures just have not "developed" enough yet; that they are "primitive" versions of our more "advanced" civilization. But is what we are living now really more "advanced" if we are damaging the very systems that we need to live? Are we doomed to the consequences of these ways of thinking as some "natural" development of what it means to be human? Or, are they simply the out-growth of the convergence of a particular set of interests and a particular set of decisions that were made within a specific set of understandings and power relations at a particular time? Is it possible that our forefathers and mothers just didn't know enough when those decisions were made? Do we know any better now, or do we at least know more about what and from whom we need to learn? If we want to live healthy lives and pass on healthy and just communities to future generations, to whom and to what are we justly responsible?

This is a central question organizing this book and the work that we do with teachers and schools. What or who else do we need to take into account if we are to live truly healthy and just lives? What other lives matter to our well-being? What other knowledge exists that may help us to solve the crises that we are facing? And what sort of decision-making system do we need to protect those lives? Stepping back from liberal democracy and beginning to recognize its history and its assumptions means that we can also begin to raise questions about its ability to really serve our communities. Some theorists in fact have begun to identify the weaknesses associated with representative forms of democracy, naming it "weak democracy" when compared to another form that gets closer to the first three fundamental principles and thus recognizes the importance of attending to fuller participation, responsibility, and the overall common good.

We turn your attention to another perspective on democracy now, as a way of introducing you to the possibility that we need not simply accept uncritically what we have inherited, and that, indeed, if we take seriously our responsibility to live well together on this planet, it is our duty to consider other perspectives.

We want to spend a bit of time looking at other forms of democratic thought and practice, especially focusing on how another theorist, Benjamin Barber, approaches the issue of diversity among humans. Then we'll take you to the work of Vandana Shiva for an introduction to what she calls Earth Democracy (2005), as a way of getting back to our interest in our responsibilities as citizens imbedded in life systems created by the larger natural world. Finally, we'll be asking here and throughout this book what this discussion of democracy means for the way we think about the purposes of public education and our roles and responsibilities as teachers working for a just and sustainable society.

Strong Democracy: Prioritizing the Needs of the Human Community

For Benjamin Barber (2003), strong democracy is a model for embracing "politics as a way of living." Politics, in this sense, refers to the ways that people come together to struggle over and negotiate conflict over different interests. As noted above, conflict is not seen as something to be avoided or denied. Rather, as a normal part of human interaction, it is viewed as both inevitable and a starting point for decision-making that can help members of a community transcend barriers and create better ways of living. As a means of defining the requirements of strong democracy, Barber writes that, "the need for *politics* arises when some *action* of *public* consequence becomes *necessary*, and when men must thus make a *public choice* that is *reasonable* in the face of *conflict* despite the *absence of an independent ground* of judgment" (2003, p. 122). You might be thinking, what does that mean? So, let's take a closer look at what each of these seven important pieces of the definition mean. Try putting these ideas in your own words as you think about what they might mean for day-to-day life, because while we might not be used to thinking about democracy that way, really it's not something to be abstracted or separated off from how we want to live in our communities.

We've already discussed the idea that *politics* is about some sort of negotiation over differences. Pushing that a bit further, Barber tells us that it requires *action*, and when approached from a commitment to strong democracy, he means actively trying to accomplish with and among others what is needed in a community. This falls in line with what we were saying earlier about responsibility—being an active citizen in a democracy means that we are willing to participate *actively* in working out how to live among other people, not simply sitting back to let others do it for us. Here, action includes *the thought* that it takes to figure something out in order to begin a set of practices. Sometimes we refer to that as the work of creating *theory* or viable explanations.

Fueled by the ideology of individualism discussed in the last section, we tend to view politics as the business of others—bureaucrats or government officials, for example—rather than what ordinary people do in the daily goings on of a community. As members of a consumer society, this idea of politics as ordinary becomes even harder to imagine because we are mostly taught to "eat" or "buy" for our own "use" what others offer, rather than to get involved in the actual making—in this case, decision-making. But, as Barber puts it, "Politics is something *we do*, not something we possess, or watch, or think about" (2003, p. 123). As a form of politics, strong democracy requires that we take action around issues of concern to our families, our neighbors, and ourselves, and, moreover, that we interact with others in the community to figure out just how to do so.

These "others" come together to constitute a *public*, the realm in which the action is taken. Here, Barber makes a distinction that political action must be public action, making a clear distinction between public and private realms of action. "Politics describes the realm of we." There are actions that we take daily in our private lives that have little or no consequence on the public good. Whether Rebecca's husband or she takes the bucket of decomposing vegetable matter from their kitchen out to the compost bin is not something that they would debate in public, and so this discussion is not part of the political in Barber's sense. However, what we do with the waste generated in households and businesses, how and where we dispose of it, how much we generate along with others in the community, and how much we try to reuse and recycle is of public consequence and thus requires some sort of decision/action by members of our communities.

Necessity simply means that we cannot avoid making such choices. Even the decision *not* to act is an action with consequences and carries with it a certain responsibility and will. So, for example, not deciding to send our waste anywhere for disposal will have public consequences and thus is an important decision. The point of necessity is that living together requires choices and decisions, whether we act or not.

Such choices must be *reasonable*; that is, they must make sense in the face of all the possible facts and knowledge presented, and in light of what is best for the community. What we must remember (what always troubles our students) is that no one can ever be 100 percent certain that the choices or decisions being made are the best or correct decisions. This is because human beings are fallible creatures. We may do our best with our ability to communicate and our ability to interpret the world and our emotional intelligences, but the fact is we are not perfect. We cannot possibly predict the future or know absolutely every detail of what may impact a certain decision. And, we have to use language to say what we know, which is always a re-presentation of the world—it's never the thing itself. This means we can only do our *reasonable* best with the information and interpretations we have brought together at the time we enter into this decision-making process. This uncertainty and the conflict that is bound to arise when fallible people come together is exactly why democratic decision-making is the most just way of trying to live together. Nobody can know absolutely what THE answer or the one right way is; so we must constantly be willing to reassess our decisions.

Finally, there would be no reason to come together at all if there were some outside, existing solution or answer to the problem we are trying to solve. So, the idea of *the absence of independent grounds* for making a decision simply means that there is no other answer or way to solve a particular problem or to make a decision around that problem than to figure it out or try to solve it for ourselves. If there were, we would not have to come together as a public body to take action to solve it.

Coming together as a community around all these criteria requires that we know how to talk to one another in ways that promote learning and understanding, as well as discernment—the ability to choose among a myriad of possibilities what is best for the group. It requires what Barber calls "public talk," the ability to listen carefully to others, to think about what is being said, and to articulate a thoughtful response. When we say "thoughtful" here we mean both well informed and compassionate. "Public talk" as the heart of democratic practice is a skill that needs to be developed by thoughtful teachers who can mediate between the multiplicity of individual experiences and voices that may be in a group of students, and the world that needs to be examined. It requires an attitude of inclusion; it requires the development of patience; it requires self-discipline; it requires thought. It requires the ability to see the importance of community and the value of all the individuals that make up that community.

In this sense, strong democracy begins from an understanding of and commitment to what cultural theorist Raymond Williams (1983) has called "equality of being." This is the idea that one person's presence and contributions in a community are as worthy and vital as any other's (Robbins, 2005, p. 10). While Barber does not use this particular concept, his ideas about democracy assume an important level of inclusion that assumes that all human members of the community are valued and thus ought to participate in decision-making, and that differences among those participants is a given. That is, we are not all "equal" in the sense of being "the same"; we all come with different talents, abilities, skills, desires, histories, and so on, but these are "healthy" ways of admitting inequality and do not entitle some to exclude or dominate others. The fact that we are alive, that we exist as beings on this planet, gives us integrity, purpose, and the right to be involved in and included as equal members of a community. Thus, strong democracy as a decision-making process and a way of life begins from the assumption that no matter what one's ability level, every person's integrity, capacity, and aliveness—his or her being—is to be respected equally. This is a very non-hierarchized way of thinking about what it means to be human among other humans, a perspective that clearly values diversity.

Checking In

So, what would a community look like if we thought this way? What would you expect to see happening among people who think about each other this way? Can you think of any specific examples? What sorts of relationships and interactions might you see if democracy of this sort were in practice? What would be going on in this community? What would schools be like? What would they be organized to do? What would you expect to see going on? What skills might be emphasized? What would the curriculum look like? What classroom practices might you see?

Earth Democracy and Sustainable Communities: Prioritizing the Needs of "Communities of Life"

But, what about the *more-than-human members*, the other species with whom we share our communities? Should our decision-making practices also include them? Clearly, they cannot sit at the table with us, but if we are to live sustainable lives, and if the planet we depend upon is to flourish, if we are to interrupt the damages being done to our ecological system, to whom are we justly responsible? Currently, we live in a culture where for the most part we are not in the habit of thinking of other creatures as part of our communities. The consequences of this attitude are all around us. Yet, all of our basic survival needs depend upon our interactions with the diverse ecosystems that create life on this planet. Our food, our water, our air, our shelter, our clothing, and according to some, our spiritual well-being all come from interactions with each other *and* with the more-than-human world. What happens if we continue to exclude other living beings from our definitions of community and well-being? Who suffers?

Should the loss of biodiversity and its concomitant social and cultural consequences be an issue that concerns teachers and the students that they are preparing to become citizens? Should we citizens have a say in how we are to live in our communities, or the condition of the communities we are leaving to future generations? Answering in the affirmative, Vandana Shiva (2005) takes some of the fundamental principles that we have defined as "strong democracy" and introduces into those the idea of our inseparability, our fundamental dependency on the living natural world as a world of intrinsic worth. In a systematic and principled undoing of the hierarchized assumptions that dominate our lives in the West, she argues that:

> Earth Democracy protects the ecological processes that maintain life and the fundamental human rights that are the basis of the right to life, including the right to water, the right to food, the right to health, the right to education, and the right to jobs and livelihoods. Earth Democracy is based on the recognition of and respect for the life of all species and all people. . . . In Earth Democracy, the concern for human and nonhuman species comes together in a coherent, non-conflicting whole that provides an alternative to the worldview of corporate globalization.
>
> (Shiva, 2005, p. 8)

This is a system of belief, of decision-making, and of day-to-day practice that strives to protect ecosystems and their integrity via economic activity that does not interfere with the ability of living systems to renew themselves. Thus, it is fundamentally concerned with the sustainability of the systems that all living creatures need to continue living into the future. It recognizes our human participation in a fragile web of life, and the right of all living creatures to flourish as a natural right. Shiva uses the terms "living economies," "living cultures," and "living democracies" to emphasize that the everyday decisions that we make are a matter of life and death and thus must be made with intelligence, care, and compassion. "In living democracies people can influence the decisions over the food we eat, the water we drink, and the health care and educations we have" (2005, p. 10). A living economy demands that we think differently about the resources that we need to live, that we recognize them as vital parts of a larger system and that we therefore act with care as we take what we need to live. It sees nature as having its own economy, one to be valued and learned from. To live sustainably means that our cultural systems, and thus our economic and political systems, are created consciously, with the Earth and her creatures in mind.

Ten Principles of Earth Democracy

1. All species, people, and cultures have intrinsic worth.
2. The Earth community is a democracy of all life.
3. Diversity in nature and culture must be defended.
4. All beings have a natural right to sustenance.
5. Earth democracy is based on living economies and economic democracy.
6. Living economies are built on local economies.
7. Earth democracy is a living democracy.
8. Earth democracy is based on living cultures.
9. Living cultures are life-nourishing.
10. Earth democracy globalizes peace, care, and compassion.

(Adapted from Shiva, V. (2005). *Earth Democracy: Justice, Sustainability, and Peace* (pp. 10–11). Cambridge, MA: South End Press)

Obviously, then, the sort of communities that we create will be structured very differently from those that have arisen out of the ideologies of individualism, efficiency, and anthropocentrism. A very different set of principles will guide our economic, social, and educational relationships. In his vision for sustainable communities outlined in the box below, conservationist farmer Wendell Berry makes clear that education for such communities should not be limited to institutionalized schooling as there are so many aspects of life that can be learned in the informal relationships we form as we develop through our lives. Adults and children need to have the opportunity to interact with each other around the values, knowledge, and practices necessary to healthy, viable communities as part of their normal, day-to-day lives. This exchange of intergenerational knowledge is an essential aspect of all sustainable communities and, as we will lay out in more detail later in the book, a critical characteristic of commons-based education. Still, it is unlikely that we will do without schools in the foreseeable future, nor would we argue that we should, given the complexity of our current culture. Thus, an educational system set up to support such communities would have to pay attention to the development of some very specific skills, attitudes, values, and assumptions. Indeed the very purpose of education would take on some specific characteristics if it were to pay attention to the living linkages among diversity, democracy, and sustainability.

Wendell Berry on Sustainable Communities

In line with the thinking of Vandana Shiva, well-known conservationist, essayist, and farmer, Wendell Berry also offers a list of suggestions for what communities aiming to be sustainable would do; what principles would guide them. We offer his list here, because it is one of the most comprehensive and thoughtful guides we've seen to date.

1. Always ask of any proposed change or innovation: What will this do to our community? How will this affect our common wealth?
2. Always include local nature—the land, the water, the air, the native creatures—within the membership of the community.
3. Always ask how local needs might be supplied from local sources, including the mutual help of neighbors.
4. Always supply local needs first (and only then think of exporting their products, first to nearby cities, and then to others).
5. Understand the unsoundness of the industrial doctrine of "labor-saving" if that implies poor work, unemployment, or any kind of pollution or contamination.
6. Develop properly scaled value-adding industries for local products to ensure that the community does not become merely a colony of the national or global economy.
7. Develop small-scale industries and businesses to support the local farm and/or forest economy.
8. Strive to produce as much of the community's own energy as possible.

9. Strive to increase earnings in whatever form within the community and decrease expenditures outside the community.
10. Make sure that money paid into the local economy circulates within the community for as long as possible before being paid out.
11. Make the community able to invest in itself by maintaining its properties, keeping itself clean (without dirtying some other place), caring for its old people, teaching its children.
12. See that the old and the young take care of one another. The young must learn from the old, not necessarily and not always in school. There must be no institutionalized "child care" and "homes for the aged." The community knows and remembers itself by the association of old and young.
13. Account for costs now conventionally hidden or "externalized." Whenever possible, these costs must be debited against monetary income.
14. Look into the possible uses of local currency, community-funded loan programs, systems of barter, and the like.
15. Always be aware of the economic value of neighborly acts. In our time the costs of living are greatly increased by the loss of neighborhood, leaving people to face their calamities alone.
16. A rural community should always be acquainted with, and complexly connected with, community-minded people in nearby towns and cities.
17. A sustainable rural economy will be dependent on urban consumers loyal to local products. Therefore, we are talking about an economy that will always be more cooperative than competitive.

(From Berry, W. (1995). Conserving Communities. In *Another Turn of the Crank: Essays* (pp. 19–21). Washington, DC: Counterpoint)

We recognize that none of this will happen overnight or without substantial reconfiguration of the beliefs, policies, relationships, and behaviors in our communities and schools. Thus, we have some suggestions for what teachers can do in their own classrooms to begin to raise the awareness of their students about the importance of democracy as a way of living, and earth democracies as living relationships in which people learn to take responsibility for the communities of life with which they are interdependent. Below you will find a few activities to get you started. Visit our website at www.routledge.com/textbooks/ 9780415872515 for more resources to help you start teaching for EcoJustice.

What Schools and Teachers Can Do

Get to Know Your Community

Community mapping is an activity that can be done with students of all ages. It generally starts with the school community itself and then moves out from there in concentric circles of relationship. If practiced over time, what develops is a multi-layered map of relationships, community assets, and resources that help to build stronger communities, as well as a clearer understanding of the sources of conflict and problems that can then be addressed collectively. The skills and attitudes that are learned in the process are those absolutely necessary to strong, earth-based democracies and sustainable communities.

Teach About Principles of Democracy

In small groups, ask students to brainstorm principles of fair decision-making. If they were to be asked to work together on a project, what principles would guide their decision-making to ensure the process is fair? Be sure to distinguish carefully between procedures and principles.

Teach About Principles of Sustainability

After introducing a definition of sustainability (see Conceptual Toolbox) to your students, ask them to brainstorm what aspects in their community contribute to, and which aspects are barriers to, being sustainable. Then, brainstorm with them ways that they might confront the barriers as a class project. Who might they get to help? What might they need to know? This process of inquiry could develop into strong community-based learning projects that actually teach them to contribute positively to their neighborhoods. See Chapter 9 for more details on community-based learning projects.

Conceptual Toolbox

Bio-diversity: The natural world is multi-layered and interdependent—from the ecology of micro-organisms to the ecology of plants, animals, and humans; renewal of species is dependent upon the diversity of living systems; biodiversity as the basis of life; to undermine it is to undermine life itself; the opposite of an anthropocentric way of thinking.

Diversity: The condition of difference necessary to all life and creativity.

Earth democracy: The decision-making power of local communities to protect the basic foundations of life, and the future of their children.

Economy: The organization and exchange of goods and services in order to meet the needs and wants in any community.

Ideology: A shared system of belief that may serve the interests of some more than others; often perceived as "natural" or "just the way things are."

Individualism: The belief that humans are independent autonomous units, that pursuit of self-interest leads to the greatest good, and that competition is natural (this is different from individuality, which recognizes each person's unique attributes and contributions).

Interdependence: The dynamic of being mutually responsible to and dependent on others; participating in a network of relationships in which the members rely upon and support each other. Interdependence includes the relationships among humans and the natural world.

Liberal democracy: A representative form of democracy moderated by a constitution that emphasizes the protection of the rights and freedoms of individuals and diminishes the role of citizens in democratic governance.

Neoliberalism: An economic and political theory that emphasizes private rights over public interests through deregulation, privatization, and a redistribution of power and resources from democratic governments to private corporate interests.

Political: The negotiation among humans around conflict.

Strong democracy: A modern form of participatory democracy that emphasizes participation, responsibility, and the common good.

Sustainable communities: Communities whose members recognize the essential interdependence among humans and the natural world and thus make decisions to protect the ability of natural systems to regenerate.

Value-hierarchized thinking: A way of thinking that depends on a ranking system where we value some and devalue others. Hierarchized thinking makes racism, sexism, and anthropocentrism, for example, possible.

Suggested Readings and Other Resources

Books and Essays

Barber, B. (1989). Public talk and civic action: Education for participation in a strong democracy. *Social Education*, Oct, 355–356.

Berry, W. (2001). The idea of a local economy. In *In the presence of fear* (pp. 11–33). Great Barrington, MA: Orion Society.

Cavanagh, J., & Mander, J. (2004). Ten principles of sustainable societies: Reclaiming the commons. In *Alternatives to economic globalization* (pp. 77–146). San Francisco, CA: Berrett-Koehler Publishers.

Goodman, J. (1989). Education for a critical democracy. *Journal of Education*, 88–117.

Henderson, J., & Hursh, D. (2014). Economics and education for human flourishing: Wendell Berry and the *oikonomic* alternative to neoliberalism. *Educational Studies*, 50(2), 167–186.

Prakash, M. S. (1994). What are people for? Wendell Berry on education, ecology, culture. *Educational Theory*, Spring, 135–157.

Quinn, D. (1992). *Ishmael*. New York, NY: Bantam/Turner Books.

Shiva, V. (2005). Principles of Earth Democracy. In *Earth Democracy: Justice, sustainability, and peace* (pp. 1–11). Cambridge, MA: South End Press.

Van Gelder, S. R., & Shiva, V. (2003). Earth Democracy: An interview with Vandana Shiva. *Yes! Magazine*, *Winter*.

Films

Merton, L., & Dater, A. (2008). *Taking root: The vision of Wangari Maathai*. Marlboro, VT: Marlboro Productions.

Tells the dramatic story of Kenyan Nobel Peace Prize Laureate Wangari Maathai, whose simple act of planting trees grew into a nationwide movement to safeguard the environment, protect human rights, and defend democracy—a movement for which this charismatic woman became an iconic inspiration.

Moore, M. (2010). *Capitalism: A love story*. Beverly Hills, CA: Anchor Bay Entertainment.

Filmmaker Moore examines the history of free-market capitalism in post-Reagan America and questions its efficacy as the basis for democratic nations.

Sundberg, A., & Stern, R. (2008). *The end of America*. United States: IndiePix Films.

A look at best-selling author Naomi Wolf's take on how democracy in America is in jeopardy, and of other countries that once had a democratic government.

Organizations and Links

The Center for Community Mapping (www.centerforcommunitymapping.org) Focuses on Public Participatory Community Mapping project planning and implementation.

Democracy Now! (www.democracynow.org)

A daily TV/radio news program, hosted by Amy Goodman and Juan Gonzalez, focusing on social justice issues and pioneering the largest community media collaboration in the U.S.

EcoJustice Education (www.EcoJusticeeducation.org)

Established as a networking and educational organization for educators and community activists actively promoting diversity, democracy, and ecological justice.

The Forum for Education and Democracy (www.forumforeducation.org)

Founded to help America's schools ensure that all young people develop the skills and abilities they need to exercise a powerful voice in shaping their own lives—and our nation's future.

The Promise of Place: Fostering Student Achievement and Sustainable Communities through Place-Based Education (www.promiseofplace.org).

A unique public–private partnership that works to advance the state of the art in place-based education by facilitating collaborative efforts in research, program design, technical assistance, resource development, and dissemination.

Chapter 3

Cultural Foundations of the Crisis

A Cultural/Ecological Analysis

Introduction

On the first day of class I walked into my undergraduate Social Foundations of Education classroom and wrote two words on the board: DRAIN and STREAM. The next 45 minutes or so went something like this:

"Take a minute and write down the definitions of these two words," I said. The students looked perplexed, but got out pens and paper and began writing.

"OK," I said after a couple minutes. "What have you got?"

"A stream is a natural body of water. A drain is manmade."

"A stream has fish, plants, micro-organisms. It is alive, a flowing body of water, necessary to human life."

"A drain is a pipe used to carry unwanted waste water away from the house or community. Like sewage drains."

"A stream supports life; a drain is a machine. It isn't alive."

"OK," I said, "so both carry water, but one is living and one is not. What happens if we collapse these together and begin to call what we formerly knew to be 'a stream', 'a drain?' "

"Yukk!" Someone groaned. "That would allow us to put all kinds of gross stuff in there and just use it to get rid of what we don't want."

"Sure, but we do that with rivers and streams too! Just take a look at the Huron River in downtown Ypsilanti. Anybody willing to swim in that?" someone called out.

"We would definitely not care about the fish or plant life, if we used the terminology drain."

"Wait a minute! I see a sign everyday when I drive into school. It says Kimmel Drain, but there's a whole wetland there. Why is it called a drain?"

"Doesn't it have to do with something agricultural?" someone asked.

"Yes, that's right, so let's think about this a bit more. Why would a community or a state like Michigan want to rename 'streams', 'drains'? What kind of action is made possible when we make streams into machines using this new description 'drain'? We have in this state a government position called a Drain Commissioner. What might the word drain allow that maybe was not as possible before, and what does this tell us about the use of words?" I was aware of some perking up going on in students who had previously been sleepy or just bored.

"OK, it would allow us to do more with the stream. We could use it to flush stuff away. My uncle has a farm; there are tiles in the field that drain the field that would otherwise be too wet to plant. The water drains into a ditch that eventually empties into a little stream nearby. I'm not sure what it's called, but it sure seems like it's being used as a drain. My cousins have gone down there with shovels to clear away logs, stones, and plants so that the water goes faster. But isn't this a good thing? Don't farmers need to drain their fields to grow the food we need?"

"What else do you suppose happens?"

"Well, whatever we're putting on those fields goes right in the stream!" someone else said.

"Like what?"

"Fertilizers and pesticides, even manure. Too much of that will not be good for whatever lives in the stream."

"We'll get sick eventually, won't we, if too much bad stuff goes in the stream? Won't it pollute our groundwater?"

"Like I said, look at the Huron!"

"OK," I continued. "Now think about this. In Detroit there is a project to uncover a stream that has been buried in a pipe for over 50 years. The now invisible stream, which used to be called Bloody Run Creek, is used to carry sewage, and has long been forgotten as a stream. Some architects from University of Detroit Mercy rediscovered it upon working on some community revitalization plans. Now, a group of community members are working hard in Detroit to have the stream uncovered and restored. They are making the argument that water is sacred and that uncovering and revitalizing Bloody Run is necessary to the health of the community. They have renewed the name, Bloody Run Creek. This is no longer a pipe carrying water; it is a stream. What might happen to one's thinking and behavior via this renaming? Imagine for a moment what happens if we link the health of the stream to the community? What if we were to name the stream 'part of our community'? Or if we were to call it 'sacred', as the folks working with the Adamah project in Detroit are beginning to do, and as many Indigenous Peoples do? What would change?"

"We'd protect it."

"We'd worship it."

"We'd nourish it, because it nourishes us."

"So, is there a difference if we name something a machine or if we name it alive? What can you tell me about the relationship between language, thought, and behavior in a community? Are there other words that infuse our day-to-day experience that are based on the idea of the machine as a dominant metaphor? Get into groups and discuss those questions for a few minutes. What other words come to mind that we might want to reconsider for their impact on how we treat each other or the natural world? And what does any of this matter to your future lives as teachers?"

We were off and running, and all I had done to begin this passage was to ask them to think about two words and pose questions that led them to consider the political and ethical implications of language, and then to link this discussion to some actual events in their own community. Their collective emotional, intellectual, and ethical energy carried us through this discussion and onward, but it required a specific examination of this important relationship between language, thought, and culture.

In the first chapters, we introduced you to the idea that the so-called "ecological crisis" is really a cultural crisis, that ecological problems like species extinction, soil loss, or water contamination can be linked to problems generally associated with social injustice, such as racism, sexism, or poverty. In this chapter, we will lay out the basic framework for understanding and analyzing how these connections come to be by offering what we call a "cultural ecological analysis." This analysis uses a multi-disciplined lens, drawing on philosophical analysis, economics, history, sociology of knowledge, and socio-linguistics, to trace how it is that we have come to think the way that we do in this culture. We will examine how humans use language to form the personal and collective identities that help to shape and give meaning to our relationships with each other and to the natural world. And, we will trace powerful linguistic forms and processes that have been handed down and exchanged generation after generation, and help to shape our day-to-day taken-for-granted assumptions about who we are and who "others" are.

What we want you to begin to understand is that our particular Western cultural mindset is created through specific ways of thinking that have a history and are powerful "maps" of the world. And as we'll see, these "maps" create a cultural system that is so strong that we may believe it to be inevitable or even natural. This system is both shaped and created within important ideological, economic, political, and social organizations (including schools and universities) that have important consequences on the natural and social systems we depend upon. But, far from being inevitable or natural, these institutions and the related mindset they represent have been created, inherited, reproduced, and shifted by the minds, hearts, and bodies of those generations of people who have lived and are currently living within them.

Culture, in this sense, is a very malleable and fluid set of meanings and relationships, created as people engage and interact and communicate with one another. Language has a huge role to play in this process because it is how we communicate, not as a simple transmitting machine, but rather, as we will point out with some specificity below, as a complex and creative process of *differentiation* that makes all meaning possible. We are all born into this multi-dimensional mix, which has been concocted over many years and is still in process. As we engage with others, immediately upon being born and perhaps even in utero, we begin the process of internalizing and shaping culture's meanings. A baby's cry has a powerful effect on those around her, sending strong messages of need or desire, and bringing an immediate response. The point is that as a form of communication the cry introduces a *difference* into the context, and the response, whatever it may be, brings yet another specific difference, initiating any number of possible interpretations and further responses: love, kindness, satisfaction, impatience, frustration, demand. The possibilities are endless. Indeed, we could say that our "knowledge" of what babies want and need has been created out of many such interactions and communications that have been interpreted and given meaning over many, many centuries. And that is why we say that language or the complex symbolic system we enter into as members of a culture does far more than simply transmit; in fact, its elements and relationships create our understandings of the world around us!

This interesting point brings us back to the importance of diversity as the condition of difference that we discussed in Chapter 2. Indeed, difference is at the heart of all creative endeavor—good, bad or ugly—whether we are talking about what happens among humans or what happens within the natural systems in which we participate. But let's back up a moment in order to make what we're saying here clear. It is very important that we all understand the very fundamental role that difference plays in all communication systems that create what we understand to be knowledge (or even intelligence), and, in fact, in the creation of all life. We'll start this by introducing you to the work of English biologist and anthropologist Gregory Bateson (1987, 2000), one of the most important contributors in the 20th century to our understanding of ecology and to culture as well, and central to our presentation of a cultural ecological analysis. Then we'll use Bateson's sense of the problems associated with modern culture to demonstrate how difference is also at work via language in the creation of all culture.

On Difference, Intelligence, and an "Ecology of Mind"

Let us begin our exploration of the creative power of difference to ecology and culture with an idea that is rather foreign to most of us in the West: that intelligence, even knowledge, is not born of the human capacity to think or make sense of the world alone. It is not something that simply occurs inside the human brain. Rather, it is the result of a collaborative endeavor among humans and the more-than-human (or natural) world. In this sense, as human communities are nested within ecological systems, we participate in and are affected by a complex exchange of information and sense-making that contributes to the well-being (or demise) of that system.

Countering the usual human-centered notion of a powerful human rationality that is objective and separate from body or from "nature," Gregory Bateson (2000) refers to an "ecology of mind" to explain the human relationship to other living systems as a living, communicating, and generative whole, all set within a limited Earthly context. In this sense, the autonomous thinking "self" is a fiction, or a human social convention (the "I" in Rebecca's example below). By contrast, for Bateson, "Mind" consists of a complex interactive system of communication and transformation where information is created and exchanged as various elements enter into relationship with each other.

Rather than thinking in terms of energy exchange as mainstream biologists generally do when thinking about how life is created, Bateson sees communication among elements in a life-system where elemental *differences* come into relationship with each other. (Think back to our example of the baby's cry earlier. Can you see similarities to Rebecca's soil example?) These differences are not static: they impact and change other elements, creating other differences that trigger yet other differences, that communicate something, and so on. This series of communicating relationships creates *a system of differentiation*—it is how things are transformed, or become different from what they were, and how we notice that they do this. For Bateson, this whole exchange of information—this "intelligence" or Mind—including our perception and interpretation of the world through our use of language, is at the heart of what we mean when we say we live in an *interdependent* relationship with the natural world.

The Map Is Not the Territory

Further, as the differentiating world impacts us (communicates to us), humans "map" that world with our discursive (linguistic, textual, and other symbolizing) forms, and thus we build powerful patterns and practices—including our words, our knowledge, our actions and interactions, indeed, our culture—that get carried forward even as they are reshaped. We are born into and learn to think and see through those patterns. As generations pass in any given culture, the interpretive, sense-making processes become deeply embedded and layered cognitive patterns. We encode the world via our linguistic patterns, and some of these we formalize and call "knowledge." In all cultures, people use words and other symbolic forms (gestures, body language, art, dance, "texts" of all kinds) to respond to the world that touches us. When we organize those interpretations into knowledge, we give them status, and they become ways of defining our relationships and behaviors toward the world. All of culture—no matter which specific culture we're talking about—is a result of this process.

A Gardener's Example From Rebecca

I am a gardener. In my garden I pick up a handful of soil, squeezing it in my fist. The force I apply sticks the matter in my hand together; it holds, and its very elasticity sends me a strong message about its possibilities. But what is going on here? The specific relationships between all of the various elements in the soil—the water content, the specific minerals, the humus, and the micro-organisms—work together to create a particular response in my hand and, mediated by the language that I use to interpret it, tell me something about what it can do for the plants growing there. And if I raise the soil to my nose and breathe in deeply, another whole set of messages are sent via the odors that this specific elemental combination creates. All these elements are in a particular differentiating relationship to each other, and to my own senses and prior knowledge about soil. That is, they form a differentiating system of communication that sends messages to me and to other elements in the garden—the plants they feed, for example. I say *differentiating* here because they are in relationships that make a difference in terms of what they form together; it is the very differences among them, those spaces of relationship, that create the specific quality of the soil as a whole, and eventually of the plants they feed. Any change in those relationships would make a definitive difference in the makeup of the soil and its possibilities for the plants, and eventually the quality of the food I might eat from them. We could say that these changes would be differences that make a difference. They would create the meaning in the system that creates all possible changes creating life.

Intelligence, then, involves a process of collaboration among all these elements as they combine and communicate with one another, as well as with me, via their differences. In fact, what I know (or think I know) is only possible because of the whole system as it engages this communication process among differences making differences, and is, thus, much more than just the operation of my own cognitive abilities.

As Daniel Nettle and Suzanne Romaine (2000) point out, there still exists across the planet at least 5,000 different languages that correspond to different cultural systems and also to specific bioregions where they originated. Many of these cultures depend primarily on oral language rather than written forms of literacy, to pass on knowledge about the "place" where they have lived for generations. Thus, as we pointed out in Chapter 2, there is an important relationship between linguistic, cultural, and biological diversity that creates different maps or ways of seeing and behaving relative to the natural world as well as toward other humans. As many of these 5,000 languages across the world are threatened by the demand for adopting particular languages as global languages—English, especially—so too are the diverse cultural knowledges and the biological diversities they represent and protect.

For some, in particular in the West, the ways of encoding the world that have been handed down and reinterpreted over many generations may actually hide us from the fact of our immersion in this wider living system. When we are touched by something in the world, we apply our words to try to explain it—differences in the natural world become differences (words, concepts) in our languaging system. We call this process "knowing the world" and, framed by a set of assumptions that defines us as separate from and superior to that world, we assume we are thinking it "ourselves," apart from the world itself, and that our words are a direct translation of that world, and we are objective observers. Yet, Bateson teaches us that, though one may *imagine* that humans are separate from, and "know," the world as an objective observer capturing the truth, one is never really "outside" that world at all. To complicate matters even more, the processes that we use to understand that which we perceive as *outside* are the same differentiating processes that produce the contexts we are in. Culture is not the same as the natural world, but *difference* as a creative, transformative effect cuts across these lines nonetheless.

Hidden by the hubris of imagined hyper-separation and a faith in our own rational superiority, we too often miss, forget, or deny the ways in which our perceptions, and the words we use to record or communicate them, are all part of the differentiating system itself. These symbolic maps we make are like road maps to understanding the world. But, just as a road map leaves out much of the reality of the land it maps, so the symbolic maps (our words and concepts) only reveal part of the world—or, as Bateson puts it, "the map is not the territory." His analysis thus carries a strong ethical imperative, not necessarily as a particular set of answers, but rather as a plea to us to recognize the larger world we live in as we pose our questions and construct our maps. If our language maps tell us that humans are separate from nature, it becomes difficult or impossible for us to see our interdependence with the natural world. As a result, we may act in ways, and through beliefs, that harm it and thus ourselves.

But, if we open ourselves to the recognition that intelligence is much bigger than our own minds or words, then we may begin to understand our specific dependence upon that which we currently treat as outside or "Other." For Bateson, the first step in creating social well-being is "systemic wisdom." That is, social well-being among humans depends upon understanding that we are dependent upon, and participants in, a larger communicating and living system. We do ourselves and others great harm when we fool ourselves into thinking otherwise. "Lack of systemic wisdom," wrote Bateson in *Steps to an Ecology of Mind* (2000), "is always punished" (p. 440). Any creature that imagines itself outside of or superior to this system of intelligence will wreak havoc upon it and ultimately upon itself.

So, we might ask, for example, which different cultural practices matter more to sustaining life? What are the natural limits of the system to which we must attend? What, in our day-to-day lives or in our political and economic practices, needs to be conserved, and what changed? These are questions that call us toward recognition of, and conscious participation in a dependence upon a living system, where everything—including our knowledge—is created within an interactive web of communication: an "ecology of mind."

Clearly, the "recognition of dependence" is not the form of intelligence that we have inherited as a "modern" industrialized culture, where along with certainty and predictability, human-centered rationality is considered superior to all other forms of relating to or knowing broader living systems. As part of this thinking, the land and creatures within the more-than-human[1] world are at our mercy, objectified as "resources" to be turned into commodities for profit and use. Such ways of defining the natural world are passed down through the generations, becoming deeply-embedded assumptions that are so unconscious they are difficult to recognize as creations of a specific set of historical events.

Language, Knowledge, and Identity

Cultural ways of knowing and the associated relationships in a culture are encoded by the particular symbolic systems, the language and communication patterns among the people. What we "know" is always a matter of what we can say about the world—that is, the particular metaphors that we use to describe it. Then we use this culturally constructed knowledge to determine how we will act. All meaning about who we are in relation to others, including more-than-human others, is created via the language we exchange in the process of trying to say something about our relationship to the world around us. Language—the symbols we depend upon, exchange and use for understanding, including body language and gestures as well as the spoken and written word, the metaphors that we internalize and then express—creates culture, encodes our thought patterns and frames the ways we will perceive, relate to, and act in the world. And these thought patterns are far from innocent or neutral. They carry with them important implications for how we treat each other, and even what we believe is possible. They carry value.

Understanding the ways that we depend upon language to understand the world disrupts Western myths of objectivity and subjectivity associated with knowledge. When we say "we know" something, we are generally not conscious of the complex system of differentiating codes that mediates our perception. Thus, it is very important to understand the direct relationship between language, culture, and thought as these affect the sustainability of any culture in relation to the life systems upon which it depends. Teachers, in particular, need to understand these relationships, examine their own use of language and assumptions about knowledge, and teach their students to do so, if we are to interrupt the behaviors perpetuating the destruction of our communities and planet.

Many linguists, anthropologists, sociologists, and philosophers study language systems as they form the basis of cultural ways of knowing. Ferdinand de Saussure, a Swiss linguist writing in the first decades of the 20th century, was one of the first to understand and describe language as a relational, differentiating system. All meaning, Saussure argued, is a result of the differences *between* particular elements. So, for example we use the letters c-a-t and the sound those letters make together to mean in general the four-legged feline that many of us keep in our houses. But, if we substitute one letter, say a "b" to make the word "bat," we are representing a different sound (Saussure calls this a signifier), which represents a different object (or signified), something one might use to play baseball, or a flying mammal that comes out at night. One letter representing one sound made a very significant *difference*.

Looking at language in this way provided the foundation for understanding the ways that language forms the basis for cultural meaning. This complex system of differentiation creates the ways that we think about ourselves and others—the meanings we give to our experiences—and ultimately the ways we conduct ourselves in relation to the world. Language mediates between the world and our understanding of it. Thus, the historic quest for the truth, the origin of meaning, is caught in the paradox of representation: what we "know" is always only a distanced re-presentation via our symbolic system. It is never the world itself. And, as Buddhists say, nothing comes into being, or is knowable, outside its relationships to something else or to a whole range of other things. Thus, difference is at the heart of all meaning. This is just how culture—our books, our buildings, our institutions, our pedagogies, our identities—is made, through our multi-layered interpretations and representations of the world. Or as Michel Foucault has written, "everything is already interpretation; every sign is, in itself, not the thing susceptible to interpretation but the interpretation of other signs" (quoted in Descombes, 1980, p. 117).

Language, Dualism, and Hierarchized Thinking

Let's take this one step further in our quest to understand how Western ways of thinking work. How is it that some people are identified as superior or inferior? Think about this example: We use the words "man" and "woman" to stand for a whole set of complicated and often unconscious cultural meanings that differentiate our identities, behaviors, and relationships as human females and males. In Western industrial cultures, these meanings can be traced through a series of *hierarchized dualisms* that help to shape our interpretations, assumptions, and our relationships. Some of the primary dualisms can be seen in Figure 3.1.

What is important to note here is that these relationships are not just about the difference between these two terms; rather, difference becomes hierarchized in the meanings given to each category. The first term in this string of oppositional pairs is always presented as superior to and independent of the second, while the second term is always inferior to and at the mercy of the first. Thus we say these pairs are "hierarchized," because one term—man, for example—is assigned more value or status than the other term, woman. This assignment of value, while it functions as if it were natural, is an *invented* superiority. We'll refer to these then as "value hierarchies."

Culture	Nature
Man	Woman
Reason	Emotion
Mind	Body
Active	Passive
Civilized	Savage
Master	Slave
Hierarchized Dualisms in Modernist Cultures	

Figure 3.1   Hierarchized Dualisms in Modern Cultures.

So, while these meanings are in no way fully deterministic of our actual beliefs or behaviors as individual men and women, traces of their effects in our day-to-day lives operate in important ways to keep domination in place. That's how value hierarchies work. For example, women have historically been assumed to be naturally more adept at professions that require them to care for someone else (nursing, teaching, social service) and these professions are given less social and economic value (women are paid less). On the other hand, men are believed to be appropriately assigned to jobs that require high degrees of rationality or decision-making skills, such as engineering, computer technology, or administration, and these professions receive more value, status, and economic compensation. Women, defined more in terms of the reproductive capacity of their bodies and their capacity for emotion than the reasoning capacity of their minds, are still seen to be best suited to and thus most responsible for taking care of children, the aged, their bosses and husbands, and so on.

These different roles and the internalized psychological experiences are a result of historically-embedded cultural constructions, passed down generation after generation through our language system and our relationships. We'll go deeper into the gender question in Chapter 5. For now, we want to make the important point that these dualisms—structured by value hierarchies—frame the ways we think of ourselves in relation to others. Thus, the ways we identify and behave are far from genetically hard-wired; they are created within a complex process of socialization that requires specific linguistic processes and forms (in the following pages, we'll define these as discourses and metaphors) that have been set up within a set of complex hierarchized relations or differences.

Sociologists of knowledge Peter Berger and Thomas Luckman (1966) refer to this process as *primary socialization*—the ways that, through interacting with others, we learn to both internalize particular maps of the world and project ourselves into those maps. Indeed, the language system that any culture uses is what any member is born into and socialized through. We learn who we are in the social process of interaction with others. Our individual and collective identities, who we believe ourselves to be as men and women, African American, white, rich, poor, physically able or differently-abled, teachers, students, wives, husbands, partners, or single, and on and on are all reciprocally transmitted and created within this symbolic system. As we interact within and use the system of codes and metaphors, we create these identities for ourselves and others.

Metaphors and the Construction of Thought

But how do metaphors construct thought and create identity? As should be clear by now, metaphor, as we use it here, is not simply the literary term we learned in English class. As linguists Lakoff and Johnson (2003) point out, our entire conceptual system is metaphorical—we are always conceiving of some aspect of the world in terms of something else, that is, with words that are not exactly that thing. This goes back to Bateson's idea that the map is not the territory. Even language itself is understood metaphorically. We often see language in terms of the metaphor of "conduit" (a direct tube or conveyor) when we say something like "I got the message," or "she got her ideas across to me." But there's a catch. Every metaphor has two effects on the thing or idea that is under discussion. First, a metaphor highlights or brings into focus some aspects of the thing or idea, and second, it hides others. For example, the "language as conduit" metaphor illuminates the ways that language does communicate meaning between people. However, it hides the ways that language is dependent for communication on the context, on the histories of the people involved and their assumptions. Lakoff and Johnson (2003) give the example of the statement "take the apple juice seat." What's your first response to that? It's probably "that's a meaningless sentence." However, if it's added that there's a table in front of you, with a glass of a different juice at each place setting, the statement suddenly takes on a meaning. The context of the glasses of juice is essential for meaningful understanding.

To go back to Bateson, the idea of language as a simple conduit hides the ways that the histories and diverse cultures of each speaker and each listener will introduce very important differences into what is communicated and what is understood. This is often overlooked when considering the metaphorical nature of language. Words have a history and a cultural context! They even have an ecological context, as we discussed in earlier chapters. Rather than assuming a "sender–receiver" understanding of language, we are arguing for an understanding of language as a complex differentiating system where all sorts of possibilities might be at play at any given moment, and are always context dependent. That is, words themselves (as a grouping of letters) have no absolute or inherent meaning. They get their meaning only as they are used in a complex set of social and ecological relationships.

Metaphors With Problematic Consequences

Lakoff and Johnson (2003) draw our attention to metaphors that are dualistic like those discussed above and laid out in Figure 3.1. Adding to this list, dualistic metaphors such as "light/dark" and "up/down" play a role in creating specific meaning associated with good and evil, or superiority and inferiority. Think, for example, of historic references to Africa as the "dark continent," or the notion of the "dark arts," as opposed to phrases like "going toward the light," "lighting the way" or a "beacon of hope." In the case of "up," there is a sense of "progress" that is seen as necessarily good: "moving up the ladder of success," as opposed to "spiraling downward and out of control."

Think About This

Can you think of other examples? Try working with these: white/ black, forward/backward.

Now let's use the tool of examining how a metaphor "highlights" and "hides" aspects of the world with a few more examples. First, let's return to the "stream" and "drain" metaphors from the beginning of the chapter. What is highlighted by the metaphor of "drain"? As was discussed, in our day-to-day context it suggests flushing away waste used for human agriculture. It hides the understandings of "stream," which suggest a body of water with other creatures living in it, implying something that should be nurtured and protected.

Next, consider this statement: "The world is a treasure chest of natural resources." What is highlighted by the metaphor of "treasure chest"? Perhaps you noted that it suggests that nature is here for the taking, or that nature is like the money in treasure chests. What is hidden by the metaphor? For one, natural resources are not unlimited. Further, to think of nature, such as a tree, in terms of its monetary value is to ignore the many other functions of the tree, its ability to process carbon dioxide and hold water, for example. (In addition, please note that the term "natural resources" itself is a metaphor that leads us to see nature primarily in terms of its use value to humans.)

Here's another set of related metaphors: "Developed countries should aid developing countries." What is highlighted by the metaphors of "developed" and "developing"? Certainly, they highlight that there is an evolutionary spectrum from low to high development among different groups of human cultures, that developed is better than less developed, and thus that the developing countries need to go in the direction of the developed countries—to become more like them. Developed also implies strength and superiority, whereas developing countries are weak and inferior.

Now, what is hidden? Centrally, the metaphor hides the reality that developed countries are the largest contributors to the ecological crisis, using far more energy and creating far more pollution per person than the developing countries. This becomes clearer if we invert the metaphor: What if we referred to the industrial countries as "overdeveloped" and the less industrialized countries as "appropriately developed"? The fact that this phrase sounds bizarre shows exactly how thought is structured by metaphors: Virtually all public discussion assumes—without thinking—that the less industrial countries need to become more like the rich countries.

Think About This

Here are a few more for you to try on your own:

- The body's defenses fought off the invading bacteria.
- This scientist is looking at a bed of clams.
- The stream is a living machine.
- The cell is the body's power pack.
- The mind is like a computer.
- The lumbermen harvested the forest.

We are not arguing here that thought is completely determined by certain metaphors or that it is impossible to think in terms different from how those metaphors encourage us to think. The fact that it is possible for us to ask you to think about both what is hidden and what is illuminated by any given metaphor points to the possibility of thinking in ways other than that which the metaphor specifies. It's always possible to use different metaphors, and in fact this is one of our central concerns that we'd like you to consider. Language shapes thought, but it is always possible to shift *how we think* and thus *how we behave* or relate to one another by using different ways of describing or representing the world.

Neither does this way of thinking mean, as many of our own students suggest, that metaphors themselves are "bad," as in bad to use and thus to be avoided. On the contrary, as discussed above, thinking metaphorically is unavoidable; that's just the way language works. We constantly map the world; the important question is "What sorts of maps might be preferable maps?" Which are harmful? The important point is to be aware of the implications of the metaphors one is using. Teachers using responsible pedagogy must be aware of the ways that language works. They need to be constantly aware of the limits of any metaphor, of how it shapes understanding, and when to unpack those limits with students. After all, if we unpacked (which suggests opening a suitcase) every metaphor we used, we would never get anywhere at all!

Still, teachers need to be aware of how their own use of metaphors operates in and influences their interactions with students. Use of metaphor can either invite students into a discussion, or exclude them. Bowers and Flinders (1990) give an example of a lesson on government regulation of the private sector. The teacher first discussed it in terms of government intervention in business, mentioning airline safety inspections, food quality rules, and the minimum wage. These aspects of an authority/power metaphor—a masculine-identified perspective—tended to include more males than females in the class. So the teacher switched to a metaphor of "protection," which brought into the discussion a girl who had previously been silent. Similarly, teachers who only use sports metaphors are likely to be more inviting to students who are excited by sports and to exclude those who aren't. Again, thoughtful teachers use a variety of metaphors to open up a topic to students who come from a variety of cultural backgrounds.

Value Hierarchies, Centric Thinking, and a Logic of Domination

Keeping in mind the ways that metaphor structures our patterns of communication, we can also begin to understand the ways language itself encodes our deeply habituated patterns of thought, behavior, and relationship. We've already introduced the notion of hierarchy that functions within dualisms. In this section, we will elaborate on the ways that language is used to create "value hierarchies," "centric thinking," and a "logic of domination." These concepts, introduced in Chapter 2 in relation to the problem of exclusion in democratic relationships or practice, suggest that language helps to structure specific sorts of relationships that reproduce domination. Indeed, the idea of "centric thinking" is itself a metaphor, indicating that we tend to give higher value to that which is located "in the center" as opposed to that which is "on the margin." Hence, social justice theorists refer to "marginalized" people as those who are devalued and hence granted less access to resources and who also have less decision-making power over the most important aspects of their lives. Center/margin is a dualized set of metaphors that are hierarchized—that is, one term represents more power or value in society than the other. We saw similar metaphors earlier in our discussion of man/woman, reason/emotion, mind/body, up/down, light/dark, forward/backward, and so on. Indeed, as we began to discuss above, many of those metaphorical pairs are used to describe groups of people believed to be "naturally" (that is, biologically) or culturally inferior. Indigenous People from North America were believed to be "backward," for example. This is how value-hierarchized thinking works through metaphor, as we will see in more detail below.

A Note About Concepts

Sometimes students get confused about our use of "value-hierar-chized thinking" versus "centric thinking." These are actually dif-ferent metaphors for the same idea. The idea is that domination occurs when we assume that some people have more value than others and thus can be seen "at the center" versus the "margins"; or at the top of a value hierarchy versus lower in a naturalized stratification. You can combine the metaphors by imagining a cone shape. The top is smaller and the base larger, like a triangle, but with mass. If you look at a cone from overhead, you see the tip as the center of a circle. That tip thus represents both the center and the top of a hierarchy. Make sense?

But, for the moment, let's look at some connections. How do dualistic relationships and the idea of "rationalism" serve so neatly as a justifica-tion for social inequality? There is *a logic of domination* (Warren, 1998) that plays within centric thinking and that follows directly from a few simple premises. First, there is the premise that the physical and emo-tional (and especially "unruly" emotion) are more tied to "nature," while the mental is more tied to "culture." Second is the assumption that what-ever is identified with nature and the realm of the physical is inferior to what is cultural and thus human (we will explore this below as "anthro-pocentrism"). Once the notion of superior and inferior realms is accepted as a truth, then it follows that whatever is defined as superior is morally justified in subordinating and ruling the inferior. The logical conclusion is that the "mental," or "rational," or "cultural," is separate from, and jus-tified in ruling, the "physical," or "emotional," or "natural." The result is, as our earlier example suggested, a whole long list of dualized pairs where one term is always seen as superior to the other: reason/emotion, culture/nature, mind/body, man/woman, and so on. You can probably add to this list by thinking about your own life experiences.

We suggest that this logic of domination, deeply rooted in Western cul-ture and operating metaphorically, underlies the acceptance and continu-ation of class inequality, along with gender and race inequalities, other forms of social degradation, and ecological devastation. If the rational is superior, and humans are rational, then humans are morally justified in dominating or exploiting nature and anything else defined as analo-gous to or "like" nature. Again, using an EcoJustice framework means that we see these problems as interrelated by the specific socio-linguis-tic (cultural) foundations that create value-hierarchized thinking. In the following chapters we will ask you to zero in on gender, race, and social class inequalities and, in particular, the ways in which these are created and reproduced in schooling. But first, a little more on how our use of language, and in particular deeply internalized "root metaphors," makes domination appear to be "just the way the world is."

To combine the ideas of the previous sections, we want to emphasize that metaphors aren't random or spontaneous. Rather, they are a product of culture. Specifically, we understand that the terms within which we think are, in fact, culturally derived ideas that carry a specific cultural history, and, moreover, they may also arise in relation to and in response to a particular ecological context.

From Jeff's Classroom

The images are powerful: smiling faces, people singing while they work, basking in the comfort of community. The culture of Ladakh has for centuries lived sustainably in the Himalayan mountains, sharing work, sharing water, and maintaining a stable society in a harsh environment. "It seems ideal," whispers a baseball-capped student in a high school global studies class, entranced by the happiness of the villagers portrayed in the film *Ancient Futures*. But in just a few years in the 1990s, this ancient culture was undermined, not by war or colonial conquest, but by the force of modern consumer culture. Bewitched by modern conveniences, entrapped by the twists of globalized economic trends, the Ladakhi are being convinced of the need to consume Western products. I've taught this film for several years, with both high school and college students. Every time, as I debrief with students after the film, they are unanimously dismayed by the degradation of Ladakhi culture. Yet, every time, nearly all assume that destruction is inevitable. "You can't stop progress," says one student, voicing what many believe. "Nobody forced them to change," says another. It always proves difficult for students to step outside the assumption of individual choice to see the impact of larger forces; to understand that when community bonds crumble, individuals are led to different choices. To understand societies as different as the Ladakhi and the U.S., we need to understand the different ways they think.

Root Metaphors and Discourses of Modernity

A key—and often ignored—form of metaphor is called a "root metaphor." As suggested by the plant analogy here, root metaphors are the buried ideological sources from which the culture draws strength and reproduces itself inter-generationally, often over hundreds of years. As the visible foliage of a plant draws sustenance from its hidden roots, so the obvious aspects of a culture draw their inspiration from ideological roots that are hidden both by time and by the power of being unconsciously assumed or "taken for granted." Taken-for-granted assumptions are all those ideas that we take to be so obviously "true" that we don't have to think about them. We take for granted that the sun will rise in the east and that if we chew food it will be easier to swallow, but in modern industrial cultures we also take for granted that humans are the most important beings on the planet, and that some humans are more important than others. The power of taken-for-granted assumptions, and the difficulty but possibility of their exposure as something other than "universal truths" is shown in the recently discredited notion that women are not suited for such occupations as Supreme Court Justice, or that a black man could never become President of the United States.

Root metaphors have a history. They were once new ideas, challenging the status quo of their time. Descartes' famous dictum "I think, therefore I am," for example, helped establish the inherent rights of the individual (think of the notion of the individual as "king" or the most important decision-maker, instead of the King) as a challenge to feudal hierarchy, but also encouraged the rejection of the supposedly "backward" conception that humans are rooted in community. It also separates "mind" from "body" and eradicated any spiritual connections to the body.

Some of the most powerful root metaphors in modernist cultures derive from the hierarchized dualisms discussed earlier. *Man* is superior because he can *Reason*. *Woman* is inferior because she lacks Reason and her value is assigned to the reproductive function of her *Body*. Just as in the examples of light/dark and up/down, the root metaphors Man, Reason, and Mind, for example, depend on their oppositional relationships to other metaphors Woman, Emotion, and Body. And the lists of metaphors within each column become analogues of each other. As these taken-for-granted analogies get passed down generation after generation, they become iconic—that is, they take on the status of truth that is very difficult to challenge because everyone, or most people in a culture, accepts it as given. C. A. Bowers explains:

> When there are several competing ways of understanding a new phenomenon, the analogy that prevails becomes over time an iconic metaphor that is a taken-for-granted aspect of thought and communication. Examples of iconic metaphors include "data," the personal pronoun "I," "emancipation," "freedom," "equality," "domination," "environment," and so forth. Indeed, most of our thought and discourse, even material expressions of culture, are dependent upon the use of iconic

metaphors that reproduce the analogies that prevailed at an earlier time due to the dominant status of a root metaphor. . . . The constitutive role of root metaphors in framing thought can be summarized by paraphrasing Nietzsche and Heidegger in the following way: language thinks us as we think within the conceptual categories that the language of our cultural group makes available. As thought is inherently metaphorical, there is always the possibility of identifying more adequate analogies, and even of recognizing aspects of cultural/personal experience that previously held root metaphors cannot account for.

(Bowers, 2003, p. 3)

The question that we'll be asking as we proceed through this book is "what are more adequate metaphors for framing thought if we are interested in a sustainable culture?" Before we get there, however, we need to dig still deeper into language, metaphor, and thought.

Discourses of Modernity

When a group of root metaphors combine, intersect, or begin to depend upon one another, they form a closely woven tapestry of exchanged and internalized meanings. This complex weave of meanings is called *a discourse*. Discourses are complex exchanges of meaning that use metaphor and that thus have a history. As we learn to talk and communicate, we use, internalize, and exchange discourse, participating in the creation and reproduction of deeply-embedded patterns of communication and belief. These patterns create practices that also communicate and create meaning and help to create beliefs. We refer to these as *discursive practices*. The beliefs and the practices they inspire become taken for granted, and less and less likely to be questioned. They just "are."

Discourses use root metaphors to structure and maintain a "that's just the way it is" perception of the world. When these discursive patterns are shared and exchanged by large groups of people, they create a complex worldview—that is, a deeply ingrained set of ideas that structures how one sees, relates to and behaves in the world. Using the concept of discourse analytically helps us to see that a worldview is in fact a combination of linguistically-created ideas; these ideas are invented but take on the function of truth. All cultures use a complex set of discourses to make sense of the world around them. We all become thinking, talking, teaching, praying individuals within and through the use of language that is shaped by commonly shared metaphors.

As we discussed earlier, Western modernist cultures use a set of hierarchized dualisms to create important taken-for-granted root metaphors. These metaphors combine to form powerful modernist discourses that have had major consequences in the lives of people and the overarching ecological systems that we depend upon. Among the major discourses that are created via root metaphors of modernity are these:

- Individualism: The idea of that we are all autonomous individuals and the concomitant separation of people from community. Root Metaphor: autonomous individual is "king."
- Mechanism: The idea that the living world works like a machine. Root metaphor: the universe is a machine.
- Progress: The idea that change is linear and good. Root metaphor: change is improvement.
- Rationalism/Scientism: A particular Western view of knowing the world as the only path to true knowledge. Root metaphor: reason is knowledge.
- Commodification/Consumerism: Discursive practice turning living things and relationships into objects for sale. Faith in the accumulation of objects as the path to happiness. Root metaphors: land is property, living creatures are profit, wealth is material.
- Anthropocentrism: Not only putting humans at the center but at the top of a hierarchy of living and non-living. Root metaphor: humans are superior and dominant.
- Androcentrism: Putting men at the center as more valuable than and superior to women. Root metaphor: man is superior and dominant.
- Ethnocentrism: Putting some cultures or groups of people at the center as more valuable than and superior to others. Root metaphor: Caucasian is superior and dominant.

This list should make it clear that modernity is far from equivalent to "industrialism," or "capitalism." In fact, when viewed from the perspective of the consequences of hierarchized and dualistic modes of thinking, it is important to see both capitalism and its antithesis, socialism, as products of the culture of modernity. Capitalism in simple terms is a set of productive relationships where those who own the means of production are in control of and may exploit those whose labor they buy. Profit for the owners is a result of the difference between the cost of production, including what the laborers are paid, and what the product is sold for. Because profit is what matters most in a capitalist system, both the people who work within the system and the land from which the raw material for production is extracted, are necessarily highly exploited. A logic of domination is thus part of the way the system works.

While the rapaciousness of capitalism is thus of enormous concern, socialist countries share the same logic of domination—especially when it comes to the land—and have been just as destructive to the environment as capitalist countries. Thus the problems we face are deeper than can be dealt with by the usual critique of capitalism that offers socialism as an alternative. They are, in fact, created through and imbedded in the deeply-held assumptions and associated discursive forms that helped to make modern industrial systems possible in the first place.

Likewise, because the culture of modernity underlies the ecological crisis, an effective response to the crisis must go beyond conventional environmentalism. Instead, we must reach for a deeper challenge to the very roots of the destructive aspects of our culture. It is important to understand that the primary discourses of modernity are created and maintained by all of us, as we participate in this culture. Thus, they have a specific history that can be traced. Furthermore, as we will discuss in more detail in Chapters 8, 9, and 10, there are many other historical and contemporary societies built upon different metaphors and discursive patterns that are far more sustainable than those based on modernity. Contrasting the primary discourses (sometimes called "master narratives") of modernist and non-modernist societies will help illuminate them both (see Figure 3.3).

The balance of this chapter will discuss the central discourses of modernity and the metaphors they use, followed by the discourses and metaphors used by sustainable societies.

Mechanism

Mechanism is the assumption that the world and everything in it functions like a machine. The mechanistic metaphor dates to what eco-feminist philosopher Caroline Merchant refers to as the scientific revolution, when such Enlightenment thinkers as René Descartes and Francis Bacon suggested that viewing living things as machines helped to see life as having understandable, predictable processes, rather than seeing them as mystical, unknowable, or having a "spirit." Astronomer Johannes Kepler, for example, said "My aim is to show that the celestial machine is to be likened not to a divine organism but to a clockwork" (Kepler, in Merchant, 1983). This idea of the cosmos as machine was a radical change that was a direct attempt to assert control over a perceived unruly natural world. As Merchant (1983) points out, the shift amounted to "the death of nature," as the organic worldview was replaced with mechanism:

> The world we have lost was organic. From the obscure origins of our species, human beings have lived in daily, immediate organic relation with the natural order for their sustenance. In 1500, the daily interaction with nature was still structured for most Europeans as it was for other peoples, by close knit, cooperative, organic communities. Thus it is not surprising that for sixteenth-century Europeans, the root metaphor binding together the self, society and the cosmos was that of an organism . . . organismic theory emphasized interdependence among the parts of the human body, subordination of individual

to communal purposes in family, community, and state, and vital life permeating the cosmos to the lowliest stone.

(Merchant, 1983, p. 1)

The fundamental social and intellectual problem for the seventeenth century was the problem of order. The perception of disorder, so important to the Baconian doctrine of dominion over nature, was also crucial to the rise of mechanism as a rational antidote to the disintegration of the organic cosmos. The new mechanical philosophy of the mid-seventeenth century achieved a reunification of the cosmos, society and the self in terms of a new metaphor—the machine.

(Merchant, 1983, p. 192)

While the mechanistic root metaphor helped the development of modern science, it also reduced the sense of the sacredness and interconnectedness of life. As Val Plumwood (2002) has argued, mechanism combined with anthropocentrism (discussed below) made it possible to abstract the natural world from our daily lives, to split nature off from human life and cut her up into parts in order to control her.

Associated with the mechanistic model is "linear thinking"; that is, the idea that events follow a line that goes in one direction. When we see systems operating step-by-step in chains of cause and effect we are using linear thinking. It also involves "reductionist thinking" where complex interconnected systems are seen as problems to be "broken down into [their] component parts, isolating [them from their] environment and solving each portion independently" (Merchant, 1983, p. 182). While reductionism helps one understand the function of the components, it hides the interconnections.

The mechanistic metaphor is expressed currently in daily language when we say that the heart is a pump, or when we see an idea as "the engine of growth," or when we describe the brain as an "information-processing" system that uses "inputs," "outputs," and "feedback" to operate efficiently, or, as in the opening example from Rebecca's classroom, when a stream is referred to as a drain. As Rebecca's students readily pointed out, living relationships such as those found in moving bodies of water can be used very differently when we see them as machines. For example, when a farm is seen through the machine metaphor, the farmer's focus is on what inputs and techniques will produce the most food, rather than on understanding and caring for the land—the soil, plants and animals as well as the humans—as living interdependent relationships. When "the farm" is thought of as "a factory" we lose the understanding of and appreciation for the connections that our bodies have with the bodies of other living creatures; we lose the understanding of the sacredness of that connection and its necessity to the life cycle.

Some Western scientists, particularly quantum physicists and ecologists, have stepped outside the limitations of mechanism by emphasizing the interconnections and interdependence of physical and living systems. These "new" perspectives in Western science echo perspectives held by Indigenous cultures that depend on oral traditions to pass on knowledge. However, the mechanistic metaphor is still dominant in most science education, and even more so in everyday speech. The consequences of mechanism include:

- a devaluation of living things from sacredness to physical objects;
- overlooking the complexity of living communities by reducing them to separate parts and cause and effect chains.

Scientism/Rationalism

Mechanism has its origins in what historians refer to as "the scientific revolution," and thus is highly dependent upon another powerful metaphor: science. But how can we possibly call science a discourse? Isn't it universal? Beginning with the idea that it is a discourse unmasks its complexity in modernist culture. First, alongside mechanism, science carries the assumption that to "know" the natural world is to be able to control it by applying rationality or reason. It emphasizes objectivity and purports to be culture-free as well as outside of morality. Keep in mind here how it differs from what Bateson refers to as an ecology of mind. It operates by using dualism to imagine that humans are radically "outside" nature, and that scientific "knowing" is an "objective" enterprise. And yet, in assuming a reductionist posture, as noted above, science is squarely a cultural enterprise, because reductionism hides more comprehensive ways of understanding the world.

The assumptions of science suggest that it is the only valid way to know the world. To question the universal nature of science as a way of knowing is not to be "anti-science." Rather, we must see science as one way of knowing rather than the only valid one. As Wendell Berry (2000a) points out:

> People exploit what they have merely concluded to be of value, but they defend what they love. To defend what we love we need a particularizing language, for we love what we particularly know. The abstract, "objective," impersonal, dispassionate language of science can, in fact, help us to know certain things, and to know some things with certainty . . . But it cannot replace, and it cannot become, the language of familiarity, reverence, and affection by which things of value ultimately are protected.

(p. 41)

Among the consequences of the science metaphor are:

- a dismissing of other forms of knowing, such as traditional or spiritual knowledge;
- a reduction of life to non-living processes;
- compatibility of the "objective" stance with the needs of industry to reduce everything to price (commodification).

Individualism

Individualism, at heart, is the assumption that humans are autonomous agents, who are at their best when independent from community and culture, and who are naturally predisposed to the accumulation of goods and materials to satisfy their own needs and wants. René Descartes' famous dictum, "I think, therefore I am," is a perfect motto for this discourse. In this assertion, the autonomous "I" is the source of all rationality, meaning, and knowledge. Further, the most effective societal arrangements are those that maximize individual success in accumulation, thus competition is promoted as good and, in fact, natural. This idea is rooted not only in the Enlightenment thinkers, such as Descartes, but in the Romantics of the 19th century, who celebrated a concept of creativity that saw imagination as a pure spring that flowed from inner experience, uninfluenced by culture. Going back to our earlier discussion of Bateson's work, this discourse has led to the idea that mind, or human intelligence, is something that grows out of individual thought and is the result of independent brain power, or natural talent.

When the individual is seen as the basic social unit, there are specific consequences: (1) thinking and intelligence begins with the individual, as in politics (John Locke), and morality (individual rights); (2) social decisions are based on the good of the individual rather than the community, as with laws that privilege private property owners over the larger community; and (3) those who do not succeed in society are seen as individual failures: either they were too lazy or they simply do not have the adequate natural talents that those who do succeed possess. Thus, the American ideal of meritocracy—a system based on the reward of hard work and talent—rationalizes individual success or failure and social inequality as simply a result of human nature. We'll be coming back to the way this works to structure policy and practice in institutions such as schools in Chapters 4, 5, 6, and 7 especially.

The individualist discourse is expressed every time we talk about individual rights and when we talk about the community as oppressive. It is expressed in schools that insist that students do individual work and get individual grades and individual intelligence tests scores; or when we think of human needs in terms of Maslow's hierarchy, putting "self-actualization" at the top while other more social relational needs—such as love—are placed below. Of particular importance is the individualist understanding of creativity, expressed every time we ask a student to "think for yourself" or "make your own meaning." By suggesting that ideas or meanings come solely from within someone's head, this phrase hides the way we exchange and create meaning via language in relationship with each other and, as Bateson teaches, in our interdependency with the natural world. In short, it ignores the cultural and ecological influences on thinking, and encourages the individual to assume they are autonomous. Further, leading the young to place high value on their own thinking puts moral authority in the hands of the young, and dismisses the claim to authority of Elders who may carry knowledge and wisdom that has been handed down across many generations, whether it is how to preserve food, or how to live sustainably with a community.

The consequences of individualism include:

- overlooking or rejecting community as necessary to individual well-being;
- a cultural focus on the individual doing what feels good, rather than constraining behavior out of respect for others;
- an emphasis on consumption as a route to individual satisfaction;
- a denial of the interconnections and interdependencies with the larger ecological systems that sustain all life;
- a fundamental inability to perceive the ways that diversity works among human communities and the more-than-human world to create all forms of creativity.

Progress

Progress as a discourse conveys the idea that certain changes are inevitable and good. Change is improvement. Modernity carries forward the assumption that change moves society forward and makes human society better off. Beyond the obvious expressions of "change as good," the discourse of progress is expressed whenever we say "oh, you can't stop progress"; or when we demand the latest product or the newest idea, assuming they must be superior to the old; or when we write histories which teach that, despite a few bad turns, things keep getting better every century.

It should be emphasized that to say progress is a discourse with certain root metaphors attached to it is not to say that other sorts of progress are never a good thing. For example, we might say that as authors writing this chapter, we are making progress toward completing this book. Instead, the issue is that we assume change to be a good thing, rather than examining the effects that social and technological changes may have on society. Among the consequences of progress as a discourse are:

- the "anti-tradition" tradition of rejecting older ways simply because they are older;
- the loss of traditional knowledge as older ways are forgotten;
- an acceptance of destructive change on the assumption that it's unavoidable, and a minimizing of the negative impacts.

Commodification/Consumerism

Commodification is a set of discursive practices (that is, practices that communicate and create meaning) by which market values overwhelm the world and turn nature, people, and even ideas into commodities for sale on the market. While some degree of commodification has existed for centuries—certainly, slaves were humans made into commodities—it is the penetration of the market into every area of life that creates a taken-for-granted feeling that it is natural, for example, to make a marriage decision a subject for television entertainment, or for seeds used by Indigenous farmers for generations to be patented by a corporation (see Chapter 8 for this disturbing story).

Consumerism works hand-in-hand with commodification. The discourse of consumerism teaches people that their identity is largely created by what products they buy. Thus people define themselves as much by what clothes they wear or what music they listen to as by the fundamental values they hold. This discourse also teaches us that happiness is defined by what stuff we possess and how much of it we can buy.

As Bowers (2001b) points out, "the culture of commodification now encompasses every aspect of adults' lives: sexual reproduction, health care, leisure activities, spiritual activities and death itself" (p. 159). The effects can be seen dramatically in the way traditional cultures change under the onslaught of commodification and begin to see the traditions they once utilized as backward or inferior. Jerry Mander (1996) writes of the impact of television and market culture on the native people of Canada's Mackenzie River Valley. Within a few years of the introduction of television, the people began to discard their own culture. According to Mander's informants:

> now the children want all kinds of new things like cars; yet most of the communities have no roads. They don't want to learn how to fish on the ice or go hunting anymore . . . Most important of all, the women said, was that TV had put a stop to storytelling. It used to be that the old people would sit each evening in the corner of the house, telling the children ancient stories about life in the North. Through that process, the elders had been the windows through which the younger generation could see their own past and traditions; it was how the children could sense their own Indian roots.
>
> (Mander, 1996, p. 352)

But, with commodified stories offered by TV shows, Elders' stories were dismissed as old-fashioned.

We express the discourses of commodification and consumerism when we assume that "everything has a price," or when we use "cost–benefit" analysis that puts a monetary value on life, when we see a forest as so many board feet, or when we value purchased music over that created within a family or community.

The consequences of commodification/consumerism include:

- loss of non-commodified knowledge, such as the ability to prepare and preserve food;
- loss of sacredness and a sense of the spiritual, as everything is reduced to market price;
- loss of local uniqueness, as one can travel around the world and buy the same fast food and other products;
- loss of cultural identities, as people define themselves more by what they purchase than by long-standing traditions;
- an emphasis on consumption (and disposal) of purchased items as a central purpose of life, thus exacerbating the ecological crisis.

Anthropocentrism

Anthropocentrism, or "humans at the center," has deep roots in Western culture. In the book of Genesis, humans are given "dominion over the fish of the sea, and over the fowl of the air, and over the cattle, and over all the earth, and over every creeping thing that creepeth upon the earth" (Genesis 1:26). Some argue that the concepts translated as "dominion" should instead be understood as "stewardship," suggesting that humans should be caretakers for the natural world rather than its undisputed rulers. What is important, however, is the cultural meaning that has developed over the centuries, which clearly places humans at the top of a hierarchy of the living and non-living world, whether as exploiters or stewards. In medieval times, the "great chain of being" reserved a rung in the cosmic hierarchy—from God down to rocks—for every different living or non-living thing. Today we are more secular, moving instead to define everything by its monetary value: What could be more anthropocentric than seeing a rock, or a beetle, or an ecosystem, solely in terms of what it is worth to *us*?

As this line of thinking and the associated metaphors are passed through generations via our words and our actions, we have learned to hyper-separate ourselves from nature by internalizing a dualistic way of thinking that rests on the "backgrounding" and inferiorizing of nature. Put bluntly, it's what makes it possible for us to drive down a highway and not be absolutely horrified by all the dead animal bodies alongside or in the middle of the road.

The consequences of anthropocentrism include:

- the rapacious killing of animal life, from the mass killing of the buffalo to the over-fishing of the seas, as well as the deforestation of whole hillsides and the subsequent loss of top soil necessary to support plant life;
- treating ecosystems as dumping grounds for waste, producing, for example, the air and water pollution that are becoming crises;
- the treatment of the non-human world as objects or commodities available for our consumption.

Androcentrism

Androcentrism is the idea that men are naturally superior to women because they hold the natural capacity for reason. According to Enlightenment thinkers, women were not fit to be part of the political decision-making or developing economic spheres primarily because they lacked the capacity for reason. Their natural reproductive capacity made the domestic realm and child rearing their natural sphere of influence. Thus defined according to the function of their womb rather than their intellectual capacity, "woman" becomes defined as analogous to "body" while "man" is analogous to "mind." And, since man is the rational creator of culture, woman is associated as closest to, even analogous to, nature. Since nature was defined as in need of control by rational men, woman, too, was to be brought under the control of her father, husband, the methodologies of science and medicine, or the State. Today, even though the feminist movement has had many successes in shifting androcentric thinking and challenging patriarchal culture, the consequences of androcentrism are many. They include:

- a "feminization" of work and professions deemed "reproductive" or service-oriented (education, nursing, secretarial) and the associated rationalization of lower pay for those professions;
- a tendency to define women as less capable of being leaders due to their "natural" emotionality and lack of capacity for "reason";
- a tendency to associate woman with nature, as in the still popular notion of Mother Nature as both mysterious and unpredictable and, thus, in need of man's controlling hand;
- a much higher incidence of violence—both physical and psychological—against women in the form of rape, domestic violence, and misogynistic messages throughout the media.

Ethnocentrism

Ethnocentrism is the idea that some people or groups of people are naturally superior to others. The very possibility of the concept "race" rests on this root metaphor. "White" and "black," for example, or the idea of the "red man" are all historically-adopted metaphors that are only possible based on the acceptance of this root metaphor and its very important relationship to anthropocentrism. What does this mean? Think back to the ways that the Indigenous People encountered in North America were defined by the Europeans who encountered them. What words were used? They were likened to "Savages." "Barbarians." "Uncivilized." "Animals." The same is true for the rationalization of the act of slavery. People of African descent were seen as enslavable precisely because they could be defined as not quite human. Now consider this: Upon what discourse and set of assumptions does the use of these metaphors rely? It would not have been possible to inferiorize some people by comparing them to animals if we did not first have the idea firmly engrained that animals are inferior to humans.

Some of the consequences of ethnocentrism include:

• the naturalization of the idea of race, and of the attempt to link economic or educational achievement, for example, to genetic or cultural characteristics;
• the rationalization of vast inequalities in income or access to what is needed to live based on the idea that some people simply deserve more;
• the carrying out of holocaust and genocide.

Anthropocentrism, androcentrism, and ethnocentrism are structured by what we have introduced as "value hierarchies" that are interwoven via dualistic analogies or comparisons ("this" is like "that") to create centric thinking and a logic of domination. Centric thinking is patterned by metaphorical relationships that present these hierarchies as natural, and thus the violent behaviors that are associated with them are seen as inevitable and just. Mapped onto our consciousness through our daily conversations, and enacted within our cultural institutions, these deeply-embedded sets of assumptions underlie and lead to the actions that have created both the ecological crises and social crises plaguing our communities. They are the cultural "maps" handed down over many generations. We create and recreate them through the words and other symbolic exchanges (discourses) in which we engage, and we have learned to accept and use them as "truths" to exploit and control each other and the natural world. The result is disastrous for the entire ecological system—both human communities and their nested relationship with the more-than-human world.

These three hierarchically structured discourses link up with other primary discourses (individualism, mechanism, progress and scientism, for example) and help to form the modernist mindset and Western industrial social arrangements that get taken for granted.

Discourse and the Processes of Centric Thinking

The analysis of centric thinking exposes the intertwined nature of these age-old patterns of hierarchized belief leading to both social and ecological oppression. Plumwood (2002) draws upon and extends the critique of centric discourses in the work of other feminists and critical race theorists by pointing out important parallels between androcentrism, ethnocentrism, and anthropocentrism. "A [dominant] centrism," she writes, "sets up one term (the One) as primary or as centre and defines marginal others as secondary . . . as deficient in relation to the centre. Dominant Western culture is androcentric, Eurocentric, and ethnocentric, as well as anthropocentric" (p. 101).

So, let's think back to the dualisms we discussed earlier. Man is the One while woman is inferiorized Other; white Europeans are the One while people of color are inferiorized Other. Human culture is the One while nature and the more-than-human world is the inferiorized Other. While social justice theorists continue to ignore the operation of anthropocentrism in this mindset, an EcoJustice framework insists on exposing the ways social and ecological violence are parallel to and even depend upon each other to keep a logic of domination, and the attending economic and political system currently ravaging the world, in place. Any serious analysis of class, gender, race, and schooling must keep this larger framework at the forefront. Otherwise, we run the risk of focusing on symptoms of social inequality or environmental degradation as if they are disconnected and not embedded in these larger cultural patterns. And, as we'll make clear in the next three chapters, this includes the analysis of social inequalities and schooling.

The primary features of centric thinking, according to Plumwood (1993, 2002) include the following:

- radical exclusion: leaving the interests of those deemed inferior outside of decision-making or without equal access to resources needed to live;
- homogenization: disregarding the unique qualities of individuals within a group deemed inferior, so that all appear to be "the same";
- backgrounding: considering those deemed inferior as secondary or inessential to one's needs or interests; they simple become part of the "background" while one's own activities are attended to as important, or essential;

- incorporation: making the particular needs and interests of those deemed inferior invisible or non-existent, thus assimilating them to the needs of the One;
- instrumentalism: valuing those deemed inferior only in terms of their usefulness to one's needs or interests. Exploitation.

These categories expose the specific ways that discourses rationalizing sexism, for example, run parallel to or even depend upon discourses rationalizing violence to animals and living systems in the natural world, which also help to rationalize racist identification and historical colonization of Indigenous groups or people of color by white Europeans. The chart in Figure 3.2 lays out how centric thinking works to create a logic of domination as it weaves among androcentrism, ethnocentrism, and anthropocentrism. In the next four chapters, we'll be providing specific examples of the ways these processes function within the context of public schooling, human supremacy, gender, class, and race.

So, what do we gain by understanding the way these discourses, value hierarchies, and centric thinking structure our culture? First of all, we begin to recognize that the patterns of belief and behavior of which we were once unaware are suddenly in front of us as the product of centuries of human action and politically motivated invention. They are not the result of nature, and they are not inevitable. They are products of centuries of human cultural labor that create an overall taken-for-granted mindset. They are, going back to Bateson (2000), "maps," but they are not the territory. And this modernist map or mindset is having a devastating impact on the world: on our bodies as they allow the production and ingestion of harmful chemicals; on our families as it becomes harder and harder to make ends meet; and on other cultures around the world as we export this way of thinking to others as "the one right way" or as the most "developed" way. And, as people are threatened, so too are other species and the overall systems upon which we depend.

As the discourses of Western industrial culture are globalized (see Chapter 8) in the name of modernity, development, and civilization, diverse and centuries-old patterns and practices that acknowledged ecological limits and human interdependencies with natural systems are swept aside, defined as primitive or "undeveloped," in favor of the "technological efficiency" of industrial methods. Monoculturalization and market-based relationships are replacing what were once rich relationships nurturing both community and biological and cultural diversity (Mander & Goldsmith, 1996; Pollan, 2006; Shiva, 1993).

While it should be clear by now that we see these particular discourses as destructive, we are not advocating for one right map, or way of seeing. Indeed a wide range of diverse cultural responses to the natural world organized via diverse cosmologies and articulated through

Radical Exclusion: The Otherized group is deemed to be both inferior to and radically seperate from the One who holds the center position.

Anthropocentrism: Non-human beings are defined as constituting a lower order of life and radically excluded from humans based on a lack of "reason." Exclusion and inferiorization stresses those features which make them different from humans. Nature is conceived of in mechanical terms such as "dead" and manipulable, thus outside the ethical responsibilities of men.

Androcentrism: Woman is defined as having a different nature and thus is excluded from man based on her lack of reason and her closeness to "nature." She becomes the analogue to radically excluded nature.

Ethnocentrism: Racialized others are deemed to be so "different" from the normalized "White Western European" group, that they are radically excluded from economic, political decision making/power. Inferiorized identities as well as less access to resources result.

Homogenization: Difference in the Otherized group are disregarded; the Other is not viewed as an individual but rather a member of a group of interchangeable, replaceable items/resources to be managed.

Anthropocentrism: Nature and animals are seen as the same in their lack of reason and reflective consciousness, thus conceived of in terms of interchangeable and replaceable parts and a serious underestimation of their individual and systemic complexity. The integrity of the individual creature as a living being is completely disregarded, thus no moral or ethical responsibility toward a particular animal or a tree, for example, is deemed necessary.

Androcentrism: Women as a group are seen as very different from men, but "all alike" as a group, especially in their lack of reasoning capacity, emotionality, reproductive function, etc. They are defined according to female "essence" in order to control and dominate then according to an inferior nature.

Ethnocentrism: "They're all alike." Individual differences among the "otherized" group are disregarded in favor of perceived group characteristics thus making possible generalized inferiorization and stereotyping.

Backgrounding/Denial: As a radically excluded, inferior and homogenized group, the Other is deemed inessential to the needs of the One. Thus, dependency on the Other by the One cannot be acknowledged or is minimized.

Anthropocentrism: Nature is the inessential background to technology and other human interests; dependency on nature is denied in favor of short-term human interests; nature's needs are systematically discounted in decision-making.

Androcentrism: The contribution of women to any collective undertaking will be denied or at best minimized. Women's work will be backgrounded and unrecognized as having real value when compared to men's contributions, defined as "real work;" men's dependency on women's labor is discounted, women's needs discounted in decision-making.

Ethnocentrism: The contributions of people of color to the general well-being or accomplishments of society is disregarded or deemed inessential, thus any dependence on knowledge, labor, or other contributions cannot be acknowledged.

Incorporation: Assimilation. The inferiorized Other is devalued as an absence, thus any interests or needs of the Other are assimilated into the needs and interests of the One.

Anthropocentrism: Nature is denied any independent definition depending completely on the primacy of the human for any meaning; thus animals, plants and other living creatures are deemed deficient and inferior because they lack human forms of thought/reason; they are not given value for other distinct traits they may have, and are thus assimilated to human needs, or replaced where possible by human order or machines.

Androcentrism: Woman is defined in relation to the man who is considered the standard or the norm; thus, she is conceived of comparatively as "deficient," a deprivation, or an absence in relation to him. Her needs are denied incorporated into his.

Ethnocentrism: Whiteness is defined as the standard or the norm, so that white privilege is unconscious and the needs, interests, and values of the other are disregarded or invisible, thus assimilated into the culture and interests of white culture.

Instrumentalism: The Other is a means to the One's ends; the One denies the Other's agency and independence.

Anthropocentrism: Since human interests are believed to be the source of all value in the world, the independent needs or interests of other living creatures are denied and deemed valuable only to the extent that they serve human ends. The non-human world is reduced to raw material and resources for human use and profit.

Androcentrism: Woman is valued primarily as an instrument to satisfy men's needs and interests. Her independent interests are denied or downplayed; she is conceived of as passive and subsumed in the agency of men. Women are reduced to objects of pleasure, labor, or reproduction.

Ethnocentrism: "Race" as a category of differentiation is created specifically for instrumental purposes, that is, to rationalize the exploitation or USE VALUE of "Others" on the basis of their inferiority and likeness to animals as beasts of burden.

Characteristics of Centric Thinking

Figure 3.2 Characteristics of Centric Thinking.

Source: Adapted from Plumwood, V. (2002). *Environmental culture: The ecological crisis of reason.* New York, NY: Routledge.

Discourses and Root Metaphors of Western Modern Cultures	Discourses and Root Metaphors of Sustainable Cultures
• **Mechanism:** sees world and life processes as being like a machine. Exhibited in such terms as "information processing" and "feedback systems."	• **Holistic/Organic:** sees world as interconnected like a living thing. Views humans and the rest of nature in reciprocal relationships of interdependence.
• **Individualism:** individual is seen as the basic social unit, autonomous from culture and tradition or struggling to escape them. Expressed in such terms as "be creative" and "think for yourself."	• **Community-centered:** sees community as basic social unit. Elders conserve and pass on traditions tha sustain community and ecology. Community includes rest of nature.
• **Anthropocentrism:** sees humans as at the center and dominant over the rest of nature. Ignores consequences of human activity. Expressed in Genesis' granting of dominion over nature to humans, and in such terms as "natural resources."	• **Ecological:** sees humans and other life and non-living as equal participants in a moral universe. Humans have moral obligation to nature.
• **Change:** seen as linear and usually progressive, but irresistible regardless. Expressed in "you can't stop progress" and in assumptions that "newer is better," experimenting on nature is good.	• **Controlled Change:** Stability is valued. All cultures change, but here change is evaluated in terms of long-term consequences. Past and future are important considerations in decisions.
• **Science:** is seen as most legitimate way of knowing; objective and culture free; seperate from morality. Reductionist - analyses complex phenomena by breaking into parts. Knowledge is only "high-status," that derived from rational thought and formal schooling.	• **Science:** is just one way of knowing. Science is holistic, focusing on whole systems rather than parts, on understanding relationships and patterns. Knowledge comes in many forms - tacit, folk, poetic, spiritual, technical, encoded in langauge, genes, plants.
• **Commodification:** or turning everything into a product for sale on the market. Expressed in idea that "education is an investment in the future."	• **Non-commodified:** traditions maintained based on intrinsic value and meaning. Markets and monetary transactions are a small part of culture.

Discourses of Modernity vs. Sustainable Cultures

Figure 3.3 Discourses of Modernity vs. Sustainable Cultures.

Source: Adapted from the works of C.A. Bowers.

different languages can be found across the planet. Many of these embrace and protect their embeddedness with the natural. Examples of these more ecological models can be found among the Ladakhi people of India (Norberg-Hodge, 1991), among the Quechua in the Andes (Apffel-Marglin & PRATEC, 1998), among the Apache of North America

(Basso, 1996), among the Inuit of Northern Canada, and many other Indigenous cultures around the world (Grim, 2001). These cultures have developed diverse systems in close recognition of their interdependence with living systems. These diverse cultural maps or cosmologies create important *differences that make a difference* among humans and the living systems upon which we depend (see also Abram, 1996). We will be introducing you to a number of these cultures in Chapters 8 and 9. Such possibilities also exist within our own industrial culture where groups of people are beginning to reclaim ways of knowing and living that also open them to recognizing the needs of the larger system and their reliance upon it. We'll introduce you to some of these communities—both rural and urban—as well.

Discourses of Sustainable Cultures

To understand the power of the worldview offered by the discourses of modernity, it is valuable to consider common discourse and metaphors shared by those societies that are more sustainable. Again, we want to emphasize the diversity among such cultures, so all of these root metaphors may not be shared by every traditional culture. What we share here, however, reflects the sharply contrasting view offered by most. Also, it should be emphasized that not all Indigenous cultures are sustainable—although those that weren't tended not to survive. This leads Gary Snyder (1990) to call the cultures we are interested in here "mature" cultures, because their patterns of belief and behavior have meant that they have been around for centuries longer than modern industrial cultures. Neither are we suggesting that traditional oral cultures are perfect models—many are marred by patriarchal relations, for example; others suffer from high infant mortality. In short, we are not suggesting some sort of Utopian vision with these examples; rather, we want to point to examples of what sorts of metaphors guide other cultures from which we could learn.

In contrast to the mechanistic thinking of the modern world, sustainable societies tend to have "holistic" root metaphors that explain all things as connected—as Western scientists have begun to learn again through ecological studies that help us see the complex interdependence in ecosystems. Rather than seeing the world as a machine, sustainable cultures view the world as an organism or sometimes as complex kinship relationships, suggesting that the different parts are living beings that are part of a larger life system. Thus, for example, many Indigenous cultures see the Earth as a mother, a giver of life, and use other kinship metaphors to name their relationships to the natural world: grandmother moon, father sky, animals as brothers and sisters, and so on. A key consequence of a holistic view is that humans are more likely to respect and revere that which they see as living (rather than as machine-like), and less likely to reduce the living to dead objects that can be studied or from which they can profit.

Sustainable cultures tend to see things through the lenses of family and community rather than the individual. The good of the community is placed above or equal to the good of the individual—and community means both the abstraction of the community as a whole and the concreteness of caring for the good of neighbors. In the Himalayan culture of Ladakh, for example, families take turns helping each other harvest crops. Among the Quechua, "chacra" is a word meaning both nurturance and plot of cultivated land.

In cultures in which community is the basic social unit, Elders tend to be seen as sources of wisdom rather than as old-fashioned or no longer of use. Elders pass on the accumulated knowledge of the society to the next generation. The Haudenasaunee Declaration of the Iroquois, published in 1979 by a group of Iroquois Elders, says, for example:

> We point out to you that a spiritual consciousness is the path to survival of humankind. We who walk about on Mother Earth occupy this place for only a short time. It is our duty as human beings to preserve the life that is here for the benefit of the generations yet unborn.
>
> (Quoted in Bowers, 1995, p. 145)

As Bowers points out,

> they are not the words of a group of older people who gathered together for the purpose of making a public statement on what they as individuals perceive as the latest threat to their existence as a cultural group. Rather, their words encode fundamental knowledge about the interdependence and fragile nature of the web of food, information and spirit that we now call an ecosystem.
>
> (Bowers, 1995, p. 145)

In contrast to the anthropocentrism of modernity, sustainable cultures are *ecological* and organized in networks rather than hierarchies. That is, nature outside humanity is seen as a moral equal, deserving of the same respect as humans. One important result is that humans are seen as having a moral obligation to animals, plants, and the rest of nature. This doesn't necessarily mean that humans are prevented from eating animals. Instead, peoples living in sustainable cultures have traditional stories (referred to as "teachings") that insist on human responsibility not to unnecessarily harm individual creatures, or overuse or pollute ecosystems. For example, many Indigenous cultures have fables about the greedy individual who kills too many animals and suffers punishment before learning his lesson.

Consider This

While we once used the term ecocentric to describe cultures that are ecologically organized, we now avoid all metaphors that repro-duce the notion of centric thinking. We feel strongly that ecological communities are not centric or organized by value hierarchies, and so we look for language that describes what they are: holistic net-works, relational, and so on. We use ecological thinking to describe an alternative to centric thinking.

Where modern society worships progress and assumes change is inevi-table, sustainable societies tend to *control change*. Unlike the myth of "unchanging primitives," all societies change—and they all understand that change must be acknowledged. Sustainable societies, however, actively evaluate potential changes, considering the long-term conse-quences on the community, as well as how a change fits with the tradi-tions from the past.

A fascinating modern example is the Amish of the eastern and mid-western U.S. The Amish have maintained a distinct culture in the face of the pressure of modernity through a process of evaluating poten-tial social or technological changes for their likely effect on their com-munity. Each innovation is pilot-tested, in a sense, by allowing limited use. A council of Elders considers the effects on the community before deciding whether to adopt or ban the innovation, or forge a compro-mise. For example, while battery-generated electricity has been allowed, especially for commercial use, television has been completely banned. On the other hand, telephones are allowed—but not in the house, where phone conversations would disrupt family interaction. Instead, tele-phones are placed along the street, so they can be used for necessary communication.

Where modern societies have made a secular religion of *science*, many other ways of knowing are valued by sustainable societies. Folk knowl-edge handed down by Elders encodes traditional knowledge about where to find food and what plants are good for medicine, but also about how to live in balance with the environment. Spiritual knowledge offers ways to live in harmony with the powers of nature.

Where Western science is analytic, breaking things into their constit-uent parts, Indigenous science is holistic, investigating the world as an interconnected whole. Kawagley and Barnhardt (1999) tell of the ability of Alaskan natives to predict fish runs through their knowledge of the historical changes in the entire ecosystem, while Western fish biologists had less success because they were focused only on isolated factors. As one Aleut Elder notes: "Bird scientists study birds. Marine mammal scientists study marine mammals. Fishery scientists study fish. They specialize even within a single category. Very few studies are done on how each species interacts with each other and under what environmental conditions" (1999, p. 135). Further, where Western science tends to make short-term observations, Indigenous science has "a long-term perspective spanning many generations of observation and experimentation" (p. 134). The Alaskan natives had been observing fish runs for 300 years, so could fit recent changes into the patterns they had seen over the years.

Sustainable societies maintain *non-commodified traditions*, that is, all or most of their relationships do not involve monetary transactions. Instead, activities are characterized by traditions that involve face-to-face relationships, community, and intergenerational knowledge. Of course, many sustainable societies have trade and other economic relationships, but they are different from modern societies for at least three reasons: first, trade is often based on barter, rather than through the abstract concept of money; and, second, while many Indigenous cultures have "markets," they are only an occasional and small part of cultural activity, rather than defining the whole way of life; and third, trade and other economic activities are generally carried out within the frame of other values—for example, trade relations may reflect the status of those participating.

An EcoJustice perspective on education asks teachers to examine the ways that this particular Western mindset has come about, how it is maintained, and how it contributes to the degradation of both human communities and the larger ecosystems contributing to and supporting those communities. The concepts may appear complex, but can be taught with appropriate modifications in elementary school. Below, we offer sample activities, as well as a Conceptual Toolbox, readings and other resources. You will also find more resources on our website at www.routledge.com/textbooks/9780415872515.

What Schools and Teachers Can Do

Sample Activities

Identify Root Metaphors and Discourses of Modernity

First and foremost, teachers should get in the habit of examining the language that is used in classroom materials and everyday interactions in schools, and, as much as possible, invite students into that examination. Ask students to identify what is hidden and illuminated in a metaphor and what the consequences of the hidden meanings are.

Unpack Inferiorization

Ask students to think about the negative words used about other cultures to demean them as inferior to Western culture (e.g. "weird" or "backward").

"Mature" Cultures Really Exist!

Study Indigenous cultures that have remained sustainable, such as those of Ladakh and the Aborigines of Australia, and look especially at how they view the world. What are the dominant metaphors used to describe relationships? See the Suggested Readings and Other Resources sections at the end of each chapter for films and materials.

Unpacking Discourses of Modernity

Introduce students to several primary discourses of modernity: anthropocentrism, individualism, progress, and mechanism, for example. After defining these concepts carefully, spend time thinking about what a culture with any one of these concepts as a central organizing discourse would be like. Generate a list of examples, and ask students to think about how they are interconnected. Then ask students to think of alternatives and write an essay about a culture of their creation that operates from alternative discourses/metaphors.

Three Thousand Dollar Death Song

Read Wendy Rose's poem about the commodification of native skeletons by museums, "Three Thousand Dollar Death Song" (available online at http://seventhgenerationnation.blogspot.com/2009/10/2.html), and ask students to write poems about the consequences of commodifying other things—trees, music, water, love.

Conceptual Toolbox

Centric thinking: The tendency to give higher value to a concept that is more "central" than another, as in the example, androcentrism (male-centeredness), which puts man as more central or important/valuable than woman.

Discourse: The exchange, internalization, and creation of a set of valued and shared cultural meanings; the exchange of cultural root metaphors that work together to create a powerful set of related and assumed meanings, such as individualism, based in root metaphors such as "individual is key," "community as oppressive."

Discourses of modernity: The specific set of discourses that together create our modern, taken-for-granted value-hierarchized worldview, including anthropocentrism, progress, individualism, science/rationalism, mechanism, and so on.

Ecology of mind: The living, generative system in which bits of information in the form of difference are created and exchanged as various elements interact with each other (as opposed to the assumption that "mind" is purely contained within the individual being).

Logic of domination: The system of thinking based on the assumption that those "higher" on the hierarchy have the right to dominate or control those that are "lower," e.g. humans over animals.

Metaphor: Using language to describe an aspect of reality that is like another. A metaphor illuminates some characteristics and hides others. For example, the conduit metaphor of communication illuminates how information can be passed from one person to another, but hides the importance of context.

Root metaphor: A metaphor that is foundational to a culture, and usually taken for granted, such as the concept of the autonomous individual.

Value-hierarchized thinking: Seeing some groups or cultures as having more value than others; or seeing humans as having more worth than any other species.

Suggested Readings and Other Resources

Books and Essays

Berry, W. (2000). *Life is a miracle: An essay against modern superstition.* Washington, DC: Counterpoint.

Bowers, C. A. (2001a). How language limits our understanding of environmental education. *Environmental Education Research*, 7(2), 141–151.

Merchant, C. (1998). The death of nature. In M. E. Zimmerman, J. Baird Callicott et al. (Eds.), *Environmental philosophy: From animal rights to radical ecology* (pp. 277–290). Upper Saddle River, NJ: Prentice Hall.

Plumwood, V. (2002). The blindspots of centrism and human self-enclosure.

Chapter 5 in *Environmental culture: The ecological crisis of reason*. New York, NY: Routledge.

Warren, K. (1998). The power and the promise of ecological feminism. In M. E. Zimmerman, J. Baird Callicott et al. (Eds.), *Environmental philosophy: From animal rights to radical ecology* (pp. 325–344). Upper Saddle River, NJ: Prentice Hall.

Note

1 Following David Abram (1999), we use the term "more-than-human" rather than "non-human" or "other-than-human" to explicitly challenge the usual "map" in our language that puts other living beings below the human. In this case, "more" refers to quantity: as in many more numbers of species than one—human—species. Thus, we are not using "more" as a value judgment.

Chapter 4

Learning Anthropocentrism

An EcoJustice Approach to Human Supremacy and Education

Introduction

In Chapter 3, we introduced you to the ideas of centric thinking and value hierarchized thinking within a logic of domination. We argued that, as members of a Western industrial culture, especially one that has a Euro-centric history, we have inherited a way of thinking and seeing the world that begins from the (often unconscious) assumption that a "hierarchy of being" is natural; that is, that life is naturally ordered within a ranking of value. Using a complex system of language and meaning that is constantly in exchange, this means that we learn to relate to one another and to the more-than-human world as if superiority of some members over others is just the way it is. And, as inheritors of this paradigm, we continue to live in ways (that is, within institutions and ideological systems) that reflect the assumption that some simply deserve to have more authority, more status, more resources, and more decision-making power (ultimately about who lives and who dies) than others. But does that make sense? Where did this system of belief come from? Who actually benefits from that set of assumptions? And who ultimately loses?

What if centric thinking is part of a cultural story that we have been born into and learned to tell ourselves and others, a complex fiction with very destructive results? In the next four chapters (including this one) we are going to look carefully at the stories feeding this worldview. We will examine how it works in our society, and especially how such a logic of domination influences and is reproduced in schools. In this chapter, we are going to challenge the assumption that humans are superior to other species. We will be linking anthropocentric discourse and its effects to a weave of other centric discourses—androcentrism, ethnocentrism, ego-centrism—to demonstrate both how saturated our social and psychologi-cal processes are with these ideas, and how they work together to support and develop each other until they seem inevitable and unquestionable. We will challenge this discourse by emphasizing again and again that the diversity of the world, the wild, unpredictable multiplicity that makes life possible, need not be valued hierarchically. In fact, we must come to love and value for their own beautiful integrity and contributions all the amazing different life forms that make this planet possible. Our own survival and theirs depends on this love.

Back to Bateson and Descartes

Let's start this exploration by going back to our earlier discussion of Gregory Bateson's Ecology of Mind, and what it might mean for shifting our assumptions about intelligence, communication, and our location as humans as members of the natural world. Recall that we discussed Bateson's idea that intelligence is constituted by a vast system of communication that includes all of life, the entire diverse planetary community, as it sends messages within a complex network of relationships. For Bateson, this system or web of life is developed and reproduces itself as patterns of communication create differences that make a difference.

A Note About Terminology

Throughout this chapter, you will note that we use a few concepts somewhat interchangeably: anthropocentrism, speciesism, and human supremacism. We use them in various parts of this chapter in part because there is a wide range of scholarship that addresses a similar set of questions, yet uses terminology that emphasizes the related issues in slightly different ways.

For example, anthropocentrism puts the emphasis on "anthropo" which refers to human, so we use it to discuss meanings associated with "human-centrism." Speciesism, a term coined by Richard Ryder, puts the emphasis on a whole range of beings and the ways that humans have devised a value hierarchy among them placing ourselves at the top (for example, see Ryder's book *Animal Revolution: Changing Attitudes Toward Speciesism*, 2000). Human supremacism also puts the emphasis on human but makes a clear linguistic and political move to link this form of centric thinking with sexism and racism by recalling the concepts of male supremacism or white supremacism. Using any one of these terms will focus our analytic attention in particular ways, but it should be noted that they are used to analyze the ways domination of the more-than-human world is discursively interrelated with other forms of domination. For the most part, we'll use anthropocentrism here, but we will also try to show you how it could be helpful to see the other points of focus.

Those differences reproduce life in all its forms; they produce the very life force (or *elan vital* in philosophical language) that keeps everything alive and reproducing. Humans live within these patterns of communication, though we may believe ourselves to be outside and "above" it. All intelligence and what we define as "knowledge" is actually created within this complex communicating world. And, as Bateson warns, to believe otherwise, to imagine that we are somehow outside and in control of all these life creating patterns and relationships, is very dangerous—suicidal in fact. Unfortunately, this is the very belief that we have inherited and now must shift if we are to stop the mass extinction currently underway, and leave a living planet for our children and the young of other species.

The historically-generated discursive patterns of relationship that we engage on a day-to-day basis in this modernist culture tell us that we were born to control and use this system for our own purposes. This way of thinking is very old in modern industrial cultures, but it is not the only way of thinking, as Bateson's work makes clear and as many Indigenous Peoples can avow. We will explore the diverse cosmological views of other cultures throughout this book and especially in Chapter 9. For now, we need to confront a specific cultural heritage that teaches us something quite different. Modern industrial cultures have developed the way they have because of a powerful belief system that insists that humans have moral and intellectual superiority over all other living members of our planet.

We can trace this belief system all the way back to the book of Genesis in the Bible, where humans are given "dominion" over all other species. The dualized system that it depends upon is emphasized in the work of the Greek philosopher Plato, but is most associated in modern terms with Enlightenment philosophers, and especially with René Descartes, a French philosopher writing in the 18th century. Recall the chart on hierarchized dualisms in the previous chapter (see Figure 3.1). Descartes believed that mind and body are separate, that the mind contains what he called *spirit*, but the body, comprised of *matter*, is bereft of spirit and thus could be understood to be like a machine. This is the basis of the mind/body dualism, and also the culture/nature dualism. While "spirit" was, in Descartes's model, the highest form of being and ultimately the realm of God, for humans the soul is where we connect to spirit. According to Descartes, nature is without spirit, or soul, or mind. It is nothing but "matter." Following this line of thought, "mind" is created through the capacity for reason—a capacity reserved for humans (actually only some humans: women and people of color were, of course, exceptions). The rest of the living world, understood as lowly matter, is thus bereft of thought or feeling, simply functioning as machines. Descartes declared that animals were without "soul" and "mind" and therefore, as biological machines, their actions were merely physical reactions. As machines, animals had brains but not minds and thus lacked the ability to think or reason. As machines, all species other than humans were thus bereft of consciousness or self-awareness.

Remember in Chapter 3 where we introduced the modernist discourse of mechanism, Johannes Kepler's idea that the universe functioned like "a clockwork"? Descartes's philosophical work is solidly within that discursive framework (supported by all the other centric discourses which put white European men at the top of the hierarchy). Since animals do not have either self-awareness or souls, but were considered mere stimulus/response machines, they could not, according to Descartes and most of his contemporaries, suffer. This, he argued was the primary "proof" of animals' inferiority to humans. As a man of science just as science was really being established as a dominant way of knowing, Descartes believed that it was within his moral right to perform vivisections (cutting of live animals)—specifically dogs—whom he defined as animal-machines (Coates, 1998). John Pentland Mahaffy (2005), in the biography *Descartes*, tells the story of how Descartes and his followers "kicked about their dogs and dissected their cats without mercy, laughing at any compassion for them, and calling their screams the noise of breaking machinery" (p. 181).

While within current philosophical debates this dualized system—culture/nature, reason/emotion, human/animal, man/woman—is being discredited, anthropocentric ways of thinking remain firmly entrenched in our day-to-day lives, economic institutions, and educational relationships. Such rationalized cruelty, unfortunately, not only continues but has taken on horrific proportions as animals are subjected to all sorts of vicious treatment in the name of human necessity. Cats, dogs, rats, mice, monkeys, apes, rabbits, cows, and other creatures are held captive in labs where their living, breathing bodies are used to test all sorts of products from cosmetics to pharmaceuticals. Until 1985, animals were still being cut open alive without any anesthesia, often chained down to hold them still; federal law now prohibits research without pain control, but animals are still routinely subjected to electrical shock, the application of harsh chemicals to their eyes, noses, and mouths, and other experimental processes that cause harm, deformities, agony, and death. Vivisection is also still practiced, especially if it can be demonstrated to be necessary to further agricultural knowledge (see the box below on the Animal Welfare Act).

Further, animals are systematically trapped and killed as "product" in a worldwide "fur trade," in which billions of dollars are raked in each year to satisfy people's desire for status, especially in expanding markets as consumer culture spreads globally. China is an especially hungry new client for the worldwide fur trade, in addition to developing their own industry (O'Connor, 2013). In the factory food industry, cows, chickens, and pigs are confined closely together by the thousands in factory farms called CAFOs (Concentrated Animal Feeding Operations), pumped full of growth hormones and antibiotics, and forced to live in cages or inside on concrete floors to produce milk, meat, or eggs for our consumption (Imhoff, 2010). Steven Best and Anthony Nocella call these industries that profit from animals "animal exploitation industries" (Best & Nocella, 2004, p. 12). In the words of Tom Reagan and Martin Rowe:

> Forty-eight billion farm animals are killed each year around the world—nearly eight times the human population, more than 130 million a day, more than five million every hour, almost 100,000 a minute. These numbers do not include the billions of other animals whose lives are taken, bodies injured, and freedom stolen in the name of entertainment, sport, or fashion.
>
> (Regan & Rowe, 2003, December 19, *International Herald Tribune*)

In our efforts to more easily sell them, living creatures are referred to as "products," "fur," and "meat." Reducing any living being to a commodity requires a metaphoric shift. Consider where meat, leather, fur, and lumber come from. Layers of language separate us from the living creatures that become our food, our homes, and our entertainment. In fact, many children, when asked where their eggs or milk or hamburgers come from, can only respond, "The store!"

Such a linguistic move from living, breathing creature to object or machine makes such misconceptions a routine part of our day-to-day lives. We learn to use the word "animal" to lump together a whole multitude of diverse species as if they had no individuality or intrinsic worth on their own. This is what Plumwood means by "backgrounding" (see Chapter 3). "Animal" has become a fundamental discursive category that we use as the foil or counter to define "human" as part of a higher order of being.

This ordering is not just about animals. For several thousand years, we have been taught that we are part of a "Great Chain of Being" (see Figure 4.1) with God and angelic beings at the top, humans next, animals, birds, reptiles, and insects further down, then plants, then rocks and minerals. Figure 4.1 is artwork from the 16th century titled "The Great Chain of Being," which helps us see that this socially constructed hierarchy had become widely understood in Western Europe by the time that Didacus Valades made this woodcut in 1579. Certainly, school curricula across Western societies have passed on this hierarchy as a fundamental schema through which to understand the world.

Turn back to the figure "Differing Worldviews" (Figure 1.3) in Chapter 1 and take a moment to compare the two worldviews. Notice the

Figure 4.1 The Great Chain of Being.

Source: From 'Retorica Christiana' by Didacus Valades (1579).

representation of a modern version of the "Great Chain of Being" illustrating the anthropocentric worldview juxtaposed with the fundamentally different ecological worldview represented by the more network-like Ecological Worldview. Can you think of examples in your own life of how the hierarchized model functions? Have you ever thought about the way the other model might work? What would change if we organized our communities, economies, and personal lives that way? This chapter is written to inspire that conversation.

Think About This

Think back to your science classes in high school, or even elementary. What did we learn about the chain of being in school? Were you ever asked to challenge this way of organizing life? Or was it presented as "just the way it is"?

The fact that we can continue to teach about the more-than-human world as if other life forms were born primarily for our study, consumption, or entertainment is due to a fundamental prejudice rooted in a value-hierarchized worldview, a judgment made *by humans* defining our peculiar characteristics as what define us as superior. This chapter puts this prejudice under question by demonstrating the ways specific qualities of other species are devalued primarily because they are not human qualities. As we will demonstrate in this and the next three chapters, an EcoJustice perspective argues for the power and necessity of patterns of relationship that protect *diversity*, and against a *hierarchized conception of being* that organizes modernist thinking. We are advocating for how we might both teach and learn together to shift toward an ecological worldview. While we believe schools can be integral in such a shift, we will examine how it is that schools and other institutions, as well as day-to-day interactions, have played a major part in keeping this violent discourse of human superiority and its consequences a "normalized" part of our lives.

"The Superior Human?"

Historically, there have been a number of common arguments made by philosophers and others about just what makes humans superior to the rest of the living world. Humans have consciousness; humans have language; human use tools; humans build and live in cities: these are just a few of the arguments that are used to rationalize our superior position and right to do as we please with inferior "others." In spite of the continuing atrocities enacted against other species, more and more people across many fields of study are coming to the same conclusion: that the arguments founding the belief in human superiority are based on false and self-interested claims. Here are a few of those claims. We hope that you'll see that, in fact, these are arguments created by and for humans who wish to dominate and control other species for our own uses (McAnallen, 2012).

Consciousness and Autonomy

As we discussed above, human nature has been defined at least since the Age of the Enlightenment by a fundamental "self-awareness" and consciousness, whereas animals and other non-human creatures are defined as lacking consciousness, making them thus inferior beings. Further, humans are defined as "autonomous"; that is, not relying on others for happiness, basic needs, or survival. Prior to the advent of the Scientific Revolution and the introduction of mechanistic definitions of the world and cosmos, these assumptions were not commonsense at all.

A variety of organic metaphors were used to define social orders up until about the 15th century. While some dominant theories during the 12th century included hierarchies—we've already discussed the Great Chain of Being—humans were viewed as embedded within an ordered organic cosmos based upon the functioning and integrated processes of earth, wind, fire, and water. The social order of ants and bees, for example, were pointed to as perfected social systems requiring cooperation and acceptance of responsibilities within a unified if hierarchized community (Merchant, 1984). As Carolyn Merchant points out, peasant life within feudal societies was also organized around a variation of organic ideology, though much less hierarchically, emphasizing instead community systems with rules based on mutuality and responsibility in their relations to each other and to the Earth. In this sense, while located in Europe, these communities were organized much like Indigenous communities around the world. It was not until Enlightenment ideas of the world operating as a machine that individual autonomy and a definition of humans as essentially selfish (ego-centric) began to be asserted along with a view of the cosmos and Earth as essentially dead machines. This set of arguments disrupted the organic view of human relations as harmonious with the-more-than human world.

In some parts of Europe into the early modern period (16th century), we see that people considered animals as having conscious will and even rights. In some communities in France and Germany through the 1500s animals could even be put on trial for behavior judged to be unjust (Coates, 1998). Pigs, weevils, and insects were all "tried" and defended in courts of law for various offences committed in communities. Pigs were put on trial, for example, for "infanticide," a sin in Christian doctrine. Clearly, if they could be tried, they must have been viewed at one time by Europeans as having intentionality and consciousness, absurd as this process of putting them on trial might seem to us today. The point is that we can trace important historical shifts in the ways that the more-than-human world has been understood in relation to humans.

So let's think about this further in today's terms. As Gary Yourofsky argues (McAnallen, 2011), we can see that animals have eyes, ears, noses, and the senses that accompany them; we see that they eat, digest, and defecate; that they use all their organs in ways similar to humans. We know that they also have brains. Why would we assume that they do not use their brains in ways similar to humans? Or, if we go back to Bateson, why would we assume that their consciousness within other patterns of communication are any less vital than the ways human thought responds to the world? Why would we assume that their forms of consciousness need to be the same as ours to be considered of equal intrinsic worth?

Many mammals, dogs and bears for example, have an amazing sense of smell, far stronger than any human. They use that sense to differentiate, track, learn, and remember all sorts of information that we could never possibly entertain. Dogs and cats have been known to detect critical illnesses such as cancer in their owners. Dolphins have intricate ultra-sonic communication and navigational capacities totally beyond anything that we can imagine. And yet, it is the human sense of sight that is linked with intelligence and used to define us as superior. But, what requires that we define ourselves this way when it's clear that (a) even Europeans have not always thought this way, and (b) we can find all sorts of evidence of diverse forms of consciousness throughout the living world?

We've talked only about animals here, but what about plants? For years we have been taught by plant biologists that plants have genes used to detect changes in light, and thus can shift their positions as needed by photosynthesis. We could say that they are thus "aware" of changes in the light. It is not the same sort of consciousness that we think of as human "thinking" or "knowing," but why do we assume it should be so to be valued? And how different are we? Here's something you may not know: the sequences of DNA responsible for light detection in plants exists in animals and humans too. Our own circadian rhythms that are connected to light and dark to regulate sleep are connected to the same genes that plants use to grow and develop. In a book called *What Plants Know* (2012), renowned scientist Daniel Chamowitz takes the reader through a series of explorations describing the specific ways that plants can "smell," feel, and are, in fact, "aware." He argues that plants have developed incredibly sophisticated means of survival. Humans "smell" by taking in chemical substances that are carried to us in the air, and so do plants, responding as needed depending on the messages those substances carry. Since they are essentially "rooted" and immobile, they have had to "develop incredibly sensitive and complex sensory mechanisms that would let them survive in ever changing environments."

[Plants] need to see where their food is. They need to feel the weather, and they need to smell danger. And then they need to be able to integrate all of this very dynamic and changing information. Just because we don't see plants moving doesn't mean that there's not a very rich and dynamic world going on inside the plant.

(Chamowitz, in Cook, p. 1; retrieved on October 26, 2013 from http://www.scientificamerican.com/article. cfm?id=do-plants-think-daniel-chamovitz)

This means that when plants are attacked by insects, for example, they send out warnings to other plants in the vicinity in the form of pheromones that let the other plants know that they need to start producing defensive chemicals to help them fight off the attack. American mycologist Paul Stamets (2005) shows the valuable role of mycelium—the network of cells that make up the vegetative part of fungus from which the fruit is mushrooms—in recycling carbon, nitrogen, and many other elements. Stamets explains that mycelium communicate with trees and plants in the forest as they work to break down plant and animal debris, creating rich soil and bringing nutrients to often distant locations for plants and trees.

An international group of plant biologists are studying the neurological signaling system in plants (Brenner et al., 2006). One member of this team, plant biologist Stefano Mancuso, discusses their work in a recent TED Talk. Drawing on the work of his team, he demonstrates that the root apex, the very tip of roots in plants, use the same sort of signals found in the brain neurons of mammals (including humans). Given the complex networks of root systems that all plants have, their actual intelligence levels measure far more complexly than human brains because each tip of each filament of root matter has this same "apex" which functions via such signals. "Plants," Marcuso (2010) argues, "are much more able to sense; they are much more sophisticated than animals . . . [yet] this underestimation of plants is something that is always with us" (http://www.ted.com/talks/stefano_mancuso_the_roots_of_plant_intelligence.html).

In this sense, plants "communicate" with each other, with animals, and with us, participating fully in an ecology of Mind, in the Batesonian sense of engaging differences that make a difference that create all living relationships in the world. We'll talk more about communication below. For now, we want to remind you that Mind is a set of relationships among everything that makes life possible.

Language

Humans, it is argued, have a developed system of language, both spoken and written, that other animals do not have. In fact, it has been argued that the most "advanced" humans are those who have developed written forms. But, again, we challenge this idea on many levels. Let's look first at the idea that other animals do not have "language."

Again, this assumption is beginning to be pulled apart as we learn the highly diverse ways that different species communicate among themselves and with others, and the ways that such communication interacts with forms of awareness or "consciousness" specific to them. They may not use the same sorts of language or cognitive systems as humans, or have the same physiological components to create the same "voice," but the systems they use are clearly developed in ways that support their own species-specific survival and social needs. Some use complex vocalizations, others physical movements, electrical currents, or some combination of these. Honeybees, for example, communicate to their hive-mates via a complex "dance," sharing information about where they have been and where to find the best pollinating plants for making honey. Ants, termites, and other insects also have complex communication patterns that aid them in finding food, building nests and colonies, and protecting each other.

Among the most interesting research on animal language systems is the study of prairie dog communities. Prairie dogs have been shown to have very sophisticated social and communication systems. C. N. Slobodchikoff and his associates studied the vocalizations that Gunnison Prairie dogs use to alert one another to the approach of various intruders. They found an amazing ability among prairie dogs to discern and express intricate differences in the size, shape, color of clothing or fur, speed of approach, and likely danger of the particular intruder (Slobodchikoff et al., 2009). Other researchers found the same ability to communicate such distinctions in other species of prairie dog, as well. And yet, these creatures, defined primarily as vermin and killed as pests or for sport, have been all but exterminated from the prairies of North America.

Some animals have been taught to use human language. Bonobos and Grey Parrots who have lived in relationships with humans, for example, have learned large numbers of human words, demonstrating the cognitive ability to use those symbols or words to communicate with humans. Anyone who has lived for any length of time with a dog knows that they learn human words—even some that we may not have intended to teach. On a similar note, closer to home for many people is their communicative relationships with their pets—or, as we like to emphasize, "more-than-human companions." Rebecca's dog, Sweet Pea, apparently even knows how to spell! Thinking the dog was asleep in her crate, Rebecca's husband Gary said, "I want to take the dogs out to W-A-L-K." Sweet Pea's head snapped up and she immediately ran to the door, joyous at the impending exercise! Obviously, we had been spelling "walk" for long enough, thinking that the dogs would not pick up on our conversation or the sounds that we use to indicate certain pending activities, but Sweet Pea showed us that she knew exactly what we were talking about. And she used her own patterns of communication to show us what she thought of it! She jumped and spun and wagged and ran to the door! And her "sister" Olive followed suit until we indeed went for a w-a-l-k! Sweet Pea and Olive, as domestic canines, are highly attentive to a wide range of human social cues, which include not only recognizing the sounds of words associated with taking a walk but also with the gestures, movements, and facial expressions that we as humans often overlook. We can only imagine what signals they get from the smells and sounds in the surrounding context that we do not pick up.

The point here is that human language is assumed to be much more complex and sophisticated, an indication of a level of cognitive ability not possible in other species. But this is, in fact, a prejudice. How many of *us* could speak prairie dog, or dolphin, or bonobo, or honeybee? And, more importantly, why do we assume that all forms of language and cognition need to be identical to our own to have value in our complex living world?

And what of those human cultures that developed without the same forms of written language, but rather passed down information through oral traditions over many thousands of years? As we will discuss in more depth in Chapters 7, 8, and 9, Indigenous cultures were defined as "savage" and barbaric—more like animals—by the Europeans who first encountered them, in part because they did not have written language. But imagine the knowledge that these cultures have of the ecosystems that they live in and continue to maintain. Their language, as we mentioned in Chapter 2, developed in accordance with the vast ecological diversity of the regions where they dwell, and was used to develop complex systems of knowledge, a whole cosmology, that they have passed down generation to generation over many thousands of years. Imagine the enormous capacity for memory that these cultures developed! Imagine their deep knowledge of the diverse species of animals and plants, including how those diverse species live and communicate.

The Elder Elephant Crisis!

In Africa, poaching and massive habitat loss devastates elephant communities. As a result, they lose elders in their communities at a much higher rate than usual, and so additionally suffer from a loss of elder elephant knowledge. Over the past 100 years, the elephant population on the continent of Africa has dropped dramatically. The World Wildlife Fund (WWF) reports that there were 3–5 million elephants roaming Africa in the 1930s and 1940s but, due to hunting for trophies and tusks in the 1950s, elephant populations plummeted. The WWF reports: "In the 1980s . . . an estimated 100,000 elephants were being killed per year and up to 80% of herds were lost in some regions. In Kenya, the population plummeted by 85% between 1973 and 1989" (http://wwf.panda.org/what_we_do/endangered_species/elephants/african_elephants/).

While recent efforts to protect the population have seen some success, what has been observed is an increase in hyper-aggression, depression, and unpredictable behaviors among herds. What is sad, but fascinating in terms of communication among species that are not human, is that scientists are reporting that this is due to a loss of elder elephants in the elephant communities. In an essay titled "Elephant Breakdown" (2005), Bradshaw et al. explain that elephants are renowned for their close social relationships. They report that "male socialization begins during infancy with the mother and a tight constellation of all mothers. But, in adolescence, males leave the natal family to participate in older all-male groups" (p. 807). They explain that the elder males in elephant societies play a critical role in the socialization of adolescent male elephants to quell aggression and learn to be adult elephants. Similarly, female elephants separated from elder female elephants aren't socialized to how to raise young elephants. Bradshaw et al. (2005) explain: "Young elephants are reared in a matriarchal society, embedded in complex layers of extended family. Culls and illegal poaching have fragmented these patterns of social attachment by eliminating the supportive stratum of the matriarch and older female caretakers" (p. 807).

What this highlights is that without elders to teach young elephants how to live and be contributing members of strong healthy elephant communities, future generations of elephants are susceptible to dangerous behaviors. This situation perpetuates a cycle in which the elephants are further separated from one another and from the habitat in which they would mostly likely thrive together as social beings. What we can learn from this is clearly that we, as humans, are not the only species teaching our young through a complex communicative system of language that passes on important knowledge on how to survive together. Further, we are reminded of the importance of elder knowledge. We are not the only species with teachers.

If we think of communication and mind in the sense in which Bateson urges us, we begin to see that we are far more connected to other species than we may want to believe, or were taught to believe. We could learn a lot from land-based cultures who continue to pass down this knowledge, but this will mean helping those cultures to protect their languages and cultures from the same destructive processes that threaten all other living communities.

Humans as the Top of the Food Chain

Humans are not regularly food for other creatures. That is, we are the ultimate predator, the top of "the food chain." Or are we? Tell that to the crocodile who attacked Val Plumwood's canoe, dumping her out, and dragging her under in its typical death spiral, hoping to feed on her (Plumwood, "Being Prey," 1996). That croc probably did not say to itself, before stalking her, "Hmmm, should I attack that person? Humans are, after all, the top of the food chain." Somehow, Plumwood lived to tell the tale; her story, "Being Prey," reminds us quite dramatically that, in spite of the people around her who insisted on hunting down and killing "the evil beast," killing in order to eat for other species on the planet is not a matter of good and evil. It is simply a matter of survival, part of the vast life system of which we are members, even when it is we who are eaten!

Or, consider the micro-organisms that inhabit the human body. All those smells we are so wont to get rid of with our soaps and potions? Those are the result of some of the activities of millions of microscopic organisms that live within and on our bodies, generally referred to as bacteria. We are used to thinking of bacteria as our enemy (germs!), but in fact we could not live without them. The microbial population, referred to as "normal microflora" or "indigenous microbiota" that inhabit the healthy human body "is estimated to consist of about 10^{14} microbial cells as compared to the 10^{13} human cells that make up the human body" (Tannock, 1995, p. 1). Think of that! Each of our bodies is home to a vast collection of microscopic species that forms its own ecological interdependencies with the other cells of our bodies. How can we possibly imagine ourselves as the ultimate predators when this is the case! In fact, our bodies are just a microcosm of the ecologies that comprise the rest of the planet! So, we could in fact, imagine Mind, in the Batesonian sense, as including all those differentiating relationships and effects of indigenous microorganisms *inside* and *with* the other cells in our own bodies. Talk about dissolving the Mind/Body split!

Living in Social Systems and Building Dwellings

Another argument given for the superiority of humans is that we have developed complex societies differentiated by status and division of labor, and we have built vast cities with buildings used for shelter, work, and other activities. Have you ever looked inside a beehive and noticed the amazing activity of bees building a honeycomb? How intricate and beautiful and perfectly suited for storing honey and supporting the hive! Bees have a differentiated society too, with a queen bee who is primarily responsible for laying eggs, and is kept alive by the coordination of the various roles of the other bees.

Or how about a termite colony? Termites live in societies with populations in the millions! They build cities of huge "skyscrapers," much higher than human skyscrapers when taking into account the relative size of termites in comparison to humans. Again, the colonies are differentiated by task: worker termites are responsible for foraging, building, and cleaning the nest, and caring for the young "brood" termites. There are also "soldier termites" who are responsible for defense of the nest. The "parents" are the termites who are primarily responsible for breeding and populating the colony.

Many other creatures also live in interdependent social groups, and build domiciles or even whole colonies. Beavers are amazing architects. They build lodges of logs and tree branches chosen specifically for their usefulness in this construction. The logs are cut and carried back to the site, and placed in intricately woven patterns to create a lodge with underwater entrances and chambers to house beaver families. Some of these lodges have been found to be immense. Imagine the strength, creativity, and cooperation it must take to do this while working underwater!

We mentioned prairie dogs earlier, and their complex, often large (though now diminishing) social groups. Coyotes, wolves, dolphins, whales, elephants, geese, turkeys, and millions of other species create groups of parents and offspring who live in mutual social relations with other adults, sometimes from different family groups. Humans are certainly not the only species to figure out that living in groups is important to survival and reproduction, or to build relationships that go beyond simple survival.

Opposable Thumbs and the Use of Tools

Another argument for the superiority of humans is that we have developed opposable thumbs that allow us to manipulate the external world in specific ways, and that we have developed tools to extend that manipulation. But apes, monkeys, chimpanzees, orangutans, and other primates all have opposable thumbs, and some even have them on both hands and feet! Wow, clearly they have it all over humans in the thumb department! And they use all four to hold things, and manipulate the world as they need to. Raccoons, too, have thumb-like appendages that they use with highly sensitive paws to sense their food. Raccoon paws are at least 100 times more sensitive than human hands. So why don't we define that as making raccoons superior to humans?

Humans have certainly developed tools and technology to help us to survive, and even to enhance our abilities to communicate and entertain ourselves. Other species also use tools, in ways adapted to their own particular needs and habitats. For example, birds use bait to fish for food (see a YouTube video titled "Clever Bird Goes Fishing" at https://www.youtube.com/watch?v=uBuPiC3ArL8). Otters use rocks to open hard-shelled creatures they need to eat, crows and their relatives fashion complex tools for daily use, and dolphins use marine sponges to stir up prey. These are just a few examples from a fast growing list of recognized animal intelligence. Further, scientists recognize that the use of tools is *learned* from elders in the species (Kenward et al., 2006). Again, we are arguing for a way of seeing that values diversity in non-hierarchized ways in order to understand the multiplicity of ways that different species live and interact as a matter of keeping this amazing living world flourishing.

Walking on Two Legs

This one is even stranger, but some actually argue that what makes humans superior is that we walk upright on two legs. Perhaps they are only referring to a comparison to other mammals (although bears can walk upright, as can primates), but what about birds? Do they count in this comparison? Or do we need to ignore that not only do birds walk upright on two legs, but they also fly! Humans actually studied bird physiology for years in order to copy it. We had to create mechanical apparatuses because we cannot do it—fly—on our own. So, why don't we use this amazing talent to define birds as superior to humans?

By now you get our point. All these arguments for human superiority are based upon a fundamental disregard of the immense diversity that has created the communities of life on this planet, insisting for self-interested reasons that this diversity be studied, catalogued, and ordered into separate parts. What has been presented to us as objective knowledge is based upon a systematic prejudice, a powerful discourse that has been used to create and organize our institutions and relationships, our most cherished "truths." As we'll see in the next sections, this way of thinking permeates many of our institutions including our economic processes and the educational systems that support those.

Think About This

Why do we need to define humans as superior? Whose interests are served? And, what are the consequences of such thinking for us and for those others we define as inferior?

Institutionalizing Human Supremacism: Examining Biotechnology, Agribusiness, and Animal Entertainment Industries

Created within a discourse of anthropocentrism, patterns of human domination are situated in a highly organized industrial and technological culture where consumerism and individual profit dominate as values. What is the role of anthropocentrism as a discourse and set of practices in such a culture, and what are the effects on both human health, and the larger ecological communities with whom we share this planet? In this section, we'll introduce you to some of the ways that the belief in human supremacy functions to keep a hyper-consumerist, commodity-addicted economy running on a global scale, how our patterns of appetite and desire are created within an industrial complex that is exploitive of the more-than-human world, and whose interests are really behind it all.

The Animal Industrial Complex

Because we are able to rationalize them as inferior beings, "animals are exploited for their meat, milk, eggs, and skin but also for sport, experimentation, and entertainment" (Twine, 2012). We eat them, wear them, use their bodies to test chemicals (even breed them in order to use them for testing) and put them in zoos or in aquariums for observation and entertainment. And all this is done for a price: that is, we pay money to eat them, wear them, or watch them. Thus, we commodify other beings, making our relationship to them very different than the many other cultures that see the more-than-human world in terms of kinship. We will have more to say about Indigenous People's cosmological relationships in Chapter 9. For the purposes of this chapter, we will be exposing the ways Western industrial cultures use other species as objects and machines, and especially how they are perceived, raised, and used as products for sale.

Scholars within the field of Critical Animal Studies have been highly critical of the ways the interests of capitalism operate to create an "animal industrial complex" which is in the business of producing animals as food, test-subjects, and objects of amusement. While we may hear arguments about animal production and consumption fulfilling necessary medical or nutritional needs of humans, or how "conservation" efforts in the fur industry "protect" animals, what is clear as we begin to examine the politics of these economic systems is that markets and profit motive is at the heart of it. As Barbara Noske wrote in 1989, "the main impetus behind modern animal production comes from . . . financial interests rather than from farmers, consumers, or workers" (quoted in Twine, 2012, p. 22). This does not mean that consumer "appetite" or medical demands are not also at play, along with a whole cultural and economic network of other processes. Rather, we emphasize that, as Richard Twine (2012) argues, that corporate accumulation of profit "has been a significant factor in industrialized animal production . . . through marketing, advertising and flavour manipulation in constructing the consumption of animal products as sensual material pleasure" (p. 16). As consumers, then, we too are being created by this industrial complex: our tastes and desires, even our sense of what it means to be "healthy," are manipulated in order to create profit for an array of corporate interests. Living organisms are modified and patented in a multi-billion dollar industry rationalized by scientific research known as "biotechnology."

What Is Biotechnology?

"Biotechnology" involves procedures that modify living organisms to serve human purposes. Of course, broadly speaking, such modification of the more-than-human world has been going on since humans began to domesticate animals and cultivate plants, mostly by generations of breeding for certain characteristics such as appearance, temperament, and performance. We can think of the domestication of animals or the cultivation of plants as part of humans' historical relationship in using other beings, and as biotechnology. In that sense it is not new. However, today we can see that it extends to genetic modification of plants and animals, cloning technology, experimentation on animals for pharmaceutical development, and so on, with changes made primarily on a molecular level (Twine, 2010). In short, the biotech industry as it has developed in the 20th and into the 21st century is primarily about the application and molecular modification of biological organisms for developing or improving commercial products—that is, as we pointed out above, for sale and consumption, and not necessarily for increasing the well-being of people or other living beings. And, the particular methods being used—the use of quantitative genetics and statistical analysis, the sequencing of genomes, and genetic selection—has sped up the ability to produce particular traits which are then patented, and thus owned by the corporations funding the research. Richard Twine explains:

> The subsequent sequencing of farmed animal genomes holds the promise of letting meat scientists know just what genes they are selecting on and improving knowledge of relations between genotype and phenotype. The molecular techniques here that I define as biotechnology are marker-assisted selection, transgenics or genetic modification (GM), and cloning. . . . Animals are assessed in terms of their transformation into a statistical representation known as an estimated breeding value (EBV) along particular indices of performance such as longevity, or meat or milk yield.
>
> (Twine, 2010, p. 15)

As Twine goes on to say, these particular techniques are of interest because they are being applied specifically as a means of increasing profitability in the animal industrial complex. Currently, pigs, cows, and sheep are patented for certain genetically modified traits. While Twine's work is primarily focused on animals, genetic modification—the insertion of genetic material from one organism into another to create particular traits, or the modification of existing genes to "switch off" their function—is also being widely used in plant biotechnology. Seeds for all sorts of grains, for example, are being modified to be resistant to certain pests or pesticides. Some are being modified so that they cannot regenerate, making it necessary for farmers, who once saved seeds each year for replanting, to buy seeds each year (see the case study on Monsanto in Chapter 8). The dangers to the biodiversity of the planet cannot be understated here.

A clear example is the genetically modified corn that is beginning to affect traditional corn varieties in Mexico. In this case, we can see that the hundreds of varieties of corn that have been developed by Mexican campesinos over many centuries can be undone in a very short time when genetically modified corn introduced into the country comes into contact with and pollinates these indigenous varieties. The resulting loss of diversity both benefits the corporate owners of the genetically modified seed and risks the protection that diversity brings. Other examples include modifying and patenting rice varieties in India (see Chapter 8 for more on the effects of globalized corporate interests).

While it is important to note that we will never rid ourselves of the use of other creatures for our own survival, how it happens—whether it is done with reverence or thoughtlessly, cruelly or with care—and whose interests are ultimately served is of utmost importance as we consider what it means to live just and sustainable lives. What is clear about our current context is that animals and other living organisms have been thoroughly reduced to "things" within a mechanized and consumerized discursive order so that "progress" (defined increasingly by individual accumulation and control) depends more and more on our not thinking of them in any other way. If "civilization" is defined by increasing technologies and consumption, and animals and other organisms are the source of raw material for the manufacture of products offered up for sale, then we are living within an ecological and cultural nightmare where nearly everything we do, in fact our very identities as happy consumers, requires the sacrifice of animal bodies. At the very least, this cultural trajectory is unsustainable, but, moreover, it is at heart unethical to the livelihood and well-being of other organisms.

Agribusiness and Concentrated Animal Feeding Operations (CAFOs)

While television and other advertising still paints images of the family farm in bucolic rural settings, this is far from the reality of agricultural business today. At the turn of the 20th century, about 39% of the U.S. population worked on farms. According to the Environmental Protection Agency, only about 2% of all Americans now live on farms, and only 1 % claim farming as an occupation. According to the U.S. Department of Agriculture census, in 1950 the U.S. had 5,382,162 farms, but by 2007 this number had declined to 2,121,107. A little under 2 million of these are considered small family farms (making less than $250,000 a year), with the vast majority (about 1,300,000) of these making less than $10,000 income per year from the farm. What this tells us is that most of the agricultural income is being made on farms making $250,000 or more; there are far fewer of these mega farms and yet they provide most of the agricultural products being sold.

One of the major contributors to the disappearance of small family farms is the increase in Concentrated Animal Feeding Operations (CAFOs), large factory operations with more than 1000 "animal units" confined in very limited spaces. According to the USDA:

> An animal unit is defined as an animal equivalent of 1000 pounds live weight and equates to 1000 head of beef cattle, 700 dairy cows, 2500 swine weighing more than 55 lbs, 125 thousand broiler chickens, or 82 thousand laying hens or pullets. Any size AFO [Animal Feeding Operation] that discharges manure or wastewater into a natural or man-made ditch, stream or other waterway is defined as a CAFO, regardless of size. CAFOs are regulated by EPA under the Clean Water Act in both the 2003 and 2008 versions of the "CAFO" rule.
> (Retrieved on January 22, 2014 from http://www.nrcs.usda.gov/wps/portal/nrcs/detail/mo/plantsanimals/?cid=stelprdb104291)

Technological developments—automation, antibiotics, animal feed, and infrastructure—have made the growth of these factory farms possible as they are able to raise more animals more efficiently at less expense. Such changes have radically changed the quality of life for the animals existing in these conditions. As Jeffrey Phang (2013), a law student at Seton Hall studying CAFOs and animal welfare wrote,

> On traditional farms, animals are afforded an opportunity to engage in natural behaviors such as walking, socializing, and resting in privacy. They also have access to open air, sunlight, and natural ground to walk on. We often take these conditions for granted when we envision a farm; however, in a CAFO there is no room for Mother Nature. In the quest for efficiency, the CAFO structure ignores the fact that the products being produced are cognitive creatures and instead treats animals like objects that simply process nutrients and water culminating in meat products for human consumption.
>
> (p. 6)

In the dairy industry, for example, cows no longer graze on fields but rather are held and fed in large barns, usually on concrete floors, waiting to be milked by large machines that attach to each cow's udder. Their manure, accumulated throughout the day of standing in one place, is sprayed off the floors into "lagoons" outside the barn. The result is highly toxic liquidized manure that is then pumped into trucks that spray this concoction onto the surrounding fields. The liquid generally does not stay on the field, but instead runs off into nearby ditches used as "drains" and eventually into local streams (also defined as drains) and the larger watershed (see Chapter 3). The same general process is also true of pig farms. So, before we even begin to talk about the treatment of the animals kept in these conditions, this approach to "farming," while considered the most efficient way of producing milk or meat, is causing enormous air and water pollution problems. Spreading the manure in such large quantities is a far cry from traditional methods that were very beneficial to crops being grown on family farms. Without the benefit of straw, hay, and other organic materials mixed in with manure, this liquidized manure is highly concentrated, releasing toxic fumes into the air. While traditional methods of using manure for fertilizer on fields certainly release strong odors into the surrounding area, they are not toxic. Researchers studying the impacts of CAFOs on quality of life in nearby communities have documented eye and respiratory problems among residents. Furthermore, liquidized manure tends to run off, rather than work its way into the soil as fertilizer. In south central Michigan, where the land was once marshy and wet, drainage tiles are placed not far under the surface so that water will drain off the field. Thus, when used by CAFOs, the fields become a conduit of highly concentrated manure often laced with growth hormones, antibiotics, and other "inputs" used to increase production or fight disease brought on by animals being kept in such close confinement. Eventually those materials are carried directly into our water sources.

The ethical issues related to animals being forced to live in such conditions are almost too much to bear if one has any sense of compassion for other living creatures. Dairy cows stand in dark barns on concrete floors, no longer able to graze on fields, rest, socialize, or feel the sunlight on their backs. Veal calves are kept in crates away from their mothers, unable to move around until slaughter. Battery hens (chickens that are used for egg production) live out their lives smashed together, 5–10 chickens in a 18" × 20" crate. They never step on soil, forage for bugs or seeds, nest, or exercise. Because they may become aggressive with one another in such close proximity, they often have their beaks removed (without anesthesia) in order to prevent damaging pecking of each other (Duncan, 2004).

Pigs used for breeding (called sows) are housed in small individual gestation cages unable to turn around or groom themselves. Thus, they are much more susceptible to disease, suffering from "urinary tract infections, cardiovascular complications, overgrown hooves, lameness, and weak muscle and bone structures" (Phang, 2012). Viewed as animal-machines, they are deprived of social interaction and normal habits of foraging and general exercise (Scientific Veterinary Committee Report, 1997).

The Ethics of Eating

We can't go on much further in this chapter and not address how food choices contribute to and complicate this discussion. Vegetarians choose not to take part in the consumption of animal flesh. Vegans choose not to consume animal flesh, eggs, or dairy products. Many of those who choose these eating habits also hold the position that not using products tested on animals or wearing animal products—like leather, furs, suede, wool, down, or silks—would alleviate a lot of animal suffering. While there is substantial support for the health benefits for a plant-based diet as well as living a cruelty-free lifestyle, the choice is complicated by several factors (Tuso, Ismail, Ha, & Bartolotto, 2013).

All too often the discussion to end or alleviate animal suffering turns quickly to the argument that one ought to be vegan or at the very least vegetarian. Such reductionist arguments are not helpful because factors of privilege associated with race, class, and culture complicate the choice. However, what is important is one's personal relationship with what it means to consume ethically. Even among the three of us we disagree on how we go about making choices about food in ways that align with our personal beliefs and ethics. While we differ in some respects, we all three agree that we have a responsibility to the life taken—plant or animal. Life is taken and in return ought to be revered and respected. In other words, we advocate that however we choose to eat, live, or make use of living beings we should do so with a deep ethical responsibility to that relationship. A good way to think of this is that if you have a commitment to the species that gives its life in order to provide sustenance, warmth, or shelter, then in return you honor and respect that animal or plant's right to live with dignity and reproduce itself. Thus, we advocate for such decisions to be made locally, and in support of living communities with value given to the more-than-human members. In other words, food systems ought to be localized and culturally relevant. No one culture should assume some perceived higher position or ethical high ground and dictate what another ought to do. Given the situation for many people in Western industrial culture it's entirely possible to be vegan, or vegetarian, and still contribute to large-scale factory farming and the monocropping of wheat, corn, and soy. We may know vegans and vegetarians who eat processed frozen meals, or spend large amounts of money on factory-produced substitutes. While this certainly lessens the cruelty to animals, it often supports unfair labor practices, the excessive use of fossil fuels, and unhealthy farming practices. Moreover, if we prioritize protecting the lives of animals over plants, we reproduce the very value hierarchies creating the problems we're trying to address.

None of this is meant to undermine those who choose to be vegan or vegetarian, but it should be clear that none of these choices occur separate from the complex and abusive culture of violence in which we live. It couldn't be more important to social justice and sustainability that we all seriously consider what it is we *need* to survive and that we make those decisions with respect to the right of all plants and animals to co-exist on this planet. So, however it is that you practice how you live on this planet, we ask that you consider how those actions either support or undermine a healthy and socially just living system.

Animal Experimentation

Perhaps the most devastating way that we use living creatures as objects is within scientific experiments and laboratories. The Humane Society International (www.hsi.org) estimates that more than 115 million animals are victimized by lab experiments worldwide every year. Some have the estimates even higher, reporting over 100 million animals used in the United States alone (www.aavs.org), and this number does not include those excluded from reports. In the United States, for example, up to 90% of the animals, especially those purposely bred for experimentation, are not reported. Thus, figures published by the U.S. Department of Agriculture are clearly underestimated. Mice, rats, guinea pigs, pigs, dogs, cats, rabbits, and other creatures are routinely subjected to extremely painful processes, kept locked in cold cages with little to keep warm, kept isolated and unable to socialize, treated brutally for being "uncooperative," transported under horrific conditions, and usually killed either in the process of or at the end of the experiments to which they are subjected. According to the Humane Society International (www.hsi.org), common testing procedures include:

1. Forced chemical exposure in toxicity testing, which can include oral force-feeding, forced inhalation, skin or injection into the abdomen, muscle, etc.
2. Exposure to drugs, chemicals or infectious disease at levels that cause illness, pain, and distress, or death.

3. Genetic manipulation, e.g., addition or "knocking out" of one or more genes.
4. Ear-notching and tail-clipping for identification.
5. Short periods of physical restraint for observation or examination.
6. Prolonged periods of physical restraint.
7. Food and water deprivation.
8. Surgical procedures followed by recovery.
9. Infliction of wounds, burns, and other injuries to study healing.
10. Infliction of pain to study its physiology and treatment.
11. Behavioral experiments designed to cause distress, e.g., electric shock or forced swimming.
12. Other manipulations to create "animal models" of human diseases ranging from cancer to stroke to depression.
13. Killing by carbon dioxide asphyxiation, neck-breaking, decapitation, or other means.
   (Retrieved on December 7, 2013 from http://www.hsi.org/campaigns/end_animal_testing/qa/about.html)

As we have been discussing, an entire animal industrial complex has been built around supplying animals for research in the medical, space, military, and food and drug fields. Animals are treated as unfeeling objects or machines, tools for the researcher rather than conscious, intelligent, and sentient beings. One particularly horrifying example from military research is reported by AAVS:

> "Wound labs" have been in use by the Department of Defense since 1957. In these laboratory experiments, animals are often suspended with slings and shot by any number of potential new weapons. In 2003, the United States Naval Board tested Pulsed Energy Projectiles (PEPs) on animals to gauge their effectiveness in creating excruciating pain followed by temporary paralysis in its victims. The weapon is eventually going to be employed to immobilize rioters, and was estimated to be ready for use in 2007.
>   (Retrieved on December 7, 2013 from http://www.aavs.org/)

These stories are horrifying, but we don't include them for the shock value. Rather, they demonstrate a direct consequence of the discourse of human supremacism: that humans can justify—and even ignore—others' suffering because we switch off the connection we have to our fellow species. Besides using their bodies for experimentation, or treating them as food factories, we also see them as "attractions," holding them in captivity to entertain us. Zoos, circuses, aquariums, and other animal themes parks have become multi-million dollar entertainment industries.

Animal Enterprise Terrorism Act (AETA)

Many advocacy and action groups have worked, and continue to work, toward the liberation of animals from labs and other forms of confinement and abuse. Gaining some momentum over the past decades, such actions did not go over well with big business. Then, in 2006, President George W. Bush, in response to pressure from corporate lobbyists, altered that legislation, signing into law the Animal Enterprise Terrorism Act (AETA). The AETA declares the right of the U.S. Department of Justice to apprehend, prosecute, and convict individuals committing animal "enterprise terror." According to the Center for Media and Democracy (2013), "enterprise terror" is defined as "any one encouraging, financing, assisting or engaged in politically motivated acts of animal and ecological terrorism" (p. 1). In Section 2, the AETA explicitly lists such activity as "inclusion of economic damage to animal enterprises and threats of death and serious bodily injury to associated persons" (U.S. Gov., 2006, p. 1). As an example of such "terrorism," an activist caught photographing the use of a front-loading tractor to pick up and move a live cow was arrested under AETA. Other activists trying to document the abuses of animals in CAFOs and labs have also been either arrested or threatened with arrest.

ALEC, the organization we wrote about in Chapter 2, ghostwrote this legislation. While we can probably all agree that no one ought to threaten death or serious injury, the idea of extending such punishment to those wishing to document abuse is more difficult to link to "terrorism." Such use of the very political system that is supposed to provide protection to the rights of individuals to organize and engage in democracy is in fact further proof that we have a long ways to go in order to address our exploitation of the more-than-human world. Despite the AETA, a movement to continue to seek justice for the more-than-human world continues, and some cases prosecuted through the AETA have been dismissed.

Animal Entertainment Industry: Zoos and Circuses

Think back to experiences you may have had with animals as a young person, or even as an adult, during field trips to the zoo or circus, or family vacations to SeaWorld. In this section we will take a look at the animal entertainment industry and how from a young age we are socialized to enjoy entertainment at the expense of the freedom of another species' right to live free, reproduce, and raise young.

Johnny Recalls Visiting SeaWorld

As a child, I vividly recall a family vacation to SeaWorld in Ohio. It was not uncommon for working class families in the area to take day trips to nearby amusement parks of various sorts. For this particular vacation, the family piled into a station wagon and drove from Detroit to Aurora, Ohio, to visit Sea World. This marine animal theme park, located over 2,500 miles from the Pacific and at least 600 miles from the Atlantic coast, held penguins, dolphins, and, of course, "killer whales." These creatures performed in shows for the entertainment of an audience of families that oohed and awed for their amazing tricks. I remember thinking that this was really, really strange and somehow not right. I wasn't some super-ethical kid in tune with animal suffering, but it seemed obvious to me that these animals did not belong in this situation. I will never forget my sister and I standing near the dirty, smelly pool, watching an orca who everyone referred to as "Shamu." I remember the orca swimming laps around the pool of water. This majestic social being with expressive eyes surfaced, dipped, and dove through the water while circling the surrounding walls. She surfaced, dipped, and dived and again continued to swim laps in the water. Occasionally, she got to join one or two other orcas and they performed tricks for special feedings as they jumped from the water, swam with humans in matching diving suits, and splashed people who had come to watch them. I remember being sick for the whole thing, but, when I asked about it, my father told me to listen to the announcer. The announcer boasted of how these animals were well taken care of, and how they were rescued from "certain peril" in the wild. He said they were fed regularly in the pools and that they loved to playfully train. They lived to perform. But to me, a boy of 9, these animals were captives, and their slavery was being made a spectacle. Thankfully, we never returned to SeaWorld as a family again.

On the face of it, the rationale behind the capturing of animals for zoos has been to provide forms of entertainment, but it is also a demonstration of domination and hegemonic power. In the third century BCE, Romans would capture elephants and fight them in arenas, which shortly after shifted to human gladiators fighting elephants and other captured animals, a tradition which continued on for centuries. Circuses also can be traced back to ancient Rome in the form of chariot races and equestrian shows, but the modern circus with which we have become more familiar over the past century emerged in England and North America as traveling shows. The most famous of these, the "Barnum & Bailey Greatest Show on Earth," set the stage for what is still, to this day, the template for several touring and non-touring circus shows, and evolved into the major circus "Wringling Brothers and Barnum & Bailey." A fixture of these shows is the animals. Early on, circuses displayed "exotic" animals, often including, in these demonstrations, marginalized people (see Chapter 7). Later, these evolved from showing animals in cages and equestrian shows to the choreographed routines with which we are familiar today, involving elephants, bears, lions, tigers, horses, dogs, and chimpanzees. These animals spend most of their lives in chains and caged, their only social contact with the animal trainers who tend them (Jensen & Tweedy-Holmes, 2007; Harris, Iossa, & Soulsbury, 2006).

Animal activists around the world are making the public more aware of the abuses to these animals through protests, films, and other forms of resistance. Less widely known however, are the ways that these captive animals themselves resist exploitation and captivity, or respond to harm. In zoos all over the world, primates—more specifically chimpanzees and orangutans, have been noted for their elaborate escape plans and protests. Historian and author Jason Hribal (2008, 2010) documents animal resistance and shares the story of Ken Allen, an orangutan nicknamed "the hairy Houdini," who found countless ways to escape over his long stay in the San Diego Zoo. Over and over, Ken was found outside his confinement, peacefully strolling the grounds of the zoo. While zookeepers and trainers knew Ken had taken to unscrewing any screw he could find and removing nuts from bolts, they couldn't figure out how he was getting loose. It was such a mystery to them that they installed video surveillance, but Ken seemed to be aware of the surveillance and would not attempt to escape while on camera. Trainers shed their uniforms and dressed up as visitors to try to monitor him, but were still unable to observe an escape (Hribal, 2010). Again and again, Ken escaped, leaving trainers baffled. Eventually, the orangutan's fame brought a local news crew to do a feature story. Ken greeted them by pelting them with his feces. The zoo spent a great deal of money and called upon long lists of experts but nothing worked. They could not contain Ken. He misled trainers, hid their tools, and defied their solutions in order to stroll the zoo freely (Hribal, 2010).

While Ken Allen is one of the most famous escape artists, his resistance is not all that unusual. A wide array of animal resistance can be noted, from tigers injured by poachers hunting down and killing their assailants while leaving others in the vicinity unharmed, to elephants injured by handlers' bullhooks finally stomping on their abusers. While we do not condone or celebrate the killing, we want to highlight that these accounts indicate that animals are aware of the situations they are in. And yet in most cases they do not resort to violence. While we may assume that they do not have the capacity to think or plan, animals have the ability to strategize, resist, and retaliate in response to unjust treatment or harm.

While countries like the Netherlands banned the use of wild animals in circuses in 2012, and the SeaWorld park Johnny's family went to in Aurora, Ohio, closed in 2007 (demolished to make way for a Six Flags theme park), many similar marine life amusement parks, circuses, and zoos still exist. Such entertainment practices are often touted as conservation efforts or even as "educational." And, in fact, we do learn from these organizations! As members of a culture framed by anthropocentric beliefs and practices, we are encouraged to see animals in captivity as somehow happier or protected from their difficult lives in the wild, and thus their captors as benevolent. We are taught that animal imprisonment is "for their own good." And, we learn that humans are superior to and have the right to determine the conditions of life for other creatures according to our own interests, whether those be observation, amusement, or profit. While zoos and circuses are important reproducers of this discourse, they are not alone as powerful ideological institutions for human supremacy.

The Animal Welfare Act (AWA)

In 1966, President Lynden B. Johnson signed into law the Animal Welfare Act (AWA), which regulates the treatment of animals in research, zoos, circuses, and the entertainment industry. This Act is intended to provide a minimum standard for the treatment and care of some animals and, while it includes several commonly cared for animals, it excludes birds, lab rats and mice, livestock—and any farm animals—and all cold-blooded animals. As you can probably imagine after reading this far into the chapter, animal experimentation, while regulated, has a number of loopholes. The food industry, for example, is protected as exempt from the AWA. While the AWA does provide some traction for advocacy groups and legal organizations who wish to end animal suffering, it is all too often unenforced or ignored.

On Learning Shame and Silence

So far in this chapter, we have presented some of the ways a human supremacist understanding plays out within our economic institutions.

Throughout the chapter we emphasize that we learn anthropocentrism within these institutions and within our day-to-day interactions that are laced with anthropocentric assumptions. We learn to suppress the pain we feel in the face of violence to others as we are reminded over and over that they are not worthy of our compassion. We are interested in exposing how it is that we, as members of modernist cultures, come to accept such horrors, how we come to view other species as deserving of such exploitation, and how anthropocentrism interacts with and supports other forms of centric thinking, such as androcentrism and racism.

What interferes with our abilities to express horror at the damages and suffering being inflicted on the living world, human and more-than-human, by modern industrial culture? What teaches us to push down the pain we may feel as we witness degradation in the more-than-human world, and turn away? Three conversations snapped Rebecca's attention back to this question, pushing her back into an awkward childhood horror, vulnerability, and silence. Here's her story:

> Over lunch, a friend told me of his daughter, a freshman in high school, who came home to tell him about her pain and disgust at having to dissect a frog in biology class. He listened and comforted her, but she went back to school with her pain neatly tucked into silence: best not to make waves so early in her career as a student in this new school. Upon sharing this story with another friend, she told me that she and a group of her female friends tried to "opt out" of these labs when she was in high school, but the school insisted that these were important lessons. Then, in a separate conversation, a graduate student told the class of her constant impulse to apologize for her sensitivity to nature, and her decision nonetheless to dedicate her life to environmental education. Confessing to the class, the student explained: "I feel, in some ways, embarrassed, which is totally at odds with my deep convictions to work on these problems."
>
> Listening to these stories, I was catapulted back to my own girlhood, and the agony I lived with on an almost daily basis as I witnessed example after example of unnecessary death or abuse of innocent animals, forests, streams, and marshlands: my brothers trapping muskrats to sell their pelts and earn a little spending money, the innocuous appearance of raccoons, possums, dogs, deer, and other creatures killed in the road, the local farmers' sport of shooting woodchucks to rid the holes from their fields, the transportation department's decision to fill in a "swamp" to build a new road, the frogs floating in formaldehyde in science class. As I tried to articulate my distress at what I saw happening, I was confronted by a general acceptance by those around me that there was no reason to question any of it. I heard: "Don't be silly." "You're too sensitive." "They're just animals! Get over it." But I never got over it. I couldn't get over it.

Like Johnny in his story about SeaWorld, I tried to protest that it seemed unfair to think of trees as "things" or to assume that animals didn't count enough to live; I tried to argue that each one must have had a worthy enough life by virtue of growing there or simply being born; the "swamp" must be home to a whole lot of living things, mustn't it? I lived with a sort of ache of distress and helplessness. Why didn't others seem to feel this way? In spite of both my parents' love of the outdoors and the lessons that they taught us about respecting each other and nature, most of my distress just fell on deaf ears, or ears already well honed to a different set of assumptions.

My words sounded childish, eventually even to me. I began to apologize when I would inadvertently wince or cry out at the sight of some awful death or abuse, or slam on the brakes to avoid being guilty of it. Mostly, I just fell silent, tucking away my pain in a dark secret place. By the time I was an adult, living on my own, I had become very adept at avoiding my pain by avoiding as much as possible any conversation, movie, course, or relationship that would require me to bear witness to the suffering in the natural world. Of course, this was not possible. And, to the degree that my agony leaked out to others, I felt exposed, small, and even ridiculous. "I'm sorry. I can't help it. I know it's stupid but . . ."

And so this wound, this haunting pain which should have developed into a passionate ability to protect what I love, instead allowed a much more pernicious cultural wound—the rationalization of violence hidden behind a veil of assumed human superiority. I could not speak coherently against the violence I witnessed almost daily as a child because I grew to believe—I was taught—that I was somehow wrong, or crazy, to see such violence as something to be questioned. If I identified with the suffering of animals, I was "off" somehow, too sensitive, and hyper-emotional. I learned to question my own pain, seeing it as a sign that there was something wrong with my priorities. I even diverted it into more "appropriate" or acceptable activities, becoming a social justice activist in grad school and for the first ten years of my life as a scholar and professor.

Looking back, I see I was being "subjected to a powerful disciplinary pedagogy" (Bartky, 1996, p. 225) that taught me to internalize a sense of shame at my agonizing love for animals and the living world. I was being taught to be ashamed of my love for and connection to the natural world, and, worse, I was being taught that such a love marked me as inferior, weak, feminine.

We'll look more closely at the gendered processes of shaming in the next chapter. For now, think about the ways you too may have been taught to silence your sensitivity to other living beings both in school, and other contexts.

K-12 Schools and Higher Education

Most schools are also heavily influenced by the discourses of modernity discussed in Chapter 3. (We'll share some great counter examples in Chapter 10.) In fact, schools and universities play a significant role in how we learn to see ourselves as separate from and superior to the natural world. In schools we learn to prioritize certain information as knowledge in connection with reason or science, and to close off or subjugate our emotional responses. In this section of the chapter, we will take a brief look at some of the common ways anthropocentrism plays out in schools and what we can do to shift these processes.

In Chapter 3, we delved into the complex interrelationship between language and culture; we emphasized how much we rely on metaphors in our day-to-day lives and as teachers. If teachers or the authors of textbooks and other curriculum materials unwittingly see the world through an anthropocentric lens, then it is highly likely that students will learn to think in ways that reinforce human supremacy. For example, when in science class we learn that the human body at homeostasis is a well-oiled machine, the implication is that, like machines, we are made up of parts that can be separated from the whole. Another example might be when we refer to the parts of a cell, like the nucleus as the "control center," and DNA as the "programming code," or the mitochondria as "the cell's power plant," etc.

In social studies, there is often talk of "managing" nature, whether it be in encouragement to use "our natural resources wisely" or in the claim that "we need to control animal populations." At what point do trees become lumber, or forests and lakes become natural resources? How is it our schools are playing a significant role in teaching people to be human supremacists or, at the very least, validating that worldview as preferred or (even worse) as fact? An example jumps out at Oregon State University, just up the road from Jeff, which has a program in "Forest Engineering, Resources and Management"—making clear that forests are just objects to be manipulated, rather than complex communities of life. When we teach using such metaphors we hide the fact that these parts are not inanimate and cannot be separated from their living existence.

Think About This

Look back at our discussion of metaphors in Chapter 3. What are some examples of teaching through metaphors that reinforce anthropocentric ways of thinking?

List a few and share them with your classmates.

Earlier in the chapter, we asked you to think about lessons learned in various classes in school that reinforce the idea that humans are at the top of the chain of being. What did you come up with? Here are a few that our students have noticed and shared:

- The "food chain," versus the "food web," to teach about health and biology.
- "An ecosystem is like a finely-tuned car," to teach in science education how many different parts of an ecosystem work together.
- "Mother Nature" as an angry, unpredictable, and retributive force. Here we see the ways gender discourses intersect with anthropocentrism.
- "The protesters were treated like animals," to teach about resistance and civil rights. This example both reinforces human supremacy but also connects it closely with racism.

These are just a few, but as you share the examples that come to your discussion about lessons it's likely that other common phrases will come up as well. A few phrases we've noticed in classrooms over the years include:

- No horsing around on the playground!
- The teacher badgered the students for an explanation.
- The children were behaving like animals.
- The boys pigged out on the birthday treats.
- Today we are going to kill two birds with one stone.

Let's think about some examples from textbooks. C. A. Bowers (1993) has written extensively on the ways the topics both included and excluded from textbooks serve to teach us certain ways of thinking about our relationship to the more-than-human world. For example, how many of you learned that plants communicate or "play" in your high school or even college textbooks? Did you read about the scientists studying plant neurology? Did you read about CAFOs and animal abuse in those books? Or how about information regarding the over-fishing of oceans, the problem of mountaintop removal, or the different impacts of fossil fuel energy versus solar and wind energy. These last two examples are getting more attention these days with the growing scientific evidence about climate change, but these issues are still considered highly volatile political issues.

What does get included? In an early examination of textbook content, Bowers (1993) draws our attention to human-centric metaphors and their effects. Think back to your own classrooms in school and the texts you used. Do Bowers's examples sound familiar?

Textbook titles and chapter headings in the early grades rather innocently announce that humans are the reference point for making sense of the world. "The Earth You Live On," "Our Regions," *Our World: Our Land and Heritage*, "What Do You Want in Your Environment?" and "Our Resources" are typical textbook examples of the unexamined conceptual order that mirrors what most students will have already encountered through television and the consumer emporiums.

(Bowers, 1993, p. 123)

Social Studies textbooks most often examine the development of modern Western civilization as it has (ostensibly) benefitted certain groups of humans over time. We are taught to see as "progress" the development of industry and technology, and the defense through wars of the systems that develop our economy as necessary. These texts do not address the huge cost to the more-than-human creatures and communities of these developments.

Since textbook publication is influenced by the largest states who purchase them (Texas, for example), what gets in depends on the political ideologies dominating those states. Texas requires that the same textbook be used in every classroom for each subject in each grade. Think about the power that state has over what publishing companies put in textbooks given the huge market the state offers. Publishers of textbook and curriculum materials and testing companies have enormous power over how and what we learn to think and do. They produce the metaphors we learn as "just the way it is."

As we have been laying out throughout this chapter, the metaphors we learn to use, both written and spoken, are ripe with anthropocentrism which weaves itself around and is reinforced by other discourses of modernity, such as mechanism, androcentrism, and ethnocentrism. We will focus on other centric discourses and the ways they work with anthropocentrism in the following chapters.

The institutionalized violence and oppression of racism, slavery, the subjugation and objectification of women, and the genocide of Indigenous Peoples—as we will examine in the next five chapters—all hinge on reasoning that the Other is inferior, not fully human, and thus "like animals." Without critically addressing anthropocentrism—one's capture in discourses of human supremacism—we are in fact making way for the abuse and exploitation of both human and the more-than-human family: the animals, the land, each other, and the oceans to which we all belong. So what would it take to begin to interrupt these discursive practices in our own classrooms? What does a pedagogy of responsibility look like?

Listening and Learning from More-Than-Human Teachers in Johnny's Classroom

In Johnny's class, students are asked to identify or seek out a more-than-human teacher for the semester, and to journal weekly what they learn from this different sort of teacher–student relationship. While at first students write about how different and challenging the assignment may be, after a few weeks the discussions about what folks are learning are rich and provide an excellent context for discussing how they might be learning to teach from participating in a different sort of learning relationship. Simultaneously, they are practicing listening to the more-than-human world. They write about sitting in "silence" and what they hear, smell, and feel. Further, the students then are asked to consider what they are learning and how that learning process is going. In efforts to build their abilities to share such often-shamed relationships, the students provide feedback to each other and report to each other on the progress of what it is they are learning.

The results are these exciting conversations and sharing of stories, as well as the students teaching each other as they share their stories. We often say, "let nature be our classroom," but how often do we just go outside and play school? The purpose of this particular assignment in Johnny's class is to go outside, or even be inside, and learn to listen to the many wise voices we often don't hear and certainly don't consider as our teachers. It's always amazing to read in the final weeks about what someone learned from the brook, the wind, the willow tree, the owl, the chickadees, the worms . . . and the list goes on.

Enacting a Pedagogy of Responsibility

Part of what we are calling for in this chapter is the development of awareness and compassion that can be developed through teaching and learning relationships that move to dissolve the boundaries between mind and body, human and animal, reason and emotion. This means that we must help our students and each other to recognize the terrible fallacy of these self-interested value hierarchies that rationalize as somehow inevitable the terror unleashed on those defined as lesser beings. How did we come to create these systems of domination, and how do they work? A pedagogy of responsibility asks that we begin to see how our own subjectivities (our identities and self-definitions) are made within that violent history of thought and practice, at the same time that we retain the ability to speak and act against it, to see and embrace our connection to others, human and more-than-human. Teacher educators are responsible for addressing these issues with future teachers, for what does education mean if not our willingness to engage in ethical and responsible ways of being in the world (Edmundson & Martusewicz, 2013)?

Jeff's Path

Unlike Rebecca and Johnny, I didn't question the treatment of animals as a child. I enjoyed zoos and SeaWorld and even took my son to them when he was young. Instead, I came to my critique of human supremacism much more gradually. Having long since come to challenge the myths of capitalism, sexism, and racism, I thought I had pretty completely stepped outside the mainstream beliefs. It was only when I encountered the work of Chet Bowers that I had that "aha" moment—that there was another central myth I had ignored: anthropocentrism. "Of course," I said to myself, "how could I not have seen that?"

This intellectual journey has opened me to see and hear this whole other part of our community. For me, this connection has been strongest when I spend time in old-growth forests in Oregon and Northern California. In those ancient groves, the voice of the community of life begins to be apparent, and the tree elders communicate the patience—and (dare I say) "wisdom"—of a whole different scale of time.

Three tasks loom large in this enactment of responsibility: (1) to create interdisciplinary curricula and practices that trace and the challenge the ways our culture has constructed a cruel belief system that naturalizes domination and terror; (2) to actively work to examine and challenge those beliefs and practices that perpetuate violence by developing our students' embodied ethical sensibilities; and (3) to learn from those other species that share our communities, and from local community members, especially Indigenous Peoples who have this wisdom. Practically speaking, this means that teachers will need to speak and learn from open hearts, to create questions and activities that insist that their students learn to think through these issues, to see the damages done and to willingly act to counter them as they learn to see differently.

Of course, these activities need to be age appropriate, and take account of students' readiness to engage in difficult conversations. It is not appropriate to engage young children in viewing or even discussing the specifics of abuse to animals or the land. But it is appropriate to engage in conversations about who deserves to be considered as members of communities and what that looks like in terms of care, reciprocity, protection, and so on.

Conclusion

We know this chapter is filled with a lot of content that can be overwhelming and even a bit depressing. Perhaps one place to start anew is to simplify all of this: make friends, get outside, listen to the more-than-human world, and share stories. Make intentional caring relationships with other species—animals, trees, a river, the songbirds that wake us up in the morning, the food that we grow, or the soil that gives us life. The point is that we learn compassion and dependency when we understand, in an ecological sense, what it means to be in affectionate relationships. We learn what it means to care and to belong without framing that understanding as human-centered. As we close this chapter, we share the inspiring words of Wendell Berry:

> Care allows creatures [and people] to escape our explanations into their actual presence and their essential mystery. In taking care of fellow creatures, we acknowledge they are not ours. We acknowledge that they belong to an order and a harmony of which we are ourselves a part. To answer to the perpetual crisis of our presence in this abounding and dangerous world, we have only the perpetual obligation to care.
>
> (Berry, 1995, p. 77)

What Schools and Teachers Can Do

As a way to get started thinking, we suggest below a few steps that pertain to what schools and teachers can do in their local community to engage in the necessary healing or reimagining of our communities and the dominant culture.

- Ask critical questions: What is a community and who should be considered important members? What do plants, animals, insects, and other creatures provide these communities, and what happens when they are gone? What happens when we treat any community member as less valuable?
- Looking at textbooks, we can ask students to consider whose interests are most represented there. What metaphors stand out to them? What are the primary points of view being represented and what are

the effects of such ideas? How are members of the more-than-human world presented?

- Engage in age-appropriate teaching and learning that explores re-thinking the assumptions influencing how we, as humans, construct meaning and thus how we learn to relate to each other and the more-than-human world. Further, commit to critically and ethically examining how we understand teaching and learning that seeks to support healthy communities that include all beings and recognize, respect, and represent belonging to an ecological system.
- Engage in critical and ethical examination of community as it is all too often defined in terms of exclusion, and work to redefine community as including all beings.
- Engage in examining the diverse ways in which all living relationships can be recognized, respected, and represented through teaching and learning among *all* members.
- Engage in supporting the diverse approaches to healing from Western industrial culture and, in solidarity, engage in showing respect to other cultural ways of knowing that differ from current dominant discourses.
- Connect with and learn about the diversity of local native species and Indigenous Peoples. Become students, *with* your students, of native languages of those peoples who dwelled in your region pre-colonization. They probably still live there!

Conceptual Toolbox

Animal Industrial Complex: The vast industrial network that exploits animals for profit, turning their bodies into meat, science experiments, and entertainment—commodities produced to satisfy corporate visions of human "needs."

Anthropocentrism: Centric form of thinking that positions humans at the center and at the top of a hierarchy of all living and non-living beings.

Biotechnology: The application and molecular modification of biological organisms for developing or improving commercial products.

Shaming: Psycho-social processes by which an inferior or diminished sense of self is internalized. "It requires, if not an actual audience before whom such deficiencies are paraded, then an internalized audience with the capacity to judge, hence internalized standards of judgment" (Bartky, 1996, p. 227).

Suggested Readings and Other Resources

Books and Essays

Chamovitz, D. (2012). *What a plant knows: A field guide to the senses*. New York, NY: Scientific American/Farrar, Straus and Giroux.

Coetzee, J. M. (1999). *The lives of animals*. Princeton, NJ: Princeton University Press.

Jensen, D. & Tweedy-Holmes (2007). *Thought to exist in the wild: Awakening from the nightmare of zoos*. Santa Cruz, CA: No Voice Unheard.

Kenmmerer, L. (Ed). (2011). *Sister species: Women, animals and social justice*. Urbana, IL: University of Illinois Press.

Merchant, C. (1990). *The death of nature: Women, ecology and the Scientific Revolution*. San Francisco, CA: Harper Collins.

Socha, K. & Blum, S. (2013). *Confronting animal exploitation: Grassroots essays on liberation and veganism*. Jefferson, NC: McFarland and Company.

Films

Mancuso, S. (July 2010) TED talk: *The roots of plant intelligence*. http://www.ted.com/talks/stefano_mancuso_the_roots_of_plant_intelligence.html

McAnallen, S. (Writer/Director). (2012). *The superior human?* Australia: Ultra-ventus.

Monroe, M. (Writer), Psihoyos, L. (Director), Hambleton, C., Stevens, F., Clark, J., Ahnemann, O., & Pesemn, P. D. (Producer). (2009). *The cove*. USA: Lions Gate.

Cowperthwaite, G. (Writer). (2013). *Blackfish*. USA: Magnolia Home Entertainment.

Monson, S. (Writer), Harrelson, B., Raz, B. C., Visram, N., Q, M., & White, P. (Producers). (2005). *Earthlings*. USA: Nation Earth.

Curry, M. (Writer). (2011). *If a tree falls: A story of the Earth Liberation Front*. USA: Oscilloscope Laboratories.

Organization and Links

CAFO: The Tragedy of Industrial Animal Factories (http://www.cafothebook.org)
This resource provides excellent materials for learning more about Concentrated Animal Feeding Operations (CAFOs).

American Society for the Prevention of Cruelty to Animals (ASPCA) (http://www.aspca.org/)
This organization is one of the oldest organizations dedicated to the humane treatment of animals. It works to investigate and make arrests for crimes against animals, and to research the conditions to which animals are exposed, and does an amazing amount of educational outreach to teach nonviolent approaches to stopping the cruel treatment of animals.

The Humane Society of the United States (http://www.humanesociety.org/)
  Similar to ASPCA, the Humane Society is a large organization in communities across the US. It offers myriad ways people can contribute and volunteer with their rescue work.
HEART: Promoting Humane Education (http://teachhumane.org/heart/)
  This organization offers great resources for teachers, with examples of how teachers are working to foster and develop compassion and respect in their classrooms.
Institute for Critical Animal Studies (ICAS) (http://www.criticalanimalstudies.org/)
  This organization is an excellent resource to connect with like-minded educators and activists working toward equality for all.

Chapter 5

Learning Androcentrism

An EcoJustice Approach to Gender and Education

Introduction

In this chapter, we'll examine how modernist discourses structured by centric thinking and a logic of domination also create our assumptions and experiences of gender, and especially what this means in terms of boys' and girls' different experiences of education and schooling. This chapter is the first of three chapters that look at how EcoJustice Education helps us to think differently—more deeply from a cultural ecological analysis—about social justice issues as they play out in schooling. We'll be delving into historical processes in order to trace the ways specific cultural ways of thinking—the root metaphors and discourses we've been discussing—are at the heart of all sorts of domination among people, and how these link to ideas and attitudes leading to environmental degradation as well. These chapters look explicitly at how schooling (though we may think of it as benign or essentially beneficial) has been used as a means of perpetuating social and ecological violence. And, we'll also be looking at educational sites as the location of important challenges to these forms of oppression.

We realize that, as you read, you may be asking questions like, "What does this have to do with me? Isn't all that sexism and racism stuff fixed already? Do social classes really exist? Didn't the civil rights movement take care of racism and inequality? We don't think that way any more, do we?" To a certain degree, you'll be right. There have been major social and political changes that have been the result of specific actions against domination and have improved the quality of people's lives. But, what we hope you'll begin to see is that we are also dealing with critical issues, and that the discourses of modernity that we discussed above, even while they may be hidden or shifted, are still impacting our lives today. The forms of social violence and inequality we'll be discussing have a history; they have deep cultural and socio-linguistic roots. To the extent that teachers can begin to recognize the metaphoric structure of these discourses, handed down over many centuries and operating in our day-to-day exchanges, they will begin to challenge the appearance of universality, or naturalness. That is at the heart of cultural ecological analysis and an EcoJustice approach to education. With this purpose in mind, let's turn to the analysis of gender and education.

A Few Definitions

Gender will be treated here as the complex ways that men and women come to identify themselves as masculine or feminine via the reproduction, exchange, and even resistance to strong root metaphors that create our definitions of these terms. In Chapter 3 we introduced you to the ways language works to create our sense of who we are in relation to our definition of others in the world. In this chapter, we will be unpacking the ways specific definitions of "man" and "woman" or masculinity and femininity have been historically created within a complex socio-linguistic system that defines women, or those who are deemed to be "like" women, to be inferior in relation to men.

This definition differentiates gender from sex, which refers to the specific biological differences between males and females—differences, for example, in genitalia, chromosomes, hormones, reproductive organs, and so on. We acknowledge that these biological differences exist. In fact, though this is not commonly discussed, we also acknowledge that sex differences can come in more forms than the two we normally think of—male and female—though these are often the only forms recognized in modern Western cultures. In fact, *intersex* is a concept used to refer to combinations of physical features (genitalia) or to describe an individual who has biological characteristics of both the male and female sexes and thus cannot be classified as either one or the other.

The important point for this chapter is that gender differences (including important differences in social, political, and economic power among men and women) are created from the representations and meanings that get assigned to these biological differences, meanings that have been passed down, internalized, and exchanged historically through complex discursive systems and presented, even experienced, as if they were biological or natural. As gender sociologist Michael Kimmel (2000) puts it,

> [g]ender is not simply a system of classification by which biological males and biological females are sorted, separated, and socialized into equivalent sex roles. Gender also expresses . . . inequality between women and men. When we speak about gender we also speak about hierarchy, power, and inequality, not simply difference.
>
> (Kimmel, 2000, p. 1)

Another important definition is *sexuality*, which is related to both sex and gender, but also different from each of these in important ways. Sexuality refers to the specific ways that sexual desire operates in our lives, and obviously intersects with our understandings of ourselves as men and women. *Heterosexuality* refers to sexual attraction and activity between males and females (or men and women). *Homosexuality* refers to same-sex attraction. Gender identities play out in complex ways as they intersect with sexuality. *Bisexuality* refers to sexual attraction to both males and females. *Transsexual* "refers to a person who identifies physically, psychologically, and emotionally as the opposite gender and may seek to alter his or her body through hormones and or sexual reassignment surgery" (Klipp, unpublished document).

Finally, we want to introduce what we mean by the concept *feminism*. Recognizing that this term raises red flags for many who may be most familiar with the media-sensationalized notions of feminists as "man-haters," or the "bra-burners" of the 1960s, we use this concept to refer to the sorts of critical and ethical analyses that examine the ways that women have been inferiorized through social and institutional processes historically, as well as in contemporary social, economic, and political contexts. Feminism comes in many different theoretical and political forms that grow out of the diverse experiences of women and men who are concerned about oppression and ecological degradation. Many feminists are clear that sexist practices and beliefs and patriarchal systems are not disconnected from other forms of domination such as racism, class-based oppression, or ecological degradation. And, because there are important differences in women's experiences across class and race lines, there are important debates that have historically shaped what different feminist groups see as critical points of focus.

African American women, for example, have been highly critical of white middle class brands of feminism as being exclusive of the unique experiences and situations of people of color. Some theorists use the term *womanist* to differentiate the work of black women about black women. Women who look explicitly at the intersection of the oppression of women and other social groups with ecological degradation call themselves *eco-feminists*. Men who are supportive of feminist concerns often refer to themselves as "anti-sexist" or as *pro-feminist* men. Some may even refer to themselves as feminists, as they work to support the intersecting concerns of social and ecological justice. This position is often challenged by women who charge that while men may support the basic causes of feminism, they cannot possibly understand the issues that feminists deal with, and therefore ought not identify as "feminist."

While we see these debates as articulating important political tasks, we take the position in this book that it matters less what one calls one's self than where one's ethical commitments lie. We will ask readers to look carefully at the ways value-hierarchized or centric thinking leads to all sorts of unnecessary violence and suffering in the world.

In this chapter, we begin by looking at how we come to experience ourselves as gendered, working from the premise that to internalize a sense of ourselves as masculine or feminine is to be created within one aspect of a hierarchized value system that we pass on through day-to-day conversations, relationships, and actions. Masculinity and femininity is learned so well, in fact, that it becomes a deeply psychological and embodied experience. We all begin to internalize gendered identities from the moment we are born into culture and interact with the exchange of language and other forms of representation. We learn a particular story about what it means to be a man or a woman, and, through these stories, we learn to "do gender." As we will discuss in this chapter, conceptions of education and the complex practices of schooling play a role in this process. But, let's back up a bit.

Revisiting Metaphor and Dualistic Thinking

In Chapters 3 and 4 we discussed the idea that modern Western culture is founded upon a set of false but powerful dualisms that present certain oppositional relationships as hierarchized and natural: man/woman, culture/nature, mind/body, reason/emotion, and so on. As a reminder, the first term in this string of oppositional pairs is always presented as superior and independent of the second, while the second term is always inferior to and at the mercy of the first. So, in the last chapter we learned how such thinking negatively affects animals and other species. Looking again at the chart of dualisms in Chapter 3, note the ways the categories in each column line up: they are analogies of one another. Man, the reasoning one, uses his *mind* to create *culture*. Woman, the more *emotional*, is the reproductive one, and hence her *body* makes her closest to *nature*, the least valued category. In this chapter, and especially Chapter 7, we'll see how comparing people to animals or defining them as less than human is one of the fundamental ways used to inferiorize them.

As we will see playing out in the history of education and schooling, because women possess the biological capacity to bear children, their essential value in Western Eurocentric and androcentric thinking is associated with their bodies, not their minds. In Cartesian terms, the body is seen as part of "matter" rather than "spirit" and thus the inferior term in the pair. Thus, women, like animals, are exploitable on those terms. Today we see such inferior status play out in some personal relationships either as wives and daughters in patriarchal families, or as women become professionals doing so-called "pink collar" or social service work (teachers, social workers, secretaries, nurses). Defined in terms of their "lack" of what men possess—reason—they have been historically excluded from all sorts of opportunities, including other occupations, political decision-making, considerations of citizenship or leadership, and forms of education that would prepare them for these roles. As a group, women's reproductive bodies (seen as the inferior opposite of "mind") have historically been used as signs that women are inherently closer to a "lower order" of life—nature—and thus (just like nature) in need of men's strong authority and control. Men on the other hand are defined as strong, unemotional, in control, aggressive, decision-makers.

Note the root metaphors at play in this discourse: Reason is equated with superiority, while reproduction and the body (and thus the naturalized association with children) are equated with a "lower order," or Nature. While these statements seem ridiculous to us today, these root metaphors have functioned historically to rationalize strong patriarchal relations throughout our society that define men and women's "natural" place in society. Think for a moment about why elementary teachers tend overwhelmingly to be women, or why men who take on typically feminized jobs such as nursing often find their masculinity challenged: "Why would a man do a 'woman's' job?!"

Of course, these beliefs are being challenged. Men are entering traditionally female spheres, and women are beginning to challenge what has been referred to as the "glass ceiling." And yet, as we will begin to unpack in the pages that follow, the specific metaphors associated with masculinity and femininity or "man" and "woman" are still strongly woven together to form a powerful historical tapestry of meaning, identity, and relationship. Gendered meanings are so internalized by both men and women as to be nearly invisible. They are normalized and taken for granted. As we will make clear below, such taken-for-granted meanings appear in school texts, in classroom practices, in attitudes and actions expressed in hallways, playing fields, or on the bus. Ultimately, violent, hierarchized definitions continue to affect relationships and opportunities for women and men in schools and throughout society to this day, even as they are challenged by feminists, womanists, and pro-feminist men.

Moreover, while we'll unpack here how they affect gender domination in particular, these metaphors link up to others that also weave through our conceptions of class, race, and our sense of who we are relative to other species. Indeed, while we cannot detail all forms here, we argue that value-hierarchized or centric thinking is at the heart of all forms of oppression.

In this chapter, we will be using this analysis to help unravel the ways that centric thinking and a logic of domination have woven through both historical and contemporary expressions of women's and men's relations to education. In Chapter 6, we examine how systematic impoverishment of people is created via systems of thinking that legitimize unequal access to decision-making power, status, and the resources needed to live. Chapter 7 goes deeply into the ways "race" has been created historically as a way to inferiorize whole groups of people, and especially the struggles by people of color to use education as a way out of oppression. As you read those chapters, and especially the ways they take up the use of "deficit thinking," think back to the ways they are interwoven with the gender domination explored in this chapter.

Historical Background

Early Education in New England Families

In the period of European colonization of North America (from the 1500s to the 1700s), education of white children was the responsibility of the family and primarily carried out for religious purposes. Puritan families, occupying for the most part self-sufficient farms during a period dominated by an agrarian economic system, worked together as a unit to produce their daily needs. Women worked alongside men as producers, and children too were expected to execute specific tasks to maintain family survival. Childhood, in this sense, was defined in very different ways than it is today. Children in white Puritan families learned many things from their parents and from each other that developed the skills needed by daily tasks on the farm. But, they also learned to read and write primarily as a means toward "individual salvation." That is, they needed to learn to read and memorize scripture.

As Joel Spring (1994a) points out, families in this context were organized as strict hierarchies "with men at the top and children at the bottom" (p. 23). Women answered to the authority of their husbands and fathers, who answered to God.

> The colonial family operated on a simple premise: "He for God, she for God in him." This meant that women were to bow to the God in men, and men were to assume the spiritual care of women. In legal matters, the married woman was at the mercy of her husband—she was without rights to own property, make contracts, or sue for damages.
>
> (Spring, 1994a, p. 23)

While they grew up under these strict controls, women were still responsible for their own spiritual development, and so girls learned to read, write, and do basic arithmetic alongside their brothers. But for girls, unlike boys, such learning was strictly intended as a means of religious and patriarchal control—they needed to learn their place in God's kingdom and their father or husband's house. Since they were considered to lack equivalent intellectual capacity, there would be no other reason to educate them. However, ironically, while men were considered primarily responsible for such education in their families, and women were subordinated to the law of God and their husbands, women often served as teachers both in their own families, and outside in schools referred to as Dame Schools where community children were sent to learn basic literacy skills.

During this early period of New England history, Quaker organizations were also involved in the education of free African American children. Reading and writing were the primary focus, though literacy rates remained low during this period. In the South, slavery made it illegal for black persons to learn to read and write. However, as slave narratives demonstrate, education was happening in secret in many slave families, and much of this work was done by women passing down traditional knowledge from African culture in stories, songs, and through specific practices being exploited by white masters. Reading and writing was also taught among both adults and children in some slave communities, albeit often in strict secrecy. Some plantation owners, however, found the education of their slaves both morally appropriate and, in some cases, economically advantageous.

> On plantations the pursuit of education became a communal effort—slaves learned from parents, spouses, family members, and fellow slaves and some were even personally instructed by their masters or hired tutors. Slaveholders were motivated by Christian convictions to enable Bible-reading among slaves and even established informal plantation schools on occasion in part because of slaveholders' practical need for literate slaves to perform tasks such as recordkeeping.
>
> (*Slavery and the Making of America*, PBS (2004), Retrieved on August 3, 2009 from www.pbs.org/wnet/slavery/ experience/education/history2.html)

Women played an important role in this process.

"Motherlove" and Girls' Education

By the early decades of the 19th century, small self-sufficient farms typical of the early colonies began giving way to new centralized forces of production as the nation began to enter the Industrial Revolution. Men and women's roles and identities began to shift as well, as some families were uprooted, leaving the farm behind so men could find work in the newly forming factories in the cities. Middle class women, remaining at home to care for children and all other domestic duties, found their lives radically changed. No longer needed to produce the necessary daily goods, and excluded for the most part from the newly expanding world of commerce, women were exiled to a new social position. From primary producers of the family's daily goods, they became transformed into consumers of now factory-produced goods.

As cities swelled with both migrating families and newly arriving immigrants, unemployment and low wages began to put stress on communities, creating fears of social and political chaos among the leaders of the middle class. Women, who in men's absence were also beginning to take on more responsibility both in their churches and their homes for religious instruction of their children, suddenly found themselves in the spotlight as newly ordained "guardians of childhood." This developing identity created an important opening that would offer educational opportunities taking both white and black women into the world of teaching. Using a discourse and set of metaphors that otherwise subordinated them, women asserted a powerful new identity for themselves that would include becoming the nation's first public school teachers.

Authorized by the aforementioned political, social, and economic shifts, a discourse on "motherlove and domestic reform" began to accentuate the differences between men's and women's worlds, heralding a "female sphere as an 'oasis' of virtue, peace and moral salvation" (Martusewicz, 1994, p. 171). If men's roles were shifting into a sphere of business and commerce, women were to become Republican Mothers, explicitly responsible for domestic peace and the care of her family. Without actually denying paternal authority, new knowledge about womanhood, attributed and functioning as "God's truth," was created using existing dualistic metaphors, and assigning to women, especially mothers, the role of preparing the nations' future citizenry. This movement became known as the Cult of True Womanhood.

Women's taken-for-granted "nature" as reproductive servants to God, her country, and her husband made her the natural choice for such a role. And, if this was the case, women reformers argued, they must be educated for such important responsibilities. To this end, Sarah Hale wrote:

> If God designed woman and the preserver of infancy, the inspirer or helper of man's moral nature in its effort to reach after spiritual things; if examples of Woman are to be found in every age and nation, who without any special preparation have won their way to eminence in all pursuits tending to advance moral goodness and religious faith, then the policy as well as justice of providing liberally for feminine education must be apparent to Christian men.
>
> (Kuhn, 1947, p. 45)

If women were to carry out the tasks and duties prescribed to them in their special domestic vocation, then it was essential that they be exposed to those specific bodies of knowledge that, as Emma Willard hoped, would "enable them as mothers, to do all that enlightened reflectiveness can for the happiness of the beings entrusted to them" (Kuhn, 1947, p. 45). Thus, the first schools for girls were to prepare them for their duties as wives and mothers. The curricula that began to be developed made it clear that "women's knowledge" was to be considered unique to women's essential nature as reproductive servants—good wives and mothers.

These new discourses on women and on knowledge did not challenge men's exclusive capacity for Reason. Rather, appropriating the very meaning system that subordinated them, these white middle class women stressed that, due to women's essential reproductive function—her body—education for women would differ as much from that of men as her "character and duties" differed from those of men.

Common Schools and the Feminization of Teaching

The girls' schools founded by Emma Willard, Catherine Beecher, and others in the early decades of the 19th century made it possible to argue for women's unique capacity to address specific social problems outside the home, and this started with the identification of their particular appropriateness as teachers. If "woman" was the natural caretaker of children, and the more virtuous of the sexes, then the morality of the future citizenry depended on her gentle hand and naturally virtuous heart. Men were clearly not the most appropriate as their more competitive and aggressive natures were now being put to the test in the burgeoning industrial sectors. These gendered discourses offered an important political opportunity for women to enter the once exclusively male public sphere, albeit in a manner circumscribed by their "nature."

The Common School Reformers argued that the most effective way to deal with the "unruly" immigrants and "dangerous social disorder" unfolding in the cities was to develop a compulsory education system whose specific purpose would be to assimilate diverse cultures into one American society. This spurred a passionate plea by Catherine Beecher, who wrote:

> Where do we find such an army of teachers . . . not from the sex which finds it more honorable, easy and lucrative to enter the many roads to wealth and honor . . . It is woman who is to come at this emergency—woman, whom experience and testimony have shown to be the best, as well as the cheapest, guardian of childhood.
>
> (Woody, 1929, p. 462)

Think About This

Look back for a moment at Plumwood's categories of centric thinking (radical exclusion, backgrounding, homogenization, incorporation, instrumentalism) introduced in Chapter 3. Using the definitions provided, which of these processes was at play in the history of education and gender shared so far? We've given you one example above. Look at the other categories and use them as analytic tools. How was centric thinking at work in these historical processes? What metaphors can you identify in use? Where are the contradictions or openings for new possibilities?

In 1840, Horace Mann, commonly referred to as the "father of public education" for his leadership in establishing the Common School movement, issued his Fourth Annual Report to the Massachusetts State Board of Education. In it he defends the idea of women as the most appropriate choice as teachers because of (1) their natural child-rearing talents, (2) their lack of distraction by other worldly forces and the lack of opportunities for other employment (thus their dependability); and (3) their "purer morals" (Martusewicz, 1994).

The idea that women were more moral and thus more fit to teach young children did not undermine the control that men were to exert over them, for, as Joel Spring (1994a) points out, a "passive type of morality was expected of teachers, not socially active moral behavior. They were expected to prevent social problems but not to actively engage in solving existing problems" (p. 124). That was men's job. And keep in mind that these women were engaged as teachers of the nation's future citizenry at a time when they were still *radically excluded* from formal citizenship themselves. They may have been given value on the basis of a "womanly virtue," but they were not considered equal to men in Reason or authority. So, while we may see this move by women into the teaching profession as an important step forward into the public sphere—and it was—it was still highly restricted by the same metaphors that were used to subjugate them. The fundamental hierarchized dichotomies and centric thinking were not challenged. In fact, we can see the ways this definition of woman was used *instrumentally*, as woman's "nature" rationalized her exploitation as a cheap source of labor. As Horace Mann argued,

> a female will keep quite as good a school as a male at two thirds the expense, and will transfer in the minds of her pupils, purer elements, both of conduct and of character, which will extend their refining and humanizing influence far outward into society and far onward into futurity.
>
> (Sugg, 1978, pp. 77–78)

In 1841, men in rural schools made $4.15 a week, compared to women who made $2.51, and in city schools men made $11.93 while women made $4.44. By 1864, men in city schools were making $20.78 a week, while women made $7.67 (Elsbree, 1939, p. 274). The reason given? Women teachers did not have to care for families because they were unmarried; and, in fact, if they were to marry, they were immediately fired. "Motherlove" may have made teaching a way out of domestic toil, but woman's "one true profession" remained, of course, the care of their husbands and the raising of children. And, while women's "moral purity" gave the profession a certain "nobility," their continued definition as essentially inferior to men and the accompanying low salaries contributed to the generally low status of teaching even for men, a general problem that remains for the profession today.

For African American women, similar opportunities opened up after the Civil War, when schools for former slaves began to appear and the need for teachers increased. The purposes of education for African American women mirrored the Cult of True Womanhood. They were to become better mothers or wives, and to serve the white community as domestic and agricultural workers. African American women attended schools like the Hampton Institute to become "teachers, nurses, missionary workers and Sunday School teachers," so that they could be in a better position to uplift other African Americans. In the 1850s, the Miner Normal School for Colored Girls was opened with the support of white middle class women eager to help black women enter higher education to become teachers in their own communities. Similarly, the Spelman Female Seminary was opened in 1881 when white New England missionaries brought religious materials and schoolbooks to Atlanta, Georgia, and helped organize a curriculum focused on the liberal arts and teacher preparation for black women (Sadker et al., 2009, p. 33).

White Middle Class Women Enter Higher Education

Accompanying the push for women to become the needed "army of teachers" for the growing numbers of Common Schools was the argument for their professional education and the birth of the "Normal School." As women won acceptance in their roles as teachers, a system of state-sponsored teacher education institutions also began to be developed to prepare them. This paved the way for women who, by the 1880s, began to demand entrance into the heretofore exclusively male domain of university education. The foundation of Normal Schools where women's "natural maternal instincts" could be organized and disciplined, introduced women to a new set of knowledges and opportunities, previously the exclusive domain of men.

By the 1870s, a few women from affluent white families began to apply and be accepted into universities, in part by insisting upon the necessity of teachers to be "properly" educated beyond the pedagogically-dominated curriculum of the Normal Schools. Women also began to argue that there was more for women to do in the public sphere besides teaching and other female-dominated professions. Some even began to argue that, contrary to the discourses on domestic reform and the ideology of mother-love, they were capable of the same education as men and should be able to enter male professions such as, for example, the medical field (Walsh, 1977). Their courageous arguments were met with powerful public opposition and even prompted the stoning of some women by townspeople appalled at their audacity in enrolling in universities and walking onto college campuses as students.

This public outrage (and fear) was backed by the medical profession, notably the work of Dr. Edward Clarke, a highly respected Boston physician who wrote a popular pamphlet in 1873 called *Sex in Education*. Clarke argued against the higher education of women and girls, citing the declining birth rates among the middle class as his primary evidence. If a woman exerted herself intellectually, Clarke argued, she would take the blood supply and energy required by rigorous study away from that necessary for her more essential reproductive organs—her uterus and ovaries. Thus, she would damage her ability to bear children and (most importantly) threaten the very social position of the middle class. Here we see the mind/body dualism at its scientific best. Clarke's "scientific proof" was so compelling and the pamphlet so widely read that it became one of the primary tools used by parents, college administrators, and professors (all men) in the attempt to prevent women from accessing higher education. Likewise, a few years later in 1880, an opponent of women's suffrage (the right to vote and participate fully as citizens in the public sphere) in Sacramento, California, wrote:

> I am opposed to woman's sufferage [sic] on account of the burden it will place upon her. Her delicate nature has already enough to drag it down. Her slender frame, naturally weakened by the constant strain attendant upon her nature is too often racked by diseases that are caused by a too severe tax upon her mind. The presence of passion, love, ambition, is all too potent for her enfeebled condition, and wrecked health and early death are all too common.
> (From the California State Historical Society Library,
> quoted in Kimmel, 2000, p. 26)

Such beliefs in women as the "weaker sex" did not prevent those women who were determined to get an education or those determined to be considered citizens from continuing to struggle for their rights, however.

In 1884, a handful of white middle class women who were among the first to obtain college degrees founded the Association of Collegiate Alumnae, an organization that debated what the proper contribution of university women should be in the larger society. What should be the purpose of higher education for women, and what would the corresponding curriculum look like? On the one hand, it was argued that, because of woman's "true nature," these women should rise in even greater service to Republican Motherhood. On the other hand, women like M. Carey Thomas argued that women were just as capable of the ideals of Reason, mental rigor, and public service defining men's higher education goals and curriculum. She wanted women to have equal access to the courses in math, science, philosophy, history, the arts, and so on, in which men were enrolled. Women were equal to men in all ways relevant to an education, and should thus also have equal access to social roles defined and claimed by men (Thomas, 1908). It was very clear from the women who took this side of the debate that women's opportunities should be expanded beyond that of teaching, nursing, and other so-called "feminine professions."

This position was hotly contested by holdouts from the Domestic Reform movement, who fought hard to define the educated woman in terms of her unique reproductive and caretaking function, arguing that university curricula should follow suit. Women's power, in this view, lay in her difference from men, a difference that would be nurtured through curricula that would deal with household arts, childcare, and domestic science.

In this debate, we see very clearly the structure of dualistic thinking, with both sides responding to what the perceived and embedded standard of power in education and knowledge was: men's capacity for reason. They each challenged the power dynamics in their own ways: equal rights advocates challenged women's exclusion from reason and refusing to be assigned the subordinate side of the binary, and motherlove advocates challenged the devaluation of reproductive definitions. The struggle in their discourse against radical exclusion maintained reason as the dominant term and thus men as the standard on both sides of the debate. And, homogenization of woman's essential nature was also articulated with men's nature and men's education as the unchallenged standard.

We will see, as we move forward into contemporary issues, that these foundational discourses are still shaping the ways we think about teaching, and about men and women's relationships to particular disciplines studied, about the purposes of education for men as opposed to women, and about the particular employment opportunities open to each via education. As we will continue to explore below, these ways of thinking about gender and education are part of an overarching logic of domination that has far-reaching effects on the ways men and women identify themselves as teachers, students, citizens, family members, and all manner of other activities and relationships. And these identifications, when taken together, have important effects in our communities. While they are always being contested, and thus shift, these historical discourses and the metaphors circulating within them create our gendered self-image as well as our capacities for action; they are internalized and become embedded in our psychological makeup—we speak them as they speak us. What do you think the consequences are for democratic citizenship, especially for Earth democracy as we described it in Chapter 1? This is an important question as we consider the purposes of education into the 20th and 21st centuries.

Checking In

So, what sorts of analyses did you come up with when looking at the early history, and the feminization of teaching? Can you see how centric thinking gets maintained in the various shifts in definition of why women should be educated and how? For example, do you see how initially women's needs are *incorporated* into those of men—her rudimentary education was required only to the extent that it made possible the religious mandates of patriarchy. We also discussed the ways *instrumentalism* operated in these discourses. What other analyses did you make? And what connections to our current context do you see playing out?

Gendered Education in the 20th Century

First, try this quiz (*answers at the end of this section*):

1. Teacher Mary Murphy was fired for misconduct in 1901 because:
   a. she had an affair with a married teacher
   b. she got married
   c. she stole the fire wood for the school stove
   d. she petitioned for equal pay with male teachers

2. In 1920 the 19th Amendment became part of the Constitution and expanded democracy by guaranteeing women the right to vote. How long did it take women to win the right to vote?
   a. 22 years
   b. 12 years
   c. 52 years
   d. 72 years

3. In what year was the Equal Pay Act (guaranteeing equal pay for women) passed by the U.S. Congress?
   a. 1933
   b. 1980
   c. 1972
   d. 1963

(McCormick, 2007, p. 22)

In 1920, the argument for equal access to male-dominated spheres of knowledge and public influence won a major victory as women in the

United States achieved the right to vote. The question of access to all sorts of previously exclusive domains, in fact, became a dominant theme of those continuing to push for the equal rights of women. However, the debates over what became referred to as "sex role differences in education" continued on into the 1970s and remain with us today, albeit in much less visible forms. The "sex role differences" position is a formalized articulation of the analogue Woman–Body–Nature. These opposing positions, though far less visible, can still be traced within both popular and academic discussion, often showing up as questions such as: What should the purpose of education be for boys versus girls? What are appropriate occupations and roles for each and how can schools help prepare them for these roles? What sorts of curricula are appropriate, and should schools provide gender-specific tracks? Why do boys perform better in math than girls? Are athletics appropriate for girls, and, if so, what sports should girls play? Named "sex role theory" by contemporary gender researchers (Bank et al., 2007), the language of essential differences continued to be asserted throughout the century.

The social regulation of bodies, particularly those of women, is highlighted by the changing attitudes toward unmarried women teachers. In the early part of the 20th century, it was common for a woman, such as Mary Murphy, to be fired for getting married, or for a married woman to be fired for becoming pregnant, because that implied she was having sex, and thus she was a bad model for her students.

Yet, after 1920, with the increasing empowerment of women and the beginnings of open homosexuality, the social ground shifted dramatically.

> Before long, unmarried women teachers took the blame not just for supposedly causing boys to become effeminate, but also for inducing female students to remain in school, to excel, and in many cases, to enter the profession of teaching themselves. In this strange manner, such women were thought to reproduce themselves, influencing their female students to avoid marriage and motherhood. . . . School officials wished to distance themselves from the growing stigma attached to spinster teachers. By mid-century, school districts around the country began hiring large numbers of married women teachers—to the near exclusion of unmarried women.
>
> (Blount & Anahita, 2004)

The social pressure to regulate women played out in the response to the increasing number of women pursuing higher education. Some people found the need to argue for it as a way for women to find suitable husbands, since their most essential role was that of wife and mother. "Academic women," as defined by Jessie Bernard in 1964, were those educated women whose husbands had earned a Ph.D. and whose most important roles were to support those men in their scholarly pursuits (Bernard, 1964). It was not unusual for women who earned Master's degrees or doctoral degrees to put aside their own aspirations once they married, in order to measure up to the expectation of "service to home and husband" still writ large upon the feminine gendered psyche.

Think About This

Today, we hear our students arguing that "staying home with the kids" is just a choice that women have, and that feminists who argue for women's equal right to jobs in the workforce devalue that choice. But, is it as simple as a "free choice"? What other factors impinge upon either choice: staying home or entering the work-force? Can you think about this using "centric thinking" or "value-hierarchized thinking" as a concept in your response?

The 1960s also saw the arrival of what is often referred to as "second-wave feminism." The feminist movement and the resulting social change led to the passage of some key laws that mandated equal treatment—most importantly, Title VII of the Civil Rights Acts of 1964, which outlawed discrimination in employment on the basis of sex, and Title IX of the Higher Education Act of 1972, which outlawed different treatment in schools that receive federal funds (see the box below for more on Title IX).

As a result, research on women and education began to assert *equity* as a dominant theme in women's social demands, including those for education. Equity was argued for in terms of equal access to the economic and educational opportunities still primarily reserved for men. "Equal pay for equal work" is both a slogan and a policy priority that has grown out of this work on the part of feminists and pro-feminist men. And, in order to get equal access to both pay and the jobs with most economic and social status, access to educational resources would have to open up.

Title IX of the 1972 Higher Education Act

"No person in the United States shall, on the basis of sex, be excluded from participation in, be denied the benefits of, or be subjected to discrimination under any education program or activity receiving Federal financial assistance." (United States Code Section 20)

In 1972, the U.S. Congress, led by Congresswoman Patsy T. Mink, passed a law that has helped ensure that women and girls are given equal access to educational resources in any educational institution that receives federal funding. Any woman who has played in school sports since 1972 has benefited from the dramatic changes that resulted; for example the number of high school girls in sports has increased by more than 900%. While this law is probably best known for what it has done for women's athletics, it actually applies to any and all forms of educational opportunities including vocational education, home economics, music and marching band, science and math clubs, and so on. It applies to boys and men too, when they are unfairly excluded from any educational opportunity in a school or university, though clearly the effects of the law have been most visible in the lives of women and girls. It does not apply to organizations such as the Girl Scouts or Boy Scouts. Since its inception, there have been many attempts to counter or change the law by those who see it as a way to limit boys' and men's educational experiences. In 1983, opponents succeeded in limiting the law when the U.S. Supreme Court passed *Grove City College v. Bell*, restricting the application to specifically educational programs within institutions.

These laws, to the extent they have been enforced, have led to substantial reductions in explicit discrimination—the kind where a counselor says "girls can't take a shop class."

Further, the laws and the effects of the feminist movement have led to significant changes in college enrollments and professional careers. For example, the percentage of doctors who are women has changed from 10% in 1970 to 34% in 2012; for lawyers, the change is from 5% to 33% in the same period.

However, it would be a mistake to suggest that gender is no longer an issue in the classroom or workplace. Sexism continues to be a "hidden curriculum"—persisting in the unconscious assumptions that are carried into the classroom every day. For example, the percentages of women in science, technology, engineering, and math (STEM) occupations has changed little since 1990, meaning only 13% of engineers are women. And women are still 85% of elementary teachers: while the legal structure has changed, this highlights there are still powerful socializing agents in the culture that encourage women to be elementary teachers and discourage men from the role.

Answers to quiz, p. 151: 1. B; 2. D; 3. D

Sexism in the Classroom and Curriculum

Charges of *sexism* began to be used to describe what were once generally accepted as simple reflections of natural differences between men and women. Sex stereotyping and bias in both public schools and higher educational programming, as well as in texts and other curricular materials, began to be uncovered and challenged. Classroom relationships and pedagogical practices have also come under scrutiny. For example, researchers began to document the hidden ways well-intentioned teachers tend to unconsciously treat boys and girls differently in classrooms based on differing expectations for each. Think back to the dualisms we discussed earlier as we take you through these examples. How are they operating in these classroom dynamics?

By closely observing hundreds of hours of classroom interactions, researchers began to tease out the taken-for-granted ways that sexism plays out in the interactions among teachers and students in classrooms. As Myra and David Sadker (1994) write of their work,

> Trained raters coded classrooms in math, reading, English, and social studies. They observed students from different racial and ethnic backgrounds. They saw lessons taught by women and by men, by teachers of different races. In short, they analyzed America's classrooms. By the end of the year we had thousands of observation sheets, and after another year of statistical analysis, we discovered a syntax of sexism so elusive that most teachers and students were completely unaware of its influence.
>
> (Sadker & Sadker, 1994, p. 2)

While these authors do not take the metaphor further, note their use of the phrase "syntax of sexism." The hidden lessons that their work exposes are indeed largely created within language exchanges that communicate powerful representations about who girls and boys are and ought to be in the classrooms studied. They emerge as the unconscious result of gendered socialization that the teachers themselves have also experienced. Thus, it is not necessary to see the teachers as bad people in their interactions with students. Rather, these interactions and the meanings they express are the consequences of the ways centric thinking operates at unintentional levels to reproduce gender domination. Remember, we learn to "do gender." Largely unconscious, this "doing" does not stop at the classroom or schoolhouse door.

In Sadker and Sadker's multi-year study, teachers were observed calling on boys more often to answer questions that required an analytic response, or simply spending more time with boys, while encouraging good penmanship and neatness, or good behavior—quiet passivity—from girls. "Girls are often shortchanged in quality as well as quantity of teacher attention" (Sadker & Sadker, 1989, p. 360). Delineating several categories for the patterns of interaction between teachers and students—praise, criticism, help and remediation, or acceptance without evaluation—Sadker and Sadker's work demonstrates the differential treatment of boys and girls in classrooms. They shared the following exchange from a 1985 classroom interaction:

Teacher: What's the capital of Maryland?
Joel: Baltimore.
Teacher: What's the largest city in Maryland, Joel?
Joel: Baltimore.
Teacher: That's good. But Baltimore isn't the capital. The capital is also the location of the U.S. Naval Academy. Joel, do you want to try again?
Joel: Annapolis.
Teacher: Excellent! Anne, what's the capital of Maine?
Anne: Portland.
Teacher: Judy, do you want to try?
Judy: Augusta.
Teacher: O.K.

(Sadker & Sadker, 1989, pp. 360–361)

Using their categories for analysis of this passage, we can see that Joel's answers are responded to with criticism and remediation as he is brought to the correct answer, and praised when he got there. Anne's answer was incorrect, but she did not receive the benefit of the same interaction with her teacher, who simply moved on to Judy.

In another example from a study conducted by researcher Peggy Orenstein nine years later, the following classroom interaction was observed. This scene, paraphrased from Orenstein's poignant book, *Schoolgirls* (1994), is an eighth grade math class in a mostly white suburban school. There is a short altercation at the start of the class, where two boys, Nate and Kyle, are talking and the teacher is reprimanding them. Allison, a quiet girl who has confided to Orenstein earlier that her main goal in life is "to be the best wife and mother I can be," has her hand up. The teacher doesn't notice Allison as she turns away from the boys to start class.

Teacher (shouting):	Get out your homework everyone! (Allison puts her hand down.)
Teacher:	OK everyone, call out the prime numbers that you found.
Nate:	Eleven! (Others in the class, boys and girls, call out answers a second or two later. As the class proceeds, Nate, Kyle, and Kevin continue calling out louder and louder, competing among themselves for the quickest and loudest response.)
Teacher:	OK. Now, what do you think of 103? Prime or composite?
Kyle:	Prime! (The teacher ignores Kyle to give someone else a turn. Kyle persists.)
Kyle:	Prime! Prime! Prime! (When he turns out to be correct, Kyle yells.)
Kyle:	See! I told you I was right!! (Amy, raising her hand, offers an incorrect answer. It's the only time she offers an answer all period. Upon realizing she is wrong, she drops her head so that her hair falls forward over her face. The teacher moves on to another student and eventually a new part of the lesson.)
Teacher:	What does three to the third power mean? (Kyle, shooting his hand up: I know!)
Teacher:	Do you know Dawn?
Kyle:	But I know!!
Dawn (hesitates):	Well, you count the number of threes and . . .
Kyle:	I know, I know, I know!! (Dawn falters . . .)
Kyle:	I know! Me! It's three times three times three times three . . .
Teacher (giving in and turning away from Dawn):	Yes, three times three times three times three. Does everyone get it? (At the bell, Orenstein asks Amy about the incorrect answer offered.)
Amy:	Oh yeah, that's about the only time I've talked in there. I'll never do that again.
	(Paraphrased from Orenstein, 1994, pp. 5–10)

In the case above, the teacher tries to engage the girls, but the boys charge on, clearly confident of their place in the classroom. The boys are already learning that they have a right to this "space," both verbally and physically. They assert a specific sense of masculinity within that space and in relation to the knowledge being offered. The teacher, by default as the girls demur, ends up giving more time to the boys, who are much more aggressive and demanding as the lesson unfolds. The teacher is responsible for a "hidden curriculum of gender" although she is unconscious of her participation in the reproduction of specific gendered relations and representations. "When female students are offered the leftovers of teacher time and attention, morsels of amorphous feedback, they achieve less" (Sadker & Sadker, 1994, p. 11). When they do not see themselves represented in textbooks as leaders, scientists, inventors, or people with the power to transform society, they are degraded by an absence defined as a lack. When they are allowed to sit on the sidelines as boys demand the lion's share of time and attention by their teachers, girls begin to falter academically. Meanwhile, boys learn that they are entitled to the attention, that their work matters more, that they are the stronger. They internalize a form of invisible privilege that gets expressed as "boys being boys." This is one way that girls' intellectual needs are once again "backgrounded" as unimportant or simply not there at all.

Researchers have also described important classroom dynamics associated with the intersection of gender and race. Jacqueline Jordan Irvine (2003) documents the ways black girls who began school as active, engaged students became increasingly withdrawn from academia as they proceeded through elementary school and into middle years. Black girls have been shown to be socialized as nurturers and caretakers in classrooms, especially in the early grades. African American boys have also been the focus of much research in recent years. As Pedro Noguera (2008) notes, "Black boys are more likely to be classified as mentally retarded or suffering from a learning disability and placed in special education and more likely to be absent from Advanced Placement and honors courses" (p. 18). As we will expand upon in the next chapters, in the case of black children, race and socio-economic status has more bearing on academic achievement than gender. Here we see the ways ethnocentrism weaves its way into the mix to create specific educational meanings, responses, and even policies.

It might be easy to write these scenes off as either outdated, something we've fixed already, or as indications of a few bad teachers in unruly, mismanaged classrooms. In 2009, Sadker, Sadker, and Zittleman updated their research, documenting how, over nearly 20 years of data collection, very little relating to the gendered interactions in classrooms had changed. Across the board, boys in elementary, middle school, and high school classrooms continue to garner more attention, learning that aggressive behavior—including harassing or bullying behavior—is considered normal for them, while girls pay the price for speaking out of turn, and also, ironically, for staying silent. As we'll explore below, boys pay the price too, albeit in very different ways.

The important point here is that pedagogical practices, curriculum, and school materials are reflective of the very hierarchized value system that creates gendered (and, as we'll see, race and class) domination, and they communicate important messages that help to create who these students become; social interactions function just like the metaphors that exist within the list of dualisms discussed earlier because they are filled with assumptions and expectations which are in turn communicated to the participants, who internalize and become the speaking, acting, thinking reproducers of gendered oppositions and power relations.

Schools are a context in which girls across racial lines begin to settle for less, keep quiet, lose enthusiasm, become passive, and often accept an other-than-intellectual definition of themselves. As Sandra Lee Bartky (1996) has argued, schools are places in which a "pedagogy of shame" inculcates a sense of inadequacy so subtle as to be simply part of girls' daily lives. By the middle school years, girls who were relatively successful academically in elementary school begin to lose interest in their studies and confidence in themselves.

The result, despite some claims that girls are out-achieving boys, is that, on average, boys and girls' education performance on standardized tests in elementary and secondary school to college has either remained the same or improved for both genders, with a slight gap remaining show- ing boys' continuing advantages in math. Girls continue to perform bet- ter than boys in reading, but that has been true since the 1970s. High school graduation rates have improved across the board for white male and female students.

On college entrance exams such as the SAT and ACT, boys have con- sistently outscored girls over the last several decades on both the math and verbal portions of the test. There is some indication that girls may do better than boys on the new writing portion of the SAT, but the research is not yet conclusive. According to the summary of the College Board assessment results, the "gender gap on the SAT-M is larger than the gap on the SAT-V, although both gaps have narrowed slightly" (Corbett et al., 2008, p. 36) (see Figure 5.1).

Learning the Double Standard: Sexual Harassment and the Dangerous Politics of the Body

Girls are achieving more academically as gender issues are being uncov- ered, analyzed, and publicized. But academic achievement is not neces- sarily the way out of unconscious violence, and is often the last thing on the minds of boys and girls during adolescence—and their experiences in schools and out during these years are vastly different. These are the

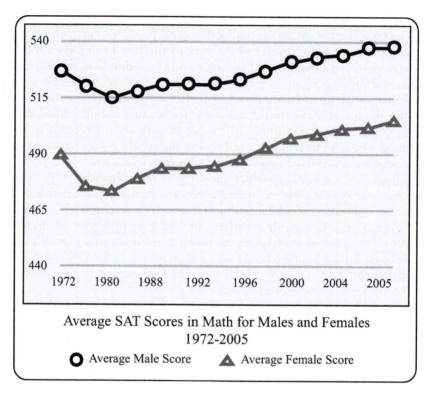

Average SAT Scores in Math for Males and Females
1972-2005

⬤ Average Male Score   ▲ Average Female Score

Figure 5.1 Average SAT Scores in Math for Males and Females, 1972–2005.

Source: CollegeBoard. (2005).*2005 College-bound Seniors: Total group profile report.* New York, NY: CollegeBoard.

years when girls begin hating their bodies, their faces, their very being. While school curricula still lack many strong images of women in power-ful positions or doing creative work outside traditional domestic roles, magazines, television, and movies bombard us with images of femininity as exploited supplicant. Just pick up a copy of a magazine and look at the advertisements. What do you see? "Glamour" is portrayed in the images of grossly underweight women wearing clothing unaffordable by 99 percent of the population, often photographed in compromised sexual positions, their bodies airbrushed to be "flawless." As Sandra Lee Bartky (1996) writes, in this context girls develop into women who are "hostile witnesses to bodily being" (p. 223). Saturated with a discourse that equates the feminine as the opposite of "reasoning" masculinity, women become obsessed with an "inferiorized body"—a body that is too fat or too thin, whose nose is too wide or too narrow and whose skin certainly lacks the perfection of alabaster . . . we are made anxious and ashamed of our "imperfections," of the myriad ways we fail to measure up.

(Bartky, 1996, p. 225)

Bartky teases apart the complex ways in which our cultural institutions—family, church, workplace, media, and schools—contribute to a "pedagogy of shame" whereby girls and women are taught to unconsciously accept an inferiorized sense of self.

Shame is the distressed apprehension of the self as inadequate or diminished. It requires, if not an actual audience before whom my deficiencies are paraded, then an internalized audience with the capacity to judge me, hence internalized standards of judgment.

(Bartky, 1996, p. 227)

Important to this analysis is the understanding that, even while we may be learning other ways of being in the world—strong ways—and even while women may outwardly fight against the definition of themselves as lesser beings, on some level deep inside there is a tendency to identify themselves as not measuring up. To feel ashamed is to accept this judgment of self. Of course, this process is not exclusive to women; shaming as a psychological process works within the hierarchizing system as a whole and so has many victims. It is one of the ways inferiorization and a logic of domination functions.

Girls and women are degraded in myriad ways in schools and other institutions, via attitudes and practices that are difficult to recognize to the degree that the language we use seems normal or natural. The definition of masculinity plays a role in this process: girls suffer humiliation as boys or men are bullied by teachers, coaches, and each other for "acting like a girl," or being "wimps" or "sissies" or worse.

Name-calling using female body parts is just one way men use "insults" to "motivate" each other to get in line. In this sense, the female body becomes a metaphor for an inferior being. Boys and men know very well that to be compared to a woman is a serious criticism meant to humiliate and degrade. Indeed, as we'll develop further below, boys who do not live up to ideal standards of masculinity—those who exhibit any signs of femininity—are often the victims of tremendous violence in school and out. Boys learn to "do gender" by performing masculine domination in relation to or on the bodies of girls and weaker boys. Indeed, schools are sites where sexually charged violence is a taken-for-granted ritual of gender performance.

Girls—and gay boys, or, more accurately, boys who *look* gay—know this very well. It's part of the hidden curriculum of gender socialization in which boys and men learn domination as a simple norm.

On "Motivation" as Violence

In an undergraduate teacher education course we were co-teaching a few years ago, Johnny and Rebecca were discussing some of the ways gender domination gets reproduced in our day-to-day inter-actions and language. Students were generating a list of terms that men use against each other that are ultimately harmful to women. The list of words all had some relation to femininity: "Priss," "little girl," "fem," "baby," "pansy," etc.; we were discussing how these sorts of words get used as put-downs. We noticed a man in the front of the class beginning to fidget, his face getting redder and redder the longer the discussion went on. Before we could ask what he was thinking, he exploded. "Wait just a minute!" he shouted, "Are you trying to tell me that if I call a guy at work a 'pu—y' [slang term for female genitalia] there's something WRONG with that??! That is ridiculous! I'm motivating them! There's nothing wrong with motivating people to work harder!"

Feminist researchers have zeroed in on the ways sexual harassment from boys saturates school hallways. As they begin to mature sexually, girls begin to hear explicit messages that relay that their true value lies in their bodies and their ability to attract boys' sexual attention—rather than in what they can demonstrate academically, or in their abilities to care for one another. Attention to academia tends to fall as girls begin to negotiate the complicated world of desire and popularity.

Girls in middle school and high schools persistently have their breasts grabbed and buttocks swatted by boys, as they are also barraged by sexually explicit taunts: "Come on, you know you want it!"; "Hey, sexy, when we gonna do it?"; "Nice a—, sweetheart!"

When brought to the attention of teachers or administrators, such instances of "catcalling" and uninvited groping are often written off as "boys being boys," in spite of sexual harassment laws being passed in all states. Even worse, girls who dare to speak up and to call attention to the problem are often blamed for being in the wrong place at the wrong time, or for "asking for it" by dressing provocatively or flirting. This reaction is not only expressed by men, but also by some women who have internalized feminine identities and carefully developed their roles and status as supportive of men. As Jackson Katz (2006) points out,

[w]omen who dare to break the customary feminine silence about gender violence are often reminded that there is a price to pay for the boldness. They certainly run the risk of evoking men's hostility and anger, because to challenge men's right to control women is to threaten men who see such control as their birthright. Sadly, women who take a strong stand against sexual harassment, rape, and domestic violence can even be perceived as a threat by some of the fellow women. Women have been trained to take care of men's feelings for so long, to stroke their egos and to curry favor with them by not holding them accountable for their sexism, that it is understandable that some women will denounce those women who expect more.

(Katz, 2006, p. 73)

A Memory From Rebecca's High School

My high school Social Studies teacher was well loved by teachers and students alike. He was always cheerful and liked to joke and tease students. He was also well known for standing outside his classroom door in the morning as we were all filing in. He had a hockey stick—a goalie stick, to be precise, wider and flatter than normal hockey sticks—and as girls walked by he would pat or whack them on the butt with the stick, sometimes lifting their skirts just a bit, and always with a jovial laugh: "Ho ho! Good morning sweetheart!" Of course that would never be tolerated now, but in the mid-1970s no one ever questioned it. We girls just laughed along nervously. I hated walking by that door in the morning, but I never thought to go to anyone to complain. It never even occurred to me that I should.

Competition among girls and women for men's attention and support—"currying favor"—is common, even taken for granted. Learning that they will be most valued for their status as objects of sexual attraction, girls are at once rivals with each other for the attention of boys and potential objects of sexual exploitation. Girls whose bodies develop early are particular targets of harassment and humiliation, often suffering not just the taunts of boys, but the resentment of their female peers as well. And, as they learn to either hide their academic or career aspirations or let go of a sense of intellectual interest and confidence, they also learn how to participate in a sexual economy of desire, often walking a fine line between double standards. Girls learn to monitor and discipline their own budding sexuality, as they play the game of sexual attraction in competition with other girls for status and value.

The much-touted "mean girl" recently portrayed in the media (Gonick, 2004), is actually a well-known player in this economy of desire, and is not really a new rendition of girlhood, as some concerned authors who see this as a new syndrome of aberrant individual girl behavior would have us believe. Caught in a double bind, girls must be desirable, but not too desirable, smart but not too smart. They should be aware of their sexuality but not freely or aggressively engage it. The only thing worse than being dubbed a "brain" and thus relegated to the unpopular "nerdy" girls, is to be laden with the reputation, "slut." And, of course, all of these potential definitions require a particular definition of masculinity at play as well. Pay attention to the way the metaphors in the following passage work:

> Girls may be "sluts" but boys are "players." Girls are "whores"; boys are "studs." Sex ruins girls; it enhances boys. In their youth, they may be snips and snails and puppy dogs' tails, but by adolescence, boys learn that they are "made of" nothing but desire.
>
> (Orenstein, 1994, p. 57)

As Leora Tanenbaum (1999) writes, becoming a "slut," whether actually "earned" through sexual promiscuity, or as a means of being "taken out" by other rival girls, is one of the most denigrating processes a girl or woman can experience, making the context of schooling hellish beyond belief.

> Slut-bashing, as I call it, is one issue that affects every single female who grows up in this country because any preteen or teenage girl can become a target. "Slut" is a pervasive insult applied to a broad spectrum of American adolescent girls, from the girl who brags about one night stands to the girl who has never even kissed a boy to the girl who has been raped . . . Some girls are called "sluts" because other girls dislike or envy them, and spread a sexual rumor as a form of revenge. Very often the label is a stand in for something else: the extent to which a girl fails to conform to the idea of normal appearance and behavior.
>
> (Tannenbaum, 1999, p. 1)

Even for those girls who "win" in this game and gain some measure of power in the gendered politics of adolescence, the price is very high, though they may not realize it fully. How do we measure either the personal or the overall social cost of girls learning to engage in abusive behavior and social violence against other girls in order to assert a sense of personal value, while at the same time learning that passivity in one's relationships with boys, teachers, employers, and other adults is a basic survival tactic? The point here is that these are neither individual aberrations (i.e., part of a "mean girl syndrome"), nor are they simply part of "natural" boy–girl or girl–girl relations. They are part of a much deeper cultural reliance on abuse, violence, and domination as a way of solving problems and relating to one another. And even the big winners, or the perceived big winners—men—pay a big price for the ways gender plays out within this logic of domination.

It Hurts Both Ways: The Making and Performance of Multiple Masculinities

Violence against women is a critical problem that, even with the accomplishments of feminists and pro-feminist men to uncover its realities, is still a matter that relates directly to the difficulties of challenging an underlying logic of domination. We are so immersed in a hierarchized cultural system that it is difficult to recognize these patterns of belief and behavior as problematic. We have internalized them as normal and so act them out or tolerate them as normal. Yet, it is important to begin to understand that girls and women are not the only ones to bear the cost of these androcentric discourses. One of the most important contributions to research on gender and education in recent years is work being done on what Michael Kaufman (1994b) calls "men's contradictory experiences of power" and masculinity.

> Masculinity may not be real in the way we assume it is, but it nonetheless is based on actual relations of power between men and women, and among men. When we talk about masculinity we're talking about gender power.
>
> (Kaufman, 1994b, p. 38)

Kaufman and other pro-feminist men have been studying how a variety of masculinities are created within androcentric discourses that begin from the hierarchized dualisms we have been discussing. They argue that if we are really committed to understanding how gender construction works within a logic of domination, it is not enough to simply focus on women's experiences. We must also look at how it is that men internalize messages about what appropriate masculinity entails, and what this means for their specific challenges. Men are affected too, experiencing both power and pain in the process. Recognizing how men's identities and experiences are also shaped and indeed limited within this meaning system is an important aspect of understanding how centric thinking works.

Just as women learn to perform femininity, men learn to perform masculinity, and each is dependent upon the other for the meanings that become patterns of belief, identity, behavior, and relationship. Men internalize cultural discourses defining masculinity in terms of the right and ability to control others through a superior rationality or raw physical power. But, as Kaufman and other pro-feminist men are pointing out, this is not a simple process and also involves serious internalization of pain by men as they attempt to negotiate these meanings and expectations. Just as women are taught that they are the more emotional "sex," men are taught to suppress emotion that is not associated with control and power over others.

Thus, while anger, domination, and forms of violence become normalized responses within an idealized masculine identity, displays of vulnerability, nurturance, submissiveness—any characteristic that would be associated with the feminine—are strictly discouraged and disparaged as signs of inferiority.

Men become men along a continuum of masculinities defined in relation to a standard of dominant or "hegemonic masculinity" (Connell & Messerschmidt, 2005). At one end are the alpha males, strong physically, powerful socially, the primary movers and shakers in a community. At the other end are those men who appear most like women: inhabiting a smaller, less muscular body, more inclined to express emotions, perhaps bookish rather than into sports.

A Memory From Johnny

I can remember in eighth grade being yelled at in school for some reason that escapes my memory. I was being screamed at by a teacher in front of the whole class. He was screaming about how disappointed my mother would be and what a failure I was going to turn out to be. I had really liked this teacher prior to this encounter and for some reason what he was saying got to me; I was trying to ignore him and got overwhelmed. It took all I had to get through that moment, but I wasn't ready for the moment that followed. When he was finished the whole class was looking at me and it took every ounce of will to not cry. I remember vividly in my mind saying to myself, "Just don't cry, just don't cry . . . just don't cry." What followed was a schoolyard fight. One of the other boys in the class brought it up and was going around saying "Johnny almost cried in class today." A group of boys immediately were all laughing, and so, when I confronted the boy with the facts, he replied, "You almost did, and you didn't do anything but sit there. You're a little bitch." At the time, caught up in patriarchal schoolyard politics, the only option was to prove my masculinity through violence. Being able to fight helped erase the fact that I did, in fact, almost cry in class.

These men are often openly "gay bashed," accused of being homosexual as a means of identifying them as other than "real" (read, heterosexual) men, and thus open targets of violent degradation and even hatred. Indeed, as Mairtin Mac An Ghaill (1994) has pointed out, schools are important sites for learning to become a heterosexual man, a process that often depends upon these forms of violence. Sexuality and gender identity are thus tightly woven around each other.

Importantly, men and boys internalize an understanding of themselves as both sexual and gendered beings at many points between these two poles of power. Masculine gender work is done both within male peer groups in the hallways or on the playing field, as well as in the expression or performance of masculinity both publicly and privately on the bodies of others. And, as we've been exploring, schools are rife with the rituals and practices associated with this gender work.

All along this continuum, men and boys are discouraged from expressing the range of emotions available to human beings. To be caught expressing any quality that might be defined as feminine is understood as legitimate cause for abuse. "Weaker" forms of masculinity are, in fact, necessary foils against which hegemonic masculinity and heterosexism are asserted. Boys who become hegemonic men learn early to create themselves as powerful by enacting domination publicly on the bodies of women and other boys who become defined as inferior and thus deserving of humiliation and often physical or sexual abuse. Many of us who have spent time in schools have vivid images of smaller boys being smashed into lockers, called names, and pushed around by bigger, more hegemonic, boys.

Kaufman adds a twist to this analysis: boys who are enacting such punishments on others, while doing so to assert their own power, also pay a price. Learning to create themselves as men within performances of domination, they develop an inability to express the vulnerabilities that they experience and must necessarily suppress. Thus, they lose the ability to communicate, to nurture, to collaborate, to behave in ways necessary to creating truly equitable social relationships and communities. They are trapped within the same logic of domination; they may be seen as the beneficiaries, but there is also a heavy cost that they experience in terms of pain, isolation, and ultimately the inability to relate in mutually caring ways. Such disability is experienced in various ways, depending on the particular quality of masculinity one learns or internalizes. Thus, most men walk a complicated line between suppression or expression of emotion, and enacting or avoiding violence. A sense of isolation and alienation is often a part of this process, unless boys and men begin to learn to identify the source of this contradictory experience and its effects in the world.

Whatever our place in this picture, there is something new in the lives of men. It is the realization that power and pain combine in our definitions of manhood; it is the acknowledgement that men's social power is at odds with our own feelings of alienation. As we give voice to the sense of pain, our personal isolation begins to fade and we discover a shared and hidden reality in the lives of men. Even more unexpectedly, as we uncover our isolation and alienation, we find that the roots of our pain are the very ways we have come to define and exercise power.

(Kaufman, 1994a, p. 58)

Is Homosexuality Genetic?

The question of whether homosexuality is determined by biology, environment or choice is difficult—and rife with consequences. After all, it has been argued, if homosexuality is chosen or created by one's experiences, then it can be changed—one can learn to stop being homosexual. Thus there is a whole industry devoted to trying to "cure" people of being gay, a position clearly indicating the idea that it is "wrong," "evil" or, at minimum, "inferior." On the other hand, if homosexuality is biologically determined, then there is no point in trying to change it. Still, deficit definitions abound. The reality is more complex. While some studies have suggested that there are genetic markers for homosexuality, there is no evidence of a "gay gene"—that is, a simple biological reason for why people are homosexual. It is increasingly likely that sexuality is a mix of biological, cultural, and experiential factors. For many, sexuality is fluid and even changes across the life-span. An EcoJustice perspective argues that it shouldn't matter: if we worried less about "what determines sexuality" and more about allowing people to feel safe with a range of sexual expression, then "the answer to the question 'why did you decide to be gay?' could be 'when did you decide to be inflexibly heterosexual?'" (Lipkin, 2004, p. 17).

Sexuality, "Heteronormativity," and Centric Thinking

As we've been discussing, while sexuality and gender are not the same terms of identity, there is a very close ideological relationship between them within value-hierarchized thinking. This is because we live in a heterosexist culture—our dominant institutions and daily practices endow heterosexual relationships and identification with more value among both men and women. Moreover, those who identify outside of the norm of heterosexuality are defined pathologically—that is, as "sick" or "abnormal"—or as having chosen a life that is intentionally outside the boundaries of "normal" male–female sexuality, and therefore not deserving the same rights and respect. The systematic practice and regulation of "heteronormativity" inculcates the day-to-day relationships and structures of meaning in schools and other institutions. To be seen as a "normal" adult—healthy and moral—is to be (or pretend to be) heterosexual. To indicate the range of expressions of sexuality outside the "norm," we use the acronym LGBTQQ, which stands for Lesbian, Gay, Bisexual, Transgender, Queer, or Questioning.

There is an urgent need for teachers to understand the consequences of heteronormativity for LGBTQQ youth—it's a life and death matter. Suicide rates among gay and lesbian youth have risen dramatically in the past decade. According to a report published by the Suicide Preventions Resource Center in 2008:

> A variety of studies indicate that LGB [lesbian, gay, bisexual] youth are nearly one and a half to three times more likely to have reported suicidal ideation than non-LGB youth. Research from several sources also revealed that LGB youth are nearly one and a half to seven times more likely than non-LGB youth to have reported attempting suicide. These studies do not include transgender youth.
> (Suicide Preventions Resource Center, 2008, p. 5)

Students who come out to friends and family, while at risk of rejection, are less likely to attempt suicide because they increase the likelihood of finding support and creating alliances with others. On the other hand, LGBTQQ youth are also at a much higher risk of becoming homeless than other youth—often from being kicked out of the house for coming out—a situation that also greatly increases the risk of suicide. It is estimated that as many as half of homeless "street kids" are gay (Lipkin, 2004, p. 53).

These tragic realities point to the preponderance of unnecessary violence in our culture that results directly from a logic of domination. What is our ethical responsibility as teachers and teacher educators if not to interrupt this vicious cultural system?

Again, while we may only perceive sexuality in dualized terms, in actuality there is a whole range of sexual identifications among both men and women. Feminist scholar Adrienne Rich (1980) introduced the term "lesbian continuum," for example, as a means of challenging what she saw as a serious misunderstanding of passion among women, even by her feminist contemporaries. For Rich, a whole range of women's bonds with each other have for too long been marginalized and hidden under the demands of what she terms "compulsory heterosexuality," the idea that heterosexuality is "a political institution which disempowers women." Rich's work helped opened the door for women scholars to explore and value the range of emotional and sensual experiences among women and among men.

For girls and boys, and most teachers and administrators in schools, however, heteronormativity is still the name of the game, dominating relationships, activities, and school rituals. LGBTQQ students are often the targets of brutal isolation and denigration from both individual acts of violence and institutional "regulations."

School is often a source of constant harassment for youth who appear gay. A significant part of school bullying is aimed at those suspected of homosexuality—or of being outside the boundaries of "normal" male or female behavior. Nearly every one in schools has heard repeated homophobic statements, and physical violence is common, too. But according to repeated studies, teachers rarely intervene, which communicates to students that homophobia is OK (Meyer, 2010, p. 103). The result of teacher silence can be deadly. Leslie Sadasivan writes of the experience of her son:

> In a classroom filled with students but no teacher, a classmate came at him with a sharpened pencil, pointed it in his face and yelled "faggot" repeatedly. Many other acts of aggression were subtle, but persistent. Over time, name-calling, pushing, shoving and general exclusion left him feeling ashamed, insecure and alone.
>
> (Sadasivan, 2001, p. 167)

Sadasivan's son eventually killed himself from the despair, despite his parents' support. While most LGBTQQ youth don't take that final step, they are under constant stress. Imagine hearing constantly that who you are at your core is the vilest thing that one can be—for males, especially, there is nothing worse than being called a "fag."

Indeed, males use epithets such as "fag" to police the boundaries of gender identity; the term is not just aimed at suspected homosexuals, but often used to attack any behavior that is seen as not sufficiently "masculine," such as small size or being in choir or even being studious. Pascoe (2007) points out that:

> Fag is not necessarily a static identity attached to a particular (homosexual) boy. Fag talk and fag imitations serve as a discourse with which boys discipline themselves and each other through joking relationships. Becoming a fag has as much to do with failing at the masculine tasks of competence, heterosexual prowess and strength or in any way revealing weakness or femininity as it does with sexual identity.
>
> (Pascoe, 2007, p. 54)

This fear of weakness reverberates: in one study, a researcher randomly informed half of the subjects that they scored high in "masculine" traits and half that they scored high in "feminine" traits. The result? "Male respondents who received feminine personality feedback subsequently reported extremely negative attitudes toward gay men" (Lipkin, 2004, p. 3).

Thus, we say that, institutions such as school implicitly "regulate" heteronormativity. First, this regulation is done by the failure of schools to challenge the bullying and harassment described above. Second, heteronormativity is reinforced by the absence of homosexuals within the classroom content:

> Within the typical secondary school curriculum, homosexuals do not exist. They are "nonpersons" in the finest Stalinist sense. They have fought no battles, held no offices, written no literature . . . invented nothing . . . The lesson to the heterosexual student is abundantly clear: homosexuals do nothing of consequence. For the homosexual student, the message has even greater power: no one who has ever felt as you do has done anything worth mentioning.
>
> (Unks, 1995, p. 5)

As a further example of the regulation of heteronormativity in schools, let's look briefly at the ritual of the prom. Social Foundations scholar and educator Pamela Smith has recently written about the prom as a particularly powerful "normalizing" event:

> Prom is a sphere where regulating adults from dominant social agencies try to guard white middle class privilege and sustain heteronormative space . . . Prom with its attendant elements rooted within unchallenged definitions of masculinity, femininity, and the inherent relations of the two, then, is essential to normalizing heterosexuality and to pathologizing any non-gender conforming identities.
>
> (Smith, 2011, p. 158)

Many proms in schools around the country forbid the attendance of gay and lesbian students. And, while this practice has been challenged successfully in lawsuits (Smith, 2011), segregated proms—by sexual preference and race—are still the norm in many places. Holding their own separate prom is one way that LGBTQQ youth express resistance to the systematic hierarchizing processes of such rituals by insisting on their visibility and right to participate in such school activities. These alternative proms are valuable forms of civil rights activism and solidarity, and operate to provide youth with at least a momentary escape from the experience of systematic heterosexism.

But teachers can make a difference. First, schools can change the climate by being proactive for kids. As Meyer (2010) notes:

> The climate of a school can have a greater and longer-lasting impact on students' lives than the official curriculum; however, it is often overlooked. It infuses all aspects of students' experiences: physical and emotional safety, academic and personal success, motivation and engagement, as well as whether they feel visible and valued by the peers and teachers.
>
> (p. 111)

Schools with comprehensive anti-homophobia policies increase the safety of LGBTQQ students. Similarly, students report a better climate when teachers are seen intervening against name-calling and harassment (Meyer, 2010, p. 111).

Next, schools and teachers can include discussion of sexuality within the curriculum. Simply including examples of LGBTQQ people in the literature, science, and social studies units tells kids that LGBTQQ people are a "normal" part of the world. And teachers can teach about gender and sexuality directly. In the widely-used film, *It's Elementary* (2007), teachers lead age-appropriate discussions that bring children's assumptions to light. In one classroom, for example, students ask straightforward questions and get straightforward answers.

School-wide initiatives can include such things as traveling photo exhibits, such as "Love Makes a Family," that include gay families along with the wide range of other families that exist today (see the resources section below).

Middle and high school teachers can help form Gay–Straight Alliance clubs as extracurriculars. Not only do they offer support for LGBTQQ students, research suggests "that schools that have GSAs are more welcoming of all kinds of diversity, including racial, ethnic, and religious as well as gender and sexual diversity" (Meyer, 2010, p. 77)

Finally, we must emphasize the importance of challenging the discourse of heteronormativity. Simple anti-bullying programs may in fact reinforce heteronormativity if they just ask teachers and students to try to interrupt or punish bullying. Merely telling kids that their behavior is "wrong" deflects us from seeing the sexual harassment that is inherent so often in bullying; much less leading us to question the harasser's underlying assumptions about gender. Challenging the discourse of heteronormativity means explicitly confronting the gender-policing role of much bullying, which tells kids who do not appear to fit heterosexual norms that they are less than human.

Conclusion

Clearly, there is something very important about the ways we come to identify and behave as men and women for our understanding of the purpose of education and its relation to citizenship in democratic communities. How possible will it be for women and men to participate in decision-making processes in their communities if gender socialization continues to degrade us via these hierarchized ways of thinking? We are asking that teachers and their students examine the ways that curricula, school policy, and their own day-to-day classroom conversations, relationships, and practices are gendered and also linked to other forms of privilege and deprivation.

Learning to reflect critically on our use of language in our everyday interactions, and to identify the ways it plays into invisible forms of domination is part of our responsibilities as women and men preparing students for healthy communities.

Communities that are democratic and sustainable cannot be based on hierarchized patterns among humans or between humans and the more-than-human world; as we have been emphasizing throughout this book, one set of patterns tends to reinforce the others. Indeed, education for a citizenship that is defined by EcoJustice requires that men and women discern the ways that androcentric language and logic works in support of other violent forms of relationship. Such understanding invites us to begin making decisions in our personal and professional lives that shift these meanings and the institutional, interpersonal, and ecological relationships that result.

Making such important shifts in recognition and action means that we get outside the isolated "silo" mentality that often accompanies social justice or environmental work. Rather than see sexism, or heterosexism, or racism, or class-based inequalities, or able-ism as the most important points of focus, an EcoJustice approach to these problems asks that we begin to see how these hierarchized relationships intertwine to become mirrors of our violent relationships with the more-than-human world, and the very systems we depend upon for life. If the purpose of education is to prepare future citizens and workers for a better world, we must begin there, examining the historically-embedded weave of destructive modernist ways of thinking. The next three chapters take us deeper into that analysis.

Teachers committed to disrupting these patterns must help their students to see what are otherwise invisible forms of violence. This means introducing them to concepts and questions that will help them to analyze their own interpersonal experiences as well as trace the larger social, historical, and cultural context within which those experiences exist. It also means that these experiences must be related to other forms within a logic of domination—anthropocentrism and racism, for example—so that these too can be disrupted. When students are asked to think about their lives using specific concepts like value hierarchy, gender, femininity, hegemonic masculinity, heteronormativity, etc., the misty illusion of normativity can begin to dissipate. Using this approach as a foundation, teachers can then look at historical events, literature, sociological studies, laws, school, and other institutional policies. Below, we offer sample activities, as well as a Conceptual Toolbox, readings, and other resources. You will also find more resources on our website at www.routledge.com/textbooks/9780415872515.

What Schools and Teachers Can Do

Teach With Powerful Concepts

- Secondary classes: Introduce "logic of domination," "value-hierarchy," and "centric thinking"; ask students to brainstorm examples of how they see these operating in their day-to-day lives.
- Secondary and upper elementary classes: Introduce and define the concept "gender" and its difference from sex, and sexuality. Have a brainstorming session about "masculinity" versus "femininity." Map the differences; discuss the dualized and hierarchized relationships between these terms. Introduce the idea of a continuum of masculinity and femininity. Ask students to write about where they fall on that continuum, and how they see these relationships playing out in their own lives.

Map Gendered Spaces

Ask students to identify spaces in the school and community that are "masculine" (boy) spaces versus "feminine" (girl) spaces. What goes on there? How are they valued by others in the community? What would happen if girls transgressed the boundaries of masculine spaces, or if boys transgressed the boundaries of feminine spaces? What is the difference between the experience and definition of such border crossings?

Flirting Versus Sexual Harassment

To get students discussing the differences between these, write these categories on the board: "verbal or written," "gestures," "physical." Under each, write "flirting" and "sexual harassment." Ask students to list different behaviors under each and to discuss why their examples are or are not appropriately assigned. (From Nan Stein & Lisa Sjostrom (1994). Flirting vs. sexual harassment: Teaching the difference. In B. Bigelow et al. (Eds.), *Rethinking our classrooms* (Vol. 1, pp. 106–107). Milwaukee, WI: Rethinking Schools.)

Interrupt Violent Language and Behavior

If you hear name-calling or see an act of sexual harassment, step in to stop it, but also teach your students (and your colleagues) to think carefully about why it's a problem. This could mean making sure your school has clear and useful sexual harassment policy, and that all students and staff are aware of what it means.

Women and Girls/Men and Boys in Conversation

Start an after-school club where girls and women mentors can begin to explore the ways that they have experienced degrading definitions of femininity and where they have felt powerful. A similar club where boys and men can begin to explore alternative meanings of being a man would be just as useful.

Work to Develop School-Wide Anti-Homophobia Policies and Practices

Work with other staff in your school to have consistent practices whenever homophobic behaviors and words occur. The best practices challenge homophobia rather than just punishing it or reducing it to bullying.

Conceptual Toolbox

Bisexuality: Sexual attraction to both males and females.

Gender: Historically and socially constructed ways that men and women come to identify as masculine or feminine.

Hegemonic masculinity: Representations of manhood that carry the most power and thus are dominant—the big strong football player, the successful, fit corporate manager.

Heteronormativity: The notion that heterosexual relationships are the "norm" and thus the pathologizing of all other forms of sexuality.

Heterosexism: The dominating assumption that heterosexual relationships are natural and normal and thus that all other forms are abnormal.

Homosexuality: Same-sex attraction.

Intersex: Refers to combinations of physical features (genitalia) or to describe an individual who has biological characteristics of both the male and female sexes and thus cannot be classified as either one or the other.

Lesbian continuum: A continuum of relationships and bonding among women.

Pedagogy of shame: The processes through which women (and other marginalized groups) learn and internalize a sense of themselves as inferior beings.

Sex: The specific biological differences between males and females—differences, for example, in genitalia, chromosomes, hormones, reproductive organs, and so on.

Transsexual: A person who identifies physically, psychologically, and emotionally as the opposite gender and may seek to alter his or her body through hormones and or sexual reassignment surgery.

Suggested Readings and Other Resources

Books, Reports, and Essays

AAUW Educational Foundation. (2008). *Where the girls are: The facts about gender equity and education*. Washington, DC: AAUW Education Foundation.

Bartky, S. (1996). The pedagogy of shame. In C. Luke (Ed.), *Feminisms and pedagogies of everyday life* (pp. 225–241). Albany, NY: State University of New York Press.

Blackburn, M., Clark, C., Kenney, L., & Smith, J. (Eds.), (2010). *Acting Out! Combating homophobia through teacher activism*. New York, NY: Teachers College Press.

Kaufman, M. (1994b). Men, feminism, and men's contradictory experiences of power. In H. Brod & M. Kaufman (Eds.), *Theorizing masculinities* (pp. 142–163). Thousand Oaks, CA: Sage.

Lipkin, A. (2004). *Beyond Diversity Day: A Q & A on gay and lesbian issues in schools*. Lanham, MD: Rowman and Littlefield.

Martusewicz, R. (1994). Guardians of childhood. In R. Martusewicz & W. Reynolds (Eds.), *Inside out: Contemporary critical perspectives in education* (pp. 168–182). New York, NY: St. Martin's Press.

Orenstein, P. (1994). *Schoolgirls: Young women, self-esteem, and the confidence gap* (1st ed.). New York, NY: Doubleday.

Unks, G. (1995). Thinking about the gay teen. In G. Unks (Ed.), *The gay teen*. New York, NY: Routledge.

Films

Chasnoff, D., & Cohen, H (Writers). (1996/2007). *It's elementary: Talking about gay issues in school.* Includes new retrospective documentary: *It's still elementary.* San Francisco, CA: New Day Films.
  A film taking cameras into classrooms across the U.S. to look at one of today's most controversial topics—whether and how gay issues should be discussed in schools.

Jhally, S. (Director), Katz, J., & Earp, K. (Writers). (2002). *Tough guise: Violence, media, and the crisis in masculinity.* Northampton, MA: Media Education Foundation.
  A film that systematically examines the relationship between pop-cultural imagery and the social construction of masculine identities in the U.S. at the dawn of the 21st century.

Lipschutz, M. & Rosenblatt R. (2005). *The education of Shelby Knox: Sex, lies and education.* New York, NY: Cine Qua Non InCite Pictures.
  A film documenting a 15-year-old girl's transformation from conservative Southern Baptist to liberal Christian and ardent feminist and her fight for sex education and gay rights in Lubbock, Texas.

Muska, S. & Olafsdóttir, G. (2000). *The Brandon Teena story.* United States: Docurama.
  Documentary about the life and murder of Brandon Teena, a young transsexual man living in Nebraska.

Organizations and Links

The American Association of University Women (AAUW) (www.aauw.org)
  A nationwide network advancing equity for women and girls through advocacy, education, philanthropy, and research.

Gay and Lesbian Alliance Against Defamation GLAAD (www.glaad.org)
  Organization amplifying the voice of the LGBT community by empowering real people to share their stories, holding the media accountable for the words and images they present, and helping grassroots organizations communicate effectively.

Gay Lesbian and Straight Education Network (GLSEN) (www.glsen.org)
  Leading national educational organization focused on ensuring safe schools for all children.

Love Makes a Family (familydiv.org/exhibits/love-makes-a-family/)
  One of the groups that helps provide touring exhibits of diverse families.

The National Organization of Women (NOW) (www.now.org)
  The largest organization of feminist activists in the United States.

Suicide Prevention Resource Center (www.sprc.org)
  Provides prevention support, training, and resources to assist organizations and individuals to develop suicide prevention programs, interventions, and policies, and to advance the National Strategy for Suicide Prevention.

Chapter 6

Learning Our Place in the Social Hierarchy

An EcoJustice Approach to Class Inequality

Introduction

This chapter will examine class divisions—that is, the persisting economic and social divisions in society. This is a familiar subject in sociology, and is usually talked about in economic terms, primarily in terms of one's relationship to the means of production (the ways goods and services deemed necessary to our society are produced and distributed). In this chapter, we will look at class stratification in a broader way. EcoJustice Education looks at the cultural habit of hierarchy and the logic of domination as the larger frame in which class divisions seem to be accepted or taken for granted as part of the natural order of things.

First, a definition: By "class," we mean a group of people who share similar social and economic positions in a hierarchized society, and thus similar identities and experiences. In industrial societies, the hierarchy includes differentiated economic relationships based on ownership of the means of production (the resources, factories, workers, means of transportation of goods, and so forth). Those who own and control the means of production occupy the top of the hierarchy, controlling access to resources and decision-making power in both the economic and broader political realms. Those who make most of the economic decisions (because they own the means of production) also make most of the political decisions, even in this so-called democracy, because, as we discussed in Chapter 1, they have more opportunity and resources to either occupy or influence those positions. Because they control economic resources and political decision-making power, those at the top also wield great influence on the ways that discourse gets organized and reproduced by the media, by institutions like schools and universities, by think tanks, political organizations, and so on. They may own movie companies, newspapers, cable channels, television and radio stations. They may own or have the power to influence textbook publishers, and other educational media organizations, as well as educational testing companies. They use their wealth to set up foundations that sponsor research in universities and thus make decisions about what gets constituted as knowledge. In this sense, they have the means to influence the circulation of cultural discourses that create meanings often taken for granted as the "truth" in our culture.

Those who appear to be in the middle, such as middle managers in corporations, may manage the work of others and also may have some decision-making power within the scope of their work around what gets created and sold to the public. But, they carry out the decisions of the top hierarchy and thus are always at the mercy of those who pay their salaries. Their perspective on their lives—their experiences and the meanings they take for granted—will be created within those relationships. Others in the middle-income layers—professionals such as lawyers and doctors and professors—have a significant degree of control over their work and their day-to-day lives, and thus may construct different understandings of the world based on the degree of authority they are free to express.

Members of the working class, on the other hand, have the least decision-making power in their work lives. Basically, they sell their labor to those they work for and their relative lack of authority or decision-making power and low economic power makes them the most vulnerable of all to the decisions of those above them. This is one of the reasons unions developed early on in our economic history, as a means of organizing as a collective bargaining body with the power to negotiate with owners around the conditions of work. As we will see in the pages that follow, each social class group lives, works, and identifies themselves through complex experiences that arise and take shape within a modernist cultural meaning system that rationalizes their position within the hierarchy.

Looking at class hierarchy in this way offers a more complex explanation of why and how a logic of domination is systematically organized and maintained through our economic system, and whom it benefits most. This more culturally focused orientation in the EcoJustice framework allows us to examine how the underlying assumptions of modernist cultures both create and are maintained by a complex economic system. And, it helps to understand the very different life experiences among different groups based on both where they are in the hierarchy and how much authority over their lives and others' lives they have, but also by how the circulating discourses define them.

Thus, we begin from this question: What are the underlying sociolinguistic systems (the language, metaphors, discourses of modernity) that rationalize the system of domination at the heart of class, creating shared or very different life experiences among people depending on where they end up in the hierarchy?

With critical sociologists of education, we are interested in the nature and quality of education received by most members of the group.

	Working Class:	Middle Class: Managerial and Affluent Professional	Upper Class: Owners of Capital
Decision-Making Power in Work	Relatively low decision making power in relation to work.	Higher decision-making power in relation to work.	Ulitimate decision making power in relation to work.
	Example: Line workers in an automobile factory generally do one discrete task with little control over how or when the task gets done, how product will be used, etc.	*Example*: Engineers who design automobiles make decisions regarding style, engine size, electonics, accessories, etc. And they manage the labor of the line workers. Affluent Professionals (doctors, lawyers) also have relatively high decision-making power over daily process and issues in their work.	*Example*: The CEOs and primary owners of the automobile industry decide what kind of cars will be made, how many, and who to hire to make it all work. These decision-makers also have a lot of power over decisions made in government because they have the means to influence both who gets elected and the interests the representatives serve.
Buy or Sell Labor	Sell labor power generally for an hourly wage.	Sell labor power generally for salaried wages.	They buy all the labor necessary to create the automobiles and control the profits that result.
Buying Power Abilty to Consume	May have relatively high buying power along with low decision-making power, but overall has the lowest buying power of these three groups.	Managers sell labor to owners of capital. Affluent Professionals (doctors and lawyers) sell labor to clients. Have relatively high buying power.	Has much higher buying power (in terms of consumption) than any other class

**Relationships to Work and Decision-Making Defining
Socio-Economic Classes**

Figure 6.1 Relationships to Work and Decision-Making Defining Socio-
Economic Classes.

Think About This: What Class Are You From?

Use the basic definitions laid out in the chart in Figure 6.1 above to think about your own families. What socio-economic class best describes the position of your family? Is that different from the way you would normally describe yourself? Use the chart provided to help you think about this question.

As we will see throughout this chapter, working class children tend to get a very different education than the children of middle management, which is again different from that received by the children of affluent professionals. We analyze these experiences as symptoms of the larger logic of domination created and reproduced culturally through the institutions, policies, and day-to-day interactions of people. Seeing class in this way makes it possible to see the ways exploitive relationships within the economic system (and educational system) are related to exploitation of the ecological system, as well as many other hierarchized social relationships that create unnecessary suffering and injustice.

This focus on shared meanings helps highlight the complex interaction of class with gender, which you've just read about in Chapter 5, and with race, which will be focused on in Chapter 7. For example, white working class women in general have different class experiences than black working class women—they often have different jobs available to them, and may have different relations with men. But, they share similar positions and identifications within the larger discourses of modernity. An EcoJustice perspective sees the larger forms and process of centric and hierarchized thinking created by these discourses as the heart of the problem. Our socio-economic system and the educational policies and relationships that support it are a product of this larger cultural system.

Historical Context

Class societies have existed for many centuries across the globe, although, contrary to common belief, not all human cultures have classes. Only those cultures that create hierarchy have class divisions, and these hierarchies may be based on social status, accomplishment, gender, or birth, but in Western societies they are based on control of property and wealth, and, related to this, decision-making at government levels.

Class societies have what is commonly called a "ruling class," that is, a class that has the most power in the making of economic and political rules—and, of course, those rules usually benefit the ruling class more than other classes. Thus, as stated above, the ruling class has more influence in terms of the meanings that get organized as knowledge, institutionalized, and taken for granted as truth. They have ideological power. Ideology is a shared system of belief that serves the interests of some more than others. As we have been discussing throughout this book, belief systems depend on discourse—the use, exchange, and internalization of specific metaphors that create beliefs and patterns of behavior. In hierarchized cultures, the ruling classes have a lot of influence on how this works, but the beliefs are also internalized—believed—by those in other classes, too. That's what we mean by ideology being a *shared system* of belief, with real psychological effects and shared experiences based on those effects. But, how does a ruling class get to rule? There are many paths.

In most class societies, a "hereditary aristocracy" developed—that is, people who were, according to the rules they created, entitled to rule by being born to the right families, and they created titles such as King, Emperor, Lord, Baron. People in other classes could not conceive of moving into the ruling class—in feudal societies, peasants did not imagine they could grow up to be king some day. Why did people believe (though not all did!) that the ruling class had a right to rule? Even if there weren't schools, the people were "educated" by the rulers, by the religious leaders who said that their god had blessed the rulers, and even by their families who had also been brought up within this specific discursive system.

As the economic system of capitalism developed in Europe from the 1400s, new classes came into being: the capitalist class and the working class. Capitalists did not necessarily have to be born into a certain family (although most capitalists did come from the aristocrats, because they had the money to invest in businesses), and workers were not bound to a certain lord's land, as feudal peasants were. Nonetheless, the barriers to mobility between classes were almost as great as before. Few workers had the opportunity to accumulate sufficient wealth to invest in profit-making ventures.

Eventually, as their economic power grew, capitalists displaced the aristocrats to take political power in most of the industrial world, often through revolutions such as the Glorious Revolution in England and the French Revolution. However, the aristocratic classes continued to have much economic power through control of land and other wealth. Across the industrialized world, property-less working people were denied the right to vote; only after decades of struggle did this right get extended to all free males (by 1860 in the U.S., 1918 in the UK, and 1920 in Canada!).

The U.S. was different from Europe because it never had a hereditary aristocracy that had power simply by the family to which they were born—there are no Kings or Lords or Barons in the U.S. However, from the very beginning of the United States, there was a small class of extremely wealthy people, whose children were wealthy for generations. Some of these fortunes were based on profits made from systems using slavery as the primary labor used to produce goods and accumulate profit, and some were based on large "royal grants" of land (that was taken from the native people). Yet these families never questioned that they "deserved" what they had. The French writer Honoré de Balzac is credited with the quip "behind every great fortune is a great crime." Though Balzac was speaking of the rich in France, a careful reading of the history of any other industrial country will find considerable truth in that statement.

Class Myths and Realities

Why do Americans, in particular, refuse to talk about class? Perhaps it's because Americans assume there aren't classes in the U.S. due to the lack of lords and kings. Most of our students say that they are "middle class" even though we know that the families that many of them come from are blue collar or working class families. Their response indicates that they understand "middle class" to mean "normal." Another reason Americans don't talk about class could be because they believe that classes are fluid—and that people move up or down based on their abilities and work ethic. Or perhaps Americans believe in the so-called American dream: "Anybody can grow up to be President." The American Dream is created through the myth of meritocracy, an entrenched belief that a person's success and achievement is based on the exercise of hard work and natural talent. The idea of classlessness, then, is created within the discourse of individualism, with the assumption that social differences are based on individual merit rather than on a socially constructed and maintained cultural and economic system creating value and status. As Benjamin DeMott points out, this notion of classlessness is relentlessly reflected back to us in the media, where both news and fictional stories share a simple theme: those who succeed are mentally or morally superior, while those who don't are inferior (DeMott, 1990). These ideas are supported within the discursive system and metaphors of modernity, as we will explore further below.

The facts, however, don't support the myths. It's true the U.S. doesn't have any hereditary titles (they are even banned in the Constitution), but that doesn't mean that powerful and wealthy people cannot pass their power and wealth on to their children. These families fill the history books as well as the mansions in the cities; they put their names on foundations and universities and museums. The gap between the wealthy and the rest of society has been growing in the U.S. since at least the 1970s, and is now one of the highest in the industrial world. According to labor reporter David Leonhardt (2007):

> Income inequality, by many measures, is now greater than it has been since the 1920's. The top 1% of earners in the United States made 19% of all income in 2005, up from 8% in 1975, according to an analysis by Emmanuel Saez and Thomas Piketty, two economists.
>
> In 1947, the median family—the one making more than half of all other families and less than half of all other families—made $23,400, according to the Economic Policy Institute. Over the next three decades, median-income more than doubled, to $47,400 in 1977. In 2005, the median family made $58,400. (All these numbers are adjusted for inflation.)

Meanwhile, the incomes of earners at the 99.99th percentile of the income distribution—those making more than 9,999 out of every 10,000 other earners—have soared over the last three decades, from less than $2 million in the late 1970s to about $10 million now.

So pay has risen for most families in the last 30 years, but not as quickly as it did in the decades after World War II and not nearly as quickly as it has for the affluent.

(Leonhardt, *The New York Times*, July 15, 2007)

Essential to the myth of meritocracy is the belief in class mobility—that is, that people can change classes if they want to work hard and exercise their "God-given talents." In fact, there is relatively little class mobility in the U.S.—that is, only a fraction of people actually change class positions from the one into which they were born—and the U.S. economic system is allowing fewer people than ever to make that shift.

One study, by the Federal Reserve Bank of Boston, found that fewer families moved from one quintile, or fifth, of the income ladder to another during the 1980s than during the 1970s and that still fewer moved in the 90s than in the 80s. A study by the Bureau of Labor Statistics also found that mobility declined from the 80s to the 90s.

(Scott & Leonhardt, 2005, p. 3)

This finding is echoed by long-time labor reporter Steven Greenhouse, noting a study that found "that men who were in their thirties in 2004 had a median income 12 percent less, after factoring in inflation, than their fathers' generation did when they were in their thirties" (Greenhouse, 2008, p. 266). Among the factors is the rapidly rising cost of education—many students avoid college due to the cost, or graduate with a mountain of debt that limits their ability to buy a home.

Similarly, given the aristocratic history of Europe, many assume that the U.S. shows more class mobility than other industrial countries. This isn't true either.

One surprising finding about mobility is that it is lower in the United States than in Canada, Britain or France. However, the U.S. rate is a bit higher than in developing countries like Brazil, where escape from poverty is so difficult that the lower class is all but frozen in place. But the United States differs from Europe in ways that can gum up the mobility machine. Because income inequality is greater here, there is a wider disparity between what rich and poor parents can invest in their children. Perhaps as a result, a child's economic background is a better predictor of school performance in the United States than in Denmark, the Netherlands or France, one recent study found.

(Scott & Leonhardt, 2005, p. 4)

The reasons for the maintenance of class and the lack of class mobility are complex and involve the underlying cultural assumptions of hierarchy, its role in rationalizing notions of empire and the global economy—and, as we'll see, the role of schools. We will look at the role of the global economy in Chapter 8. Here we will focus on the ways that class stratification is created and maintained via a specific cultural mindset and the associated institutions and relationships; in particular, schools. You will no doubt notice that the analysis that we present here has a lot in common with the analysis of gender in the previous chapter, and the analysis of race in the next chapter. This is because an EcoJustice analysis sees all forms of domination and social inequality as a result of the same interlocking cultural discourses and ways of thinking. By now, this analytic framework should be getting clearer: The way we think about gender, class, race, ability, sexuality, and so on is the result of the ways discourses of modernity wrap themselves around our daily interactions, our beliefs, behaviors, policies, even our family relationships. It might help to revisit Chapter 3 just to reacquaint your self with those discourses. We'll be discussing some of them as we go here, but it is important to keep in mind that none of these categories—gender, class, race—function alone. People live within and among the meanings that each imbues us with. So, women who are poor and black, for example, experience domination in ways that are both very different from, and yet are built upon, the same hierarchical structures as women who are poor and white. Androcentrism interacts with ethnocentrism, racism, and other specific discourses in ways that are unique. But let's take a deeper look at the meanings of class in this cultural mix.

Class and the Logic of Domination

To understand why all these class differences persist—and continue to grow—we need to start with the concepts discussed in Chapter 3—hierarchized thinking and the logic of domination. In relying on these concepts, EcoJustice education differs from a social justice approach, which either uses class as a starting place for understanding most other inequities, or focuses primarily on conditions leading to one specific form of injustice, such as sexism or racism, for example. The EcoJustice approach, on the other hand, acknowledges that the issue of class is crucial to consider, but that class must be seen in the context of the deeper cultural assumptions reproducing value hierarchies.

Remember that the logic of domination presents as natural the idea that one group of people has the right to dominate others—including non-human others—because this group claims some form of inherent superiority and uses specific metaphors to support that belief. When class was based purely on birth, as in medieval times, that was seen as sufficient justification for inequity. But, with the end of purely hereditary positions of authority, other forms of justification are necessary to explain and rationalize the vast inequality within industrial societies. These explanations include deficit theories presented by social scientists, supported by popular notions of meritocracy, and the testing movement that supports those explanations.

Deficit Theories

A major way that the logic of domination is applied to and justifies economic stratification is through explanations that are known as "deficit theories." Sociologists and psychologists have long asked, "What are the primary causes of social inequality?" Deficit theories have been the most common ways that social scientists have answered this question. Basically, their explanations of social differences focus on identified "deficits"—or the qualities that are seen to be lacking by a person or group of people who are on the bottom of the social ladder.

Genetic Deprivation Theory

For example, imaginary genetic differences in intelligence were once commonly used as a justification for class as well as racial and gender differences (see the section on Meritocracy and Intelligence Testing, below, for more discussion). In this case, it was believed that an individual's biologically-endowed mental capacity was at the heart of their ability to succeed or not. So, groups of people who remained in the working class or in poverty generation after generation were identified as genetically "deficient" or "deprived." While the most direct statements of this position have been largely discredited, it remains in the popular mind, even if people often don't say it out loud.

The Pervasiveness of Deficit Thinking

Recently, an acquaintance said to Rebecca that he had heard that if all the wealth in the world were redistributed evenly to all the people in the world, the same few people who are currently rich would again be rich within three months. "And I believe it!" he exclaimed. Rebecca said, "Oh, so you believe that they are genetically superior?" "No! They all work harder, and some people are just lazy!" "Hmm . . . so does that mean your father who worked so hard all his life is somehow inferior? He's just lazier?" The man paused, then exclaimed. "Maybe it is genetics!"

As you look at other deficit theories below, you may find yourself think-ing "well, that seems true—what's so wrong with that idea?" If so, you're falling into the same trap that so many educators do: seeing poverty and school failure as caused by the behavior of the poor rather than as a predictable consequence of a system based on domination and hierarchy. Newer deficit explanations that are commonly used include:

Cultural Deprivation Theory

Students from homes in poverty have been identified by some sociologists, psychologists, and other educational professionals as "culturally deprived." That is, they are believed to be from a culture that failed to teach them key habits, skills, and ways of thinking leading to educational or economic suc-cess in mainstream society. Their position in the social hierarchy is deemed to be a result of belonging to social groups who lack the proper values and skills needed to succeed. These values might include, for example, two-parent homes and marriage. Families where unmarried single mothers pre-sided are often deemed "morally deficient" (Polakow, 2000). Mainstream habits believed to be lacking include the ability to delay gratification and to plan ahead. Skills include "school readiness," such as using scissors and knowing the alphabet, while values include the belief that working hard in school will lead to college and to life success. Families that don't prepare their children for school in these ways are deemed to be deficient.

Of course such skills and habits are valuable (for Western schooling, at least). The problem is in how we understand why some children get those skills and others don't. The term "culturally deprived" suggests that the home culture or value system of the students is inferior. It locates the problem of social inequality within the family or the individual, but this time, instead of the individual's genetic system, it is in the family value system where the problem is believed to reside. This perspective thus "pathologizes" poor and working class families. That is, it deems them to be socially and morally "diseased." As the bias in the notion of cultural deprivation became evident, the use of that terminology has faded in use. However, the assumptions behind it have not. Instead they are couched in other terminology that is equally pathologizing, such as "at risk."

Being "At Risk"

Today, many poor and working class students are often called "at risk" students, meaning that they have a greater risk of failing than other stu-dents. While lower academic achievement is statistically true, the expla-nation for the person being at risk is generally couched in deficit terms: that such students come from a home situation that doesn't provide the necessary values, basic skills, and attitudes for school success.

Some readers might think, "But, isn't this true? Some kids don't learn skills such as counting or letters at home, while others do. They are deprived, right?" Among the problems with this way of thinking is that it begins from a white middle class standard of what success is, and it is focused on what working class kids and their cultures lack in comparison, rather than giving any value to their strengths. Explaining school failure as resulting purely from individual/family deficits deflects an analysis of the ways that a hierarchical society discriminates, discourages, and deters a person from success, or excludes him or her from the opportunities necessary to culturally defined achievements. For example, parents in a society such as the U.S. that creates many low wage jobs without health insurance may be working multiple jobs to provide for their family—leaving them little time to teach their children those expected basic school skills, or little extra money to provide books, videos, music, and other skill-building resources in the home. These are often the same families who don't show up for parent–teacher conferences—perhaps they had bad experiences as children in schools and so have a negative perception of what schools mean, or who they are in relation to schools. Remember: Class is more than a measure of how much wealth you have; it is also a culturally created, institutionally reinforced social and psychological experience. And, it gets carried around and performed in work settings, and all sorts of other public situations. We'll see how this works in schools in more detail below.

A Modern Example: The Hidden Class Bias in Ruby Payne's Work

Somewhere in your career as a teacher you will probably encounter a workshop or some other presentation of the ideas of Ruby Payne, whose best-known work is titled *A Framework for Understanding Poverty* (Payne, 2001). Payne claims to be trying to help educators understand the different assumptions of poor and working class kids—what she calls "the hidden rules of poverty"—including some "survival skills" of poverty such as "I know how to get a gun, even if I have a police record," or "I know how to get someone out of jail."

While these rules may appear to be consistent with the emphasis on culture and hidden assumptions in the book you are holding, they have a very different root and are saturated with particular definitions and meanings that derive from the ideologies and discourses we've been discussing. As Anita Bohn (2006) points out,

> Payne's books and lectures present a superficial and insulting picture of children and families in poverty. Poor people, according to Payne, are scofflaws perpetually looking for a fight or some other good time when they are not busy milking the system . . . One teacher told

me after an Aha! Process workshop that something she learned in Payne's seminar was "poor people can't think abstractly."

(Bohn, 2006, p. 15)

This idea is clearly based on deficit thinking. Consider the curricular decisions that might be made by a teacher who takes away that understanding of her students from a Ruby Payne workshop.

Payne offers teachers and administrators something very seductive: simple and comfortable solutions to complex school problems. Payne's facile answers allow teachers and administrators to place the blame for low-income children's lack of academic success entirely outside the schools.

(Bohn, 2006, p. 15)

Payne's work is an example of how a logic of domination infuses so much of our popular consciousness and day-to-day thinking—even ideas that attempt to bridge the gap between classes can end up reinforcing the divide, unless they are built on a critical understanding of the assumptions of domination.

Meritocracy and Intelligence Testing

The idea of "meritocracy" is the partner of deficit theories. It is used to argue that those who are successful in a class-defined society have achieved their position through their own merit: they deserve it because of their individual hard work and superior natural abilities. Those who fail do so because they are lazy (they lack the value of hard work) or they lack intelligence (natural ability). Here we see clearly the ways that the discourse of individualism plays into the justification of social inequality: Social success is purely a matter of individuals making the right choices, using the right values, and exercising personally developed skills and talents. As long as an individual does so, she will find her proper place in the social system. In this story, each person gets what he or she deserves. Competition is the name of the game and the resulting unequal distribution of resources and power is really quite "natural."

This ideology saturates our culture and is generally used to contrast with the "bad old days" when people gained power and privilege simply by being born into the right family and class. The need to have the population believe that existing society is indeed a meritocracy has, in turn, been a key impetus for the rise of aptitude testing.

For a long time, "merit" was determined through individual judgment. The rewards in a hierarchical society, such as job offers, promotions, and admissions to universities, were decided by those in positions of power—who were, of course, mostly white male Protestants, who not surprisingly mostly found merit in other white, male Protestants. By the 1920s, however, the bias of this system was too obvious to be avoided, and threatened to undermine the legitimacy of the established order. A more "objective" method to determine merit was needed.

Coincidentally, the field of mental testing was just being born. The entire structure of intelligence and admission testing—first IQ tests, then SATs, GREs, MSATs, and so on—is built on the idea that it is possible to scientifically and fairly measure individual intelligence and thus objectively and efficiently decide where students best fit in schools (vocational versus college-bound tracks, for example), and who should get the precious slots in top-ranked colleges, the jobs in prestigious law firms, and all the other rewards of success.

The history of the creation of testing is revealing. The testing movement, which began with Benet's tests of mental ability in France, took off in the U.S. during World War I with the creation of the Army Mental Tests, designed to classify the ability of military recruits. Here are some sample questions. Consider which groups of people would tend to score well on tests with questions like these:

10. "There's a reason" is an "ad" for a
drink revolver flour cleanser
19. Crisco is a
patent medicine disinfectant tooth-paste food product
38. The Pierce Arrow car is made in
Buffalo Detroit Toledo Flint
(Quoted in Owen, 1985, p. 181)

One can imagine what a recent immigrant or a rural black person might make of these questions. The bias in favor of those familiar with middle-class culture seems obvious to the reader today. But, based on these tests, Robert Yerkes and Carl Campbell Brigham made broad generalizations about innate mental ability that, not coincidentally, matched up with the existing race and class structure of U.S. society.

Brigham detected four distinct racial strains in American society. At the pinnacle were the Nordics, the blond, blue-eyed original settlers and the group to which Brigham naturally assigned himself. At the other extreme was the American Negro. "Between the Nordic and the negro," Brigham wrote, "but closer to the negro than to the Nordic, we find the Alpine and Mediterranean types. The Mediterraneans were particularly worrisome, Brigham said, because they had bred "conspicuously" with the Amerind and the imported negro.

(Owen, 1985, p. 183)

We consider this completely racist today, but those in the most prestigious universities in the U.S. took it as objective fact. After all, Yerkes was a professor at Harvard, Brigham at Princeton. The racist assumptions that most so-called educated people carried were now being clothed in the aura of "science," and were being used to justify the inequalities in the social structure. We'll discuss the racist use of science in the next chapter in more depth.

Brigham went on to help create the SAT. While the questions in the SAT are not as blatantly biased as the Army tests, they still carry class biases. Look at the following question from fairly recent tests, and think about who would be more likely to know the answer to the question, just by how they grew up.

RUNNER: MARATHON

(A) Envoy: embassy
(B) Martyr: massacre
(C) Oarsman: regatta
(D) Horse: stable

Other questions consider inheritances, ballet, symphony orchestras, and the like. Isn't it likely that students from affluent backgrounds are more likely to know something about marathons, regattas, inheritances, and high-culture music because they may have experienced or discussed those things with their families? Even though the particular form of analogy questions has been removed from the newest version of the SAT, it's impossible for test writers to escape the culture and class bias that is inherent when a person from a particular culture writes language that must be interpreted by people who may not share the same history.

As a result of questions like these, and many other factors, test scores on SATs and IQ tests, as well as other mechanisms that supposedly deliver meritocratic results, are significantly related to class differences. That is, children of higher-income families usually score higher than children from working class families (see Figure 6.2).

This strong correlation between income and scores has stayed the same for decades. It almost looks like the College Board just checks your family income and assigns a score. Of course it doesn't, since these are averages that contain plenty of exceptions. But it powerfully shows the effects of class advantages, including the SAT test prep classes that so many affluent students take.

Some readers may point out, "I've worked really hard to get where I am. Does this analysis of meritocracy suggest that my effort is meaningless?" No, it doesn't. But let's ask another question: Is a value hierarchy natural? Are some people worth more, somehow, than others? That is, do some people really deserve to eat better, live in big homes, have

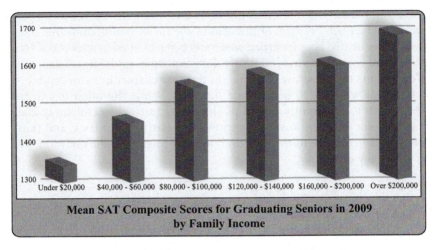

Figure 6.2 Mean SAT Scores for Graduating Seniors in 2009 by Family Income.

Source: CollegeBoard. (2009). *2009 College-bound Seniors: Total group profile report.* New York, NY: CollegeBoard.

access to health care, and possess all sorts of luxuries and privileges while others go without? Is that condition the result of something natural, or is it a result of unjust and fictional cultural discourses that convince us of its inevitability?

Further, the general belief in meritocracy as a true measure of fair achievement misses the fact that many working class and minority people may also work just as hard and are just as intelligent, but they are made to suffer both material and ideological injustices due to a logic (a taken-for-granted way of thinking) that defines some as inherently superior and thus deserving of the good life, while others are inferior and thus deserving of less of what society has to offer.

And as we will show below, schools are far from neutral institutions in this cultural process. Or, put another way, schools are far from immune to the discursive system that creates value-hierarchized thinking. Indeed, as some critical sociologists of education have shown, deficit thinking and meritocratic myths pervade schools. We'll get to this in a moment. First, let's play with some conceptual reversals.

Turning Deficit Thinking on Its Head

By thinking about how deficit theory is rooted in hierarchical thinking and the language of the logic of domination, we can see how culturally

bound it is to see certain people—the poor, for example—as simply inferior due to what they seem to lack. One way to highlight this is to turn it
on its head: What do the poor have that the more affluent don't? Well,
survival skills, for one. They know how to survive on a lot less money,
often by making or doing for themselves what others buy or pay for. For
example, they may be able to grow a garden and make a nutritious meal
from simple ingredients, know how to sew their own clothes, do home
repair, or fix a car. Or, they may have "street smarts"—the knowledge
and skills for how to navigate often-dangerous neighborhoods and hostile government representatives such as police.

Or, to turn another assumption over, what do the more affluent lack
themselves? One characteristic missing in the affluent may be empathy.
Brantlinger (2003) interviewed affluent parents and teachers and found
that in advocating solely for their own children, they displayed a singular
lack of concern for children from poor and working class families. The
affluent parents advocated for tracking (see below), Talented and Gifted
programs, and other ways of separating their children from students they
saw as likely to drag their own children down. Yet nearly all insisted they
were liberal people who favored integration and equality in society. But,
because they were caught up in the discourse of hierarchy, they failed to
see how their own actions undermined the possibilities of equality.

Similarly, we can turn the concept of "at risk" on its head by pointing
out that children from homes in poverty are at risk for being discriminated
against, for being given low expectations, and for being forced to go to
inferior schools. Further, as Ayers and Ford (1996) incisively point out:

> Being "at risk" is a kind of pathology . . . In our society today, "at
> risk" functions as a kind of witch-hunting metaphor: void of any
> credible data, it is a label in search of content. It offers a thin surface
> of scholarship and pseudoscience to cover the thickest and most per-
> sistent stereotypes about poor and African-American people. After
> all (they are) mostly "at risk" of being black and poor.
> (Ayers & Ford, 1996, p. 5)

The strangeness that might be apparent in these reversed concepts is an
illustration of how deeply ingrained value-hierarchical thinking is in us—
after all, we have been taught since birth that people "deserve" to be
where they are.

Reproduction of Class in Schools

Far from being viable explanations of social inequality, widely shared
assumptions about the deficits of poor and working class students
are themselves responsible for the reproduction of socially stratified

communities. As critical sociologists of education have been exposing since the late 1970s, this belief that the children of poor and working families are intellectually and culturally inferior has led to vastly different forms of education for them as compared to children from other classes. Value-hierarchized thinking and related assumptions are so integral to the cultural system in which we live that they also actively structure what goes on in our institutions, including and especially in our schools.

Try this activity before going on:

Think About This

Step 1:

Think about the kind of schoolwork you experienced most often in your K-12 years. Of course, you had many different teachers, but which of the following best fits your experience:

School A: Work was worksheets and rote memorization, often without any understanding of purpose. Teacher was primarily an authoritarian figure; attitude toward students was control, often harsh and arbitrary.

School B: Work was getting the right answer and learning the correct methods. Teacher was rule-based authority; classroom management was based on rules to be followed.

School C: Work often encouraged creativity and critical thinking. Teacher was facilitator, management was through negotiation.

School D: Work often was analytic, aiming at learning to understand and control. Teacher was leader, management was by expectation of high behavior.

Step 2:

Next, which of the following best fits the economic nature of the neighborhood of the school that you most considered in choosing your answer in Step 1.

W (working class): Most people work in factories or service jobs in non-management jobs.

X (middle class): Most people work in middle management or skilled job areas where they are mainly answering to people above them, and may have supervisory responsibility. This often includes teachers and principals in most schools.

> *Y (creative professional class)*: Most people work in highly skilled professional jobs where they have substantial control over their day-to-day lives, and the lives of others—doctors, lawyers, advertising execs.
>
> *Z (executive elite)*: Most people are in top management of businesses or similar positions.
>
> Now consider them together. If you chose *A* in Step 1, did you choose *W* in Step 2, or *B* with *X*, *C* with *Y*, *D* with *Z*?
>
> Ask other people around you. If you're like most groups we have taught, you will find that more people had those matches more than anything else.

So what's this all about? The tendency for those matches is an example of the ways in which schools tend to "reproduce" class differences in U.S. society. We have used the concept of reproduction previously in the book. It means that a hierarchical division in society—such as gender, race, or class—is maintained by some social arrangement where the dominant discourses circulate and cultural meanings are exchanged and internalized by the members or participants. When we say that schools tend to reproduce class, therefore, we mean that aspects of how schools are organized and the practices and relationships that take place there tend to make it likely that people who are born into a class will stay in that same class. We are taught to stay where we "belong."

It's important to note here that the concept of reproduction does not argue that there is a conspiracy—there is no secret group designing schools to make sure that working class kids can't succeed, while affluent kids get all the goods. Rather, the discourses, beliefs, and practices that circulate in a school help to create the specific conditions whereby we come to expect some students to succeed and others not to. Also, remember that reproducing some belief or tradition in society isn't always a bad thing. Traditions and practices should be conserved when they support equitable and sustainable ways of living, but traditions that maintain division and domination need to be identified and challenged. This is what critical scholars, including EcoJustice scholars, do when they analyze the ways that deficit perspectives operate in the structure and function of schooling. So, if there's not a secret cabal designing schools to maintain the class structure, why does it happen anyway? The claim that both the overall organization of schools, as well as the day-to-day interactions within them, reproduce class is based on a long trend of research in education and sociology. Samuel Bowles and Herbert Gintis (1976) found, for example, that differences in schooling accounted for a significant part of the lack of mobility between classes. They identified what they called a "correspondence principle"—that the hierarchy of schools corresponded to the hierarchy that workers later face in the workplace, such that schools function to teach young people how to follow the rules of hierarchy.

The exercise above with Schools A through D is based on the work of Jean Anyon (1989). She studied a group of schools and found that the economic background of the neighborhood tended to predict the kind of preparation students were offered in schools, the expectations of the teachers, the sorts of classroom activities prevalent, and the curriculum materials. Working class kids were trained to do rote work such as math worksheets, where the main point was following directions and completing the procedural steps as shown by the teacher, thus preparing them for little else but rote jobs in the factory. Kids from middle managers' homes tended to learn to follow rules, and the most important goal was getting the right answer. Critical questions or controversial issues were not only ignored, they were actively discouraged. Anyon suggests that these students were being prepared for jobs as middle managers—following and enforcing rules. Kids from professional neighborhoods were asked to do creative, independent work, such as making a script and filming it, or creating math problems for each other. This kind of work prepares students for selective colleges and professional jobs where they would be expected to make decisions and invent new approaches. Executive elite schools (mostly elite private schools) tended to emphasize logic and conceptual understanding, expecting students to reason through a problem to arrive at a solution. Anyon argues that this work particularly prepares students to run large organizations (as well as preparing them for highly selective colleges).

But . . . It's Not So Simple

At this point, many of our students object that it's not that simple. "I lived in a working class neighborhood and I had several teachers who taught us to think creatively." "I went to a so-called middle class school, but got in to Yale." They're right, it's not that simple—there are plenty of exceptions. Schools are complicated places and are constantly challenged by many forces in society—they are, as we say, "contested spaces" offering often unpredictable possibilities. However, exceptions are just that: variations on a general rule. When we talk about reproduction, we're talking about the overall impact: what happens to most people, not a few individuals. Further, even the exceptions and contests simply serve to reinforce the system.

Academic Achievement, School Funding, and Social Class

This early work by critical sociologists of education helped us to understand some of the specific ways that school practices and policies could be linked to social class and directly related to school achievement. More recently, Anyon surveyed a variety of studies and notes "We have long known that social class, or socio-economic status (SES), is highly correlated with educational achievement: Generally, the higher the resource background of the child's family, the higher the achievement" (Anyon, 2005, p. 65). One study found that up to 85 percent of the variation in standardized test scores across schools was accounted for by the percentage of low-income students in the school.

One part of the answer is economic—because of the strange way of funding schools in the U.S. (based on local property values), schools in poor neighborhoods or cities may have less than half the money per student of schools in affluent neighborhoods. Despite the claim of some that "money doesn't matter," the evidence is that student achievement is deeply affected. Lee and Burkam (2002) found:

> However school quality is defined—in terms of higher student achievement, more school resources, more qualified teachers, more positive teacher attitudes, better neighborhood or school conditions, private vs. public schools—the least advantaged U.S. children begin their formal schooling in consistently lower-quality schools.
>
> (Quoted in Anyon, 2005, p. 66)

Jonathan Kozol has described with wrenching clarity the effects of low funding in his book *Savage Inequalities* (1991). Larger class sizes, poorly maintained buildings with ceilings that leak and heating systems that don't heat, science labs without equipment—all characterize schools in poor communities. These deficiencies not only lead to poorer quality education, but also send a message to students that they don't matter. One student in Camden, New Jersey, showed Kozol a tattered copy of a Dickens novel, and says "You see this book? . . . That's the book they gave me. Pages are missing. *A Tale of Two Cities*. We don't even have enough for every student. There are just ten students in that class! . . . Ten people! They had only seven books. Why are we treated like this?" (Kozol, 1991, p. 154).

Kozol points out that students know what schools in affluent neighborhoods look like, and that those neighborhoods draw district boundary lines to keep poor and minority students out. One student writes a poem:

America the beautiful,
Who are you beautiful for?

(Kozol, 1991, p. 112)

These economic differences are nothing more or less than specific manifestations of a logic of domination, for which the unspoken assumption is: "Why should we fund schools in neighborhoods where the poor live? They aren't worth it."

School District Transfer Policies

At another level, the gap between good and bad schools grows because of the decentralized arrangement of schools in the U.S. Assignment of teachers in many schools in based on transfer policies that allow considerable freedom to individual teachers to change schools. Good teachers can move from low-achieving schools to high-achieving schools where the teaching is easier and more respected—and is often paid more. The resulting brain drain in many districts leaves the schools in the poorest areas with the newest and least prepared teachers.

Tracking

Sometimes the different qualities of education exist in the same school—most commonly in high schools. In fact, about the same time intelligence testing was invented, the comprehensive high school came into being with different levels of coursework for different groups of students. Tests were used to measure the supposed "native intelligence" of students who were then sorted into different tracks in schools: from "special education" to vocational to college-bound tracks.

Did you go to a high school that had, for example, different English classes labeled something like "Honors," "Standard," and "Basic," or even as simple as English A, English B, or English C? If so, you experienced a common form of class reproduction known as "tracking." In tracking systems, students are guided, or "tracked," into different courses offering different levels of challenge. The decision about which track a student is placed in may be made by guidance counselors and teachers, by tests, or even by the student or their parents, but once it's made, it's very hard to change—students rarely change tracks during their high school career.

History of Tracking

The separation of students into different tracks has a 100-year history in the U.S. that is directly connected to the rise of intelligence testing as well as specific developments in our industrial history. In the early 1900s, business leaders wanted to bring working class students into the high schools so they could be socialized for factory work, but these leaders didn't believe that working class students could do the academic curriculum, and they certainly didn't want to raise the expectations of working class students that they could aspire to professional jobs. In a 1912 report by an influential business organization, the case was made that separate education was needed because students had different abilities. Note the metaphors used to describe children in the following passage:

> Differing as students do from one another, they may nevertheless be divided into three great educational classes:
>
> 1. The abstract minded and imaginative children, who learn readily from the printed page. Most of the children whose ancestors were in the professions and the higher occupations, so-called, are in this class, as well as many from the humbler callings.
> 2. The concrete or hand-minded children. Those who can, only with extreme difficulty, and then imperfectly, learn readily from the printed page. These children constitute at least half of the children of the nation, being that half who leave our schools by the end of the sixth grade.
> 3. The great intermediate class.
>
> (Quoted in Nasaw, 1979, p. 127)

Note the dualistic metaphors of abstract-minded (mind) and hand-minded (body), and the negative description of the hand-minded, indicating their inferior place. The assumption of a natural hierarchy implicit in this language made it an easy step for the writers of the report to go on to suggest substantially different education for each class. Indeed, separate educational tracks were rapidly implemented across the U.S. by the end of the 1920s.

After World War II, the emphasis on channeling "manpower" reinforced the separation of students. First, the military draft was continued after the war in order to maintain a large standing army, but with deferments for college students, meant to support the need for scientists and other knowledge workers. Since college deferments went primarily to middle and upper class students, they had the effect of steering low-income and minority children into the military. Next, the Cold War contributed. After the Soviet Union was the first to put a satellite into orbit with Sputnik in 1957, there were widespread claims that the U.S. was falling behind scientifically. The resulting passage of the National Defense Education Act put money into scholarships and into creation of new science curricula, all designed to channel "talented" students into colleges to study science and technology. Finally, many working class students were steered away from the four-year colleges into the newly created system of community colleges. These two-year colleges focused on "vocational education," and promised a pathway to four-year colleges that was only rarely available. The result of all this was the further sorting of students by class, again using discourses that create the myth of meritocracy as rationalization (Spring, 1989).

The next push for sorting arose in the 1970s, partly as a response to the upheavals of the 1960s. Pushed by the Nixon administration, "career education" aimed to (1) focus all education toward one or another career path and (2) increase enrollments in vocational courses at both high school and community college levels. But, as Ira Shor notes, "Career education repeated the same politics as the community college movement before it: the promise of democracy and success with the delivery of unequal education and credentials for the social hierarchy" (Shor, 1986, p. 35).

Current Tracking Practices

Although the language used to justify tracking today does not explicitly suggest that students from a particular class are destined to be in a corresponding track, it may not be surprising to hear that there is a strong correlation between track level and social class. Students from families in the executive and professional classes (primarily white) are much more likely to be in Honors courses, while students from working class backgrounds are far more likely to be in Basic-level courses.

Proponents of tracking, or homogeneous grouping, argue that it is simply giving students the most appropriate education for their ability. Once again, deficit thinking is so unconscious that even those who have all the best intentions fall into its ugly trap. It's frustrating, they say, for students with poorer skills to be in a class that is too hard for them. Similarly, it's said to be frustrating for an advanced student to be bored waiting for weaker students to catch up.

But the research is clear, according to Jeannie Oakes. While some studies have shown a small advantage for the upper track students, "[n]o group of students has been found to benefit consistently from being in a homogeneous group . . . However, many studies have found the learning of average and slow students to be negatively affected by homogeneous placements" (2005, p. 7). Oakes goes on to examine the specific differences that underlie these life-changing placements, and finds that

> tracking brings with it very different expectations for student achievement, access to subject matter and critical learning opportunities, instructional strategies, and resources (including teachers). These disparate expectations, access, and resources have a predictable effect on student learning: low track students fall further behind.
>
> (Oakes, 2005, p. 225)

Among the ways that a culture rooted in domination helps maintain tracking is by normalizing the situation: The assumption that some should be raised above others leads many people to see tracking as normal and necessary, and hides from them the clear reality that tracking is fundamentally unequal. This also helps explain why, even when students are given a choice of track placement, working class students usually tend to choose lower tracks. Not only do they want to be with people like them, they often don't believe they belong in the higher track. As we have pointed out throughout this book, value-hierarchized thinking is an internalized psychological condition that gets created as these meanings circulate, get exchanged, and create the very structure and processes in our institutions.

Examining the Culture of Schools

While we have mainly been looking at the overall or "macro" structures and organization of schools, another key process of class reproduction is found in the more day-to-day or "micro" processes in the culture of the school and surrounding community. Remember the concept of culture as webs or "systems" of meaning? Those webs are created by any local group, a school community, for example, interacting over time and developing routines of work, exchanging and internalizing culturally-embedded assumptions about who people are and how they interact, and habits of interaction with others.

These local cultures, while unique and diverse, are also always framed within the larger cultural assumptions of the society—such as the assumptions of superiority in the logic of domination and the assumption of individualism. In fact, this is precisely how all societies bind themselves together—via historically created, nearly invisible discourses that create webs of cultural meaning. It's how people identify as members of a society or culture.

Schools themselves develop cultures too. Students and teachers interact within webs of meaning that are largely patterns of taken-for-granted ideas. As we discussed earlier, looking at Jean Anyon's work, many schools in poor neighborhoods reproduce a pattern of low expectations in the curriculum and teaching methods employed. Low expectations are a symptom of deficit thinking, and get reinforced through the particular metaphors that circulate within a classroom to describe and rationalize the situation. Both the actual words used by teachers, as well as the practices engaged in, communicate how the participants feel about who they and others are in the school.

In much the same way that we discussed a "pedagogy of shame" relative to gender in schools, Haberman (1994) suggests that there is "pedagogy of poverty" in some schools, a kind of silent bargain between teachers and students under which teachers offer little challenge to students—who, in turn, offer little open challenge to the teachers. New teachers who try to have higher expectations are faced with resistance by students who are used to the status quo, until the teacher gives in and offers a simpler task that allows them to disengage. If teachers don't lower expectations, counselors may undermine them by transferring students out of their classes into less demanding classes, or veteran teachers will encourage them to "just give the students a worksheet." Even parents sometimes participate in this culture of low expectations by complaining if students have too much homework (Haberman, 1994; Edmundson, 1998).

It's important to see the power of the language and practices used by people who have the best of intentions in order to, ironically, maintain low expectations. Deficit theory is not just an abstract analysis made by sociologists or other researchers—it gets translated into both popular attitude and actual classroom relations. For example, counselors will say the work is "too hard" in justifying student transfers into less challenging classes. Note the absolutism of "too hard"—it's not that it's difficult work that needs more time to master, but work that "these students" will never master, so they shouldn't even try. Or consider a teacher who refers to the often-traumatic family lives of students, calling them, for example, "hurting puppies," a phrase that Jeff has heard from many teachers. While it may originate in some form of compassion, this infantilization of the students as puppies suggests that they are too weak or damaged to be able to do challenging learning. Note the underlying value-hierarchical pattern in the language: Students are consistently referred to in ways that define them (and their families) as inferior.

Cultural Meanings and Gaps Between the Dominant Culture and "Others"

Another aspect of class reproduction occurs in the gap between the culture of students and that of teachers. Most teachers come into schools with a middle or professional class point-of-view, while in many cases few or none of their students share the same class, especially in schools in impoverished communities. Again, using the lens of culture as webs of meaning, we can see that students are bringing different cultural meanings into the classroom than those of their teachers. What metaphors of the student–teacher relationship does the typical teacher bring into such a classroom? Perhaps it's a "helping-hand" metaphor where the teacher is there to help the low-income student up the "ladder." On the other hand, student assumptions might include, for example, the idea that K-12 school is simply something one must endure before getting on with the "real life" of earning a living, or that people who carry books and do homework are "nerds." Thus the metaphors such students may be using include "teacher as dictator" to be circumvented or challenged, and that doing schoolwork is giving in to authority.

Because deficit thinking is so pervasive in schools, when teachers find that students don't carry the same cultural understandings of school, they tend to assume that students are flawed in some way: "They just don't get how important school is." Again, the act of ascribing negative labels to students for their different assumptions and behaviors is a "pathologizing" process. That is, teachers treat students as if they have some pathology—or disease. Unable to interpret students' situation using a deep cultural analysis, teachers may instead individualize a student's problem, defining it as if it were the student who is "ill" or has a problem. For example, if a teacher sees a student asleep at her desk, a pathologizing approach would be for the teacher to assume that the student is lazy and uninterested.

Think About This

Here are some more situations in which students are often patholo-gized. For each, think about how they might be pathologized, and then come up with some other explanations for the behavior that is described. Try to think of differences rooted in a broader cultural context—in different ways of making meaning of a situation.

1. A student attends class regularly but never turns in homework.
2. A student refuses to make eye contact with the teacher when the teacher is talking directly to him.
3. A student never brings her book to class, or takes it home for homework.

There could be a world of other explanations for the sleeping student. Perhaps she works late at a job so she can help the family pay its rent. Perhaps the class is indeed uninteresting. Maybe she really is lazy and uninterested in school—but whatever the symptom, the cause is always created within a larger context than the individual herself. Teachers who opt to blame the student without asking about this larger context may be, as William Ryan (1976) suggests, blaming the victim.

The last example in the box, which occurs often in schools in low-income communities, was dramatized in the 1988 film *Stand and Deliver*, about a real Los Angeles math teacher, Jaime Escalante. A Latino student in Escalante's math class never does homework. Escalante, rather than pathologizing or blaming the student, finds out that for a student to carry a book home is to risk violence on the street. Escalante solves the problem by finding the student a second book to keep at home.

Identity and Resistance: The Psychological Consequences of Class

It should be clear by this point that social class is not just a descriptive category. It is not just about income or money, or who can buy what. It's a lived experience that leads to specific subjective understandings of who we are as we go about our day-to-day interactions. One part of working class identity is rooted in internalizing the deficit explanations of a hierarchized society: "I'm not as smart as those middle class kids, so I don't belong in college." And that perspective is obviously no accident, and should come as no surprise. Jeff's students in a predominantly white working class high school frequently voiced such statements. Demonstrating the ways in which a "pedagogy of shame" operates in terms of class as well as gender, young men and women in these classes would often preface statements with "I know this is probably wrong," or "I know I don't know much, but . . ." They often dismissed the idea of going to college with rationalizations like, "I don't need to go; my friend will get me work." But, in less guarded moments, they would make it clear that they didn't think they were good enough.

Story From a Colleague

A colleague of Rebecca's who is now a professor of educational psychology tells her students of a moment in her own life when the psychological conditions of working class life were made clear to her. A guidance counselor who knew she was very bright and could be successful in college submitted an application to a division one university for her. When she received the admissions letter, she was thrilled and went to share the good news with her father. To her dismay, upon hearing his daughter's excited news, he looked up with sad eyes and said, "Oh honey, I'm so sorry. Our family doesn't go to college."

As Linda Valli (1986) points out, working class students have more difficulty imagining that they have alternatives to a life of low-wage labor. Under capitalism, in fact, alternatives are limited, and their families' experiences have taught them so. But they have also been taught to locate the problem in themselves, and, to the extent that possibilities exist, they are not perceived as such by these students. They have internalized the messages that saturate our culture: some people are just better, smarter, and more deserving than others. Some folks go to college and some go to work (if there is work to be found). Some use their minds, others use their bodies.

Children of affluent families, on the other hand, tend to develop identities that are based in a belief that schools are on their side; that if they follow the rules they will gain society's benefits. From their first teachers, their parents, these children also learn to see themselves as different from working class children. As noted above, Brantlinger (2003) studied affluent professional parents and found an ideological component. Affluent parents differentiate themselves and their children from those who aren't like them, who don't share the same values—namely the poor and working class children, who are seen as less intelligent, less interested in school, and less supported at home. The deeply-rooted assumptions of superiority and inferiority are once again shown in Brantlinger's interviews with affluent parents, who rationalize why their kids should not have to go to school with working class kids: "My kids would not be challenged"; "teachers have to deal with more problems with lower-income kids."

It is also important to recognize that none of us is simply the dupe of an overarching system. All people have agency that includes the ability to exercise power even in contexts saturated with hierarchized meanings. As we pointed out above, schools are contested spaces, and students resist the imposition of all sorts of meanings and processes as a regular part of their lives there. Unfortunately, much of the time their resistance to the degrading processes of school is seldom supported with good pedagogy, with instruction that helps them makes sense of their class-based circumstances. This is particularly true for working class students. As many writers have found, another important part of working class identity is formed as an opposition to school and its worldview. British sociologist of education Paul Willis (1977) looked closely at a group of working class boys in England who called themselves "the lads." Like many young people in contemporary schools, the lads vigorously challenged the school's attempts to control them. They rejected the work they were assigned, questioned school authority, and made fun of those who did follow the school's demands. But, in their very resistance to school, the lads left themselves with no options except the same working class jobs their parents did, thus ironically reproducing the class system despite their resistance. Just saying "no" to an oppressive situation doesn't necessarily keep it from exercising its effects. The lads said "no" to school for themselves, but didn't challenge the way of thinking or the system that underlies it—they didn't challenge capitalism, and even less did they challenge the logic of domination.

Sennett and Cobb (1972) described working class schools where teachers regularly picked out a few who seemed likely to succeed and labeled the rest as "ordinary." Many students responded by breaking school rules. But, say Sennett and Cobb, "This counterculture does not come to grips with the labels their teachers have imposed on these kids; it is rather an attempt to create among themselves badges of dignity that those in authority can't destroy" (1972, p. 84).

In contrast, Weis (1990, 2004) and Everhart (1983) found that students often followed two contradictory stories. They believed that school was necessary in order to go to college, which was believed to lead to good jobs, but they did not value school knowledge or school authority. Thus, the attitude was often "what do I need to do to pass?" as opposed to working for top grades, let alone finding anything of interest in school assignments.

In working class African American culture, Fordham and Ogbu found a similar oppositional identity. Fordham and Ogbu's highly controversial thesis suggested that this identity was characterized by a folk theory of "making it" that was rooted in friends and community rather than education, and that stigmatized school success, isolating students who were academically successful because they were seen as "acting white" (Fordham & Ogbu, 1986; Fordham, 1996). Though some scholars have challenged Ogbu and Fordham's concepts, many teachers have seen compelling evidence that students of color sometimes identify school success as "acting white."

Clearly, the psychological burdens of class cannot be lifted simply by teachers pretending that class differences don't exist, or by urging students to change their assumptions about the world. Teachers must understand the different meanings that students bring to the classroom and offer validation to students as people without validating a discourse that oppresses students.

Conclusion

As we noted at the beginning, Americans have a hard time with class. But, to challenge domination rooted in class, teachers have to train themselves to see it. Teachers who don't see class almost inevitably reproduce its effects through various forms and practices linked to deficit thinking that fundamentally inferiorize and degrade their students. We have tried to give you some tools in this chapter to see class and its effects. Ask yourself questions such as these:

- Do your teaching materials ignore class to the same extent that they used to do for race and gender?
- Do you and your colleagues use deficit language in talking about students, and is Ruby Payne's work (or similar) used without being problematized?
- Do you repeat the myths of meritocracy or challenge them?
- Does your school have ability grouping or tracking? What are the consequences?
- Does your school or district have other policies, such as transfer policies, that encourage separation of students or that encourage the best teachers to go to the highest-income schools?
- Does your school allow working class students to resist school in ways that produce failure rather than change?

If even a few of these questions get a "yes" answer, then your school is supporting the logic of domination that reproduces the hierarchy of class. Some of them you can challenge on your own. For others you will need allies to make a change. We encourage you to look for allies in fellow teachers, among parents, and with students. Just as awareness of racism and sexism took a long time to develop, new thinking about class won't happen overnight, but it is part of a pedagogy of responsibility.

The following section offers you activities and other resources that will help get you started. We also encourage you to use the additional resources found on our website at www.routledge.com/textbooks/ 9780415872515.

What Schools and Teachers Can Do

At the Community Level

- Get involved with groups in your state who are challenging the use of standardized tests for high-stakes decisions regarding students.
- Help to organize educational campaigns to educate your community about inequitable school funding that allows wealthy school districts to spend twice the dollars per student as some poor districts.
- Challenge teacher assignment practices that cluster the most effective teachers in the high-income schools.

At the School Level

- Interrupt deficit thinking: When colleagues use deficit explanations, encourage them to consider alternative explanations that take account of larger socio-economic structures and cultural roots of centric thinking.
- Work with colleagues to change tracking systems in your school. A group of determined teachers has frequently been able to persuade administrators and parents to alter the schedule. As an alternative, push for close examination of teaching practices across tracks.

At the Classroom Level

- Challenge the silence in schools and prejudicial assumptions in curriculum regarding class—make it an explicit topic of your classroom. Middle and high school teachers can use resources such as Howard Zinn's *A People's History of the United States* (1980), or Bigelow and Diamond's *The Power in Our Hands* (1988) to look closely at the struggles of working class people for dignity and decent lives.
- Tell students explicitly what the expectations are for assignments and behavior. Middle class teachers often assume that students know

what is expected, and then blame working class students who don't meet the unspoken expectations.

- Challenge all students to rigorous and interesting assignments that ask them to think in a variety of ways and develop a variety of skills. Don't assume the kids from poor socio-economic families can't do analytic work, and don't assume kids from middle and upper class homes don't need to develop memorization skills.

Conceptual Toolbox

Class: A group of people who share similar social and economic relationships in a hierarchized society, and thus similar identities and experiences.

Class reproduction: The version of reproduction theory that investigates the ways that schools and other institutions serve to maintain the class divisions through a variety of hidden assumptions and practices, such as tracking.

Deficit approaches: Flawed ways of discussing students or others who don't succeed academically or economically by pointing out what the individuals lack. Deficit approaches may blame lower intelligence, cultural deprivation, cultural modes of behaving, or poverty, for example.

Meritocracy: A system of rewards based on hard work and talent; the idea that our position in the socio-economic system is natural and deserved; a flawed way of explaining academic achievement as rooted in individual merits of the student. To say "the U.S. is a meritocracy" means to say that most of the people who succeed do so because of their own ability, morality, and hard work.

Pathologizing: An effect of deficit thinking that suggests that those who don't succeed have some sort of disease or flaw, rather than trying to understand the behavior on its own terms. An example would be "pathologizing" a student who doesn't do homework as lazy, without knowing what their life outside of school is like.

Tracking: A school practice of dividing students, supposedly by ability, into different sequences of classes. Lower tracked classes usually have lower expectations, a less challenging curriculum, and less-qualified teachers.

Suggested Readings and Other Resources

Books and Essays

Anyon, J. (1989). Social class and the hidden curriculum of work. In J. Ballantine (Ed.), *Schools and society: A unified reader*. Mountain View, CA: Mayfield Publishing.

"Class Matters," a special section of the *The New York Times*, at www.nytimes.com/pages/national/class/index.html

DeMott, B. (1990). *The imperial middle: Why Americans can't think straight about class*. New York, NY: Morrow.

hooks, b. (2000). *Where we stand: Class matters*. New York, NY: Routledge.

Kozol, J. (1991). *Savage inequalities: Children in America's schools*. New York, NY: Harper Perennial.

Oakes, J. (2005). *Keeping track: How schools structure inequality*. New Haven, CT: Yale University Press.

Valencia, R. R. (1997). Conceptualizing the notion of deficit thinking. In R. Valencia (Ed.), *The evolution of deficit thinking: Educational thought and practice* (pp. 1–12). London: Falmer Press.

Films

Hayden, J. (1998). *Children in America's schools*. Columbia, SC: Carolina ETV Network.

Organizations and Links

National Center for Children in Poverty (www.nccp.org)
The nation's leading public policy center dedicated to promoting the economic security, health, and well-being of America's low-income families and children.

The National Center for Fair and Open Testing (www.fairtest.org)
Excellent materials on the problems with and effects of standardized testing.

Rethinking Schools (www.rethinkingschools.org)
Teacher-run publication that publishes a quarterly journal that includes many ways to teach about class, tracking, and social justice. Large archive of past articles.

Chapter 7

Learning Racism

An EcoJustice Approach to Racial Inequality

(Co-Authored by Gary Schnakenberg)

Introduction

In the last three chapters, we have been discussing some of the specific ways that a logic of domination manifests itself in our lives through our relationships and institutions. An EcoJustice framework helps us to understand the ways that value hierarchies insinuate themselves into our day-to-day interactions making notions of superiority and inferiority almost "second nature." This mindset or sensibility—even "common sense"—is created through a historically-embedded discursive system that leads to the exploitation of groups of people as well as the more-than-human world. As we've been saying, a logic of domination manifests itself in all sorts of ways; once we can begin to identify how it works, we can also decide to stop contributing to it.

In this chapter, we will explore how racism is also a result of this same complex system, unique and complex to be sure, but also a matter of using a value hierarchy as if it were natural and inevitable to control, exploit, and meet specific interests. We trace some of the ways race as a category gets created historically, the particular discursive practices that legitimated it, and how it functions in our day-to-day interactions and in institutions such as schools to maintain powerful systems of control and exploitation.

There has been a range of explanations for why racism exists. Probably the most simplistic explanation is that racism is expressed through stereotyping and limited understandings by "bad" or "ignorant" people who don't know better, or are just plain immoral. This point of view is tempting because it individualizes the problem, locating racism within specific people or their works, or "at an earlier time in our history," thus relieving ourselves of any responsibility. We find this limited understanding to be common within popular notions of racism.

Another, more complex, point of view defines racism as a product of our economic system and related social structures. Here, the idea is that the needs of a cheap source of labor in a capitalist system has led to the exploitation of certain groups of people, in particular people of African descent and other people of color, who receive unequal and unjust remuneration for their work as compared to whites. Justice, in this perspective, calls for a "politics of redistribution" wherein the resources being produced and opportunities offered in the system are fairly doled out.

A third important perspective on racism examines the ways people of color are defined as inferior within complex socio-cultural processes. In this point of view, the effects of deficit thinking play the most important role in constructing perceptions of inferiority, creating a racist society. All other issues, including those related to unfair distribution of resources and stereotyping, should be understood to grow from the ways cultural differences are represented. Resistance to this form of racism is referred to as a "politics of recognition," as people of color demand recognition and value of their cultures and full existential equality with those who are in positions of power.

Arguing against the false dichotomy that these two scholarly positions reflect, feminist philosopher Nancy Fraser (1997) proposes instead that issues related to unfair distribution of resources and issues related to cultural identities are inextricably woven together via the discursive practices of our culture. That is, cultural processes that define some people as superior and others inferior are used to rationalize a hierarchized economic and political system that allows some to accumulate more of the wealth and power. We find her position closely aligned with an EcoJustice analysis of race and racism, the primary difference being that EcoJustice Education includes the more-than-human world and the problem of anthropocentrism in its analysis of cultural violence.

Let's begin with a definition. In this chapter, we discuss "race" as a culturally created discursive category used for the express purpose of defining some people as biologically and culturally inferior to others. Race is a result of a specific manifestation of the logic of domination as it has been applied to particular human cultures. Or, in Val Plumwood's words (2002), it is a particular assertion of "centric thinking," where one group, believing and defining itself to be superior—and having the means to control the organization of knowledge through specific institutions like science, schooling, and the media—uses language to present a particular illusion that begins to function as truth. In the case of race, as in class and gender, it has been a very pernicious and destructive "truth."

Remember that we defined discourse as the creation, exchange, and internalization of specific meanings that are created using language, specifically metaphors. So, when we say that race is a discursive category, we mean that the discourse of racism begins by constructing certain definitions of people using and adding on to established age-old metaphors. Think back to Chapter 3 again, and the idea of hierarchized dualisms: culture/nature, reason/emotion, mind/body, civilized/savage. From the civilized/savage pairing we can uncover a few more root metaphors that have had particular power in the creation of race. For example, let's take light/dark. Which of these terms has more value? Which is associated with civilization and which with "barbarism?" Which with ignorance, and which with knowledge? Have you ever heard Africa described as the "Dark Continent?" Europeans gave the continent this name because (since they had no knowledge of it) they believed no knowledge of it existed. But what about the intimate knowledge of the landscape of interior Africa held by the Baluba, Kongo, Oromo, Dogon, Fulani, Maasai, Herero, and *thousands* of other peoples who dwelt there? What other meanings are created by the "Dark Continent" label? How is it positioned in relation to the concept of "Enlightenment?" And where did the so-called "Age of Enlightenment" originate, according to our history?

We are asking you to consider with us that language was used to first inferiorize whole groups of people whose skin and other physical features could be pointed to as signifiers (or proof) of their assumed natural inferiority. This inferiorization was then used to rationalize the brutal exploitation of them as they became defined as "less-than-human." Think, for example, about all the images in the history of North America that present native peoples as "savages." Along with millions of bison, the people who populated this continent were systematically "removed"—read, "killed"—nearly to extinction in the name of a self-proclaimed Manifest Destiny. How? They were defined as barbarians, less-than-human, and as barriers to taking possession of the land and its resources deemed necessary for empire building by the European colonizers: less-than-human, "like animals," and therefore not worthy of any sort of ethical consideration or equal respect.

But, wait a minute! What idea has to be firmly in place in order to define some people as inferior based on their supposed similarity to animals? Why should that comparison work to rationalize killing or enslaving them? A key idea in an EcoJustice analysis of race and racism is that as a culturally created, discursively based phenomenon and set of experiences, racism (and even more broadly ethnocentrism) rests firmly on a foundation of anthropocentrism. That is, as we discussed in Chapter 4, in a dualized system the meaning of "human" depends upon a related, oppositional category: "non-human" or "animal." These two categories exist in a hierarchized relationship, with humans given more value. Thus, in order to successfully inferiorize and subjugate a group of people based on their likeness to animals, we must first have a deeply entrenched belief that animals, and in fact all beings in the natural world, are inferior to humans. Racism rests on, and depends upon, anthropocentrism. In the sections that follow, we trace the history of the development of racism as a modern discourse, created and rationalized within a specific cultural, economic, and educational context.

Race as an Illusion Rooted in Racism as a Discourse

"Race" is a conceptual and discursive category that works to systematically classify human difference based on socially constructed meanings. Many researchers and popular news writers have repeatedly debunked the idea of race as a classifying system representing significant genetic characteristics common to groups—in other words, race has absolutely no genetic basis but rather is a social construct influenced by a set of discursive practices. Skin color is only that: skin color. The genes that determine skin color do not have any relationship to the genes that determine blood type, physical athletic ability, talent, or intelligence. This is a very different thing from saying that race is not "real," however. The concrete and material impacts and results of these discursive practices and this social construction on people's day-to-day lives are very real, sometimes reaching the levels of determining life and livelihood, if not life and death.

To be sure, differences and variation exist within humans (as well as among other species that inhabit the Earth). It is fairly safe to posit that most inhabitants of the West African country of Ghana would have some basic differences from most of the inhabitants of Norway, primarily skin and hair color. However, what do these differences really mean? While some mitochondrial DNA can indicate where our ancestors came from and can therefore be used to trace migrations they might have made, DNA cannot determine anyone's "race." According to the work done on the Human Genome Project (completed in 2003):

> DNA studies do not indicate that separate classifiable subspecies (races) exist within modern humans. While different genes for physical traits such as skin and hair color can be identified between individuals, no consistent patterns of genes across the human genome exist to distinguish one race from another. There also is no genetic basis for divisions of human ethnicity. People who have lived in the same geographic region for many generations may have some alleles [DNA sequences] in common, but no allele will be found in all members of one population and in no members of any other. Indeed, it has been proven that *there is more genetic variation within races than exists between them.*
> (U.S. Dept. of Energy Office of Science, 2007; emphasis added)

In other words, using our example of Ghanaians and Norwegians above, if you discount the characteristics that result from millennia of habitation in very different latitudes, the person from Ghana might show more genetic similarity in other ways to the Norwegian than she might to someone from Somalia!

Readers might well ask why the illusion of race is so persistent if it has no genetic underpinning. Discourse is a powerful thing! Let's look at some of the different elements that went into creating race.

Historical Emergence of Racism as a Discourse

Contrary to the opinion of many, dark-skinned African people were not always seen by Europeans as "naturally inferior" or "closer to animals" in ways that marked the discourses of racism with which we are so familiar. In fact, historical accounts exist of black African Moor soldiers and sailors in Viking sagas and early Spanish histories, and while mention is made of their appearance frightening their paler-skinned opponents, comment is also made regarding their courage, skill, and strength. No reference is made to their being "brutish," "savage," or any other derogatory quality—they were merely dark-complexioned opponents in battle. The *Cantigas de Santa Maria*, a 13th century Spanish manuscript of songs, shows in an illumination a pair of black Moorish nobles playing chess while being waited on by both white and black servants; another shows a black man as part of a group of nobility receiving gifts from a sultan (Brunson & Rashidi, 1992; DeCosta, 1974). European artists' depictions of Africans from the Renaissance often showed people who looked like dark versions of European nobility; frequently, exotic depictions of princely beings. These images were based on idealizations since most Europeans had never seen a black African, but our point here is that while perhaps not accurate or free from the projection of white imaginaries, the images did not portray the subject as inferiorized. This is a far cry from renditions of Africans from a few centuries later. The reason for this difference rests upon the paired experiences of colonization and slavery.

As nearly every American schoolchild has heard, late 1492 saw the arrival in the Caribbean of a Genoese sailor, in the service of the King and Queen of Spain, who had been trying to reach India and the Malay Archipelago. Christopher Columbus (or Cristóbal Colón; we will use the more familiar Anglicized-Latin version) landed on a small island in the present-day Bahamas, and subsequently reached the islands of Hispaniola and Jamaica, coming in contact with indigenous Arawak and Carib people along the way. Since he was a European steeped in Western discourses of science, Christianity, anthropocentrism, and centric thinking, Columbus's arrival in the Caribbean also meant the arrival of the seeds of American racism.

The story of Columbus and the basics of early Spanish colonization of the Caribbean islands and mainland are well-known elements of high school World History courses. Columbus's aim was to find passage to Asia in order to enable the Spanish Crown—which had only just expelled the Moors from Grenada, and finally controlled their entire territory—to undercut the monopoly on trade in luxury items controlled by the Levantine Arabs and the Italian city-states like Venice and Columbus's home of Genoa. Goods and commodities from the Malabar Coast of India, the islands of modern-day Indonesia, and from China's Silk Road had brought immeasurable wealth to Italian merchants and financiers, and the Spanish monarchy desired a share in that wealth to help consolidate control over their newly united territory. Of course, Columbus failed totally in his primary goal, but the Spanish monarchy succeeded in theirs by gaining access to the wealth of what was, for them, the "New World."

Race and the Conqueror Model

Value hierarchies shaped in a logic of domination common in Western culture created the framework and context in which Europeans saw the people with whom they came into contact and colonized. Starting in the Middle Ages, Europeans were familiar with the intellectual model of the "proper" ordering of the Universe, the "Great Chain of Being." This idea, as we introduced it to you in Chapter 4, developed early in the Common Era and was articulated by early medieval Church philosophers (remember, the only ones in Europe at the time with any formal learning), who ordered all things in a hierarchical relationship: God was at the top, followed by angels and saints, followed by human beings, then animals, then plants, then non-living elements of nature. Of course, there was a perceived "natural" hierarchy among humans as well: the Pope (as God's representative on Earth) and the clergy, then kings and nobility, then commoners of various types, and so on. It is no accident, by the way, that this idea was most strongly associated with the Church in the conflict-ridden early Middle Ages (prior to 1000 CE) as a way to assert its own power and control over rebellious rulers and nobles. It remained strongly influential, however, through the Renaissance and into the 1500s.

The European colonizers saw the cultures of people they colonized as they presumed them to be—and this presumption was a necessary part and parcel of the process of their colonization. Other cultures and people, especially those that did not wear clothing like Europeans, share the range of skin tones common among Europeans, eat similar foods, share marriage and family practices, follow similar or analogous religious rituals, etc., were simply not fully human. And, since "human" was at the top of the earthly pyramid, if one was not fully human, one was simultaneously (1) "lower" in the value hierarchy, and therefore (2) closer to animals. Steven Newcomb (2008), a Shawnee/Lenape and founder of the Indigenous Law Institute, uses the concept of a "conqueror model" to explain the mindset that enabled Europeans to frame the cultures of those native peoples of the land masses to the west of Europe as ripe for domination and colonization. The conqueror model relies on anthropocentrism to allow colonizers to justify mistreatment, enslavement, and often annihilation of the Indigenous Peoples living on the lands they wanted to claim. Along with the Great Chain of Being, Europeans carried with them discursive assumptions of nightmares of animals and wild uncivilized tribes, "demons" who dwelt in the "Wilderness" (defined Biblically as a "place apart" where Jesus strove against Satan), and then believed to have found exactly that when they came into contact with other cultures.

The role of Christianity and, in fact, the entire Judeo-Christian heritage of Western thought in the European conquest of the Americas cannot be underestimated. Not only was Man (the gender-specific term here is intentional) given "dominion over the Earth" by God in Genesis, but the covenants of the Old and New Testaments identified those who were God's "Chosen" and those who would be granted access to the Kingdom of Heaven. Although the covenant of the New Testament was rather more inclusive than the very rigid, ethnically-based one of the Pentateuch, it still maintained that only those who accepted the tenets of the "True Faith" could gain salvation and avoid consignment to the fires of eternal damnation. And, according to this thinking, if one did not willingly come to this Truth, it was evidence of one's wickedness and perhaps alliance with the Devil.

Such notions may seem overly simplistic today, but in Columbus's time (and for centuries afterward) they were as real and true to Westerners as the notion of the Earth traveling around the Sun is to us. In fact, these ideas established a discursive and legal framework that created a set of material realities that in turn determined the outcomes of the lives of millions of indigenous inhabitants of the Americas.

As mentioned above, Columbus sailed west financed by, and on behalf of, the Spanish monarchy. Upon his return to Spain after reaching these "new lands" and claiming them for Spain, Pope Alexander VI issued a series of bulls which granted to the monarchs and their descendants "all of the islands and mainlands . . . discovered or to be discovered to the west and south . . . provided that none . . . be in the actual possession of any Christian king or prince . . ." (Davenport, 1917, cited in Newcomb, 2008, pp. 83–84). In other words, the fact that Indigenous People of the Americas were not Christian was justification for their conquest and domination (it should be noted as well that Pope Alexander VI was a Spaniard). Forty-one years earlier, the King of Portugal had requested papal authority to make claims along the coast of West Africa, and Pope Nicholas V complied, giving Portugal the right to "invade, capture, vanquish, and subdue all Saracens [Muslims], pagans, and other enemies of Christ, to put them in perpetual slavery, and to take away all their possessions and property" (Davenport, 1917, cited in Newcomb, 2008, p. 84). The "Voyages of Discovery" valorized in many textbooks were undertaken with the goal of the conquest and subjugation of newly discovered lands, which were sought for that very purpose. It would be good if we could shake our heads sadly and wonder at the attitudes of the era, but Newcomb points out that these papal decrees have continued to serve as the basis for policies and decisions regarding indigenous land rights all the way to our current era! We will return to that topic a little later in the chapter.

Though Columbus did not create slavery, he brought it and the slave trade to the Americas. Upon seeing the native inhabitants of the islands for the first time, he wrote in his journal about their friendly and peaceable nature, but also that they could be trained to "make good and skilled servants for us" (Fuson, 1992). Columbus sought to discover in the Caribbean the wealth he had set out to find in the (East) Indies, but obviously needed to change the approach to accessing it. Without the lucrative spices and trade in other luxury goods that so enriched merchants and bankers in the Levant and the Italian Peninsula, the natural resources of the new discoveries would have to provide the means to this wealth. Although encouraged by the sight of small amounts of gold decorations on some of the native Arawak inhabitants—and despite enslaving native people to gather it from rivers and streams, the only sources of gold in the Caribbean; no gold 'mines' exist in the islands—the region never proved to be a source of gold or silver in any significant amount.

The native inhabitants Columbus enslaved were both sent to Spain to be sold and put to work in the island colonies, but they proved to be an "inefficient" source of labor. Some, especially on the larger islands like Hispaniola and Jamaica, were able to run away to the inaccessible interior; a great many more simply died from diseases, living conditions, or from being hunted, "punished" for failure to meet quotas, or being otherwise murdered (coincidentally, the ecological systems of the Caribbean and later the American mainland were severely disrupted by the arrival of rodents, livestock, and exotic plant species from Europe). In addition, some contemporary writers reported mass suicides by people who would rather die than endure continued life as slaves. Within 50 years of Columbus's arrival, the native cultures of the Caribbean islands' peoples were extinct—whether the Arawak people themselves became fully extinct is another issue, with many historians believing that elements of native culture survived in isolated pockets and blended with later runaway Africans in several areas to create a syncretic "Maroon" culture. Especially after Columbus brought sugar cane plantings to the Caribbean on his second voyage (he had been trained in the nascent sugar industry in the Madeira Islands as a young man), a large supply of labor became of paramount importance in creating the basis for wealth to export to Europe.

Slavery had existed in the Iberian Peninsula since the times of the Roman Empire, but on a very small scale for most of its history. The papal decrees mentioned above had given Portuguese raiders the Church's blessing to enslave "infidels and heathens" in their explorations along the African coast, which provided opportunities to take slaves in greater numbers. Slavery of Africans had other sources, as well. On the east coast of Africa, the Arab slave trade from Africa to Arabia, from ports such as Dar Es Salaam, Mombasa, and Zanzibar, are well documented. Slavery also existed among African groups, with people becoming slaves through defeat in battle, debt, or as a type of relationship to seal alliances or treaties with other groups.[1] However, this type of slavery was far different from its counterpart in the transatlantic slave trade. In the typical intra-African slave practice, individual slaves were in that condition for specific purposes, and often they were slaves for a specified period of time, not for life. Sometimes slaves could become adopted by the village with whom they were bonded or by specific families. Even if former slaves might be barred from the highest levels of status in a group, they could become full-fledged members of that group, marry, and enjoy all rights and obligations.

In the European slave trade that brought somewhere between 20 million and several hundred million kidnapped Africans to the Americas as chattel, the factor that made them slaves was their skin color. Nothing else about them mattered. Not surprisingly, the practice of the slave trade, in which hundreds of black people at a time were marched in chains, held in coastal forts, and crammed like cargo into ship holds increased a sense of superiority among whites involved and reinforced the discourses of inferiority that were already in place.

We cannot leave this topic without noting two potentially controversial points. The first is to acknowledge that we have not fully examined the horror of the African slave trade in the context of this chapter. This is not meant to minimize that horror or to somehow skirt the way that the prosperity of the American colonies and later the independent United States was built upon an economic foundation provided by slaves; it is merely that this topic would take us in a different direction and take far longer than we intend within this book. Interested readers can easily find research and commentary on this topic, and we encourage you to do so.

The second is to note that not only did Africans have slavery in their own societies, but also participated in the trade with Europeans.[2] The earliest European raids kidnapped black Africans directly and brought them to the ships, but this practice was soon abandoned and slaves were bought from African leaders and rulers who raided other groups in the interior and were paid in metals, jewelry, and especially firearms. This fact is lamented in accounts of several former slaves who wrote after obtaining freedom of their kidnap and betrayal by those of their "own complexion" (Tunde, 2000). A king in Dahomey (modern Benin) wrote to a British governor that, while they did not sell their own people to slavers, "we do indeed sell to the white men a part of our prisoners and we have a right so to do. Are not all prisoners at the disposal of their captors? And are we to blame if we send delinquents to a far country? I have been told you do the same" (quoted in Anquandah, 1999, p. 104). Nigerian writer Wole Soyinka, 1986 Nobel Laureate in Literature, has said in interviews that healing from the deep and profound wounds of slavery requires that Africans acknowledge this fact, a sentiment echoed by African American scholar Kwaku Person-Lynn (2006). However, this point should not be used to bypass, minimize, or excuse the role of Europeans, because they created the situation and set the rules of this cruel and racist institution, which should be correctly classified as "genocide." Rather than being the result of defeat, or bad luck, or a failed crop, the enslavement of black Africans in the European transatlantic slave trade resulted from a set of overlapping discourses based on value hierarchies and a mindset of domination. Further, as King Sugar in the Caribbean, and later King Cotton in the American South made certain members of the planter classes rich, the naturalized inferiorization of those whose skins happened to produce more melanin than Europeans was increasingly supported by an emerging discourse of science.

Science and Race

As the 18th century progressed and Europeans became more aware of people in faraway areas of the world, men of science (for it was almost entirely men who engaged in this pursuit) began to turn their attention more and more to issues of human differences. The term "race" started to be applied in a more specific way than had previously been the case. The word in English meaning 'people of common descent' came into use around 1500 from the Middle French term "razza" (probably adopted from Italian), denoting a particular lineage or breed, but in usage throughout 16th and 17th century English this meaning was broad enough to include meanings as diverse as wines with a characteristic flavor, a generation, a group of people with the same occupation, or a tribe/nation. By the end of the 18th century, it had come to be applied as a classification system of human characteristics based on coloration, but that included elements of group character, intelligence, "refinement," and other more esoteric qualities. Around the time of the American and French Revolutions, it had acquired its modern definition as "one of the major biological [sic] divisions of mankind, distinguished by color and texture of hair, color of skin and eyes, stature, bodily proportions, etc." (*Webster's Unabridged Dictionary*, 1983). In large part, the acceptance of this specific usage reflected the work of science and scientists.

Earlier, we made the connection between the so-called "exploration" and "Voyages of Discovery" undertaken by Europeans and the goal of conquest and domination. Science played a role in this by producing knowledge about far distant places, their flora and fauna, and people. By becoming "known," lands distant from Europe and their human and non-human inhabitants were placed in inferior positions. This is one of many ways that "knowledge is power." Science helped make the "Wilderness" predictable through knowing about it in advance (Latour, 1987). Sea voyages included "naturalists" whose job it was to collect specimens of plants and animals (occasionally human remains, and, as we shall see, humans) that were brought back home where they were studied. In this way, European collectors, be they institutions or wealthy individuals, already "owned" bits and pieces of the world far away from them, and constructed their knowledge about it not in its own context and on its own terms, but in their particular European context. The living things that inhabited specific biomes around the globe and the knowledge surrounding them became commodified through this process of collection.

Taxonomic Classification

Going back at least to the time of Aristotle, taxonomy, or the science of classification, was an important aspect of scientific activity. During the 18th and early 19th centuries, this taxonomic craze intensified as more and more species were "discovered" and scientists had to figure out where they fit in the hierarchical schemes they had invented—which, naturally, grew out of their sense of the world created by the discourses in which they had been steeped. The world and all its living organisms presents a scientific project of staggering complexity, so, to a great degree, the classification system created to organize knowledge and how to "correctly" think about it became a project of simplification, of making it "legible" by imposing a structure that made sense. But "made sense" to whom, and for what purpose?

The classification system based on a ranked hierarchy still in use for the animal kingdom—and, in fact, the designation of an "animal kingdom" itself—was developed in the mid-1700s by a Swedish botanist known by his Latinized name of Carolus Linnaeus (Carl von Linne in Swedish; English speakers would call him "Carl Lind" if he was alive today). As discussed in Chapter 4, anyone who has completed high school biology is at least somewhat familiar with the Kingdom/Class/Order/Genus/Species organizational structure developed by Linnaeus, as well as his "scientific" two-part naming system (such as Homo sapiens, or Pinus strobus for the Eastern White Pine). These names represent very well the power of discourse, since species known to and used by Indigenous People for millennia do not "exist" in the scientific sense until they have been designated with the proper Linnean name and placed properly in the taxonomy.

By itself, there is nothing inherently "bad" about classifying. It is a process of answering the question, "what other things is this like?" and is part of how people make sense of the world (think back to Chapter 3 and our discussion of Bateson's notion of the "map" and the territory). Indigenous People themselves classified groups of plants and animals in ways that made sense to them and their lives—for example, sometimes classifying by their uses, other times in kinship relations to humans. Linnaeus used a system of structural and functional similarity to group living things together. He deserves credit for breaking the "Great Chain of Being" and categorizing humans biologically along with other animals, for which he was criticized by some. However, two points stand out. First, the Linnean taxonomy, like other "systems," is based on a mechanistic concept of nature. As we mentioned in Chapter 3, mechanism takes apart a whole and views it as the sum of the functions of its various parts. This mechanistic conception has had serious negative consequences for the more-than-human world, as well as for humans. Second, through the power of scientific discourse, one and only one classification system came to be seen as "the valid one"; all other schemes and names became backgrounded and subsumed, made inferior, to a particular take on what constituted "knowledge" or "truth." The Linnean system, based on form and structure, would come to play a major role in how "race" was considered and studied through the rest of the 18th century and beyond. As humans "functioned" in terms of their organs and physical systems pretty much identically, it was form and structure that captured the imaginations of many European scientists. "Imagination" is perhaps the most operative word.

In order to not be misled by what was visible at the surface—that is to say, skin color and hair texture—scientists had to undertake analyses that went beyond superficial appearance. Many of these investigators used comparative anatomy as a way to identify and analyze variation in human form and structure. Since there were no X-rays, MRIs, or CAT scans in the 18th and early 19th centuries, the way to do this was through the examination of human beings, or human remains. In a logical assumption, the nervous system was thought the best indicator of complexity, and therefore the skull as receptacle of the brain—the most complex part of the most complex system—was thought to be the best human anatomical variable that could be observed. One of the most important figures in the history of racial classification, Johann Friedrich Blumenbach, had a collection of nearly 250 human skulls.

Following Linnaeus, Blumenbach originally identified four subgroups of humans based on (unranked) geographic origin (see Figure 7.1): "Caucasian" (European, or "white"), "Ethiopian" (African, or "black"), "Mongolian" (Asian, or "yellow"), and (Native) "American" (or "red"). After the voyages of Captain James Cook in the late 1770s in the South Pacific, the "Malay" ("brown") group was added. Also like Linnaeus, Blumenbach emphasized the unity as well as mental and moral equality of all humans and was emphatic about the equality of Africans and Europeans (Gould, 1996). He was an opponent of slavery. He noted that some parts of bodies, even those of Europeans, were darker than others and that exposure to sun caused changes in complexion from summer to winter (Painter, 2003).

Yet, despite all of this, and even acknowledging that perceptions of beauty lay in the eyes of the beholder, Blumenbach created a hierarchical schema based on perceptions of "beauty." This schema placed the skull of the Caucasian in the position of "best" and moved away in both directions to the "farthest removed" African and Asian examples with "Malay" and "American" representing respective intermediary positions. It was Blumenbach who first used the term "Caucasian" in reference to whites, based on the "beauty" of the people of the Georgian region of the Caucasus Mountains. Thus, as the late American paleobiologist Stephen Jay Gould pointed out, it is ironic that this least racist of Enlightenment-era writers on the subject switched from an unranked classification based on geography to a double-ranked hierarchy—but was still "caught in his culture's surrounding preferences for linear hierarchies" (Gould, 1998, p. 504).

Further evidence of this fascination with skull shape and size is part of one of the most tragic and fascinating stories about the construction of race by European scientists. Born eight years prior to Blumenbach's publication of the first edition of his work, Georges Cuvier (1769–1832) became chair of animal anatomy at the Museum of Natural History in

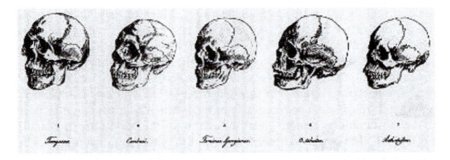

Figure 7.1 Blumenbach's "Five Races." In Blumenbach's classification scheme, the white, or "Caucasian," skull is in the center due to its designation as "most beautiful." The others move away in a double hierarchy, with the "American" and "Malay" skulls in intermediate positions between the "least beautiful" "Mongolian" (left) and "Ethiopian" (right) examples.

Source: This illustration appeared in Blumenbach's 1798 *Über die natürlichen Verschiedenheiteinm Menschengeschlechte [On the Natural Varieties of Humankind]*. Leipzig: Breitkopf & Härtel.

Paris around 1800. He also believed in the importance of the study of skulls as key to understanding variation among humans and other animals. Facial and cranial structures gave insight, it was believed, into the size and shape of the brain. Working in the time he did after Napoleon's invasion of Egypt, Cuvier was able to utilize mummies of both humans and animals in his studies, and instructed travelers to acquire bodies after battles between "savages," giving guidelines for getting clean bones and skulls (Fausto-Sterling, 2001).

In 1814, a woman from the Cape Colony of southern Africa arrived in Paris, known by the Dutch name given to her by a Boer family for whom she had been a servant. Saartje (or Sarah) Baartman was most likely descended from the Khoikhoi, a herding people from far southern Africa related to the San, or "Bushmen," although these were hunter/ gatherers. Because of the clicking sounds prominent in their language, the Dutch East India Company employees who set up the first colony there called them "Hottentots," mimicking what they heard as the "babbling" of the Khoikhoi language. Baartman had come to London around 1810 and had been exhibited at shows in Piccadilly Circus and around England as a curiosity, appearing first to audiences in a cage and then walking around the stage platform. After coming to Paris, also as part of a public exhibition, she was examined by a panel of scientists that included Cuvier at a scientific institution early in 1815. After her death in December of that year (at the approximate age of 30), Cuvier received permission (from French authorities, not from anyone linked to Baartman herself) to dissect her cadaver. These "objective and scientific" investigations offer insight into the manner in which race and gender were constructed by white males, and perhaps reveal more about the researchers than they do about the supposed subjects of their study.

Fausto-Sterling (2001) wrote that Baartman's head and facial features were examined closely for the purpose of comparison: to see where she fit in relation to "the lowest race of humans, the Negro race, and the highest race of monkeys, the orangutan," according to a publication by Henri de Blainville in 1816. His report linked "Hottentots" more closely to orangutans than to "Negroes." At the same time, as a woman, Baartman fell into a common scientific framework of the period that linked human females with apes (according to Fausto-Sterling, males were differentiated from other primates by invoking language, culture, intellect; females were differentiated by comparing sexual anatomy). Here we see a double inferiorization of Saartje Baartman through her association with nature and "lower" animals.

Again, interesting contradictions abound. Cuvier was also opposed to slavery, and believed that all humans were descended from a single creation; some other scientists of the time believed that different "races" were actually separate species. Again, according to Fausto-Sterling, as an expert in anatomy Cuvier represents a change from earlier ideas about geographic origin or degrees of "civilization" to a biologically-based, scientific analysis and construction of race. An important point she raises that we easily forget when examining this history from our vantage point is that Linnaeus, Blumenbach, Cuvier, de Blainville, and their various contemporaries did not believe that organisms evolved into new ones. They all predate the theories of evolution advanced by Darwin and Wallace in the mid-19th century. Instead of the Darwinian view that traced differentiation among species by looking "upward" from lesser to greater complexity and from earlier to more recent, Cuvier and others who emphasized skulls and the human brain and nervous system started with humans at the "top" and classified all other animals "downward" from this. Rather than discovering some underlying "natural" organizational system, they projected their own self-serving anthropocentric (and androcentric) conceptions onto others' bodies. Those subject to the effects of this projection had no voice in the matter. What Fausto-Sterling (2001) stated regarding Saartje Baartman could be applied to all victims of such "scientific" constructions of race: "Baartman's bodily differences were constructed using the social and scientific paradigms available at the time. The historical record tells us nothing about her agency, and we can only know how Europeans framed and read her" (p. 360).

Charles Darwin and the Advent of "Social Darwinism"

The publication in 1859 of Charles Darwin's *On the Origin of Species* was a watershed moment in human intellectual history. Many writers in numerous fields have addressed Darwin and this work, as well as Alfred Russell Wallace's independent development of essentially the same idea, so Darwin's story and that of this work will not be related here. Suffice to say that few works have been "quoted" so frequently and read so seldom. In its 500 or so pages, Darwin barely mentions humans (or apes, for that matter). However, the appearance of *On the Origin of Species* had a significant impact on thinking about race that continues in some quarters to the present day.

The first effect was that ideas of the polygenists—those who believed that races were actually separate species—were discredited, and largely faded from mainstream view. Rather than separate Divine origin, evolution by natural selection meant that human difference occurred over time as a result of random mutations that better enabled some organisms to survive in their particular environment. Not all mutations did this; some caused species to become extinct. There is no way to predict what will be beneficial or not, or what mutations will appear. Nonetheless, many applied the theory to develop a notion of linear "progress" that became an important element of discourses on race. Just as Cuvier and others began their examinations of human difference from a position of the superiority of the "Caucasian" male, this idea of "progress" began from the position that Europeans and European society were the standards against which all others were measured.

Because the phrase is so well-known, some readers may be surprised to know that Darwin never wrote "survival of the fittest." This term was coined by British philosopher Herbert Spencer (who, incidentally, also first used the term "evolution") in applying Darwin's ideas to topics he himself did not address. The "survival of the fittest" concept had several effects. First, it naturalized competition as part of a "struggle for existence." In the process, it detoured from Darwin's ideas: organisms do not consciously "struggle" in this way; they do not know if a mutation has taken place that may require millennia to become widespread in their species. They are simply born, live, and die, and pass on whatever was in their genes. This idea of competition grew out of and had more application to the burgeoning industrialization and class divisions that were occurring in Britain than it did to Darwin's idea of natural selection. A second and related effect was to justify genocide and colonization (the dash to carve up Africa culminated in the Berlin Conference of 1884, when Europeans sat around tables and drew lines on maps to delimit "their" possessions; the "taming" of the American West took place at the same time), and to undermine any suggestion of social welfare for the poor in Europe. That people were not as well off as those (whites) with the most resources was taken as evidence that they were not as "fit," nor deserving. This Social Darwinism helped define as "natural" the hierarchy of races that had been constructed and classified through the discourses of science.

Eugenics

The influence of Social Darwinism and its attendant scientific gloss was responsible for the creation of the "eugenics" movement in the late 19th century. The term means "good genes" and was first used in 1883 by Francis Galton, a cousin of Charles Darwin. Galton and other eugenicists wanted to show that all human cultural and behavioral difference was hereditary, and therefore they supported selective breeding to improve humanity by reducing the "corrupting influences" of "inferior races." The Great Columbian World Exposition, better known as the Chicago World's Fair in 1893 (named to commemorate the 400th anniversary of Columbus's landing) and the St. Louis World's Fair of 1904 (commemorating the centennial of the Louisiana Purchase) both had eugenics exhibits. The St. Louis Fair had "living dioramas" of Indigenous People from around the world in their "natural habitats," putting on public display the hierarchical sweep of human "progress." Eugenics (and therefore racism) reached into American popular culture quite deeply. County fairs throughout the United States had "Fit Families" competitions (readers can probably guess quite easily what winners of these looked like), and F. Scott Fitzgerald has Tom Buchanan talk approvingly about the ideas of a eugenicist in *The Great Gatsby* (though, it must be said, Fitzgerald does this to say something dislikeable about Tom's character). Common high school textbooks contained what strike us today as shockingly crude examples of racism, and had titles like William Atwood's (1922) *Civic and Economic Biology*. Eugenics lost a great deal of steam after its association with and popularity in Germany during the Nazi era, and has since moved to the fringes of discussions on race, but the focus on measurement and quantification that made it seem "scientific" and therefore true due to prevailing discourses remained alive and well. The emphasis on quantification in social science and the emergence of "race science" appeared at the same time and developed together (Carter, 2009).

As mentioned above, the "survival of the fittest" orientation of Social Darwinism contributed to the naturalization of competition that was at the base of industrial capitalism. By the time *The Great Gatsby* and Atwood's biology textbook were published, this orientation had become part and parcel of the American education system. Schools were built and organized on a "factory" assembly line model, with standardized tasks and students sitting in straight rows under the supervision of a teacher/manager. Performance was quantified in report cards. Individual students were hierarchized by their performance, and there was the practice of "tracking" organized groups of students by "ability levels" (as discussed in Chapter 6). Migrations of African Americans from the southern United States to other regions and the arrival of immigrants complicated matters. In a move that would have certainly been familiar to Saartje Baartman, schools had to find a way to measure student ability "objectively," based on scientific principles, to determine where children should be placed in the hierarchy. Rather than facial-cranial examination (though in the early 20th century these had not disappeared), school systems turned to the newly-developed IQ test (see Chapter 6 and later in this chapter for more on this).

Race and Europeans

Ideas of racial classification were not limited to those groups we now identify as "people of color." Early 20th century geographer Ellsworth Huntington (1912) referred to "Scandinavians" as a race (p. 259). In the decades before the Civil War, Irish in America were considered a "lower race" and described in derogatory language remarkably similar to that aimed at blacks, often because both were involved in similar kinds of jobs. As Takaki describes:

During the mid-nineteenth century, anti-Irish stereotypes emphasized nature over nurture and descent. The Irish were imaged as apelike and "a race of savages," at the same level of intelligence as blacks. Pursuing the "lower" rather than the "higher" pleasures, seeking "vicious excitement" and "gratifications merely animal," the Irish were said to be "slaves" of "passions."

(Takaki, 1993, p. 149)

As other European whites immigrated to the U.S., similar attitudes were displayed—well into the 20th century. In his book *Dreaming up America*, writer Russell Banks discusses how this played out in his own boyhood:

When I was growing up in the 1950s and 60s, my father and other Anglo American men of his generation used to refer to Italians as "Guineas." I never knew what a Guinea was until I was an adult and saw that it was a nineteenth-century word for Africa, and thus for Africans. What that means to me is that as recently as the 1950s, Italians and other Mediterraneans were seen as racially different from us white folks.

(Banks, 2008, p. 32)

Johnny and Rebecca both have memories of the same sort of pejoratives being used, albeit in very different contexts. Johnny, growing up Italian in Detroit, recalls being taught to defend the family honor against such slurs. For Rebecca, one of her parents' best friends was Italian, and "affectionately" referred to in the community as "that Guinea Wop!"

While this sort of hold-over name-calling remains to this day, generally, over time and through various means, these and other Europeans were able to gain the status and privilege of being "white" (Allen, 1994).

In his provocatively titled book *How the Irish Became White*, Ignatiev shows the process by which the Irish were able to move from being seen as comparable to blacks to being seen as different: "To enter the white race was a strategy to secure an advantage in a competitive society" (Ignatiev, 1995, p. 2). The Irish, Ignatiev shows, took advantage of the existing color line in the U.S. to cooperate in pushing free blacks out of jobs such as construction and delivery.

To be acknowledged as white, it was not enough for the Irish to have a competitive advantage in the labor market; in order for them to avoid the taint of blackness it was necessary that no Negro be allowed to work in occupations where Irish were to be found.

(Ignatiev, 1995, p. 112)

Once again, we see that race and racial differences are an illusion, constructed out of the struggles of people within a hierarchical system that allows only a few to be on top.

We have explored the discursive foundations of racism at some length in order to highlight how a logic of domination has shaped many areas of modern thought—even those areas we tend to think about as objective and beneficial, such as science. Further, other modernist discourses—anthropocentrism, mechanism, and "progress," for example—were woven through the scientific and Christian doctrines that came to rationalize colonization, slavery, and genocide. The Enlightenment replaced conceptions of "Divine Will" with notions of "Reason" and "Free Will" as essential human characteristics. However, it severely limited who was to be identified as fully human; that is, having the capacity for the power of rationality, and thus freedom. Enlightenment thinkers and their inheritors merely shifted power from priests and kings to themselves. Racism became a naturalized meaning system used to rationalize a set of Eurocentric economic, political, and cultural interests that also has critical ecological consequences, as we have discussed in previous chapters and will continue to explore below. Educational institutions became part of an organized system used to keep a logic of domination serving particular social and economic interests.

Racism and the History of Education

This section will take a brief but distinctive look at the history of education as it has been affected by racist discourse. We'll look specifically at examples from the experiences of African Americans, Indigenous Peoples, Latino or Hispanic peoples, and East Asian Americans. These examples do not mean to exclude the experiences of other marginalized groups—it is part of the nature of the discourse of race that it is expressed toward any group that is outside the center defined by the dominant culture. In addition, some more contemporary manifestations of racism will be discussed later in the chapter.

African Americans

Education for slaves is a complex story. In colonial times, some degree of literacy was encouraged for slaves, as it contributed to their acceptance of Christianity. However, many Southern states banned writing for slaves, for fear it would be used for communication for resistance. And, after the slave revolt of 1831 (led by Nat Turner), Southern states often prohibited teaching slaves to read. After all, reading not only enabled communication, it encouraged reflection and thought.

The abolition of slavery did not end anti-education policies for African Americans. Southern whites enforced the policy of segregation, technically meaning that whites and blacks were separated in many institutions—separate schools, buses, restaurants, even bathrooms—but in fact meaning that there was vicious discrimination against black people.

Thus, African Americans were forced to establish and fund their own community schools. Despite segregation, the question of what the purpose of education ought to be for African Americans sparked a debate within the black community, and they chose a variety of ways to respond. Some backed the approach of Booker T. Washington (1856–1915), who believed that blacks should focus on learning useful industrial and commercial skills and become necessary to the white economy. To this end, he helped found Tuskegee Institute (1881) and many other similar institutions which trained black people in a wide variety of vocational skills. Black nationalist Marcus Garvey (1887–1940) led another approach, arguing that blacks across the world should unite and ultimately create a separate black-ruled country of their own, which was usually understood to mean on the continent of Africa. Harvard-educated W. E. B. DuBois (1868–1963), who helped found the National Association for the Advancement of Colored People (NAACP), took a third approach, advocating civil rights for blacks, and challenging the laws of segregation. Directly confronting the position that blacks were intellectually inferior to whites, DuBois argued that his people were just as capable of pursuing advanced study, and furthermore had the right to equal opportunity in education at all levels. Such pursuit, he insisted, was the only way for blacks to gain entry into white-dominated economic and social spheres.

No matter which position was taken, education was highly valued in African American communities, as it was for their white counterparts. School-related activities were often considered the core of community life. Black schools in the South suffered from underfunding since no tax money from white taxpayers was spent to educate black children. In spite of this inequality, however, many of the schools attended by black children were as good (and some better) than their all-white counterparts. Many Southern black teachers were educated in the best teacher education institutions in the North—University of Wisconsin-Madison, University of Chicago, and Teachers College—but were prohibited from teaching in white schools (Ladson-Billings, 2004), a fact that is often overlooked when considering the history of segregation. As historian Vanessa Siddle-Walker (1996) wrote:

> It is true that these schools were often treated unjustly and victimized by poor resources. But, in spite of legalized oppression, many teachers and principals created environments of teaching and learning that motivated students to excel. They countered the larger societal messages, which devalued African Americans, and reframed those messages to make African American children believe in their ability to achieve. This belief—that even under the oppression of segregation students, teachers, and principals could push to reach their highest potential—is the central message of segregated schooling.
>
> (Siddle-Walker, 1996, p. 219)

In short, as legal scholar Charles Lawrence (1980) argues, the problem of segregation was not that black children attended black schools taught by black teachers, it was that segregation reinforced a pervasive discursive and legal system that defined African Americans and their community as inherently inferior. As we've been discussing throughout this book, and as Gloria Ladson-Billings (2004) so clearly articulated, "Issues of race and racism permeate U.S. culture—through law, language, politics, economics, symbols, art, public policy—and the prevalence of race is not merely in those spaces seen as racially defined spaces" (p. 5).

While the legal structure of segregation in the South drew the most attention, the discourse of racism and the practice of segregation was alive and well in the North as well. Many southern African Americans (and whites) migrated to the North looking for work during WWII. They went to New York, Detroit, Chicago, and other urban centers where war manufacturing held the promise of jobs, swelling the cities. As a result of discriminatory housing and employment policies, African Americans were often pushed into the lowest-quality housing, and given the lowest-paying and most dangerous jobs. A discriminatory practice called "redlining" by banks and real estate companies prevented black families from moving into white neighborhoods. When a black family succeeded in attaining housing in areas dominated by whites, there were often violent consequences; white residents organized, black homes were vandalized, and the family members were accosted (Sugrue, 2005). Consequently, as in the South, Northern schools too became deeply segregated, not by law, but by where people were allowed to live.

In 1954, the NAACP brought segregated education into the national spotlight through the well-known Supreme Court case, *Brown v. Board of Education*. Patiently waiting for the right case, chief NAACP lawyer Thurgood Marshall found the example of Linda Brown, one of several black children kept in segregated schools by the Topeka Board of Education. Marshall offered a wide range of evidence to the Supreme Court regarding the inequality of segregation, and in 1954 the Court found in Brown's favor, overruling the 1894 case of *Plessy v. Ferguson* (from which came the claim that separate facilities, such as schools, were permissible if they were "equal") and insisting that "separate educational facilities are inherently unequal."

Southern whites, of course, were dedicated to the discourse of racism and resisted the ruling. It took many years of legal effort for schools to be even partially integrated. In the end, the federal government withheld funding to any state that did not comply with the mandate to desegregate. But the *Brown* decision certainly helped encourage many other struggles against segregation and racism. Collectively known as the Civil Rights Movement, young people held "sit-ins" in segregated lunch counters and organized bus boycotts; marchers walked for voting rights and registered blacks to vote, often at the risk of their lives and jobs.

In the North, in cities like Detroit, whites simply left the city for the newly developing suburbs, causing "defacto" segregation of the schools, or segregation by private decisions rather than by law. "White flight," along with decisions by the automobile industry to relocate many of its plants, caused Detroit's tax base to decline, leaving the school system and other municipal services in a shambles. Policy-makers, who had done little to help with the disparities in housing in earlier decades, now found that the schools could not be properly funded.

In 1974, another important lawsuit—*Milliken v. Bradley*—was filed against the Governor of Michigan. The suit charged "that the Detroit, Michigan, public school system was racially segregated as a result of official policies." A district court reviewed the case, finding that the system was in fact segregated, and ordered the adoption of a plan that would desegregate outlying school districts (U.S. Supreme Court Oyez; retrieved on July 24, 2010 from www.oyez.org/cases/1970-1979/1973/1973_73_434). The case was appealed, but in a 5–4 decision the Supreme Court ruled that there was "no showing of significant violation by the 53 outlying school districts," thus affirming defacto segregation and dooming the Detroit school children and others in urban centers like it to inadequate education.

Brown v. Board of Education ended the formal legal structure of segregation and helped to affirm the Civil Rights Movement. Certain kinds of progress have been made with the help of these political actions, including the election of thousands of black officials in Southern states where none had been elected in decades. But there have also been important questions raised on the part of some African American scholars about the actual outcomes of desegregation for the African American community. Their critique has opened debate over the wisdom of what some call the "assimilationist strategy" of the Civil Rights movement. Gaining access to educational and economic opportunities gave some blacks more status and buying power within consumer culture, but left those who were impoverished behind and fragmented the African American community. While segregation resulted in systematic inferiorization, as we have pointed out, it also forced the creation of important social bonds among the people based on strong values of mutuality and interdependence. Desegregation opened the doors to competition and individualism—every man for himself—creating an important double bind in the African American experience. Any situation denying people the right to decent housing, satisfying work, and a good education should, of course, be challenged, as this movement did. Yet, the real problem—a culture steeped in naturalized "supremacy" and hierarchy—was not necessarily challenged. And, as Cornel West (1993) has argued, the political demand for access, while important in terms of challenging the bonds of poverty, also inadvertently denied the differences inherent to African American culture:

> These courageous yet limited black efforts to combat racist cultural practices uncritically accepted non-black conventions and standards in two ways. First, they proceeded in an assimilationist manner that set out to show that black people were really like white people, thereby eliding differences (cultural, historical) between whites and blacks . . . Second, these black responses rested upon a homogenizing impulse that assumed that all black people were really alike—hence obliterating differences (class, gender, region, sexual orientation) between black peoples.
>
> (West, 1993, p. 17)

Ironically, by demanding opportunities to compete within a white Eurocentric system, blacks (and other dominated groups who followed this strategy) reinforced the very logic of domination defining them as inferior. And as we shall see in the examination of current conditions in schools, the failure to challenge that underlying problem has led to other over-simplified analyses of inequality and education.

Indigenous Peoples

Many people associate the term "genocide" with the Nazi Holocaust or with the mass murders in Rwanda, but don't associate it with Indigenous People who lived in North America.[3] Yet the genocide of Indigenous Peoples was far larger, if spread over a longer period of time. It also took a variety of forms, from direct murder to the control and destruction of the sources of their livelihoods, the spread of disease, and, in addition, the use of schooling to destroy Indigenous culture.

From missionary schools to government-run reservation schools, education had long been a tool for incorporating Indigenous Peoples into the dominant culture. In the late 1800s, the boarding school became the favored approach for dealing with the "Indian problem." Children from native tribes were taken away from their families, put on trains, and sent far away for months or years at a time so they could be completely surrounded by white culture. If the native families didn't want to send their children away, they were threatened with loss of food rations and other support.

Once safely away from tribal influence, the students were not allowed to practice their tribal customs or speak their native languages (Ramsey, 2010). They were forced to cut their hair, wear the clothing of white culture (the boys had to wear military uniforms of the very men who had slaughtered their people), taught English, Christian doctrine, and vocational skills. Similar to the African American youth who attended Tuskegee Institute, they were also carefully taught individualism, industriousness, and consumption as a way of life. As Adams notes, according to one person involved, "We need to awaken in him wants. In his dull savagery he must be touched by the wings of the divine angel of discontent" (Adams, 1995, p. 23). The explicit purpose, as indicated by the title of Adams' book, was "Education for Extinction"; that is, to extinguish native culture and completely assimilate them into white culture: "Kill the Indian, save the man." Thus the discourse of racism was deeply embedded in education for Indigenous People, and even though the boarding schools mostly closed by 1930, dominating attitudes about tribal culture have certainly not disappeared.

With the closing of the boarding schools, control over education was turned over to the reservations and tribal leaders. By now, however, the dominant white model was so established that little to no effort was made to make these schools places where traditional Indigenous culture would be reinvigorated. Instead, schooling remained much the same as it had. While segregated and severely underfunded, education for native children replicated a white model emphasizing Eurocentric values because that approach was seen as the way to access economic opportunities.

Of course, this situation led to double binds similar to those experienced by the African American community, as even educated Native Americans were neither treated as equal to whites nor did they retain the power of their own communities and cultural traditions. As we will see in Chapter 9, however, there is currently an important movement to reclaim traditional Indigenous knowledge as a major approach to education for Native Americans and First Nations people in Canada, a shift that has much to offer us as we seek remedies to the ecological crises we face.

Latinos/as and Chicanos/as

For people of Mexican ancestry—both those who had been in the U.S. and those who moved to the U.S. in the 20th century—white attitudes were often characterized by racism, ranging from seeing them as "vermin to be exterminated" (Spring, 1994b, p. 63) to a threat to American culture. One white professor in the 1920s warned against the "Mexicanization" of the Southwest. Takaki summarizes his statement this way:

> The benefits derived from the "restriction of European and the exclusion of Oriental immigration" should not be nullified by allowing Mexican immigration to create a "race problem" that would "dwarf the negro problem of the South," destroying all that was "worthwhile" in "our white civilization."
>
> (Takaki, 1993, p. 330)

Education for Mexican Americans became a battleground. Employers who counted on Mexican children as cheap farm labor didn't want to encourage them to go to school at all, and, often, compulsory school-attendance laws were widely ignored. "Mexican children who did attend school faced segregation and an education designed, in a manner similar to Indians, to rid them of their native language and customs. School segregation for Mexican children spread rapidly throughout Texas and California" (Spring, 1994b, p. 67). A central component of this segregated education was learning English—and discouraging or even outlawing the use of Spanish.

For Puerto Ricans who had become instant U.S. citizens, there was a similar path. Within a short time after the war, U.S. officials moved to set up a school system. Chief among the goals was "Americanization," as students were encouraged to honor U.S. traditions and celebrate U.S. heroes such as George Washington (Spring, 1994b). But, there was more struggle over which languages were used. Although some U.S.-imposed school leaders attempted to require English only, Puerto Rican students and teachers successfully resisted and eventually won the permanent right to teach and learn in Spanish. For Puerto Ricans who came to the U.S., however, their experience was much more like that of the Mexican Americans—English only and deculturalization.

For the many other people of Spanish-speaking countries who have come to the U.S., the struggle to maintain their language and culture against the pressure to become "American" has been an ongoing concern, particularly within the schools. For those who have come into the U.S. without documents, the struggle has also been whether their children could attend school at all. Many states actively discouraged or even prohibited undocumented children from attending public school. However, this was dramatically changed by the 1982 Supreme Court case of *Plyler v. Doe*, where the Court found that it was unconstitutional to prohibit undocumented children from attending school just like any other child—pointing out that children do not have control over their parents' decisions and should not be prevented from life opportunities as a result. This decision only applies to K-12 education, though, and many U.S. states restrict the ability of undocumented people to attend public higher education.

Another major area of controversy regarding children for whom English is not the native language is around bilingual education, or education in which two languages are used as a medium of instruction, with the goal of having the student become literate in both languages. While many Spanish-speaking families favor bilingual education as a way to maintain their culture, some whites are often led to oppose it on the grounds that it might discourage students from learning English or from becoming "American." Most famously, in 1998, California passed Proposition 227, a measure that limits bilingual education and mandates a transition to English instruction after as little as one year of learning the language.

East Asian Americans and Education

After the U.S.-Mexican war of 1848–1850, which resulted in a U.S. that spread from Atlantic to Pacific, the U.S. began to reach out across the Pacific for trade and influence. One of the results of this increased contact was a surge of immigration from China, first to work as gold miners, then as 90 percent of the workforce that constructed the Western segment of the transcontinental railroad. Once the railroad was completed in 1869, the Chinese moved into many areas of work—and began to compete more directly with whites. One consequence was the Chinese Exclusion Act of 1882, which prohibited immigration from China (while immigration from Europe was being actively promoted).

Schools for Chinese children were rigidly segregated, and focused on teaching English and Christianity. There was little opportunity in these public schools for Chinese language and culture. As Ramsey notes: "Although other ethnic groups, most notably the Germans, were able to maintain their mother tongues in the public schools of California, bilingual education was largely discouraged among the Chinese" (Ramsey, 2010, p. 92).

The reason for the differential treatment is not a big mystery. While German and other northern European immigrants had Protestant Christianity in common with the dominant American culture, Chinese culture and religion was far different and easy to dismiss as "heathen" and thus inferior.

The discourse of racist domination that ascribed certain characteristics to African Americans was similarly applied to Chinese. "Like blacks, the Chinese were described as heathen, morally inferior, savage, childlike, and lustful. Chinese women were condemned as a 'depraved class,' their immorality associated with a physical appearance 'but a slight removal from the African race'" (Takaki, 1993, p. 205). Note the ways the discourse of ethnocentrism winds its way around androcentrism and anthropocentrism via these metaphors.

A fairly typical belief was expressed at a California Senate hearing by a Reverend H. H. Hill, who noted that "Chinese immigration, if left to itself, will simply be a flood of heathenism poured on American soil" (Ramsey, 2012, p. 44). The obvious answer, of course, was to teach Christianity as part of "civilizing" the Chinese.

Similar segregation and English-only schools were inflicted on the Japanese immigrants, who had started arriving in the 1890s and lived primarily in Hawaii and the West Coast.

The larger Chinese and Japanese communities responded by creating their own private schools to teach their home language and culture. "In 1909, for instance, Hawaii had over seventy Japanese language schools that enrolled around 7000 pupils" (Ramsey, 2010, p. 159). Despite occasional attempts to shut them down and laws mandating the teaching of "Americanism," many of these schools were able to stay open (Ramsey, 2010).

The discursive construction of race as a normalized category used to determine what people deserve educationally, economically, politically, and socially has a long and complex history, and these events have not gone without powerful challenges and resistance from among the affected groups and their allies. While it is beyond the scope of this chapter to examine those events, a summary of some of the more important legislative and policy decisions in American history, as well as the Civil Rights movements that accompanied them, can be found on our website (http://cw.routledge.com/textbooks/9780415872515/). See also our list of resources at the end of this chapter. The balance of this chapter will examine the ways racism continues in our contemporary day-to-day lives, in particular within educational institutions.

The Persistence of Racism Today

Inevitably, when we talk about the history of racism, some students say "but that's all in the past. Didn't the Civil Rights Movement change all that?" And, since November 2008, this has included some version of "the U.S. has a black president, so racism isn't really an issue anymore." While the civil rights struggles of past decades have certainly made some changes, the reality is that racist distinctions and even outright discrimination based on race are still widely prevalent. Only a small part of these are the overt expressions of hatred such as racial epithets or an open refusal to hire someone because of their race. More common are the institutional and subtle interpersonal differences that result in continued racial gaps and internalized racism. We will consider some of the general patterns in the U.S. and other Western cultures before focusing on the particular role of schools and education in maintaining racial hierarchy.

Economic Disparities

By nearly every social and economic indicator, wide economic and educational disparities exist between whites and people of color. These disparities are rooted in the historical ways that racism as a normalized discourse and way of thinking has been internalized in our culture. One key indicator of the historical legacy is in the figures on "net worth"—or the total value of what a household owns minus debts (including assets such as inheritances, house ownership, etc.). According to U.S. Census Bureau figures, "in 2000, the household median net worth was $79,400 for households with a non-Hispanic White householder, $7,500 for households with a Black householder, and $9,750 for households with a Hispanic householder" (Orzechowski & Sepielli, 2003). In other words, the average wealth of a white family is over 10 times that of the average black family. When we suggest that this is a historical legacy, we mean that partly due to the long discursive history of inferiorization, black and Latino families have often not been able to acquire the assets that stable and fair employment would provide. This is a clear example of the ways unequal resource distribution intersects with ideologies on race and racialized identities (Fraser, 1997).

The ongoing figures are just as shocking. According to the Children's Defense Fund:

- Black children are more than three times as likely as White children to be born into poverty and to be poor, and are more than four times as likely to live in extreme poverty.
- One in three Latino babies and half of Black babies are born into poverty.
- Black babies are almost four times as likely as White babies to have their mothers die in childbirth and are more than twice as likely as White babies to be born at very low birth-weight and to die before their first birthday.
- A Black boy born in 2001 has a 1 in 3 chance of going to prison in his lifetime; a Latino boy a 1 in 6 chance; and a White boy a 1 in 17 chance.

(Children's Defense Fund, 2007, pp. 15–16)

The Children's Defense Fund calls this the "cradle to prison pipeline," emphasizing that being born into poverty greatly increases the likelihood of ending up in prison.

Disparities in the Criminal Justice System

On top of that, however, are laws that are clearly written to favor the lifestyles of whites. For example, in the U.S., possession of 5 grams of crack cocaine (more commonly used by blacks) has been given the same minimum sentence as possessing 500 grams of powder cocaine (more commonly used by whites). This is what has come to be known as the 100-to-1 sentencing disparity. (In 2010, the Fair Sentencing Act reduced the disparity to "only" 18-1). According to Steven Shapiro, legal director of the American Civil Liberties Union, "Judges should not be required to close their eyes to the fact that the 100-to-1 disparity is unsound in theory and racially discriminatory in practice (ACLU, 2007). The law's effect on the disproportionate number of African Americans in United

States' prisons is staggering. While drug use rates are similar among all racial groups, African American drug offenders have a 20 percent greater likelihood of receiving a prison sentence than their white counterparts, and African Americans now serve virtually as much time in prison for drug offenses as whites serve for violent offenses.

Environmental Racism

A major problem that too often goes unacknowledged by white communities is the disproportionate location of poor families and families of color in proximity to a toxic environment. Degraded soil, air, and water, and the disposal of hazardous waste are all problems that dominated groups must struggle with at much higher rates than those in the dominant culture. In the early 1980s, African American civil rights activist Reverend Benjamin Chavis brought attention to

> racial discrimination in environmental policymaking, the enforcement of regulations and laws, the deliberate targeting of communities of color for toxic waste facilities, the official sanctioning of the life-threatening presence of poisons and pollutants in our communities, and the history of excluding people of color from leadership of the ecology movement.
>
> (Bullard, 2000, p. 278)

In the decades since, environmental justice activists have worked hard to expose the public health threats of pollutants in our communities, especially as these hazards reflect racist policies and laws.

Incinerators and other hazardous waste facilities are much more likely to be built in neighborhoods where poor people of color and Indigenous communities live today than they were 20 years ago. For example, in Los Angeles county, "hazardous waste, treatment, and storage facilities were found to be disproportionately located in areas where African American and Latinos live" (Boer et al., 1997). As Robert Bullard (2002) writes, environmental degradation is much more likely to be experienced by peoples who have also been systematically excluded and exploited economically:

> The systematic destruction of indigenous peoples' land and sacred sites, the poisoning of Native Americans on reservations, Africans in the Niger Delta, African-Americans in Louisiana's "Cancer Alley," Mexicans in the border towns, and Puerto Ricans on the Island of Vieques all have their roots in economic exploitation, racial oppression, devaluation of human life and the natural environment, and corporate greed.
>
> (Retrieved on January 29, 2014 from www.ejrc.cau.edu/ PovpolEj.html)

In Detroit, Michigan, for example, the largest trash incinerator in the world burns 4,000 tons of garbage every day, a process that is converted into energy in the form of electricity. The incinerator costs Detroit residents over 1.1 billion dollars, and ravages the local neighborhoods with toxic pollution linked to high asthma rates and other illnesses.

Pollutants resulting from burning trash are linked to cancer, respiratory ailments, skin diseases, and birth defects in disproportionate levels for working class communities and people of color. Today, Detroit has higher rates of respiratory illness than the rest of the state of Michigan. Children living near the incinerator are hospitalized three times more often than the state average for asthma. Those growing up near toxic sites have been shown by neuroscientists to have severe learning disabilities, and shorter life expectancies. Death rates for asthma among children in Detroit is twice the state average (Wasilevich et al., 2008).

Other dangerous toxins include high quantities of lead, a highly toxic metal, found in housing, soil, and water sources in poor communities. Despite lead's toxic characteristics, it was used for centuries in paint, gasoline, batteries, ceramics, and many other products, creating major public health problems. According to the Center for Disease Control (CDC), approximately 250,000 children between the ages of one and five years have over the CDC-recommended safe level of 10 micrograms of lead per deciliter of blood (www.cdc.gov/nceh/lead). Medical research demonstrates that exposure to lead has serious neurological and probable behavioral effects on children. According to the American Academy of Pediatrics (2005), the most definitive effects of the toxicity of lead poisoning are cognitive impairments; however there is convincing evidence that other aspects of brain or nerve function, especially behavior, may also be affected. The same organization reports that students with elevated levels of lead are not only less attentive and hyperactive, but also show low rates of graduation from high school, evidence of reading disabilities, and increased aggression (American Academy of Pediatrics, 2005).

These economic, legal, and environmental differences create marked differences in quality of life for people of color and the poor. To understand such differential outcomes, one must first trace the historical roots of contemporary discourses that define people of color and other dominated groups as inferior, and thus unworthy of the same opportunities for safe and healthy lives as middle class whites. And yet "deficit" explanations (introduced in Chapter 6) still dominate social scientists' explanations for such immoral outcomes, blaming the very people suffering the most. How is it that we continue to accept degraded ecosystems that threaten life as "just the way it is?"

The Psychology of Race

> This wound is in me, as complex and deep in my flesh as blood and nerves. I have borne it all my life, with varying degrees of consciousness, but always carefully, always with the most delicate consideration for the pain I would feel if somehow I were forced to acknowledge it.
>
> (Berry, 2010, *The Hidden Wound*, p. 4)

Although conscious or intentional racism may have declined, there is continued evidence that people make subtle, often unconscious racial distinctions that have a major impact on others' experiences and well-being. This should come as no surprise when we consider the ways our sociolinguistic system works to shape the ways we see ourselves and relate to the world around us; however, most of us are not aware of the ways we have internalized, engaged with, and reproduced the general meanings in the system, both as people of color and as whites. This is, in fact, how culture works and gets passed on without our being necessarily aware of it. As Wendell Berry (2010) suggests, for those of us identified as white, it is a "hidden wound."

Internalized Assumptions of Racism

There are a number of studies that suggest that whites tend to quickly assume negative stereotypes of people of color. Greenwald, Oakes, and Hoffman (2003) conducted an experiment in which subjects were simulating the role of a police officer and confronted with people holding either weapons or tools. The subjects consistently were more likely to incorrectly see weapons in the hands of black people. The authors of the study suggest that this may help explain why blacks are more likely to be mistakenly shot by police officers.

An interesting ongoing study indicates the almost imperceptible ways that racism may be internalized in our culture. The "Implicit Association Test" is part of Project Implicit, run by the Harvard University, the University of Virginia, and the University of Washington. In the race version of this experiment, subjects are asked to associate white faces with positive or negative words, and black faces with positive or negative words. The time it takes to make the associations is measured. If you can associate positive words to white faces faster than to black faces, then the experimenters suggest you may have an unconscious preference for whites. It turns out that the large majority of whites consistently show this preference.

Try It Yourself

On the web, go to www.implicit.harvard.edu and follow instructions to get to a list of tests, or go directly to https://implicit.harvard.edu/ implicit/selectatest.html and take the Race IAT. There are other interesting tests you might try as well.

Millions of people have now done the IAT, and the results are quite consistent. Does it mean that most whites are conscious racists? Of course not. This research does not allow that kind of conclusion. But it does suggest that we should be aware of the potential for unconscious bias, even when we think we are non-racist. We are born into a culture where a well-established logic of domination continues to create negative, inferiorized images of people of color in all sorts of places: media, literature, "science," and day-to-day practices and assumptions. The unconscious bias described above can even affect medical treatments. Green et al. (2007) were trying to understand why doctors in emergency rooms, faced with patients showing symptoms of a heart attack, were less likely to prescribe a procedure for breaking blood clots to African American patients than to white patients. They found that doctors who showed more unconscious preference for whites on the IAT were indeed less likely to offer that clot-busting procedure to blacks. Imagine what it means for the physical and psychological well-being of people of color when they are disregarded and disrespected in these ways on a regular basis. The psychology of race means something very different depending on what racial identity has been ascribed to a person.

White Privilege

No matter who we are or where we live, as members of modern industrial cultures, we are born into and begin internalizing the same historically-rooted system of hierarchized cultural meanings. However, depending on any number of discursive categories—gender, race, class, ability, or sexuality, for example—our experiences, opportunities, and quality of life will be very different. As the dominant group in the U.S., Canada, and other industrial countries, whites often don't recognize that being identified as white carries a host of unseen/unconscious privileges.

Peggy McIntosh is among those who have tried to bring the experience of "whiteness" to light. She suggests that white privilege is "an invisible package of unearned assets that I can count on cashing in each day . . . like an invisible knapsack of special provisions, codes, maps, passports" (McIntosh, 1998). Sometimes when we introduce this topic, some of our white students react defensively saying, "I'm not privileged! No one gave me special treatment! I've worked hard to get where I am!" And of course they have worked hard. But, so have others who may still not have access to the same day-to-day assets or "cultural capital" as those of us who are identified as white clearly enjoy. As we discussed in the chapter on class, meritocracy—the idea that hard work and talent get us where we belong—is a myth.

McIntosh offers a long list of examples of such resources. For example, as a white person:

- I can if I wish arrange to be in the company of people of my race most of the time.
- I can go shopping alone most of the time, pretty well assured that I will not be followed or harassed.
- I can swear, or dress in second-hand clothes, or not answer letters, without having people attribute these choices to the bad morals, the poverty, or the illiteracy of my race.
- I can be pretty sure that if I ask to talk to the "person in charge," I will be facing a person of my own race.
- I can take a job with an affirmative action employer without having my coworkers on the job suspect that I got it because of my race.

(McIntosh, 1998)

These are just a few of the 50 items McIntosh includes in the latest version of her article. Together, these experiences constitute a normalized cocoon in which most white people walk around, oblivious to the value of the "knapsack" they carry. Conversely, for people of color, the lack of access to those experiences that most whites take for granted creates unnecessary challenges that affect many aspects of daily life, from self-concept and general outlook to education and employment opportunities.

Driving While Black

Jeff, while driving a car, has never been pulled over by a police officer without there being a plausible reason, such as speeding, and has received a more-or-less justified ticket or warning each time. But every single black acquaintance he has talked to has been pulled over repeatedly, and often given no ticket and no explanation other than "suspicious driving." One African American academic colleague described being pulled over several times in the course of a few months, never receiving a ticket. This experience is commonly referred to as the "crime" of "driving while black."

Racial Microaggressions

Another related way that racism circulates to create very different psychological and material realities are the subtle racial messages referred to as "racial microaggressions." Most prominently examined by Dr. Derrald Wing Sue, microaggressions, are "everyday insults, indignities, and demeaning messages sent to people of color by well intentioned white people who are unaware of the hidden messages sent to them" (Sue et al., 2007). Sue, an Asian-American educational psychologist, gives the example of boarding a plane with an African American colleague and being told they could sit anywhere. Later, several whites board, and are also told to sit anywhere. Shortly thereafter, a flight attendant asks Sue and his colleague to move to the back of the plane for the purposes of balancing weight. When the two men point out that they, as people of color who had boarded first, were being asked to move to the "back of the bus," the flight attendant sharply denied any racial bias.

It is their very invisibility to white people that makes microaggressions a companion to white privilege. As Sue points out "most White Americans experience themselves as good, moral and decent human beings who believe in equality and democracy. Thus they find it difficult to believe that they possess biased racial attitudes and may engage in behaviors that are discriminatory" (Sue et al., 2007, p. 275).

Sue and his colleagues have identified nine different categories of microaggression, including the claim of "color blindness" in the airplane example. Claims of color blindness are interesting because they simultaneously deny racism as systematic, and refuse to acknowledge the different cultural experiences of those they address. Another example is "ascription of intelligence," expressed when a white person says of a person of color "she is so articulate." The hidden message sent in this statement is that people of color usually aren't articulate or intelligent.

In Jeff's Classroom

Jeff carried out a classic example of a microaggression while, ironically, teaching about microaggressions. Jeff and his African-American co-teacher—let's call him Robert—had created a series of improvisations (mini-skits) for students to act out some examples of microaggressions. In one, two white women are walking down the sidewalk and see two black men walking toward them. One of the women instinctively clutches her purse tightly, and the other questions her action as a microaggression. In the class, two female students came to the front of the room to act it out. Jeff figured that they needed to have someone represent the black men to get the skit going, so said to Robert "here, let's play the black men." Robert started to get up, then stopped and said he couldn't play a black man. That was the first layer of microaggression—Jeff failed to realize that asking a black man to "play" a black man in a roomful of white people put him in an uncomfortable situation. (To help understand this is problematic, consider this: Jeff would not have asked a person in a wheelchair to "play" a person in a wheelchair, because being in a wheelchair is not something one can choose to play or not play.)

But then a further microaggression occurred. Several students asked about what had happened between Jeff and Robert. Robert tried to explain that he didn't want to play a black man. The students, out of genuine curiosity, kept pressing: "But why was it an issue for you?" Robert, frustrated that the students wouldn't accept his answer, and not willing to put his soul on the table, finally had to leave the room. The students' reluctance to accept his answer failed to accept his need to maintain his dignity and personhood, and reduced him to an item for study.

When examples of microaggression are exposed, whites often insist that they didn't intend harm, and that the person of color is being "overly sensitive." Finally, they will suggest that it's a minor issue and that the annoyed person of color should just "let it go." But these responses all deny the validity of the experiences of people of color, which may include several microaggressions every day. The white person sees only the single event, lacking the knowledge to see the pattern that event fits into. It should be pointed out that other dominated groups such as women and people who identify outside the heterosexual norm also experience microaggressions that come in their own specific forms.

Race and Schooling

Of course, schools are contexts that are rife with such differential experiences. As in the case of socio-economic class, it is conventionally claimed that schools are "the great equalizer," giving everyone an equal chance to compete and succeed. But the glaring, uncomfortable truth remains that schools are places where the violent results of racism are played out through unequal funding, disproportionate punishment, tracking, and day-to-day social relations, especially in deindustrialized urban schools (Robbins, 2010).

Jonathan Kozol's study of funding inequalities, in his book *Savage Inequalities* (1991), was described in Chapter 6 in relation to class, but racial differences add a key dimension. For example, in New York, funding in the mostly white suburbs on Long Island was at least twice that spent on students in New York city (predominantly students of color), resulting in major differences in the availability of resources, quality of the buildings students attended, ability to retain the best teachers, and so on. Others have studied the relationship between resources and the rate at which children are assigned to special education classes, finding that, especially in areas where school funding is low, black boys are much more likely to be identified as having "learning disabilities" than any other group (Noguera, 2008).

Zero Tolerance

Further, in every state (except Vermont) school districts have established "zero tolerance" policies following the passage of the Gun-Free Schools Act in 1994, ostensibly to deal with increasing violence in schools. Researchers are finding that the policy is being used to exclude and criminalize urban and poor youth, especially those of color, for offenses that are more related to "disruptive behavior" than actual criminal acts. According to the *The New York Times*, and as shown in Figure 7.2,

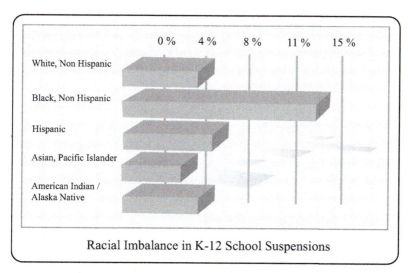

Racial Imbalance in K-12 School Suspensions

Figure 7.2 Racial Imbalance in K-12 School Suspensions.

Source: NCES. (2009). Table A-28-1. Number and percentage of students who were suspended and expelled from public elementary and secondary schools, by sex, and race/ethnicity: 2002, 2004, and 2006. Retrieved September 14, 2010 http://nces. ed.gov/programs/coe/2009/section4/table-sdi-1.asp.

[s]ome 15% of the nation's black students in grades K-12 are suspended at least briefly each year, compared with 4.8 percent of white
students, according to federal data from 2006, the latest available.
Expulsions are meted out to one in 200 black students versus one in
1,000 white students.

> (Eckholm, 2010; retrieved on September 14, 2010 from www.
> nytimes.com/2010/03/19/education/19suspend.html)

Sociologist of education Christopher Robbins's (2010) work points to:

> An intensification in the social control of youth and a related celebra-
> tion of technology, particularly its use in producing "order," "being
> tough," "sending a strong message," "establishing authority," "teach-
> ing a lesson"—the semantic smog of such catchphrases strangely suf-
> fusing discourses about, and informing responses to, youth in schools
> as much as other ever-shifting targets in the "culture of cruelty."
>
> (Robbins, 2010, p. 115)

> Children have had criminal charges brought against them for behav-
> iors as trivial as tossing peanuts on a bus, to an eight-year-old being
> suspended for pointing a chicken finger at a teacher and saying "pow-
> pow," and any other range of behaviors that teachers (and admin-
> istrators) have deemed "disruptive" to the classroom environment
> or "threatening" to school officials. These are common practices of
> zero tolerance at the local level, not statistical aberrations, as the
> overwhelming majority (over 70%) of documented expulsions due to
> zero tolerance are for "disruptive" behaviors or behaviors defined as
> "disorderly conduct" alone.
>
> (Robbins, 2010, p. 117)

Zero tolerance policies sanction the exclusion of those youth already
defined by the larger society as "problems" without us troubling ourselves
to look at their larger social or economic situations, the cultural context
with which they are so defined, or our own internalized assumptions.

Academic Achievement and Race

Given these historically-created conditions, it should come as no surprise that academic achievement by students of color is far behind that of
whites. According to the National Center for Educational Statistics at the
U.S. Department of Education (2009):

> White students . . . had higher scores than Black students, on average,
> on all assessments. While the nationwide gaps in 2007 were narrower

than in previous assessments at both grades 4 and 8 in mathematics and at grade 4 in reading, White students had average scores at least 26 points higher than Black students in each subject, on a 0–500 scale.

(Vanneman et al., 2009, p. iii)

The variety of explanations for the achievement gap parallels the wide range of explanations for gender and class inequities that were considered in the previous two chapters. One set of explanations is what we have referred to as "deficit theories," which explain the cause of differences in achievement as lying primarily in genetic or cultural differences. As we have been discussing throughout this chapter, all racist (or sexist, or classist) discourse is a form of "deficit thinking," often rationalized by "scientific" explanations, but it behooves us to look specifically at the ways in which it plays out in educational research.

Deficit Explanations of Achievement Differences

The most pernicious deficit explanation is the one that points to genetically-based "intelligence" as the cause, arguing that people of color, primarily African Americans, have a lower intelligence quotient than those whose ancestry is primarily Caucasian. As described in Chapter 6, racist assumptions have underlain intelligence testing since its development in the early years of the 20th century, and these theories rest on much older hierarchized assumptions—many of them created within science, as we have pointed out. But, despite repeated rebuttal, some educational scholars continue to press their claims for biologically based racial differences in intelligence.

The most recent major attempt was in the book *The Bell Curve* (1994), in which Richard Herrnstein and Charles Murray claimed evidence of persistent racial differences, even when socio-economic status was taken into account. In fact, they argue that both class and race differences in socio-economic status are significantly related to intelligence, and that intelligence is largely inherited—essentially suggesting that African Americans are poorer than whites because they are biologically inferior.

These claims have been decisively answered by, among others, biologist Steven Jay Gould in the second edition of *The Mismeasure of Man* (1996). Among the many pieces of evidence against racial IQ differences is the case of mixed-race people. If there really were inherited racial IQ differences between people of African ancestry and people of Caucasian ancestry, then we would expect to find that mixed-race people would consistently have IQs in between, and that those scores would vary based on the percentage of "white" or "black" ancestry in one's history—that is, the more African in your genes, the lower your score. But the reality is that there is no such variation.

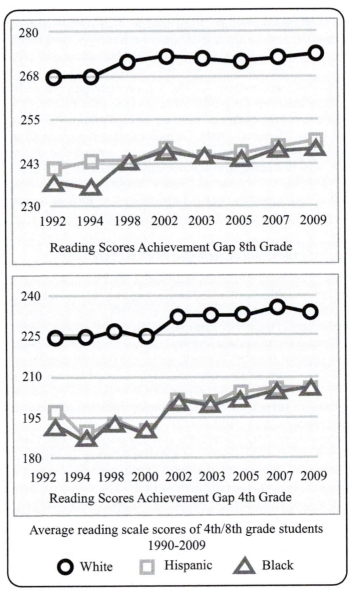

Figure 7.3 Average reading scale scores of 4th/8th grade students 1990–2009.

Sources: NCES. (2009). Table A-10-2. Average reading scale scores of 8th-grade students, by selected student characteristics: selected years, 1992–2009. Retrieved from National Center for Educational Statistics http://nces.ed.gov/programs/coe/2010/section2/table-rgp-2.asp. NCES. (2009). Table A-10-1. Average reading scale scores of 4th-grade students, by selected student characteristics: selected years, 1992–2009. Retrieved September 14, 2010, from National Center for Educational Statistics http://nces.ed.gov/programs/coe/2010/section2/table-rgp-1.asp.

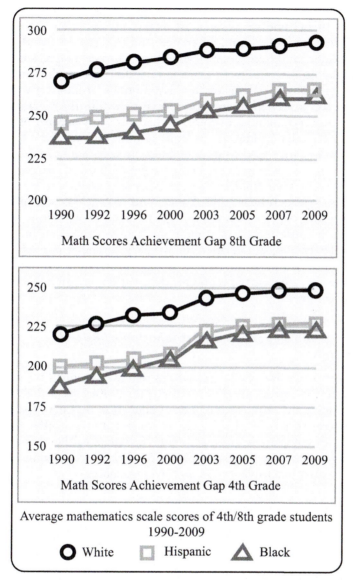

Figure 7.4 Average mathematics scale scores of 4th/8th grade students 1990–2009.

Sources: NCES. (2009). Table A-12-2. Average mathematics scale scores of 8th-grade students, by selected student characteristics: selected years, 1990–2009. Retrieved September 15, 2010, from National Center for Educational Statistics http://nces.ed.gov/programs/coe/2010/section2/table-mgp-2.asp. NCES. (2009). Table A-12-1. Average mathematics scale scores of 4th-grade students, by selected student characteristics: selected years, 1990–2009. Retrieved September 14, 2010, from National Center for Educational Statistics http://nces.ed.gov/programs/coe/2010/section2/table-mgp-1.asp.

The more pervasive "cultural deprivation" theories among educational scholars are in some ways even more dangerous since they begin from the acknowledgment of cultural differences and so seem less overtly racist as explanations for differences in academic or socio-economic achievement. But, make no mistake, these explanations derive from the same discursive roots and rely on constructed assumptions of inferiority, this time locating the source of inferior performance within the value system of families and communities of color. In this sense, any number of variables are pointed to as leading to academic failure: families who don't value education or don't read to their children or keep books and magazines in the home; women who prefer single parenthood to marriage and so can't supervise their children properly, or prefer welfare to work; people who live in dangerous neighborhoods, and so on. Note the intersection of sexist (androcentric) assumptions here. Such explanations may seem plausible because indeed in some poor African American homes there may be fewer books, and often the primary caretaker is a woman who may have to accept welfare in order to properly care for her children. But these are symptoms of economic deprivation, not an indication of an inferior culture.

Reproduction Theory as an Explanation of Racial Disparities

In Chapter 6, we discussed explanations that take seriously the relation of schools to the reproduction of economic disparities. Reproduction theorists examine the different qualities of education that manifest in tracking. Different tracks in schools prepare students for very different futures. Students of color are disproportionately assigned to the "lower" tracks that prepare students for little beyond the workforce. Jeannie Oakes, in the most comprehensive studies on tracking, shares:

> Racial disparities associated with tracking are national patterns that appear in three contexts. First, many schools that serve predominantly poor and minority populations offer a lower percentage of high-track classes when compared to affluent schools . . . Second, in racially mixed schools minorities are typically underrepresented in high-ability classes . . . A third context of racial disparity related to tracking is in classes that are purportedly at the same track level but turn out to be quite different [at high income vs. low income schools].
>
> (Oakes, 2005, pp. 228–229)

Reproduction theory, however, doesn't account for the reality of racial differences *within* social classes. From an EcoJustice perspective, the discourse of racism creates specific experiences that go beyond those of class and add on to class-based domination. In addition, reproduction theorists often ignore the political activism that has led to real changes in schools, such as Multicultural Education and Bilingual Education (Nieto, 1996). Finally, reproduction theory leaves out psychological and cultural issues, and fails to explain how language inscribes specific racially-charged meanings on our very psyches.

Social Psychological Explanations and Culturally Responsive Teaching

Social psychologist Claude Steele has identified an important example of the psycho-social consequences of racism on school achievement. When African American college students were given a test after being told it measured their intelligence, they performed worse than a similar group of black students who were not led to believe the test measured intelligence. However, there was no difference between two groups of white students given the same information. Steele suggests that this differential is the result of "stereotype threat," the fear that one will confirm the truth of a stereotype—in this case, the stereotype that African-Americans are less intelligent. Stereotype threat highlights how a discourse rooted in hierarchy winds itself into our deepest thoughts, even into our unconscious assumptions.

Cultural issues are at the heart of another explanation referred to as "cultural clash" or "cultural incompatibility." In this explanation, the school culture and home culture are so different that students have difficulty adjusting, often performing poorly as a result. This research focuses attention on the dynamic relationship between school and home, rather than blaming the home culture. It has led directly to an important innovation in teacher education called "culturally responsive teaching" (Gay, 2000), or "culturally relevant teaching" (Ladson-Billings, 1994).

When teachers use culturally relevant approaches, they bring the students' home culture into the classroom. Gloria Ladson-Billings's pioneering study *The Dreamkeepers* (1994) portrayed a number of successful teachers of African American children using pedagogical strategies that valued and utilized the students' cultural understandings. For example, one teacher had parents teach local skills, such as baking sweet-potato pies, within a curriculum about food. Another teacher had her second-grade students bring in (non-graphic) rap lyrics to study poetry and literary technique. Note how culturally relevant teaching challenges the devaluing of home culture that is characteristic of deficit thinking so prevalent in schooling.

However, the cultural clash approach doesn't explain why some students still succeed in conventional schools, despite coming from cultures with values and practices much different than most schools. To account for this, John Ogbu and his colleagues (Fordham & Ogbu, 1986; Fordham, 1996), whom we mentioned in Chapter 6, argued that one must consider the historical relationship between a group's culture and the larger society around it. Specifically, Ogbu argued that "voluntary" immigrants have a very different relationship to society and schools than do "involuntary" immigrants. Voluntary immigrants, which in the U.S. are said to include many Japanese and Koreans, for example, have joined a culture freely, and tend to share the values and ideology of the culture, and thus tend to succeed in schools shaped by dominant discourses. "Involuntary immigrants," who in the U.S. include African Americans and many Latinos, come to a culture in circumstances that are usually not of their own free will, leaving them in a lower social status because their culture is valued less. This effect lasts, Ogbu suggests, far after the actual time of arriving in the new culture. Ogbu has found cross-cultural examples that show the power of this pattern. For example, in Japan, students of Korean descent are valued less and do poorly in school. In Sweden, low-status Finnish students do poorly in school. Interestingly, both Koreans and Finns do as well as others when they move to a culture in which they do not have a history of colonization and discrimination. Ogbu's research highlights the power of a systematized logic of domination as it insinuates itself into every aspect of the psychology and behavior of its victims.

According to Ogbu, due to a history of inferiorization, involuntary immigrants may see limited value in schooling. Rather, many see schools as trying to take their cultures and identities from them. As a result, these students often openly resist the agenda of school. Students who conform to the culture of school may in turn be put down by their peers. In the case of African American students, Fordham and Ogbu found evidence that doing well in school is often seen as "acting white" (Fordham & Ogbu, 1986). This concept is highly controversial among both scholars and African Americans. Some writers point out that most African American students voice the belief that school is important to their future. However, this may be more a result of students saying what they think they are supposed to say, while their actual behaviors of avoiding schoolwork and refusing to attend suggest very different actual attitudes.

Recall our discussion of "the lads" in Chapter 6 whose very resistance to school ironically ended up continuing the reproduction of class differences. If we consider culturally different students as resisting domination by the larger culture, we are recognizing them as actors, not just passive victims of a system. While the actions they take may be contradictory or unproductive in important ways, they make sense to the actors involved. It's hard to blame students for responding negatively to an institution that tells them that they are worthless and that doesn't value their culture. Understanding the complex educational experiences and achievements of students of color requires an examination of specific historical and situational factors, and exposes the over simplifications common to deficit explanations.

Conclusion

As with the challenges raised by critical race theorists regarding the complicated nature of desegregation, we must confront the ways that a narrow focus on academic achievement overlooks the problem of a radically-hierarchized and essentially racist cultural system. Surely we cannot stop being concerned about what and how and even whether students of color are learning: but what should such learning be for? What kinds of communities do we want? Are we simply aiming to prepare students from dominated groups to become consumers of/in the same exploitive system ravaging our world? Or, are there other goals on which we should be focusing? Can "achievement" within the existing system ever *really* lead to a challenge of its complex problems?

When we raise these questions, we confront who we are as educators in this system, and what our responsibilities are in the face of its embedded violence. As we ask you to confront the issues we've put before you in these last three chapters, we recognize the pointed discomfort that such an exposure may cause. Some of our white students have reacted angrily, retorting that they should not be made to feel guilty about something they had no direct part in creating. Students of color in our classes have also expressed anger. Heated responses are certainly understandable when reading about the pain and suffering caused by such injustices. However, we want to be clear that asking you to confront yourselves in this reading is not about assigning personal blame. Rather, we are asking that you begin to confront the complexity of a culture whose circulation of meanings creates the hierarchized relationships, institutions, unequal opportunities, and "truths" from which we either benefit or suffer. Making the historical construction of these meanings visible helps us to identify our unwitting complicity in their perpetuation, and, more importantly, to begin to do the personal and professional work of shifting the system. As we tell our own students, it's one thing to be complicit in racism when we don't know how it works, it's quite another to be complicit by refusing to act when we do know.

Racism in the 21st century is complicated, especially in the classroom. Decades of white liberalism have washed racism over with the sentiment that, while such beliefs exist in day-to-day relationships, talking about it in classrooms will change things. The reality is that while talk is something, it does not necessarily extend into cultural change. As stated in this chapter, we are born into racism because the underlying structures of meaning in our culture present domination as natural. Though it is still taboo to admit overt racist behaviors, it has become somewhat routine to discuss racism through a white liberal lens. Here is one more story.

From Johnny's Classroom

In my undergraduate "Schools in a Diverse and Democratic Society" course, we were discussing the vivid segregation in our local communities, focusing on the racist nature of school policy and discussing its systemic roots in our culture. The discussion was lively, as it often is, but this class meeting took a very insightful turn. This particular section of undergraduate students was about 40 percent persons of color. The class took care to be supportive and to share honestly assumptions they held about both education and society. One African American gentleman shared a very profound and real perspective. He said that he and other students talked regularly about how weird it was that the classrooms are presented as some sort of safe place for white people to talk about racism, but you don't see any of those people taking action outside of class, and it's not exactly safe for the minorities. "It's almost like a whole generation of white people learn how to behave in classrooms, but only in classrooms. White teachers and students don't even see their classroom behaviors as a privilege. In fact, they can study racism as some sort of liberating progress from racist roots and it's even better if they happen to have a person of color in class to testify."

White instructors can present racism as a subject, but for most of the world's population it is a lived experience: white students can study it while their minority peers live it. Classrooms and schools are saturated with the same cultural hierarchies we've been discussing and these shape race education too. Understanding this will help us to push things beyond covering race within the safety net of white curiosity, but there are no easy answers.

Obviously, interrupting the processes and institutionalization of a logic of domination is difficult work, requiring teachers who are willing and prepared to step up and teach in ways that challenge the naturalization of inequality, and engage students in authentic opportunities for confronting its effects. It means confronting the ways we unconsciously internalize value-hierarchized meanings and experiences everyday and it means choosing to raise the important questions in everything we do as teachers: in the content we teach, in the activities we create, in the relationships we create with our students, in the assumptions that will continue to surface. What is education for, and what kinds of communities do we all deserve as living creatures sharing this planet?

These are the essential questions we pose to prospective and practicing teachers and teacher educators everywhere as a matter crucial to reclaiming diverse, democratic, and sustainable communities. Fair, engaged decision-making for healthy communities cannot happen when major segments of the population are defined and treated as less able or excluded from participation. Getting students outside their comfort zone in conversation is important, but asking them to engage in actions that work together toward ending violence is even more so. In the final three chapters, we push you to consider what this means in your particular contexts as we examine the larger system of globalization, and responses from Indigenous cultures and other communities around the world who are beginning to resist modernity's impact.

In the section that follows, we offer suggestions for activities, readings, films, and organizations that can help you to teach about race and racism. We also invite you to look at the wide array of resources on our website at www.routledge.com/textbooks/9780415872515.

What Schools and Teachers Can Do

Challenge Deficit Thinking/Language

Challenge the use by colleagues of deficit explanations for low achievement by students of color. Offer alternative explanations from a cultural ecological analysis that look at the logic of domination.

Discuss White Privilege

Read Peggy McIntosh's *White Privilege: Unpacking the Invisible Knapsack* with your students and ask them to come up with other examples of the privileges of whiteness.

Step Forward

If you have a level of trust built within your class, do one of the variety of activities available where participants "step forward" or "step back" if a statement applies to them, e.g. "If your ancestors were forced to come to this country, take one step back" (for example, Paul Kivel's exercise at www.paulkivel.com/resources/classandrace.pdf).

Talk About Racism and Injustice

Even young elementary students can have straightforward conversations about race. See Rita Tenorio's "Raising Issues of Race with Young Children" or Alejandro Segura-Mora's "What Color Is Beautiful?" in Pelo's *Rethinking Early Childhood Education* (2008) for examples.

Conceptual Toolbox

Culturally responsive (or relevant) teaching: Instruction that includes and connects to the strengths of a child's home culture as a way of inviting the child to learn. It is directly opposed to deficit approaches.

Discourse of racism: A culturally created way of thinking, speaking, and acting that is rooted in seeing some people as inferior to others. Note that the discourse of racism rests firmly on a foundation of anthropocentrism.

Race: A culturally created discursive category used for the express purpose of defining some people as biologically and culturally inferior to others.

Racial microaggression: Everyday insults, indignities, and demeaning messages sent to people of color by well-intentioned white people who are unaware of the hidden messages sent to them.

White privilege: The mostly hidden benefits that accrue to those who identify as white, based on the assumption that white is "normal." Examples include the ability to go shopping without being followed or harassed, and the likelihood of having school materials that reflect their people's culture and history.

Suggested Readings and Other Resources

Books and Essays

McIntosh, P. (1998). White privilege: Unpacking the invisible knapsack. In P. S. Rothenberg (Ed.), *Race, class, and gender in the United States: An integrated study*. New York, NY: St. Martin's Press.

Segura-Mora, A. (2008). What color is beautiful? In A. Pelo (Ed.), *Rethinking early childhood education*. Milwaukee, WI: Rethinking Schools.

Siddle-Walker, V. (1996) *Their highest potential: An African American school community in the segregated south*. Chapel Hill, NC: University of North Carolina Press.

Spring, J. H. (1994b). *Deculturalization and the struggle for equality: A brief history of the education of dominated cultures*. New York, NY: McGraw Hill.

Takaki, R. (1993). *A different mirror: A history of multicultural America*. New York, NY: Little.

Tenorio, R. (2008). Raising issues of race with young children. In A. Pelo (Ed.), *Rethinking early childhood education*. Milwaukee, WI: Rethinking Schools.

Zinn, H. (1995). *A people's history of the United States*. New York, NY: Harper and Row.

Films

Adelman, L. (2003). *Race: The power of an illusion.* California Newsreel. Three-part series examining the social construction of race and its history.

Else, J. (1992). *Eyes on the prize: America's civil rights years.* Alexandria, VA: PBS.
Essential series on America's Civil Rights movement, 1954–1985.

Lesiak, C. (1992). *In the white man's image.* PBS.
Examines the use of boarding schools to destroy Native identity.

Films Media Group (2011). *Indian school: Stories of survival.*
Also examines the use of boarding schools to destroy Native identity, but includes several personal accounts of the educational system.

Organizations and Links

Facing History and Ourselves (www.facinghistory.org)
Organization that offers classroom materials for teaching about hatred and tolerance.

Rethinking Schools (www.rethinkingschools.org)
Teacher-run organization that publishes a quarterly journal that often includes teacher writing on working with issues of race. Large archive of past articles.

Teaching Tolerance (www.splcenter.org/what-we-do/teaching-tolerance)
A project of the Southern Poverty Law Center, Teaching Tolerance provides a wide range of teaching materials on teaching about racism and hatred.

We Shall Remain (www.pbs.org/wgbh/amex/weshallremain)
Site based on the PBS series *We Shall Remain* on Native American History.

Notes

1 For example, accounts of African slavery can be found in the writings of the 14th century traveler Ibn Battuta in his journeys across the Sahel. Chinua Achebe's seminal African novel *Things Fall Apart* (1958), as well as Buchi Emecheta's *The Bride Price* (1976), feature slavery in the West African context as important elements of their stories and illustrate the complexity of the practice in the African setting.

2 This point was raised by Henry Louis Gates in a PBS television series about Africa, and created a firestorm of controversy from many sources. However, other African and African American scholars, such as Cornel West, have mentioned this involvement, and, despite any merits of the criticism of Gates on the point, we agree with those who have said that acknowledging African involvement in the European institution is not the same as saying that Africans were responsible for the slave trade.

3 There is controversy over use of terms for the Indigenous People of North America. There are problems with "American Indian" and "Native American," though both terms are used by many Indigenous People themselves. Most prefer tribal names when possible, especially when referring to specific groups. When referring more generally, some prefer just the term "Native." In Canada, the term "First Nations" is widely used. We will use Indigenous People often, with the other terms interchangeably.

Chapter 8

Learning About Globalization
Education, Enclosures, and
Resistance

Introduction

In this chapter, we will look at how the culture of modernity has been
exported across the world and the economic, ecological, and cultural
impacts that it is currently having on human communities and their surrounding ecosystems. There are those who describe this process as a modern form of colonization. Others see it as an important way to insure
universal human rights, and still others believe that globalizing Western
industrial economic systems will end poverty and bring "undeveloped"
countries into the civilized world.

We recognize that interactions among people from different cultures
can teach us a lot, and, indeed, we will be discussing that in the next chapter when we focus on Indigenous perspectives. EcoJustice scholars are
particularly interested in the ways Western industrial models of economic
development exploit both people for cheap labor, and the land other peoples have lived on for centuries. Cultures that have different values and
different relations to the land that they inhabit are being convinced, either
through strong modernist discourses or economic threats, that their cultural ways of being—their values and relationships—are inferior, and
they should thus become like members of Western consumer cultures.

Examining the ways that language and cultural practices of modernity
have spread, we argue that "discourses of modernity" have been globalized. In particular, the discourse of "progress," or the idea of linear
change as improvement to the quality of life, rationalizes the spread of
modern cultural and economic ideas and practices from the global North
to the global South.[1] Thus, industrialization and participation in the
world market is put forth as a necessary improvement over subsistence
forms of living, and traditional cultures find themselves being pressured
to "modernize" or "develop" (note the strong metaphorical implications
of these concepts and they ways they support the discourse on "progress"). We agree with those who see globalization as growing out of earlier forms of colonization, and in particular the ways Eurocentric and

ethnocentric ways of thinking produce assumptions of superiority. Modernist cultures often see themselves as simply having the right to move into other lands in the name of development because of the belief that they are essentially superior.

But it's not all a sad story—this chapter will also consider the ways in which people around the world challenge the culture of globalization to maintain ways of living that are often far older and far more sustainable. A central aspect of these older ways of living is that much of how they live is rooted in community relationships rather than valuing the individual's rights above all else—knowledge, as well as land and other material resources, are held in common rather than being owned by any individual.

What Is Globalization?

In mainstream sources, "globalization" is seen simply as describing a world that is tightly knit together, where one can buy products from anywhere on the planet, communicate instantly to the other side of the world, and thus make the world "flat," as often phrased by *The New York Times* columnist Thomas Friedman. Media pundits like Friedman sing the praises of large multinational corporations who are seen as spreading "freedom and democracy" or "feeding the world" as they export a specific set of economic relations and expectations across the world. But are these economic frames really democratic? Who is making the decisions when people are moved off the land they have occupied and cultivated for centuries just so that large industrial farms can be established? Are their families really better off working in factories for a daily wage? What are they forced to give up for two dollars a day? One of the premises behind such changes is that cultures who have been living in small communities that do not depend on the exchange of money or a consumer-based society must be poor and undeveloped, in need of what we in the West take for granted. And, certainly, there are many people in the world whose lives have been improved by access to medicine, electricity, and other benefits. But, globalization has also meant that millions of people have been forced to enter into a global market in which foods that were once part of their daily lives are no longer grown, and extended families that once depended on each other and lived in strong supportive communities are pushed into urban centers to look for low-wage work and live in squalor. What is actually being globalized across this supposedly "flat" world?

In this chapter, we examine the cultural foundations of economic policies and practices that now dominate the world, and the specific ways in which the "world's social majorities" (Esteva & Prakash, 1998) are responding. In saying globalization is "imposed," we take issue with the assumption that modernist ways of living are inevitable, examining the ways that other cultural ways of knowing are asserting themselves in direct resistance to the overwhelming consumption-oriented ideologies now ravaging the planet's ecosystems and human laborers. The system that is being exported in the name of bringing "development" to the poor countries of the world is based on the same hierarchized ways of thinking that we have been discussing throughout this book—what Derrick Jensen (2006a, 2006b) calls "an occupier" mentality whose primary interest is in control and accumulation. Under globalization, this means control of the resources and labor of other regions of the world, rationalized by notions of superiority and inferiority. Indeed, a close look reveals a worldwide class system emerging, with small "third world" nations now laboring for two to three dollars a day—a wage on which they cannot feed their families—while the multinational corporations for whom they work take control of the forests, water, soils, and seeds upon which they once depended for life, and pocket the profits. Yes, the world seems to be getting smaller and smaller as communication and travel to the far reaches of the planet are ever more available to those who can pay to get there. But who gains and who loses as we export and impose our modernist ways of being far and wide?

What mainstream definitions of globalization ignore is that this tightly knit world is not equal on both ends of the string. In fact, the rich industrial countries have created, control, and thus benefit far more from the global system. The rich impose their culture, set the rules of the game, and enforce the rules that benefit them. The rules are rooted in the philosophy of neoliberalism (which we talked about in Chapter 2), which emphasizes private rights over public interests, pushing governments to deregulate and privatize to benefit property interests over people. Of course, not everyone sees this process positively. In fact, there is widespread resistance by the world's "social majorities," taking many forms.

Two conflicting paradigms of resistance to globalization should be examined before we go further. As Martin Khor of the International Forum on Globalization (IFG) and the Third World Network argues, the first paradigm involves seeing the system as inevitable. That is, we recognize that we are choosing to work in a system of globalization that we feel we are trapped in, and we ask whether the rules of the game are fair particularly to the weaker partners: "Or, are they being twisted and manipulated by the strong partners in order to keep the weaker down?" (Khor, in Cavanaugh & Mander, 2002, p. 13). In this paradigm, we would work within the parameters of the system in order to try to refine the rules to be more just, but we would not take on the system itself.

A second paradigm, Khor tells us, recognizes the first as somewhat anthropocentric in nature. That is, even if we could make the rules fairer for the human participants, the catastrophic ecological consequences and the overall quality of life on the planet would not be altered.

If we continue to emphasize high growth, but the growth is more equitably shared and the poor are made to come out better, the whole system of industrialism still goes on and the ecological degradation is not countered. So, what have we gained in paradigm one if we and all other members of the planet are still in peril? This second paradigm questions the inevitability of industrialization and globalization as the best economic system, and rather sees these as having detrimental effects on systems of life worldwide. This paradigm sees the debate over the North–South distribution of material resources as irrelevant because in 20 or 30 years the whole system will blow up anyway (Khor, in Cavanagh & Mander, 2002, p. 13).

This paradigm instead suggests the need for a community-based, self-reliance model that honors reciprocity, mutual care, and sharing that are the basis of "the commons," a concept we'll discuss in detail below. In short, it doesn't matter if people are "equal" if we are forced to live on a destroyed planet, and further, there are existing ways of knowing and being in diverse cultures across the planet, still in practice, that are far more sustainable, and lead to happy healthy living systems. As you may recognize, these are two fundamental premises of the EcoJustice Education perspective we've been discussing throughout this book. We'll introduce you to some of those practices, and the people who are enacting them as forms of resistance and subsistence, in this chapter.

The Commons and Their Enclosure

In the analysis that follows, we use the "cultural and environmental commons" (Bowers, 2006; Cavanagh & Mander, 2004; *The Ecologist*, 1993; Shiva, 2005) as concepts that can help us pay attention to the non-monetized relationships and practices that people across the world use to survive and take care of one another on a day-to-day basis. The "commons" is a concept that allows us to recognize both the interactions between cultural and ecological systems, and the ways that certain practices, beliefs, and relationships are oriented toward the future security of both. We will consider the "cultural commons," which includes non-money-based economic and social exchanges including: work-for-work; strong communitarian beliefs, practices, and relationships; alternative forms and spaces of education; democratic decision-making; and efforts to create more sustainable, ecologically-sound relationships with natural systems. Aimed at protecting the ability of both human communities and natural systems to live well together into the future, these are the sorts of day-to-day relationships and practices that function to nurture the larger communicative system of intelligence—or Mind—which Gregory Bateson (2000) describes as essential to life (refer back to Chapter 3 for a review of Bateson). What we will be interested in, then, are the specific practices that open us to an awareness of, and promote the nurturance of eco-ethical consciousness, as well as those enclosure practices that become barriers to such an understanding, and may thus damage living systems, including human communities.

We will also use the term "environmental commons." For modern industrial cultures, the most basic concept and practice of the "commons" dates back to ancient English law, where peasants shared land for grazing their animals, as well as decision-making practices for how to do so without over-taxing the land and thus degrading it for future use. While we may borrow this concept—"the commons"—from that ancient time and place, diverse cultures across the planet have also developed ideas and practices designed to protect what they need from the natural world to survive: gathering, developing, exchanging, and protecting seeds for future planting, protecting water sources, nurturing and protecting forests, caring for and protecting the soil and biodiversity more generally. These forms we refer to as the "environmental commons" (Bowers, 2006). Key to defining the commons are (1) that they are not owned. They belong to everyone, and thus, (2) they do not require money to be accessed. Fundamentally, when the cultural and environmental commons intersect, our practices are aimed at protecting the larger life-systems we need and thus we are actively engaging and protecting an "ecology of mind" in the Batesonian sense. This includes an acknowledgment of the vital nature of each, and represents our attention to security, to social and ecological well-being. The purpose of education within this context is thus systemic wisdom in which learning is oriented toward understanding and acknowledging the ways in which we interact with, depend upon, and impact a larger system of intelligence. While they may not involve schools as we know them, such educational processes are visible, albeit in diverse ways and via diverse languages, wherever communities are depending on commons-based practices for survival.

The cultural commons may include food cultivation and preparation, medicinal practices, language and literacy practices, arts and aesthetic practices, games and entertainment, craft and building knowledge, bartering, decision-making practices, and so on. These practices are generally very old, dating back in modern Western cultures to a time when our economy was based primarily on small self-sufficient farms, organized around agrarian values that protected the land and its creatures, and when our economy was more community-based. For many of us in the West, our commons have been so eaten away by processes of commodification that it may be difficult to identify them as still existing (Bowers, 2006). And yet, as many of the stories of resistance and subsistence we share below will demonstrate, they do exist as non-monetized assets. The commons are forms of wealth in the community (sometimes seemingly in the most unlikely places) that help to nurture our relationship within life-giving systems and thus awaken us to a conscious participation in the wider systems of intelligence surrounding us.

Enclosure

Woven into the long history of the world's diverse ecological and cultural commons, and now causing severe threats to the sustainability of diverse ecosystems, is the practice of enclosure, which privatizes and commodifies what was once freely shared, cutting people off from the life-giving relationships offered by the commons.

Enclosure was central to the transformation of England (and later other European countries) from the feudal arrangements of medieval times to the capitalist structure of modern England. In the feudal system, most of the land was controlled by the nobility/aristocracy and farmed by the peasants—tenants who had the right to make a living on the land as long as they gave a significant share of their crop to the lord of the manor. Every manorial estate also contained significant areas of land that were used by everyone for pasture, hay, wood, and water—the "commons."

But, beginning in the 13th century and accelerating in the 18th century, the landowners began to realize they could make more money by using the land in ways other than tenant farming, such as raising sheep or doing large-scale farming, so they began to pass laws—"the Enclosure Acts," allowing them to "enclose"—literally, put up fences around—both the tenant-farmed land and the commons land. This, of course, left the peasants with no way to make a living, forcing them off the land and devastating communities. As refugees in their own country, peasants had few options but to go to the cities and work in the rapidly growing factories for very low wages, thus feeding the growing industrial system. Referring to both social and ecological consequences of such changes, Gary Snyder wrote:

> The arguments for enclosure in England—efficiency, higher production—ignored social and ecological effects and served to cripple the sustainable agriculture of some districts . . . the enclosures of the eighteenth century created a population of rural homeless who were forced in their desperation to become the world's first industrial working class.
>
> (Snyder, 1990, p. 32)

Thus "enclosure" refers first to putting land formerly available for common use into private hands for the private gain of the owners. But, as we are defining the commons to include the cultural commons, so we define enclosure as any privatizing of material or cultural resources that were once freely available to all. For example, in recent years municipal services—such as the provision of potable water—once the shared right and responsibility of communities, are being bought up by privately owned agencies or corporations and sold back to the public, who consequently lose decision-making control over quality and access.

A School Memory From Rebecca

I remember learning in social studies classes about all the ways that the Enlightenment period helped to rescue people from feudalism. We were never taught to think about the ways peasant people's subsistence lives were good for them, or the ways the loss of their lives on the land caused them to be harmed or exploited in ways that may have been even more degrading. Instead, we were taught of all the ways that industrialization and ideas about "democracy" that grew out of this period represented a kind of cultural "evolution." When I first began to read about "enclosure" and the "commons" it totally flipped my worldview on its head. I remember reading a novel by John Berger called *Pig Earth* (1979), a wonderfully poignant story about peasant life in France just on the brink of industrialization. Now I can't help but feel a little tug of resentment about the stories that I learned as truth, and their damaging effects on current world policies and ways of thinking. What Europe experienced 300 years ago or more is now happening all over the world.

Energy companies now control our ability to provide heat to our homes, unless we are fortunate enough to own or have access to a fairly large source of wood to burn, a situation open to fewer and fewer people in the world. As people are moved off the land, they lose access to the right to provide their own food, heat, water, and housing. As subsistence is devalued by market ideologies, the people are impoverished and forced into exploited labor.

In modern industrial cultures like ours, enclosure has become so taken for granted that it would be difficult to imagine any other way of living. Unless we grow our own food and husband the animals needed to provide meat, most of our food is provided through grocery stores that acquire food from around the world via a handful of huge privately owned multinational corporations. But food production was, until very recently, the responsibility of small family-owned farms who both provided for themselves and also took their produce, meat, and dairy products to a local market. Today, small farms are almost non-existent. Even our entertainment has been privatized. Take music for example: Where once families and friends or neighbors gathered regularly to freely sing and play instruments together as a common form of entertainment and art, now music valued as "good" is done by professionals who sell their works to recording companies, undermining the notion that anyone can sing for fun and social pleasure.

Think About This

What practices can you name that have been privatized in recent years? Talk to family members—see if they can remember examples of practices that used to be available for free but now are usually paid for. Examples might include: gardening/farming; food preparation and preservation; entertainment; children's play; carpentry.

Founded upon deeply embedded cultural assumptions that define humans as in charge of and outside of all natural systems, and cultural "progress" as a creation of autonomous individuals seeking material accumulation, enclosure claims everything and anything to be up for grabs for the market and private profit. When the commons are enclosed by processes of privatization, they are no longer available to people who need them to survive unless those people can pay. If the people cannot pay, they are generally blamed as deficient in any number of ways (remember deficit thinking and "victim blaming" from previous chapters), and left to fend for themselves. Enclosure is thus a process of exclusion created and kept in place by a complex cultural mindset that presents hierarchical relationships of value as natural.

Enclosure as a Way of Thinking

It is important to keep in mind that enclosure practices are founded upon very old ways of thinking that, going back to Bateson again (Chapter 3), are mapped onto our consciousness via the language and interpretive practices that we use, and thus function ideologically as if they were "natural," so that we are not able to think in terms of the systems upon which we depend. To summarize, these include the belief: (1) that people and human relationships are more valuable than non-human creatures or relationships between humans and non-humans (anthropocentrism); (2) that human nature is fundamentally based on the self-interest of autonomous, atomistic individuals (individualism); (3) that some individuals are more deserving of the goods and services needed to live than others (ethnocentrism, androcentrism); and (4) that this system of value is most efficiently articulated by processes of exchange governed by private ownership of the means of production, and the exchange of money as representative of relative worth in the system (capitalism, consumerism, commodification). Thus, individualism, meritocracy, ethnocentrism, and anthropocentrism form a primary ideological foundation encoded, articulated, and exchanged in our very linguistic system and reproduced in our institutions (Bowers, 1997; Prakash & Esteva, 1998). Erroneously assuming theses ideologies to be natural human characteristics, Garret Hardin (1968) famously refers to this process as "the tragedy of the commons." In truth, as many authors have pointed out, what Hardin identifies is actually the tragedy of enclosure (Cavanagh & Mander, 2004). And, as the work of Gregory Bateson demonstrates, such practices are tragic, indeed ultimately suicidal, because they cut us off from systemic wisdom: recognizing and protecting the living patterns and relationships that embed us in a necessary system of interdependence. Practices and ideologies of enclosure do not arise from some part of humans' essential individualistic "nature." They are culturally created and maintained, and they contradict those collaborative interdependent relationships that help us to survive. As you can see, much of the process of enclosure involves making private property out of what was once freely shared. A central aspect of this "privatization" involves the process of "monetization," or putting a price on things that once were available to all. Another way to see it is as "commodification," or turning things—both alive and not—into products to be sold on the market (refer back to Chapter 3 and our discussion of discourses and root metaphors). This process is both material—that is, part of an actual production process—and ideological, or part of a shared system of belief woven from the internalization of meanings via discourses of modernity. Internalizing these ideologies as "truth," we accept enclosure as normal and lose sight of the commons because we are immersed in a belief system that makes money and the accumulation of things more important and even more "real" than protecting life.

Globalization: Enclosure Through Ideology and Trade

If commodification is the underlying discourse and enclosure is the political policy underlying globalization, let's consider how they get enacted institutionally to rationalize the global project. First, we consider the discourse of progress and the ideology of development, and then turn to the international institutions that frame global discussion based on the beliefs and interests of the industrial world: the General Agreement on Tariffs and Trade (GATT), its descendant, the World Trade Organization (WTO), the International Monetary Fund (IMF), and the World Bank (WB); and some of the international agreements that enforce those interests, such as the North American Free Trade Agreement (NAFTA).

The Discourse of Progress and the Metaphor of Development

You might recall that in the Chapter 3 discussion of metaphor we looked at an example in a textbook that said "developed countries should aid developing countries." We pointed out how language carries many assumptions, including the idea that modern countries were better or "more developed" than those who are "developing." The main goal of those "less evolved" countries should be to "improve themselves" by becoming more like the modern countries. This idea that "West is best" is a taken-for-granted assumption by those from the global North, but it is also believed by much of the leadership of countries of the South—largely because most of them are educated in Northern or Northern-influenced schools. So, when they learn math and science and history, they also learn Northern/modern assumptions about what kinds of scientific information to trust, what kinds of research and data really matter, which traditions are valuable, and which are simply "behind." All of these ideas of what constitutes cultural and economic "advancement" rely on specific dualized and hierarchized metaphors (advanced/behind, developed/undeveloped, for example) and are part of the overarching discourse of modernity, in particular the discourse of "progress." These fundamental discourses created the hierarchized thinking that made colonization possible. As described in Chapter 7, European "explorers" searching for resources for their home countries arrived on the shores of other continents, and, defining all of inhabitants as less-than-human, used violence to take control of their lands and often their bodies for the labor needed to move the furs, trees, gold, and silver back to Europe. As William Cronon (1983) has documented in his now classic history, *Changes in the Land*, the land and its creatures were defined as valuable "commodities" to be taken and used by the now occupying colonists.

An updated version of this mentality, rationalized by the same logic of domination and discourses of commodification, is now being exported around the world to support a globalized economic and cultural system. Under the mantra of "spreading democracy and freedom," resources and labor are the targets of exploitation and profit is the motive. To "develop" a nation is to bring it under the rules and ideology of an industrial mindset. And, similar to the Native American boarding schools used to defeat the resisting tribes, a specific system of formal education is being exported as one of the primary means of accomplishing this hegemonic feat.

Concurrent with learning to value modern ways of thinking is learning to devalue one's own cultural patterns. Many students from the South in Westernized classrooms come to see their home culture as inferior—as backwards and primitive. When they become leaders in their home countries they pursue policies that ignore or even destroy local cultures in favor of Western ways of living—all with the best of intentions. However, for an overwhelming majority, these students become stuck in a kind of no-man's land: They are neither able to "make it" in the competitive world of the global market, nor are they a part of their home culture. Thus, they join the ranks of the world's "homeless" poor, their fates an international example of the intersecting politics of distribution and recognition (Fraser, 1997).

The Institutions of "Progress"—GATT, WTO, IMF, World Bank

The ideology of development is undergirded by a series of global institutions that essentially set the rules for trade and business among the capitalist countries—which today means nearly every country on the planet. To understand how these global institutions came into being, a little history is necessary. The larger picture is the history of colonization of most of the world by the European industrial countries. Between roughly 1500 and 1900 AD, the economies of most countries of the global South were enclosed by the colonizing countries—that is, they were reorganized to benefit the colonizers. For example, in India, the ancient trade of cloth-making was destroyed so that British factory-made cloth could be sold. Indians were limited to growing the raw materials for British factories, or working in the factories themselves. Many other countries of the South became forced to be suppliers of raw materials for the industrial countries.

After World War II, the wealthy countries came together to consider the post-war world. They saw that the war had been in part caused by the chaos of the worldwide Great Depression of the 1920s and 1930s, and wanted to create a system that would prevent another depression. In addition, they saw that the tides of history were going to force them to give up most of their empires and allow some form of independence to the countries of the South. Of course, they didn't give up those empires without a fight in many cases—the terrible wars in Vietnam, Algeria, Angola, and elsewhere were the deadly last gasp of the period of colonization.

However, being officially "independent" hardly meant that the former colonies controlled their own destinies. Their economies were still enclosed by their former colonizer—for example, British companies controlled much of the economy of Ghana, Kenya, and other African countries. Further, the newly independent countries had neither the income (having few people with enough wealth to tax) nor the political traditions to run a modern country.

So the Western policy-makers considered these connected problems: (1) they wanted to have global rules and agreements to avoid the chaos that had contributed to the Depression; (2) they wanted to have an international "bank" that would help countries in economic difficulty, to avoid the defaults that contribute to depressions; and (3) they wanted the newly independent South to have functional nation states (which of course would be integrated into the Western economy). Further, the policy-makers all believed that free markets would be the best way to encourage economic development. All this framed the 1947 "Bretton Woods" conference (named after the town in New Hampshire in which it took place) among 44 Western capitalist nations, but dominated by the victors in World War II. This conference created a set of policies and organizations that exist today and which exercise much control—though usually hidden to most people—over much of the world's economy: the General Agreement on Tariffs and Trade (GATT), the International Monetary Fund (IMF), and the International Bank of Reconstruction and Development (now known as the World Bank). We will consider each of these institutions briefly.

Perhaps the most important is GATT, which in 1995 morphed into the World Trade Organization, or WTO. GATT was, as its name implies, a mechanism for making agreements among countries about trade and especially about "tariffs"—or the taxes a country sets on goods that are imported from other countries. But, based on the assumptions of enclosure, the "agreements" were dictated by the Western industrial countries to benefit their own industrial economies. For example, Tanzania grew a fiber called sisal, which makes good rope, and Tanzania wanted to build rope factories. But tariff policies under GATT allowed the rich countries to put high tariffs on imported rope, which made the price of Tanzanian rope too high to sell. So Tanzania had to give up making rope and just sell the raw material—sisal—to the rich countries. Rope, of course, is much more profitable than sisal, and so the rich countries got richer while Tanzania stayed poor.

Today, the WTO, which has as members most of the world's countries, is even more powerful than GATT. According to the WTO, it

> is the only global international organization dealing with the rules of trade between nations. At its heart are the WTO agreements, negotiated and signed by the bulk of the world's trading nations and ratified in their parliaments. The goal is to help producers of goods and services, exporters, and importers conduct their business.
> (Retrieved on December 20, 2009 from www.wto.org/english/thewto_e/whatis_e/whatis_e.htm)

Exactly as prescribed by neoliberal theory, however, the rules are written by and for the corporations based in the rich countries. And though these corporations may be based in those countries, the WTO policies are often harmful to the people and ecosystems within those countries as well. According to the International Forum on Globalization (IFG), "The WTO's trade rules have regularly trumped domestic regulations, weakening protections for clean air, wildlife, safe food, fair trade and human rights" (IFG, 2003). The following areas have been particularly impacted:

Clean Air

The U.S. Clean Air Act was weakened in response to a WTO ruling which found that the law "discriminated" against foreign producers.

Wildlife

In two WTO rulings, the U.S. was forced to weaken the U.S. Marine Mammal Protection Act and the Endangered Species Act, relaxing protections for dolphins and endangered sea turtles. The WTO ruled that countries could not differentiate between products based on how they are produced, known as production process methods, so long as the final product is essentially the same.

Safe Food

The European Union (EU) currently faces hundreds of millions of dollars in trade sanctions from the U.S. because it has not eliminated a ban on hormone-treated beef as required by the WTO. The EU enacted the ban in response to public and scientific concern over the health risks associated with hormone treated beef. In its ruling, the WTO effectively declared that health regulations enacted in advance of scientific certainty were not allowed under WTO provisions.

Fair Trade

The EU currently faces hundreds of millions of dollars in trade sanctions from the U.S. because it has not eliminated the Lome Convention, a preferable trade arrangement with its former colonies in Africa, the Caribbean, and the Pacific (ACP). This arrangement was an example of trade being used to successfully advance social and economic goals—or "fair trade." In 1997, the EU was instructed to eliminate the convention or face $190 million in trade sanctions from the U.S. per year.

Human Rights

The WTO was used to successfully threaten two U.S. human rights laws modeled after successful South African anti-apartheid laws. The EU and Japan launched a WTO challenge against a Massachusetts law penalizing companies doing business with Burma's brutal military dictatorship. The WTO case was suspended and ultimately unheard because a U.S. corporate group simultaneously pursued a challenge all the way to the U.S. Supreme Court where it was struck down.

(IFG, 2003, pp. 1–2)

These examples highlight the insanity of a way of thinking that privileges economic growth over life, but which is taken for granted as "good business practice."

Similarly, the IMF and World Bank, the other two organizations created at the 1947 Bretton Woods conference, operate primarily under the direction of corporate interests. These sister organizations provide grants, loans, and economic advice to countries, primarily those of the global South. The grants and loans are made largely (1) to ease financial troubles; and (2) to build infrastructure projects that will encourage industrial development, such as dams and airports.

The money, however, comes with strings attached. In order to get the money, a country usually has to agree to a "Structural Adjustment Program," a budget-cutting plan which generally includes: cutting social services such as education and health; reducing government employment and salaries, thus putting people out of work; and selling off—privatizing—national assets that were part of the national commons, such as water systems and natural resources. These conditions mean that the country is virtually under the control of the IMF bureaucrats.

That control is enhanced by the fact that most of the money comes as loans which must be paid back, with interest. Some countries pay out as much as half of their entire government budget in loan and interest payments. And, since most can't raise enough money to make payments, they have to take even more loans, eventually getting stuck under a mountain of debt. In a now famous speech given at the Havana Debt Conference in 1985, worker activist and later President of Brazil, Lula da Silva said:

The Third World War has already started—a silent war, not for that reason any the less sinister. This war is tearing down Brazil, Latin America, and practically all the Third World. Instead of soldiers dying there are children; instead of millions of wounded there are millions of unemployed; instead of destruction of bridges there is the

tearing down of factories, schools, hospitals and entire economies . . .
It is a war by the United States against the Latin American continent
and the Third World. It is a war over the foreign debt, one which has
as its main weapon interest, a weapon more deadly than the atom
bomb, more shattering than a laser beam.
(Global Research, January 2004; retrieved on September 13, 2010
from www.globalresearch.ca/ index.php?context=va&aid=20918)

The money being paid out by countries of the South outweighs all the
foreign aid that the rich countries contribute to the South. So, despite the
claims by the rich countries that they are generously helping the poor, the
net flow of money is from the South to the rich countries. As summarized
by journalist Kevin Danaher:

Despite all the rhetoric about development and the alleviation of
poverty, the central function of these multilateral lending institutions has been to draw the rulers and governments of weaker states
more tightly into a world economy dominated by large transnational
corporations.
(Danaher, 1994, quoted in Bigelow & Peterson, 2002, p. 77)

A Treaty of Domination: NAFTA

Finally, we must mention the last pillar of this whole system of domination—specific trade treaties. The best known in the Americas is the North
American Free Trade Agreement, or NAFTA, which included Canada,
the U.S., and Mexico, and took effect in 1994. NAFTA sharply cut tariffs (import taxes) on goods flowing between the three countries. The
claim was that this would simply increase trade among the three. It did,
but not in a balanced way. One major effect was that U.S. corn, which
was very cheap because of mass production and subsidies from the U.S.
government, rushed into Mexico and undercut Mexican corn. Mexicans
bought the cheaper U.S. corn, which put millions of Mexican farmers out
of business. Many of those farmers were forced to find work in factories
owned by U.S. and Canadian corporations at wages far lower than the
companies were paying to workers in their home countries, throwing millions out of work in the U.S. and Canada and forcing others to take large
pay cuts.
    Further, some of the land previously owned by corn farmers, which
had once produced food for local consumers in Mexico, was bought up
by U.S. and Canadian agricultural companies, which now grow vegetables to ship thousands of miles to the U.S. and Canada so that consumers in those countries can have fresh vegetables all year round. Mexican

activists point out that NAFTA opened the doors for business and money to flow more freely between countries, but that it kept the door closed to the flow of people between countries. So the farmers who were forced off the land cannot easily come to the U.S. or Canada to find work. Instead they must try to sneak across the border, and be forever stigmatized as "illegal immigrants."

One other important aspect of NAFTA is that it makes illegal any and all restrictions on "free trade," allowing corporations to sue anyone who it sees as presenting barriers. Thus, for example, a lawsuit under NAFTA has forced Canada to repeal a law banning a chemical that caused nervous system damage (retrieved on September 5, 2010 from www. globalexchange.org/campaigns/ftaa/topten.html).

Neocolonialism: Control Through Discourse and Money, Not Guns

The term often used to describe this process of domination is "neocolonialism," or a new form of colonialism. Where neoliberalism—freedom for private property—is the philosophy, neocolonialism is the result. Under traditional colonialism, the rich countries controlled the South directly, maintaining governments as colonies mostly through military force. Under neocolonialism, military force isn't always necessary (though possible, as shown by a series of U.S. military incursions), because the control is exercised over the whole economic system through money and the assumptions of enclosure. To sum up neocolonialism and its application of neoliberalism: The rich countries control trade by controlling the institutions and treaties that set the rules for trade, which makes sure that most of the money that is earned flows to the rich countries. Then, when the countries of the South have trouble making a living, the rich countries loan them money under conditions that give more control over the South to the rich countries and that send even more of the wealth toward the rich countries.

Monocultures Versus Biodiversity

As globalization creates an increasingly "flat" world dominated by Western corporations, the rules of profit and progress also change the ecosystems and the ways we grow food. Complex ecosystems and an endless variety of crops are being replaced with vast areas of land planted to a single crop—a monoculture.

Imagine a forest, perhaps one you know. Note the wide variety of plants, from the tall trees to the young trees to the amazing variety of ground-level plants. Think about the birds you hear, the squirrels and others who run through the trees, the other animals that stay away from noisy humans and so are only sometimes seen—deer, bear, panthers, fox, coyotes, raccoons, possums—not to mention the endless insects.

Now imagine a different forest where all the trees are the same and planted in rows. There are virtually no other plants, just rows and rows of one tree, usually a single variety of pine, like cotton fields. This is really not a forest at all. Rather, it's a plantation. Hardly anything else lives on this plantation. It's good for one thing—providing wood pulp for paper-making—and it's very efficient at producing a great deal of wood pulp per acre. The entire system of modernity and capitalism runs on simple goals—efficiency and profit. For this way of thinking, all those other animals and plants in our natural forest are just wasting good land that could be producing more wood pulp and more profit.

Why Does Biodiversity Matter?

Remember that we talked about diversity as a condition of difference necessary to life in Chapter 2. Further, our ecosystems rely on the complex interactions of this rich array of different species, which feed off each other, use the waste products of one to aid another and protect each other. Next, there is resilience built into diverse systems. If disease strikes one species, others generally survive. But in a monoculture struck with disease, everything dies. Also, biodiversity means that nature can find the species that is suited to every ecological niche. Sometimes, humans help that process along. Indigenous Peoples have developed endless varieties of crops suited to the varying ecosystems in which they live. It is estimated, for example, that the Inca and other Andean farmers had at least 3,500 kinds of potatoes, each one suited to particular elevation and microclimate, and having specific uses (Apffel-Marglin & PRATEC, 1998, p. 3). Finally, there is the often-raised argument about benefits to humans, such as the medicines that often come from the vast diversity the planet offers—as it's often put, do we want to lose the cure to cancer because we destroyed the plant that bore the secret?

We refer to these tree farms, and indeed to all modern farm crops, as monocultures.

On the other hand, the natural forest is characterized by significant biodiversity—a wide range of living species, from the many bacteria in the soil to the variety of plants, each in its own niche, to the animal and insect life that lives on the plants and on other animals.

All the forces of globalization we have considered work to impose monocultures and destroy biodiversity. Habitat is destroyed by the growth of modern cities and suburbs. As the environmental commons—the source of diversity—is enclosed, it is often turned into fields for monoculture crops. Even the seeds themselves, once considered as unquestionably part of the commons, are now being controlled—enclosed—by a few large corporations claiming patents on their genetic structure (see the case study on Monsanto later in this chapter). When global institutions such as the World Bank finance projects in the global South, they finance diversity-destroying projects such as dams and the cutting of rainforests for pasture and farming.

It's important to see that even the so-called "Green Revolution," which claims to have sharply increased the yields from crops, is based on diversity-destroying monoculture crops. In this process, a very small variety of seeds are used in widely different climates, but, in order for them to thrive, these seeds must have heavy doses of pesticides and fertilizer. Farmers who can't afford these expensive inputs are pushed aside, and the methods that had been passed down over generations about how to grow crops in *this* particular soil with *these* particular seeds are lost forever (Shiva, 1993).

Diversity of Cultures and Food Production

This loss of biodiversity through cultural destruction highlights another point: that cultural diversity and biodiversity are related. Each of the thousands of human cultures that once existed had learned, through patient observation and experimentation over hundreds and even thousands of years, how to live with the diverse species in their particular ecosystem. But, when their commons are enclosed and they are driven off their land, all that knowledge of plants and animals is lost along with the land. Like the Andean farmers with their thousands of varieties of potatoes, every local culture developed food growing and gathering systems that sustained both the culture and the ecosystem. As journalist Michael Pollan points out, humans can live healthful lives with an amazing variation in diet—from the Inuit who have subsisted on fish and blubber to the Masai of Africa who lived on meat and milk from their cattle, to agricultural peoples who lived largely on plant crops. One estimate is that humans have eaten some 80,000 species, with 3,000 in widespread use (Pollan, 2006, p. 117). In every case, the diet was determined by what was compatible with the local ecosystem, rather than crops from far away being imposed. People in local, land-based cultures developed and maintained a specific ethical relationship to their food source that was based on recognizing that their survival depended on maintaining the carrying capacity of the land, and the intrinsic value of other species.

In its place, an industrial-based global food system has emerged, with government subsidies granted to huge monocrop farms both in North America and abroad where farmers are no longer able to cultivate the land to provide food for their families and local communities. Rather, large agribusiness or "factory farms" with many hundreds of acres or many thousands of heads of cows, for example, are given government subsidies to produce commodities for the global market. Small farmers, unable to compete with these large industrial farms (whose subsidies drive down prices), sell out to housing developers creating new suburbs, or to other farmers who have been convinced to "get big or get out."

Globalization and Small Farms

In Northern NY, Rebecca's grandfather and great grandparents made a good living from dairy farms that consisted of under 200 cows, some chickens, and enough acreage to grow the hay and corn to feed them. Milk was sold to local dairies who in turn bottled it and sold it to the local grocers in nearby towns and villages. Since WWII, however, and the introduction of farm subsidies that benefitted big farms, milk prices have dropped considerably, making it difficult for small farms to survive. Today, the countryside is now dotted with the broken down remains of small farms. No longer able to compete with subsidized CAFOs (concentrated animal feeding), the land is either going fallow, or being sold to developers for new housing. And, the prison industry has taken over where there was once a thriving farm economy.

Making this system possible is our ever-growing reliance on fossil-fuel-based technologies as the basis of fertilizers, pesticides, and methods of cultivation and transportation. On average, fruits and vegetables that arrive at our tables in North America have traveled 1,500 miles to get there. On the positive side of this system is the seemingly infinite variety of produce available (to those who can pay) all year long, which many of us now simply take for granted. Bananas from the Caribbean, apples from New Zealand, tomatoes, oranges, and grapes from California—all available every month of the year. The downside of this, of course, is the reduction in quality of many of these varieties as they are picked early, ripened artificially, processed in large quantities, and shipped halfway around the world to be packaged, then shipped again to various places across the world to awaiting consumers. In a world experiencing the ever-rising effects of climate change and decreasing levels of cheap oil, this system is clearly not sustainable. In fact, as we begin to face "peak oil," the point at which total production of oil begins to decline, we must face the looming reality of a food production system that will become ever more expensive and destructive to the planet's ecosystems. And yet, this is the system being pushed upon "developing" countries around the globe, whose own people now have to earn a wage (usually very low by our standards) in order to buy foods from other countries that they once may have grown in their own backyards! While their own farmers are forced to grow crops for export, people in these countries have been forced off the land to look for work in urban centers, many of them ending up in ever growing slums. So, when the World Bank claims to be feeding the world, or the United States complains of an "immigration problem" in the Southwest, it is important to understand the larger economic context within which people are being forced to go hungry or try to migrate.

Schooling in the Service of Globalization

In Chapter 6, we introduced the concept of schools as "reproducers" of class differences; that is, rather than serving to reduce the gap between classes, schools often tend to recreate the assumptions and habits that maintain class differences. In the same way, schooling tends to reproduce globalization by transmitting the assumptions that underlie globalization without questioning them.

First and foremost, official school curricula rarely question the assumptions of enclosure and domination. The "right" of individual property ownership is generally treated as a given, as is the right of corporations to buy up the land of others as a matter of "progress" and "development." Indeed, just to note how strange it sounds to suggest that the rich countries are "overdeveloped" is to see the power of an assumption to shape our perceptions.

Further, K-12 schools rarely teach about the impacts of globalization, about the WTO or the IMF, despite their enormous impacts on the world. These institutions are rarely mentioned in textbooks or curricula. When they are, it is almost exclusively in economics books, which focus on the benefits of capitalist economics. In fact, capitalism is often presented as economics, period. Or, if other forms are presented—such as communism, for example—they are usually criticized as authoritarian forms that limit people's freedom. Examples of non-industrial economies that are based on the commons and subsistence relationships, if addressed at all, are treated as "primitive." Thus, the texts invariably repeat the myths that "Free trade, in the long run, will improve life for everyone around the world," or "The WTO is a democratic organization" (Au, 2000, p. 4).

A "Tragic" School Memory From Jeff

Jeff remembers carefully studying Hardin's (1968) *Tragedy of the Commons* in high school. As presented by the teacher, it was laughably obvious that ranchers sharing a common patch of land to graze their cows could never be trusted to conserve it—each of them would also add one more cow, then one more cow, until the land was overused. "It's human nature," the teacher said, "to pursue one's own interest without concern for the larger consequences." We were never told that, in fact, common grazing areas have been part of human culture for thousands of years, and that it only stops working when a different culture—modernity—creates different assumptions about morality. Why? I'm sure the teacher didn't know about these large areas of history—because she hadn't been taught about them either.

Another layer to the role education plays in reproducing the practices of globalization is that modernist forms of schooling itself have been globalized. The decreasing diversity in the model of schooling implemented, or imposed, around the world presents a serious threat to the ability of future generations to see beyond or outside the illusions presented by globalization. Spring (2009) shows that schools worldwide increasingly focus on high-status knowledge and on Western thinking about development. Further:

> Global discourses exist about the knowledge economy, lifelong learning, global migration and brain circulation, and neoliberalism. Illustrative of major global institutions affecting worldwide educational practices and policies are the World Bank, Organization for Economic Cooperation and Development (OECD), the World Trade Organization (WTO), and its General Agreement on Trade in Services (GATS), the United Nations, UNESCO, and other inter-governmental organizations (IGOs), and nongovernmental organizations (NGOs), such as human rights, environmental, and women's organizations. Another factor is the impact on local schools of the development of English as the language of global business.
> (Spring, 2009, p. 2)

Globalization and Resistance: Case Studies

The following case studies offer examples of ways that globalization impacts people and ecosystems. It's easy to see this as a relentlessly negative story, and much of it is indeed discouraging. However, many of the case studies also offer examples of resistance; people often find ways to fight back against the seemingly unstoppable forces of globalization. Others of the case studies offer "subsistence" more than resistance—that is, people finding a way to survive the destruction of community that is often the legacy of globalization.

To help you draw some connections between the case studies, consider these questions as you read:

- What surprises you?
- What patterns do you see across the world, including both the industrial world and the South?
- What seem to be effective ways, both individual and collective, that people use to resist the impacts of globalization?
- What can you learn from people who are finding ways to subsist—survive—within a community devastated by the global economy?

Case Study #1: Global Food Companies Versus Farmers

Most of us have little idea where our food comes from. We imagine Farmer John hoeing some vegetables or maybe driving a tractor in his fields. In fact, farming has become a complex, industrialized business. As in other areas, corporations have moved to enclose and privatize knowledge, going so far as claiming patents for the DNA of living things, thus treating as private property the specific genetic material of living creatures (see Chapter 4).

How do you think a farmer gets his or her seeds to plant next year's crop? Until recently, the primary source of seed was last year's crop. The farmer would save some of the corn, for example, to use as seed for next year. However, with the advent of farming as a large corporate business, seed companies began to develop and sell seeds that were "new and improved," if used with the right fertilizers. Farmers began the practice of buying seed.

Next, companies moved rapidly into the business of genetic engineering of seed varieties. Monsanto, by far the biggest of these companies, perfected a model of controlling knowledge and thus controlling farmers. As the Center for Food Safety summarizes:

> In order to ensure its role as an industry leader in the field of biotechnology, Monsanto has employed three main tactics: it has bought or merged with most of the major seed companies to gain an important level of control over seed germplasm; it has acquired a multitude of patents on both genetic engineering techniques and genetically engineered seed varieties, thus dominating the market in biotech crops;

and it has required that any farmer purchasing its seed must first sign an agreement prohibiting the saving of seed, thereby forcing farmers to repurchase Monsanto's seed every year. These tactics have afforded this one company unprecedented control over the sale and use of crop seed in the United States.

(Center for Food Safety, 2005, p. 7)

You can see in these tactics how enclosure—control—is a central motivation for Monsanto. This kind of control produces predictable profits, and, more importantly, reduces competition. If nobody can grow soybeans without Monsanto seeds, then Monsanto is in a perfect position to dominate the industry and increase its profits.

Monsanto's efforts toward control have been tremendously effective. "Monsanto's varieties of genetically engineered seeds have effectively pushed other seed varieties off the market. Indiana soybean farmer Troy Roush says, 'You can't even purchase them in this market. They're not available'" (Center for Food Safety, 2005, p. 10). A key step in the enclosure process is controlling all of the knowledge and practice in a field. To the extent that some knowledge is still shared by the community, the domination by the industrial world (in this case Monsanto) is threatened. The next tactic for Monsanto has been to aggressively sue any farmer who may have used seed that has some of Monsanto's patented genes in it. The problem here is what's called cross-pollination: The pollen from any plant travels beyond the field in which it was planted on the wind, on birds, on bees. If pollen from a plant grown from Monsanto seed breeds with a non-Monsanto plant, then Monsanto claims that the farmer who grows this hybrid must pay Monsanto.

Many farmers have settled out of court with Monsanto rather than face the legal costs of fighting, and some in the U.S. have lost in court. But one farmer in Saskatchewan, Canada, fought back. Percy Schmeiser's farm was first contaminated with Monsanto-owned seeds in 1996–1997. He planted his fields with seed he saved from his previous crop, as he always had. Monsanto somehow got some of his crop and determined that many of his plants had the "RoundUp Ready" gene in them (genetically engineered to withstand the spraying of the weed-killer RoundUp). It was never clear how his crops were contaminated with RoundUp Ready seeds—whether pollen blew in from other farms or whether it fell off farm trucks. But it didn't matter. Monsanto sued Schmeiser for using their seed without paying for it. Rather than giving in, he countersued and showed that he had never used RoundUp on his fields. His legal battle with Monsanto lasted nearly 12 years, until a final decision by the Canadian Supreme Court in 2008. Although the Court found that Monsanto's patent on the seed had been infringed, it charged Schmeiser with no damages—basically calling it a draw.

You can see here how the process of enclosure spreads from buying seed to making seed to patenting life to controlling what is grown by nearly every farmer of major cash crops in the U.S. and Canada.

Other Resistance to the Enclosure of Food

There are many other ways that people and organizations are challenging the corporations that control so much of our food supply: seed savers, organic farmers and others who opt out of the corporate food system, and those who resist the pressure by the global food companies to accept what some call "Frankenfoods."

In many European countries, there is widespread resistance to genetically engineered crops, and some of those countries even have laws banning or limiting engineered crops. In the U.S., however, there has been relatively little mass resistance, with one exception: milk. Some years ago, the global food companies created a hormone, rBGH, that when fed to cows increased milk production. It rapidly spread in use by the dairy industry. The hormone also had a number of side effects, including pain and injury for cows as well as possible consequences of added hormones on the development of children and an increase in various cancers. A movement grew up opposing the use of rGBH. As concern about rGBH milk spread, a number of dairies stopped using it and advertised that their milk was rGBH-free. Consumers became concerned enough to vote with their wallets by buying organic milk and other milk that was rGBH-free. Today, there are a declining number of dairies who give rGBH to their cows. This example suggests that it is possible for informed people to change what the food corporations offer.

Another form of resistance to corporate enclosure of food is to opt out of the corporate food system. One path to opting out is to grow or purchase organic food. Farmers' markets, food cooperatives, and Community Supported Agriculture (consumer supported farms) are often sources of organic food, and even conventional grocery stores commonly offer organic food. However, global food corporations are heavily involved in organic food now, too. What this means is that while their products may be grown without pesticides or chemically-based fertilizers, they are most likely still coming from large subsidized monocultures, and will still travel many hundreds of miles before reaching our table. As Michael Pollan (2006) points out, it may be better to buy non-organic food from a local farmer whom you know and can talk to about his or her methods, than from a large corporate organics producer. The best option, of course, is a local organic grower who produces using traditional methods, generally grows a diverse crop, and uses no chemicals.

Indeed, some farmers opt out of the global food system. One of the best-known examples is Virginia farmer Joel Salatin (www.polyfacefarms.com), who raises food animals on what he calls a "beyond organic" farm, whose stated goal is "to develop emotionally, economically, environmentally enhancing agricultural enterprises and facilitate their duplication throughout the world." Salatin's farm uses techniques that don't require purchases from global food companies and that were once part of the commons—rotating pastures, fertilizing with animal manure, use of worms and compost for soil enhancement.

Finally, there are organizations dedicated to maintaining the diversity of seeds rather than limiting them. Non-profit groups such as Seed Savers Exchange (www.seedsavers.org) encourage the saving and distribution of "heirloom" seeds—the thousands of plant varieties that have been developed and shared over the ages before the global food companies moved to limit and control the crops—mostly to grow crops that were the most profitable, not the best tasting. If you haven't ever had heirloom food, go to your local farmers market and try an heirloom tomato—you'll never want to eat a supermarket tomato again!

How does this connect to education? For one, the domination of Monsanto and other food corporations is maintained when we don't know where our food comes from. The European refusal to buy genetically-engineered food is a result of widespread knowledge about the consequences for farmers and consumers. But, in the U.S., there is little discussion in the mass media. Schools can put the discussion in front of students. Students can explore how much of their food comes from genetically-engineered crops as opposed to coming from organic or local food, and can compare heirloom varieties of, say, tomatoes with industrial varieties mainly designed to survive long-distance travel.

Case Study #2: Basmati Rice and the Neem Tree: Who Owns Life?

Imagine your ancestors had composed a song hundreds of years ago. It was sung at family celebrations and was familiar to every child. As it was passed to each generation, it was changed a little bit, but it was still the family song. But then, one day, a music company came to a family event and recorded the song. Before long, a representative of the company came to your family, holding a piece of paper that said the company now owned the song, because it had changed one note in the song and claimed a copyright on the "new" song. The company said that your family must pay every time you sang the song, because you were using the company's property. The police officer who came with the company rep backed up the company's position, saying that the government would force you to pay.

Seem ridiculous? Yet this is exactly parallel to what happens with plants and seeds in a globalized world. Corporations such as W. R. Grace go into Indigenous communities, take seeds that are the product of generations of breeding, change a small number of genes through genetic engineering, and then claim patents on the seeds, the same way that patents are taken on new forms of windshield wipers or coffee-makers. The corporations claim the knowledge of how to produce these seeds as "intellectual property." But the communities who developed the seed call it "biopiracy." Much of the struggle against biopiracy has taken place in India. One example is the case of the neem tree. Another is the plot to steal basmati rice.

The neem tree, known as "the curer of all ailments" in India, has for thousands of years produced various benefits. Over the generations, communities across India learned how to turn the seeds and bark into natural pesticides, contraceptives, and medicines. The communities used the tree for fuel and timber. But, in 1985, the W. R. Grace company claimed a patent on a fungicide from the neem tree (one of many patents claimed on products from the tree). The company started manufacturing neem products, and bought up most of the available seed, driving the price up, which meant that many traditional users could no longer afford it (see Shiva & Holly-Bhar, 1996).

Organizations in India started resisting in the early 1990s. Grassroots organizing led marches on the Grace company building and petitions with a million signatures opposing Grace's control of neem. Meanwhile, legal challenges were mounted by Navdanya (www.navdanya.org) and other Indian organizations.

The legal case was finally won in 2005, when W. R. Grace's patent was revoked by the European Patent Office, which said there was no new invention in the fungicide. Note that this decision doesn't question the right of a company to own products produced by centuries of community work, just that they hadn't changed this product enough.

Next, the case of basmati rice shows an attempt not just to own a community-created product, but to own life—to own a genetically engineered version of basmati rice (the fragrant rice that is often a component of Indian cooking). In 1997, the Rice-Tec company was granted a patent on a variety of basmati rice, despite it being only slightly different than the dozens of varieties of basmati rice that have been created by generations of farmers using traditional methods of crossing plants. Rice-Tec's patent threatened to put out of business hundreds of thousands of Indian farmers who grow their own varieties of basmati rice; they were even threatened with having to pay Rice-Tec for using their own rice.

Widespread opposition from India created a campaign to overturn this patent. The campaign was successful in 2001, when much of the patent was revoked by the U.S. Patent Office (Retrieved on December 15, 2009 from http://navdanya.org). As with the neem tree, the decision was made not because the Patent Office objected to patents on living things, but because Rice-Tec could not prove that its rice was sufficiently different from traditional basmati rice.

The WTO and GATT have played a key role in companies' efforts to own living things such as community-developed seeds and products. One of the key aspects of the trade agreements were TRIPs, or Trade-Related Intellectual Property rules, which essentially insist that all countries accept patent laws that protect corporate "intellectual property" above local values and above the generations-long development of crop varieties.

It is important for educators to see that much of the world does not accept Western valuing of privately owned property above all else. Moreover, it is important for educators to help students problematize claims that appear reasonable at first glance, such as corporations' claim of ownership over their own "inventions," but which hide the larger questions of patenting life and stealing collective knowledge or inventions. To return to our song analogy at the beginning, on first glance, a corporation that owned a new song would seem to be reasonable in wanting others to pay for the use of it. This is what keeps musicians and music companies in business. But hidden behind that "reasonable" claim is the long history of the song's development in families and communities.

Slow Food

While on the topic of food in a global system, it is hard not to consider how all of these examples, especially the ones directly about food, relate to diverse efforts around the world to localize both food production and consumption. Directly impacting and leading resistance to multi-national corporate domination of food is the Slow Foods movement (Petrini, 2007). This movement developed in Italy from a philosophy that stands for the diverse cultural pleasure of meals, for the importance of good-tasting food, and for a direct and local relationship to food. It is a response to cultures facing rapid monoculturalization through food as a result of today's modern myths about world hunger and market economics. They have helped local communities emphasize the importance of eating food that tastes good and is good for living systems. Health, enjoyment, and the preservation of cultural food habits that support healthy living are promoted in association with a localization movement shared by farmers and local consumers across the globe.

Slow Foods launched a massive campaign to unite world food security movements in the yearly event called Terra Madre. The movement began out of the need to support small farmers and to combat the global systems undermining local food movements. The unifying event brings consumers, educational institutions, food preparers, agricultural researchers, and several non-profit organizations together to craft a manifesto and work toward resisting the impact of an attempt by global markets to control food. Your local community more than likely has co-ops and farmers who either participate in Terra Madre or stand for the same ideals.

Case Study #3: Detroit, a City Left Behind

Detroit's relation to the processes of globalization is unique in that it really represents what happens when corporations no longer need a community. In many ways, Detroit's story can be understood as what happens to the people in industrialized communities as they are left behind by companies in the search for cheaper labor and less restrictive environmental laws. In this sense, Detroit's story is about survival, rather than resistance.

Until the 1950s, the city was a thriving and powerful city with gorgeous wide boulevards lined by big old shade trees, and beautiful architecture both in its downtown buildings and throughout the residential neighborhoods. The booming auto industry and all the associated manufacturing and service businesses attracted immigrants from all over Europe as well as African Americans and poor whites from Southern states looking for work in the factories. In the late 1940s and early 1950s, as the decision was made to invest in a super-highway system and not mass transportation, white residents began to find new housing opportunities outside the city, and a ring of suburbs began to develop. Cheap gasoline, a love of the automobile, and these new highways were used to move white workers into work and back out to their homes and families. As we discussed in Chapter 7, black families were not equally welcome.

Banks and real estate companies used "redlining" tactics to prevent African American families from buying homes in dominantly white neighborhoods, isolating these families in the city. Meanwhile the "Big Three" automakers also decided to relocate outside the city, moving many of their factories and with them many jobs. In this sense, "outsourcing" of work and economic collapse was a reality for poor whites and African Americans well before American jobs in the auto industry actually left the United States.

As white families and the manufacturing sector left, property values in Detroit fell, as did the tax base supporting city services such as public education, garbage and trash pickup, street maintenance, and sewer and water utilities. As the quality of education, housing, and public health services fell for remaining residents, segregation continued, and racial tensions became high. In the late 1960s a riot erupted, resulting in fires, violence, and other destruction that sent even more white families fleeing the city. Detroit had become a veritable war zone in just two decades as the people who had built it and the auto industry with their labor were pitted against each other for what little the city had left to offer.

Today, the results of these historic events can be seen in the abandoned and burned out buildings, abandoned lots, and general blight across this once beautiful, flourishing city. Now considered one of the world's "shrinking cities," as more and more people leave, Detroit has 40,000 abandoned lots, many of which are "brownfields" contaminated with lead, mercury, and other toxins, and the city is considered a "food desert": the last major grocery store left in 2007 because it could not make a profit. Liquor stores and fast food restaurants are found on every other corner. Obesity is a problem among teenagers, diabetes is on the rise, and the elderly are finding it more and more difficult to find sufficient food.

But this is not the whole story, not by a long shot. As a result of being forced into these dire circumstances, many residents of Detroit have turned to each other for help, developing important relationships of mutuality and care that can be understood as a revitalization of the Detroit commons (Martusewicz, 2009; Bowers & Martusewicz, 2006) and a turn toward simple subsistence activities as a means of survival and general well-being. While this story is really more about forced subsistence than actual intentional resistance to the effects of industrialization and a globalized economy, it is no less powerful. Remember what we said in the above section about the commons being those shared relationships and activities that do not require money but often lead to important caretaking. Some of the most important aspects of the Detroit revitalization effort include informal bartering—work-for-work where someone offers to roof his neighbor's house in exchange for the repair of a car, for example, or one woman cares for her neighbor's children one day so that her own children will be cared for the next. Elder care by neighbors is another important example of a commons practice being enacted among neighbors. Many of Detroit's residents are aged with little or no health care support except that offered by generous neighbors who may go get groceries, help with daily tasks, or simply visit to make sure they are all right.

There is also a strong and growing public art network in Detroit. Poets, muralists, and musicians share their talent in open poetry slams, on the walls of buildings, in storefront galleries, and local clubs. They also teach often-free classes to interested youth in after-school, weekend, and summer sessions. In the case of this city and others in the United States, we can see that the people are experiencing the downside of an industrial process that has left them by the wayside as corporations "globalize" to look for cheaper workers and less stringent environmental or labor laws in the so-called "developing" countries. What we see, then, is not so much "resistance" on the part of Detroit residents, as much as a strong will to survive a tragic neglect and abandonment.

Probably the most organized way that Detroit residents are responding to the neglect and abandonment they've experienced is by addressing the lack of nutritious, culturally-relevant food by growing gardens, raising chickens, and keeping bees. A local system of urban agriculture is developing across the city that is turning the empty lots into raised beds and community gardens. In Detroit, over 1,500 gardens have been created, supported by neighborhood folks with a network of non-profit community organizations whose purpose is to help teach about and provide resources for the cultivation, harvest, preparation, and preservation of food. These activities form the basis of an ancient food commons that, for Detroit and other urban areas across the United States, has its roots in southern slave culture, plantation life, and reconstruction agricultural practices, all the way back to ancient African traditions.

One organization, the Black Community Food Security Network, for example, uses African traditions, rituals, and knowledge to help raise awareness of the need for fresh healthy food to counter the killing effects of food insecurity in the city. They have created an urban farm that includes large vegetable plots as well as an apiary to both teach and feed the community. Another organization, EarthWorks, was founded by Brother Rick Samyn, a Franciscan monk who upon his return from Vietnam realized the dire circumstances that Detroit's food system was creating for the health of its residents. On little more than an acre of land, several tons of food are harvested each year to contribute both to the Capuchin Soup Kitchen as well as local farmers' markets held in church parking lots across the city. EarthWorks is supported by other organizations— the Greening of Detroit, in particular—in a growing network of urban farmers. These organizations work hand in hand with residents sharing knowledge and labor to create gardens, large and small, that are feeding many city residents. The Greening of Detroit's Garden Resource program offers people all sorts of classes about planting, cultivating, harvesting, preparing, and preserving food, as well as actual material resources in the form of a tools lending service, seeds and seedlings, compost, and physical labor when it's needed to till soil or help harvest.

In sum, while the city residents certainly would not choose to be in this situation and would no doubt welcome a return of jobs and a strong capitalist economic system, what they are creating is in many ways more sustainable than what the industrial system once offered. They are engaging in practices that their grandparents and great grandparents once knew well, and left behind believing them be (as one of Rebecca's students from Detroit once remarked) "backward." But, as we've been discussing throughout this chapter and the book, such beliefs are really a matter of the ways the particular discourse of "progress" has been perpetuated by our culture, and internalized by us as members of that culture. Living in ways that are simpler, that require us to develop "give and take" relationships with, and get to know, our neighbors and the land we occupy, is not "backward" or inferior at all. In fact, as we are seeing in this city, such methods and interactions are proving to be full of nutritious and environmentally sound alternatives to the current industrialized systems being exported across the world as more "developed."

Case Study #4: Living Outside Globalization in Cuba

Cuba's story is interesting because of its former relationship to the global industrial economic system via trade agreements with the Soviet bloc, its ability to resist the global food crisis that has been brought about in part by the inequalities in the structures of the world economy, and what it now offers as a model response to the problem of "peak oil." Peak oil is a concept that refers to the moment when we have reached maximum global petroleum extraction, after which oil production and the quality of what gets extracted declines. "Fueled" by industrialization, current processes of globalization require large inputs of petroleum for both the production and transportation of goods.

Prior to 1990, Cuba's agricultural system was focused on the production of export crops—in particular sugar cane—for the world market, particularly (after the Cuban revolution in 1959) for the Soviet bloc countries. Most of the land in Cuba was under production for this conventional "monocultural" system, requiring high inputs of fossil-fuel-based pesticides and fertilizers, and large gasoline powered machinery. These were imported primarily from the Soviet Union. Due to this commitment of land to sugar cane, and using their earnings from its export, the country imported "an estimated 57% of its caloric intake" (Norberg-Hodge et al., in Cavanagh & Mander, 2002, p. 172). To insure that the people of Cuba were fed, a rationing system was used to provide a low-cost but highly nutritious diet to Cuba's population.

The end of the Cold War and the collapse of the Soviet Union led to important changes in Cuba's relation to the global market and especially in its approach to agriculture and the supply of food. Cuba's trade relations began to collapse in 1989 when the U.S. tightened its embargo and the Soviet Union could no longer provide the goods that had been imported, including petroleum to fuel its modes of transportation. During a period referred to as "the Special Period," Cuba experienced an 80 percent decrease in pesticide and fertilizer imports and a 50 percent decline in food imports (Norberg-Hodge et al., in Cavanagh & Mander, 2002). Plunged into a food crisis, Cuba responded by drawing on both the knowledge of a well-established scientific community and using older traditional knowledge to create a locally-based, decentralized system of sustainable agriculture. Under Castro, Cuba's population has been well-educated, with 96 percent literacy and substantial numbers gaining college diplomas. Prior to the crisis, a strong base of research on agro-ecological methods was already established. This research was put into action alongside that of the older generation of farmers as the

Cuban government responded to the crisis with strategies that lessened the country's reliance on fossil-fuel-based fertilizers, pesticides, and tractor cultivation, and encouraged people to begin to engage in small scale farming.

Many of the huge state-controlled farms were dismantled and turned over to smaller worker-controlled collectives, called Agricultural Production Cooperatives, through the policy and practice of "usufruct": granting the right to occupy, use, and make a profit from the land for specific purposes—in this case, food production for local needs. Farmers on these collaboratives, along with individual smallholders, descendants of generations of small farmers, began to grow vegetables and raise the animals needed to feed the people of Cuba with fewer inputs and using older more sustainable practices. These included, for example, using animal waste and "green manure" (the practice of growing nitrogen-rich plants to be tilled into the soil) as fertilizers, methods of diverse crop plantings and crop rotation, the use of natural enemies to combat pests, and soil conservation. One way that science was brought to bear on traditional knowledge was through a return to animal traction in place of machinery, and the improvement of plows that helped to turn the soil in such a way as to conserve precious topsoil. Oxen were reintroduced as a primary way to prepare the fields, using the knowledge of old-timers in the raising of the necessary number of animals.

By the late 1990s, the food shortage was largely over, but the cost of food had increased significantly, especially for those in urban areas. As a result, small community gardens in the urban centers also began to spring up as Cubans, much like Detroiters, responded to the food crisis by turning small patches of vacant land and roof-tops into productive and profitable agricultural space. As Peter Rosset and Martin Borque (2002) point out,

> the proliferation of urban farmers who produce fresh produce has also been extremely important to the Cuban food supply. The earlier food shortage and resultant increase in food prices suddenly turned urban agriculture into a very profitable activity for Cubans . . . formerly vacant lots and backyards in all Cuban cities now sport food crops and farm animals, and fresh produce is sold from stands throughout urban areas at prices substantially below those in farmers' markets.
>
> (Rosset & Borque, 2002, p. xviii)

By the late 1990s, these activities had created an alternative food system in Cuba. Farmers across the country were addressing food shortages and resisting worldwide food crises plaguing other countries by offering locally produced, high quality, and nutritious foodstuffs. Locally and regionally produced food has offered Cubans self-sufficiency and an important form of economic security as the country no longer relies on the world market to meet the nutritional needs of its people. Cuban agriculture is more ecologically sound as the land and those it feeds becomes healthier and more productive. One of the results of turning to small locally controlled farms and urban agriculture has been a demonstration that redistributing land to small farms and using methods that demand fewer inputs actually increases the relative productivity of that land on a per acre basis. And further, it offers high status employment to the Cuban people as farmers are held among the most respected of professions.

In short, what began as a crisis brought on by a victory of capitalism over communist methods of production in the Soviet bloc, has turned into a much healthier way of providing food for the Cuban people, an inadvertent resistance to the effects of global power.

Case Study #5: Ladakh

A powerful example of the impact of globalization is shown in the case of Ladakh (mentioned in Chapter 3), also known as Little Tibet, in the Indian province of Kashmir. The Ladakhi people have for centuries forged a comfortable subsistence in a harsh mountainous region, where the growing season is only a few months. The culture, rooted in Buddhism, is centered on community and cooperation. Families help each other with harvesting crops and take turns leading their animals to grazing pastures. They share the limited supplies of water for irrigation and drinking. As part of surviving in the difficult terrain, they even have developed ways to limit population growth, including birth control and a tradition of sending children to Buddhist monasteries. Helena Norberg-Hodge, a British anthropologist who has spent decades learning the culture of Ladakh, notes that a singular characteristic of the culture was that the people were happy, despite their limited material possessions.

But globalization came to Ladakh, starting in the 1960s. A highway was built, allowing far easier access than had existed before. Industrial products, such as electrical appliances, cars, and motor scooters began to fill the streets. Then the Indian government started shipping in cheap grain, more to dump the products of industrial farms in India than to help Ladakhis. The cheap grain undercut the carefully balanced economy of Ladakh, making their grain less competitive, and pushing many people to take jobs in the cities. At the same time, Indian and Western movies made modern culture look attractive—and as Ladakhis were persuaded of the value of Western goods, they were forced into the cash economy to make the money to buy those goods.

Even education played a role in changing Ladakhi culture. As families were drawn into the cities, their children were drawn into formal schools.

But these schools didn't teach Ladakhi culture, they taught in an Indian language—Urdu—and then switched to English for high school. School materials tended to glorify Western ways of living, and prepared students for college but not for the traditional culture. Unfortunately, many students failed college entrance exams, and so were left with few options in the modern economy, and no skills for the traditional economy. We often see education as one of the unqualified benefits of modernization, but Ladakh's experience shows the ways that modern education serves more to assist the process of globalization than it helps the people (Norberg-Hodge, 1991).

In just a few years, Ladakh was changed from an independent subsistence culture to a part of the global economy. While globalization certainly brought some gains, it also brought poverty—whereas everyone in the traditional culture had a comfortable home, the new culture created a large class of poor people living in shacks. Family and community ties have been broken, violence has increased, and even tension between ethnic groups has increased dramatically.

An important lesson from Ladakh, therefore, is that so many of the problems we see in modern culture are not the inevitable product of "human nature," but instead are the consequences of a specific culture. Because the changes happened so quickly, and were documented, we can see that the process of globalization is not natural, but is instead imposed from outside, benefiting the globalizers but not the victims.

But Ladakh also offers lessons in the ability to challenge the imposed rule. Among the groups trying to protect Ladakhi traditions is the Women's Alliance of Ladakh. Since 1994, this organization of over 6,000 women—most of whom live in traditional villages across the region—has been resisting globalization with two main goals: to raise the status of rural women and to strengthen traditional culture and agriculture. The main activity of the Ladakhi Women's Alliance Center in Leh (the capital city) is to work on the ground in the villages and in the city to educate and promote Ladakhi traditions.

Globalization works to systematically marginalize women. As pressures to modernize draw men and children away from villages in Ladakh, women are left with more work and less decision-making rights. Rebecca and Johnny visited the Women's Alliance Center in 2006, and met women from surrounding villages who regularly organized and hosted monthly exhibitions, celebrating and teaching others local knowledge and skills. Women who are concerned that future generations will not learn or value the importance of harvesting oil from apricot seeds, spinning wool, preparing local foods, dying and weaving, sharing stories, music, dance, and art gathered to showcase and educate the community, thus passing on these important aspects of Ladakhi living.

The Women's Alliance Center also takes direct political action. They were specifically influential in the passing of a ban on plastic bags, as well as regularly organizing clean-ups. Leh has no municipal trash system in place, as the very notion of trash is a product of modernization. In traditional Ladakhi living everything is used and reused and nothing is ever trash, even human excrement.

The Ladakhi women travel to villages to educate and unify women, and to aid in resisting market propaganda which promotes a way of life that undermines the traditions of Ladakh. The efforts are summed up by local WAL member Dolma Tsering, who said, "Only a few years ago women were considered backward and ignorant. Now we're respected as one of the most influential voices in Ladakh" (www.isecf.org.uk).

Efforts to mobilize women and strengthen the local via intergenerational exchanges and skills comprise some of the leading efforts in the world to resist globalization through local action. This happens as women gather to cultivate a plot of land in a Detroit neighborhood, gather in a local knitting circle, trade handmade items in trendy urban nightclubs, or join the WAL in the Himalayas.

Try This Out

Find out where efforts to localize and share important skills are happening through women in your neighborhood and community. Grandmothers, mothers, and daughters have been and will continue to sustain life through many traditional practices at home and collaboratively in communities. We need to recognize this important work, value it, and learn from it.

Case Study #6: Resistance to Water Privatization

In 2001, the bottled water company Perrier leased a piece of land from the owner of a private hunting preserve in Mecosta County, Michigan, and was granted a license by then-Governor John Engler for less than $100 per year allowing the company to pump 100–300 gallons of water per minute out of the local aquifer. Pumped out of the ground and piped 11 miles to Stanwood, the water is bottled and sold back to the public as the popular brand Ice Mountain, now owned by Nestlé Waters of North America. It is advertised on their website as "100% Mountain Spring Water" (www.icemountain.com), though anyone who knows the landscape of this region of the lower peninsula of Michigan knows there are no mountains anywhere near the plant.

Shortly after pumping began, several grassroots organizations began to protest this privatization scheme, arguing that it had negative effects not only on the local environment, but also that it represented a negative precedent in terms of moving control of their local resource out of the hands of the public and into a multinational corporation. In short, the groups were protesting a clear act of enclosure against their environmental commons. Led by the Sweetwater Alliance, local people staged peaceful "canoe-ins" along the stream to publicize what was happening to their watershed.

Then, later in 2001, "Michigan Citizens for Water Conservation (MCWC), along with four individual local residents, filed a lawsuit in Mecosta County Circuit Court seeking to prevent the pumping, arguing that it was not a legally defined 'reasonable use' of water and violated state and federal regulations regarding water rights" (Lydersen, 2003). The lawsuit cites studies finding that pumping 400 gallons a minute will reduce the flow of water in lakes and streams fed by the spring by as much as two and a quarter inches. Nestlé argued that pumping the water out of the Mecosta aquifer would have "no harmful effects on people" and would actually be "good for trout fisherman" by lowering the overall water temperature in local streams. But, the opponents to Nestlé argued that the larger issue was that Nestlé should not be allowed to extract billions of gallons of water a year from the area for profit and with nothing returned to the local communities or state beyond the permit fee.

> "At the gut level people believe water is for everybody," said Holly Wren Spaulding, a member of the Sweetwater Alliance, noting that the grassroots movement against the plant has included a wide coalition ranging from Native American tribes to Navy SEALS. "People think it's wrong for a transnational company to be allowed to come in and take water and profit from it."
>
> (Lydersen, 2003; retrieved on January 31, 2010 from www.alternet.org/story/16044)

Spaulding goes on to note the ways that Nestlé's octopus-like tentacles are spreading over Michigan, with plants waiting to open in nearby Oscoda County and other parts of Michigan where residents are less informed or organized to oppose them. Several members of the Sweetwater Alliance were detained by police for simply walking into a local grocery store wearing anti-Ice Mountain buttons.

In early December 2003, the courts made their decisions. Judge Lawrence Root ordered Nestlé to completely stop pumping water in 22 days, effectively closing the plant. But Governor Jennifer Granholm shocked activists by filing an amicus brief that convinced the appeals court to grant a stay to the order, allowing Nestlé to continue taking water for profit out of Michigan. While serving as Attorney General, Granholm had voiced strong opposition to the Ice Mountain project, but clearly the multi-million dollar water privatization industry had found its way into the hearts and interests of state officials.

Water privatization is a worldwide enclosure issue, and includes not just bottling and selling water for profit, but also the privatization of public water utilities. For example, in Highland Park, Michigan, an urban city surrounded by the city of Detroit and suffering from the same economic abandonment discussed earlier, residents working with the Michigan Welfare Rights Association successfully blocked a water privatization scheme. With Highland Park's tax-base severely affected by white flight and the loss of auto industry jobs, utilities in the city fell into disrepair, as residents were forced to pay ever-increasing water bills. The city hired an emergency financial manager, whose solution to the economic crisis was to raise prices even further. When some residents were unable to pay, water was shut off to their homes and the bills were added to their city taxes. To make matters worse, the people in Highland Park who were already suffering from the impoverishment of the city were often blamed for their inability to pay, and charged with being bad parents when social services were legally forced to remove their children from their homes. The inability to pay eventually led to the city seizing some residents' property, evicting them for failure to pay, and finally putting forth a plan to sell the utilities to a private firm.

Residents organized with the help of grassroots activists including the Sweetwater Alliance and the Michigan Welfare Rights Association, who helped them inform their neighbors of their rights and the negative effects of privatization. Led by ordinary citizens determined to push back and regain control of their commons, these Highland Park residents took on the city council and won. The problem of high prices and a failing utilities is far from solved but their success in bringing to their neighbors' attention the exploitive attitudes and practices of private firms has proven to be a stronger force than expected.

In Bolivia, another now-famous case has been used by Michigan residents and others around the world as a rallying cry in the fight against the enclosure of water rights. "Remember Cochabamba!" is a powerful proclamation by communities organizing to protect their water commons. Cochabamba is a town of about 800,000 people located high in the Andes. Suffering from the highest rates of poverty in South America, Bolivia had been following the rules of international lending agencies, selling most of its airline, railroads, mines, and electric company to private—usually foreign-controlled—companies. In 1999, the World Bank offered a concession to International Water, a subsidiary of Bechtel, as it recommended that the municipal water supply of Cochabamba be privatized. The privatization meant that the price of water immediately increased, making access difficult for the Cochabamba residents, most of whom live on less than $100 a month. Outraged, the citizens organized, accusing the government of "leasing the rain." They formed La Coordinadora de Defensa del Agua y la Vida (The Coalition in Defense of Water and Life) and mobilized millions of Bolivians who converged on Cochabamba and marched through the streets in protest, supported a general strike, and successfully shut down the city for four days (Shiva, 2002, p. 102). At this mass protest, the people issued the Cochabamba Declaration, demanding the protection of universal water rights. Responding to their protest, the government asserted that it would reverse the price increase, but it didn't happen.

> La Coordinadora organized a peaceful march demanding the repeal of the Drinking Water and Sanitation Law, the annulment of ordinances allowing privatization, the termination of the water contract, and the participation of citizens in drafting a water resource law. The citizens' demands . . . were violently rejected.
>
> (Shiva, 2002, p. 103)

Attempting to silence the protestors, the government declared martial law and police assaulted the protestors with tear gas and batons. Activists were arrested and in the end 175 people were injured, and one young man killed. But the people stood their ground and on April 10, 2000, after eight days of violent conflict, Cochabamba stunned the world when the government announced that Bechtel had left, claiming the government had broken its contract.

The victory was felt by water activists around the world, and the farmers in the outskirts of the city returned to irrigating their fields in traditional ways. Yet, even as the people of Cochabamba assert their rights to control their water, Bechtel is suing the government of Bolivia, and "investors who were part of the private company that sparked the water war in Cochabamba are now up in the mountains, quietly taking control of the key lakes and water sources for the city" (Watson, 2003):

> "Privatization is very important because the water is more important than the gold now," says [Gonzalo] Ugalde. "The gold is for a few people, but the water is for all people, all around the world. If you obtain control of the water, you can obtain control of the people."
>
> (Watson, 2003; retrieved on January 31, 2010 from www.cbc.ca/news/features/water/bolivia.html)

Case Study #7: The Zapatistas

On January 1, 1994, the state of Chiapas, Mexico, woke up to find that many of the cities were occupied by a guerrilla army, the EZLN, commonly known as the Zapatistas. But this was no ordinary guerrilla movement, out to take over the country. The primary demands of the Zapatistas included economic and social justice as well as more decision-making power for local communities. The uprising of January 1 occurred on the day the NAFTA treaty went into effect. This was no coincidence—the Zapatistas believed (correctly, as it turned out) that NAFTA would be devastating for the small farmers of Chiapas, because the flood of U.S. corn would undercut the price of local corn.

Although the EZLN was pushed out of the cities by the Mexican army, negotiations and international support led to significant changes for the Indigenous People of Chiapas. On a visit to Chiapas, Jeff saw some of the results: cooperatives such as an organization of women making beautiful fabrics and a co-op that buys and roasts organic coffee from small producers. Further, many of the villages, called base communities, gained significant freedom to make decisions separate from local government. Land was gained for the landless, as those who had occupied unused estates were often allowed to stay on the land. Local health clinics and schools outside the state system offer community-controlled services. It seems that the Zapatista uprising has unleashed considerable creativity as people find new ways to survive under the pressure of NAFTA's brutal globalization.

One of the spokespeople for the EZLN, known only by his pseudonym "Subcommandante Marcos," has written widely about the issues facing the people of Chiapas and elsewhere. He often points out the larger issues behind their struggles:

> All cultures forged by nations—the noble indigenous past of America, the brilliant civilization of Europe, the wise history of Asian nations, and the ancestral wealth of Africa and Oceania—are corroded by the American way of life. In this way, neoliberalism imposes the destruction of nations and groups of nations in order to reconstruct them according to a single model. This is a planetary war, of the worst and cruelest kind, waged against humanity.
>
> (Marcos, 2001, p. 562)

Conclusion

In this chapter, we have examined the ways that the discourses of hierarchy and domination are manifested in the everyday lives of people around the globe. Globalization is not a natural process but one designed for the benefit of a small group of corporations and the people who own them. Globalization is not inevitable and widespread resistance, as we have noted in this chapter, is growing, rooted in the increasingly obvious disparity between those who benefit and those who don't. One indication of the resistance is that whenever the WTO meets now, it must hide behind legions of police who are mobilized to keep the massive demonstrations from shutting down the WTO. When the powerful use armed force, it's because the assumption of inevitability—which leads people to accept globalization—has broken down and forced the elites to reveal that power to kill is ultimately all they have to offer.

In the next chapter, however, you will see a sharp contrast. Not all cultures have been completely enclosed by greed and power, and those who work to maintain or revitalize traditional indigenous practices offer a much different vision of how to live with the other species on our planet. In the following sections, we have provided activities, primary concepts, suggested readings, films, and organizations to help you bring this information to your students. You'll find more resources at our website at www.routledge.com/textbooks/9780415872515.

What Schools and Teachers Can Do

What's in the News?

Work with students to collect and analyze news stories that show the impact of globalization, such as lead-poisoned toys from China, losses of diversity in ecosystems, and job losses in industrial cities in the North.

Diggin' Up Dirt

Assign students (in teams or as individuals) to research one of the following corporations: Monsanto, Cargill, Conagra, or Tyson Foods.

Ask them to look for and write a report about the following information:

(1) The location of its headquarters or base of operations.
(2) A list of its holdings: the brands produced and distributed by the company.
(3) A summary of a major litigation in which your corporation was involved: Who, specifically, was involved? What circumstances surrounded the case? What was the outcome?
(4) An examination of how the circumstances surrounding the case relate to class discussions, readings, and films.
(5) A response to the question: How do the actions of these companies affect the production and distribution of foods we eat every day?

(Activity created by Ken Boisselle, Melissa Chapman,
and Gary Schnakenberg for their course Food for
Thought at Souhegan High School, 2006)

Transnational Auction

Conduct a "transnational capital auction" to demonstrate the way that capitalists encourage poor countries to compete against each other. Put students in groups, representing poor countries from the global South, while the teacher represents Capital. Countries "bid" for Capital by offering low minimum wages, low taxes, and lax enforcement of child labor, while avoiding rebellion. (Drawn from Bigelow & Peterson, *Rethinking Globalization* (2002); see p. 108 for more details.)

Mapping and Mentorship in the Cultural Commons

Have students find out who in the community has skills such as carpentry, food preservation, music-making, etc. Students choose a mentor with whom to learn a commons-based skill. They then share their experiences and knowledge gained from the relationship.

Conceptual Toolbox

The commons: The non-monetized relationships, practices, and traditions that people across the world use to survive and take care of one another on a day-to-day basis. This includes both the "environmental commons," such as land, air, water, seeds, and forests, and the "cultural commons," which include practices, skills, and knowledge used to support mutual well-being.

Enclosure: The practice of privatizing that which was once freely shared as part of the commons.

Globalization: The ways that the culture of modernity has been exported across the world, and the economic, ecological, and cultural impacts that it is currently having on human communities and their surrounding ecosystems.

Monoculture: Growing of a single species in an ecosystem, as a form of industrial agriculture. As the opposite of biodiversity, monoculture destroys diversity.

Suggested Readings and Other Resources

Books and Essays

Bigelow, W. & Peterson, R. (Eds.). (2002). *Rethinking globalization: Teaching for justice in an unjust world*. Milwaukee, WI: Rethinking Schools.

Ecologist, The. (1994). Whose common future: Reclaiming the commons. *Environment and Urbanization*, 6, 106–130.

Mander, J. & Tauli-Corpuz, V. (2006). *Paradigm wars: Indigenous people's resistance to globalization*. San Francisco, CA: Sierra Club Books.

Shiva, V. (1993). *Monocultures of the mind*. Atlantic Highlands, NJ: Zed Press.

Shiva, V. (1997). *Biopiracy*. Cambridge, MA: South End Press.

Films

Cavalcanti, O. B. (1992). *Life and debt*. Oley, PA: Bullfrog Films.
Addresses the impact of the International Monetary Fund, the World Bank, the Inter-American Development Bank, and current globalization policies on a developing country such as Jamaica.

Garcia, D. K. & Butler, C. L. (2004). *The future of food*. Mill Valley, CA: Lily Films.
Presents key questions about the history and politics of the introduction of genetically modified foods into our food supply.

Ankele, J., & Macksoud, A. (Writers). (2001). *The global banquet: Politics of food*. Maryknoll World Productions.
A documentary dealing with social justice, human rights, globalization, and hunger.

Morgan, F., Murphy, E. P. & Quinn, M. (2006). *The power of community: How Cuba survived peak oil*. Yellow Springs, OH: Community Service, Inc.
A film about how Cubans have adapted to limited energy resources and the continued and strengthened U.S. embargo.

Page, J., Beeman, C., Norberg-Hodge, H. & Walton, E. (1993). *Ancient futures: Learning from Ladakh*. Bristol, England: International Society for Ecology and Culture.
Examines the root causes of our environmental and social crises through a look at development processes currently occurring in Ladakh, India.

Organizations and Links

Global Exchange (www.globalexchange.org)
An organization that offers research and connections for social and environmental justice, which has done much to challenge so-called "free trade" and develop the idea of "fair trade."

IFG, International Forum on Globalization (www.ifg.org)
A North–South research and educational institution composed of leading activists, economists, scholars, and researchers providing analysis and critiques on the cultural, social, political, and environmental impacts of economic globalization.

ISEC, International Society for Ecology and Culture (www.isec.org.uk)
A non-profit organization concerned with the protection of both biological and cultural diversity, emphasizing education for action.

NEF, New Economics Foundation (www.nef.org)
An independent think-and-do tank that inspires and demonstrates real economic well-being.

The Oakland Institute (www.oaklandinstitute.org)
   A policy think tank whose mission is to increase public participation and promote fair debate on critical social, economic, and environmental issues in both national and international forums.

Note

1 To denote the less-industrialized countries, we use "global South" instead of "Third World," and for the industrialized countries, "global North" instead of "First World," because the latter terms imply a hierarchy of value. We understand that these terms are imperfect.

Chapter 9

Learning From Indigenous Communities

Introduction

A few years ago, Rebecca and a graduate student were presenting at a national conference about work that the student had done to try to teach a group of high school students to analyze a problem in their community using an EcoJustice approach. She discussed both what a deep cultural critique might have looked like, and the ways of thinking that would have prevented the problem from occurring in the first place. The talk, attended by 20 or so mostly white academics, was generally well received and the question and answer part of the session was quite lively. Then, a man stood up at the end of the session and said, "I appreciate the story you shared and your commitment to this sort of education; I appreciate this discussion, but where is Indigenous knowledge in all of this? In what you have relayed to us today, it appears that you, or the white intellectuals you draw on, have invented these solutions that you propose." The student tried to respond but she was pretty tongue-tied by the powerful presence of this man. So, Rebecca gave it a try: "Well, sometimes I feel between a rock and a hard place: I think if we tried to discuss this situation by applying Indigenous ways of knowing, we could be accused of speaking for you, or some form of incorporation. And, yet, if we do not, we run the risk of appearing as though we believe we have the answers, as you say. So, what would you have us do?" The man was thoughtful for a moment, and then said, quietly, "Just, pay respect. You have a lot to learn."

That was a critical lesson and comes back to me (Rebecca) often. The tensions in that brief encounter are so real and so important: There are many, many cultures on this planet who for hundreds, even thousands of years developed highly complex ways of knowing and being that recognize the human interdependence with all the other creatures with which we share this world; we cannot be them; we ought not speak for them; but neither ought we ignore what they have to teach us. Throughout this book, we have been asking you to look carefully at the roots and practices of a modernist, Eurocentric industrial culture. This is an important process because it forces those of us born in it to ask ourselves both what needs to be changed about the cultural system that shapes us, and, also, what should be conserved. But there are other diverse ways of knowing and being that could help us to understand our own culture, and to become more ecologically sustainable.

In Chapter 7, we introduced you to the ways a "conqueror model" or mindset (Newcomb, 2008) was developed and justified within official Christian rulings by the Pope in the 15th century. Columbus and subsequent colonizers used specific hierarchized metaphors and linguistic codes to rationalize the domination (even the attempted elimination) of Indigenous Peoples in the so-called "New World." We discussed the ways that official, federally-sponsored schooling was used to delegitimize or eliminate the spiritual and psychological realities of Indigenous Peoples beginning in the 19th century in North America.

In this chapter, we shift our perspective, looking instead at what the conqueror mentality sought to destroy: the more eco-centered worldviews that many Indigenous Peoples are currently seeking to protect or revitalize in their communities as a means of addressing what some refer to as the "bio-cide" of the last 500 years.

Exploring Indigenous Traditions

There is no way to be comprehensive in one chapter, so we have chosen to focus on:

1. Oral traditions and storytelling as a central part of day-to-day practices, moral education, spirituality, and community life.
2. Ancient knowledge of the complexities of ecosystems—the animal and plant life upon which we depend—and a moral system for protecting them; this is dependent upon a specific and deep understanding of "place."
3. An emphasis on the centrality of diversity—linguistic, cultural, and biological—needed to protect life.

We begin from the assumption that Indigenous cultures should have a right to exist as they see fit, like any other culture, without foreign cultures being imposed on them. But beyond this, they also offer alternative pathways and centuries-old wisdom for how to live on the planet, and as such they can offer valuable lessons to an increasingly unsustainable modern world.

One of the challenges in writing a chapter like this is trying to organize it in such a way that makes sense. Most Indigenous Peoples do not separate community from nature, or knowledge from the spiritual realm, or education from any of this; rather, these perspectives on community, nature, and education are intimately woven together through their particular worldview via the oral traditions, ceremonies, and day-to-day practices that make these beliefs concrete. Wisdom about how to live and sustain community is part and parcel of the spiritual beliefs, rituals, and traditions. Education is not separated off from these but is part of the relationships and storytelling that cut across all these realms. In this sense there is no separation between the sacred and the secular.

In fact, Indigenous Peoples living in traditional ways really do not have a sense of the secular in their life ways. This may be difficult for those of us who have grown up in modernist cultures to understand because we are so accustomed to "science," "religion," "law," and "education," for example, operating independently of one another as they are understood to be separate realms. In the sections that follow, we try to show how education is an integral part of all aspects of Indigenous cultural practices and communities, including and especially their spiritual beliefs and traditions.

Defining "Indigenous"

Currently there are some 350 million Indigenous People in the world, approximately 6 to 8 percent of the world population.[1] This includes around 550 tribes in the United States speaking over 175 distinct languages (Nelson, 2008, p. 3). We define as "Indigenous" those peoples who predate any other groups living in a particular region, and who define themselves through a "spiritual link to the land" (Adamson, 2008, pp. 28–29). This is not uncontested conceptual terrain. Even among the people whose work we draw upon here, there is disagreement about who is "Indigenous" and who is not.

Are We Romanticizing Other Cultures?

Whenever we mention the lessons offered by Indigenous cultures, some people—mostly white academics—immediately claim that we are "romanticizing" those cultures—seeing them as ideal or perfect cultures and ignoring their problems. While we agree that such misrepresentation can be a serious form of racist accommodation or incorporation, we are quite adamant about the importance of recognizing the deep knowledge in these cultures. In showing respect for widely varying Indigenous cultures, we try to avoid over-generalizing, as in "*all* Indigenous cultures are in harmony with nature." There are indeed some common patterns among sustainable cultures, but that should not be read to mean that those patterns are true of all.

One difference between learning from a culture and romanticizing a culture is in the concept of "learning." When we talk about learning from an Indigenous culture, for example, we are interested in the diverse but explicit principles in those cultures that deal with how to relate to nature or specific knowledge of an ecosystem, with the goal of understanding our own culture more fully in order to change it as necessary. Alternatively, those who romanticize or exoticize these cultures may want to take on specific practices of an Indigenous culture, such as sweat lodges, in an attempt to "be like them," as if incorporating the rituals and spiritual practices of a completely different culture were possible or desirable. While often couched in feelings of awe for other cultures, such practices are actually part of "othering" those cultures, and thus may reproduce racist tendencies.

Further, we can acknowledge the challenges faced by a culture without detracting from the lessons we can learn from it. For example, the culture of Ladakh (in northern India), which we have mentioned a couple of times in this book, has high infant/child mortality and has issues with ethnic division. None of that, however, undermines the fact that the Ladakhi have lived sustainably for hundreds of years in a difficult mountain environment without noticeably reducing the region's ability to support life. Many members of these cultures who spend time in the modern world decide to return to the traditional practices and beliefs of their communities. Some cultures have tentatively adopted some aspects of modern culture, particularly technologies that help make their lives easier without undermining their community.

Building on the case studies in the previous chapter, we want to emphasize that none of these cultures exist closed off from the political and economic pressures of modernization; rather, while they may indeed be able to draw on ancient beliefs and traditions that indicate knowledge of an interrelatedness with nature, they are also always negotiating and contesting the contexts that they live in, perhaps accommodating ideas from other sources, and they always have. They are not "untouched." So, while we challenge old ideas from modernist discourses that defined them as "primitive," they are not static or closed cultural systems.

Further, as we will see below, many of the stories told within oral traditions of Indigenous Peoples are about what went wrong, and what needed to be learned from particular experiences and situations. These stories are passed down to instruct the younger generations how to avoid problems their ancestors already confronted. And, because these cultures were rooted in specific bioregional places, their knowledge of those places is very old. How could they not understand their environment in precise and complex ways? At times it seems to us that the worries about romanticizing Indigenous Peoples is another, newer form of skepticism on the part of white scholars about whether this knowledge should be considered valuable, whether it is in fact knowledge at all. Their protests seem to us a way of justifying not paying attention to it.

On the other hand, misrepresenting other cultures to fit some fictional or Utopian vision of the world is not a useful approach either. Painting a picture of a culture as exotic and Utopian is a form of othering that may appear to celebrate them, but in fact only perpetuates misunderstanding. And, as Linda Tuhiwai Smith (1999) has so clearly shown, these issues seem to be problems within dominant modernist scholarship and often divert our attention away from what we might learn from Indigenous cultures. Indigenous scholar Melissa K. Nelson puts it this way:

> The issues of romanticization and exotification seem to be more of a concern and practice from outside, from Euro-American academia and the New Age movement respectively. Certainly Native Peoples are concerned and upset when they are stereotyped and romanticized; this form of racism needs to change. But the question of whether Indigenous Peoples were, historically, environmentalists or not, is almost irrelevant . . . On the one hand, given the rich philosophical worldviews and life practices of land and kin, it is absurd for Indigenous Peoples to question whether or not they were or are environmentalists . . . On the other hand, many Indigenous groups, tribes, and villages made and make ecological mistakes.
>
> (Nelson, 2008, p. 13)

As Nelson goes on to say, the point really is how these cultures learned from these mistakes, and what they did with the knowledge gained. One of the most important points for this chapter is the way that Indigenous Peoples pass on to future generations what they have learned through the rich tapestry of stories, languages, traditions, ceremonies, and day-to-day practices. Their stories are full of metaphor, allegory, and pedagogy, demonstrating centuries-old understanding about the complex contexts in which they live. They have much to share with those of us who are still so alienated from the land that supports us.

Educating Through Diverse Oral Traditions

In his book *Wisdom Sits in Places*, Keith Basso (1996) describes the intricate ways that the Apache peoples use stories about events that happened in spaces and places to teach moral lessons. In one example, he shares a story about a young girl returning home to her reservation from boarding school in order to attend a girls' puberty ceremony. She goes to the ceremony with pink plastic curlers in her hair, an "ornamentation considered fashionable" by her school friends. According to tradition, young Apache women are expected to wear their hair loose at such ceremonies. A few weeks later, while the girl was having a meal at her grandmother's house, the old woman abruptly told the tale of a young Apache policeman who had become too enamored with the ways of white men.

It happened at Ndee Dah Naazjne (Men Stand Above Here and There) [a place on the Apache reservation]. Long ago, a man killed a cow off the reservation. The cow belonged to a whiteman. The man was arrested by a policeman living at Cibecue at Men Stand Above Here and There. The policeman was an Apache. There, at Fort Apache, the head army officer questioned him. "What do you want?" he said. The policeman said, "I need cartridges and food." The policeman said nothing about the man who had killed the whiteman's cow. That night some people spoke to the policeman. "It is best to report on him," they said to him. The next day the policeman returned to the head army officer. "Now what do you want?" he said. The policeman said, "Yesterday I was going to say HELLO and GOODBYE but I forgot to do it." Again he said nothing about the man he arrested. Someone was working with words on his mind. The policeman returned with the man to Cibecue. He released him at Men Stand Above Here and There.

(Basso, 1996, p. 54)

When asked about the story, the grandmother said "I shot her [the granddaughter] with an arrow." Sometime later, Basso was talking with the young woman about the incident. She explained: "I sure don't like how she's talking about me, so I quit looking like that. I threw those curlers away." They were passing within a few hundred yards of Men Stand Above Here and There, and Basso pointed it out to her. She "said nothing for several moments. Then she smiled and spoke softly in her own language: 'I know that place. It stalks me every day' " (Basso, 1996, pp. 56–57).

In traditional Apache culture, stories about how to "live right" are intimately connected to the places and the land where the people have lived for centuries. Moral lessons are directly linked through these stories to actual places and the elements of the landscape of those places: the streams, trees, rocks, and so on. Thus, the land is imbued and encoded with the wisdom of the culture through the stories told about place. Everyone in the culture knows the stories, and, when one is told, it is often used as an "arrow" to try to teach someone who has gone astray how to live according to the ethical code of the community. In the case of the young woman, the story about the Apache policeman who had been too accommodating to the whites was told to urge her not to behave so much like white people. Other stories in Apache culture are directly linked to how to live in relation to the soil or the water, and are linked to place names that again imbed the moral code in the land itself.

The power of storytelling is integral to many forms of Indigenous education. Navajo educator Gregory Cajete writes about the essential role of storytelling to education, and, in particular, the development of specific capacities for creativity, flexibility, synthesis, and imagination that it affords the people.

> Indigenous education imparted an awareness of story that provided a context through which imagination and the unconscious could develop at all stages of life. Indeed, Indigenous storytelling engaged all levels of higher order creative thinking and imaging capacities. Indigenous storytelling developed a fluency of metaphoric thinking and mythic sensibility that served Indigenous people in their understanding of their own psychology and maintenance of their spiritual ecology . . . The basis of traditional Indian education is embodied in the structures of thinking related to the creative process were engendered as a part of Indigenous storying. These disciplines were attention, creative imagination, flexibility and fluency of thinking.
>
> (Cajete, 1994, p. 139)

As Cajete goes on to point out, what we call the "disciplines" or content areas in modern education are forms of stories that explain and describe particular approaches to knowledge. "The difference," he tells us, "between the transfer of knowledge in modern Western education and that of Indigenous education is that in Western education information has been separated from the stories and presented as data, description, theory, and formula." Students in modern cultures have lost the sense of story that accompany these traditions and instead are taught to see the disciplines as separate domains of "expertise," that include some and exclude others. These are domains of status and power because they have succeeded in taking the narratives that circulate and defined them as Knowledge. But Cajete argues that we should allow teachers to return to their roles as storytellers, and encourage students to become active listeners. "A curriculum founded on American Indian myths in science might revolve around stories of human relationships to plants, animals, natural phenomena, and the places in which Indian people live" (Cajete, 1994, pp. 139–140).

Ancient Knowledge of Living Systems: The Importance of Education in Place

Indigenous People take a holistic approach to create diverse knowledges of the world that include spirituality, in contrast to the specialized and often reductionist approach of Western science. When we use the word holistic, we refer to the Greek word "holos," meaning all, encompassing, or total. Hence, for Indigenous Peoples, the forms of knowledge that they hold about the world—the physical, biological, linguistic, spiritual, social, economic, and so on—also embrace the great mysteries of the living and non-living world, and the impossibility of fully knowing or controlling those mysteries. These are multiple approaches to knowledge formed from great respect for what the Earth offers, and an understanding that all human beings are a part of a much larger set of forces or "laws"; we are not external from them and certainly not in control of them. This recognition and deep respect forms the basis of Indigenous spirituality and is woven through their ceremonies and day-to-day practices.

Understanding and knowledge of these laws is handed down over many centuries, and sometimes referred to as "original instructions." For example, according to the Indigenous Law Institute (ILI):

> The spiritual, Earth-based lifestyles of our ancestors were in keeping with the original instructions given to them by the Creator, which were handed down for thousands of years through oral tradition. The natural world wisdom and understanding of our ancestors still exists in the languages, ceremonies, and sacred places of our respective nations and peoples. Traditional Native Law is found in the Kanaka Maoli Law of the Native Hawaiians, the Seven Laws of the Lakota, the Twelve Laws of the Shawnee, the Laws of the Kogi, and so forth. But by the word "law" we are actually talking about a conceptual and cultural alternative to the technological and chemically laden culture of empire and domination. The I.L.I. asserts that Traditional Native Law is an essential source of environmental wisdom and understanding for the planet today.
> (Retrieved on January 31, 2014 from http://ili.nativeweb.org)

So, what we refer to as "holistic" approaches is a sense of the world and the universe—the lives of people as they co-exist with other living creatures—as governed by laws given to the people by the Creator as original instructions, and passed down over many centuries. Knowledge for Indigenous People is about recognizing how these laws unfold or are expressed in a particular place among the specific creatures living in that place. Education occurs as the young interact with their Elders, listening to their stories about the ways their people, in their place, learned to respect the laws of the Creator.

The advantages of such approaches—and limitations of the reductionist approach common to modern societies—are illustrated by an example from Alaska. Barnhardt and Kawagley (1999) describe a meeting of Athabascan Elders from the village of Minto with a group of scientists employed by the state Departments of Natural Resources and Fish and Game. The scientists included two fisheries specialists, a moose specialist, a beaver specialist, and a hydrology specialist. The scientists tried to explain their research to the Elders, while the natives wanted to discuss the various impacts on fish runs from policy, technology, and over-development. After the various specialists described their research, an Elder asked about the Bureau of Land Management (BLM) burn policy. Since none of the scientists were fire specialists, they didn't know what to say. The Elders went on to explain the relation of the people and the beaver to the river and the fish, pointing out that when the BLM allowed fires to burn, it made the beavers move their dams, which in turn affected the fish runs.

Among the technological issues was the use of radio-tracking devices, which, when inserted into fish, made them unusable for the natives. The vaster native knowledge was demonstrated when Peter John, the Chief of the village, pointed out:

> "If you want to know where pike spend the winter, come and ask me. How do you think I lived to be this old? I can tell you exactly where we go to get the biggest pike and where the pike spend the winter. But I don't want to let those snowmachiners in Fairbanks know." In the course of Peter John's presentation, he pointed out that the fish and game people had referred to statistics that went back only thirty years to determine how many pike had been there in the past. "You are talking about thirty years. Our record goes back three hundred years" . . . at which point he proceeded to explain the seasonal fluctuations that were recorded in their knowledge base going back more than ten generations.
>
> (Kawagley & Barnhardt, 1999, p. 124)

While Western science offers some tools for understanding ecosystems, it tends to ignore the complex interactions within ecosystems, which only people who have a long familiarity with a region can understand.

The Importance of Identity in Place and Space

Indigenous knowledge systems are regionally and tribally specific, dependent upon thousands of years of observing and passing on knowledge of the particularities of the land itself, the animals, and other life forms that dwell there. Thus, Indigenous knowledge (IK), or native science, is "place-based," and "holds the memories, observations, stories, understandings, insights and practices for how to follow the natural laws of a place (Nelson, 2008, p. 12). And again, because these knowledges are imbedded in specific and diverse ecosystems, they take multiple forms. So, for example, while the Annishinaabeg hold ancient wisdom about how to navigate the waters of the Great Lakes and how to harvest wild rice (manooman) along its shores (LaDuke, 2008, p. 207), the Quechua of the Andes understand the particularities of the soil on those mountain slopes, and how to grow many varieties of potatoes in a mountain climate

(Rivera, 2008, p. 197), and the Hopi in the southwest of the United States understand how to read the clouds, and to cultivate specific varieties of corn with little rainfall.

This diverse knowledge is essentially about how to survive within a particular ecosystem and bioregion, and is thus at heart, practical. But it is also shot through with an appreciation for the cycles and mysteries of life, and is thus spiritual. Recognizing their essential imbeddedness in and dependence upon the well-being of a specific set of living relationships, such knowledges emphasize responsibility toward the creatures and their interrelatedness in the system itself. In this sense, Indigenous knowledges are also tied to a spiritual experience and identity, not in a transcendent sense (it is not about how to move beyond where they are), but rather, of a consciousness that is tied to complexities and mysteries of life in a particular ecosystem.

Thus, traditional ecological knowledges are composed of a "sacred orientation to place and space" not only in the sense of physical place but also in the sense of consciousness—the way people understand themselves and come to think (Cajete, 1999, pp. 3–4). As in every culture, language is central to the creation of a specific way of seeing and being—of identifying oneself in relation to others in the world. For Indigenous Peoples, this means that many metaphors represent their relationships with specific animals and plants, the landscape, climate, the moon, and sun, which they understand to be essential to their survival. Gregory Cajete explains, for example, that Indigenous Peoples in North America use specific metaphors to recognize and name their directional relationships with the sun:

> Thus, north may be referred to as "to the left side of the sun rising"; south, "to the right side of the sun rising"; east, "to the sun rising"; and west, "to the sun setting" . . . Orientation is essential for Indigenous people because each person belongs to a place. Understanding orientation is essential in order to grasp what it means to be related.
> (Cajete, 1999, p. 7)

Indigenous knowledge systems can thus be understood to reflect a "sacred ecology," a way of understanding and representing the world that honors the complexities of interdependent relationships necessary to all life. Julio Valladolid Rivera talks about the difficulty of making sense of this way of thinking in today's modern world:

> How to convey the profound feeling of affection and respect that the [Quechua] peasant feels for the "Mother Earth" (Pachamama), or the joy and gratitude towards his or her mountain protectors ("Achachilas" or "Apus") the peasant experiences of the birth of an alpaca, who is treated like a 'new daughter', is a truly difficult chal-

lenge. One must live the life of the Andean countryside in continuous conversation with the stars, rocks, lakes, rivers, plants and animals, both wild and cultivated, the clouds, the frosts. One must relish the taste of the rains, listen to the corn growing, observe the colour of the winds—feeling oneself at all times accompanied by our deceased ancestors.

(Rivera, in Appfel Marglin, 1998, p. 51)

This broad and sensual understanding of place is a rich tapestry passed on generation to generation through the relationships created in community. The woven threads of meaning created within this specific metaphorical and allegorical system envelop the community in ceremony and oral traditions that follow the cycles of the seasons, the sun and moon, include a constant remembering and honoring of those who came before, and function pedagogically to acculturate the young. In this sense, place is much more than the area where a group of people live; it encompasses their very sense of themselves as a people. As expressed by a Pueblo Elder: "It is this place that holds our memories and the bones of our people . . . this is the place that made us" (Cajete, 1999, p. 3).

It is in this context that Indigenous education must be considered as a set of moral practices, a lifelong process of becoming. Indigenous Peoples offer not just different teachings, but entirely different ways of thinking about teaching. Speaking specifically about education, Gregory Cajete describes a specific metaphor, "look to the mountain," which captures both the "ecological vision" and the notion of "a journey to a higher place":

Climbing these metaphoric mountains of orientation to gain the unique perspective afforded by each embodies the age-old process of Indigenous education. It is a way of developing the ecological understandings and relationships that ensure the attainment of life's needs. Journeying to that sacred mountaintop, one can begin to envision a sense of relationship, not only to one's self and one's community, but also to the natural world. This was the guiding sensibility that allowed Tribal people in the Americas to establish an abiding resonance with the places, plants, animals, and other natural entities with which they related and through which they came to know themselves as The People.

(Cajete, 1994, p. 93)

This sense of the sacred interconnections and deep understandings of place passed on generation to generation was and is Indigenous Peoples' key to survival. This "resonance" with place, especially their sense of affiliation with the animals with whom they share the land, calls our attention to the particularly damaging effects of modern cultures' hyper-separated sensibilities, begging a closer look at anthropocentrism in modern industrial cultures.

Indigenous Relationships With Animals as Integral to Community

In his book *The Animals Came Dancing* (2000), Howard L. Harrod begins his study with an assertion that we've also been working from in this book. "Human experiences of other beings in their environment," he writes, "are shaped by distinct cultural patterns. These patterns are encoded in a people's language, appearing concretely in the naming of the nonhuman beings that are part of particular ecosystems" (p. xvii). This naming is the way a particular group of people represents their relationship to and experiences of the larger world. Gregory Cajete (2000) writes that most native languages do not have a specific word for "animals" but rather name each species, an indication of the integral role each creature plays in the lives of the people. "Animals were partners with humans . . . With this attitude of partnership and mutual participation with animals, native cultures gained many important insights in the dynamics of animal nature and practiced their knowledge for human benefit and survival" (p. 152).

Harrod's study examines specific cultural meanings and knowledge of the Indigenous Peoples living on the plains of North America from 1750 to 1850, a period of great crisis for these people "as the buffalo were destroyed and their Indigenous ways were dramatically altered with the emergence of reservation life" (2000, p. xix). Echoing our own suggestion earlier in this chapter, Harrod begins his book by encouraging contemporary Euro-Americans to reflect on our own taken-for-granted relations with animals and other non-human creatures as a means of deepening an understanding of our own culture. "If these views are brought to the surface of awareness and examined closely, then the contrasting Northern Plains understanding of animals will become much clearer" (2000, p. xxviii). Having largely dissociated ourselves from what Cajete calls a "natural instinct for affiliation" with animals, contemporary modernist people may find it difficult to relate to the ways Indigenous Peoples understand and interact with animals, or the idea that animals are often understood to be their kin and their teachers. In this section, we ask that our readers entertain a worldview different from their own as a means of opening insight into our relationship with the more-than-human world with whom we share our local communities.

The notion that Indigenous Peoples practiced a "sacred ecology" that included many stories of the ways of animals does not mean that they refrained from killing animals, sometimes in ways that may appear brutal to those of us who do not generally witness the deaths of those creatures we eat. As an Annishinaabeg Elder recently reminded us in a day of teachings at Trent University,[2] every living creature kills in order to live. We all eat and therefore must kill to do so. For many Indigenous Peoples, the act of taking the life of an animal requires a specific appreciation and honoring of the sacrifices that animals make for humans. This sensibility is practiced through ceremony and is an essential part of the knowledge system of Indigenous cultures that hunt. Animals transform themselves to become food and this is an ecological reality. However, it is also necessary to understand that the taking of life was always framed within a complex symbolic system recreated and enacted in rituals, ceremonies, and traditions and creating a rich imagery and perception of animals as part of a complex kinship system.

While it is impossible to give a good sense of the complexities of these traditions especially in terms of all the variations in Indigenous knowledge systems across tribes, it is helpful to recognize the important roles that animals play in creation stories and the original instructions underlying traditional Indigenous ways and practices. Stories of the beings who created the world often revolve around the roles of animals as essential players in bringing the Earth into being. In a version of this story common across many North American tribes, water birds are enlisted by a creator being to dive below the surface of a vast sea of water in search of earth. According to the version told by Northern Plains Indians, this creator being was floating on the water crying and fasting, seeking assistance to accomplish a great task. He appeals to a Grandfather for assistance. The Grandfather grants him the power to call on the water birds for help, but the birds are only able to bring up a small amount of earth from the bottom. Finally, it is turtle who is able to retrieve the necessary quantity of earth to create the world.

> When turtle finally emerged from beneath the waters, the Creator took the mud from his four feet and spread it out to dry; when it was dry, he blew the soil toward each of the four directions and then swinging his arms in a circular motion, he cast forth the remaining earth, and the world arose.
>
> (Harrod, 2000, p. 31)

There are many versions of this story among North American Indigenous Peoples, and, depending on the tribe, different creatures appear, often a turtle, but sometimes a muskrat, a duck, or other waterfowl.

These narratives also include tales of beings who represent seasonal powers. Annishinaabeg stories, for example, relate the power of the Grandfathers in spring thunderstorms. Cheyenne origin stories include a woman and a man who had been created after the formation of the world and placed in the north and south respectively:

> The woman in the north was in control of Winter Man, the power who brought snow and cold as well as sickness and death . . . the man in the south was in control of thunder, the power associated with spring and summer rains and the growth of animals and plants.
>
> (Harrod, 2000, p. 35)

The stars, the moon, and the sun also have roles in these stories, including clear responsibilities for the creation of animals, or for the particular cycles of life. The moon is called Grandmother, for example, and she is directly responsible for fertility, both of the earth and human women whose menstrual cycles follow the cycles of the moon.

Many stories in Indigenous oral traditions tell tales of near starvation and hardships that are often resolved by the gift of animals. Passed down generation to generation over hundreds of years, these stories are an important way of educating about animals and their participation in the people's lives. In these stories, lessons are often offered for the sorts of attitudes required to take the lives of animals: don't show pity, be respectful, and don't take too many. Further, as Cajete writes:

> The understanding gained from animals about ecological transformation was portrayed in many forms, and wherever Indian people hunted these traditions abounded. Once again, while each tribe reflected these understandings in unique ways, core understandings were similar from tribe to tribe. The essential focus was relationship and the guiding sentiment was respect. The central intent revolved around honoring the entities that gave life to a people . . . Through observation and interaction with animals over generations, Indigenous people understood that animals could teach people about the essence of transformation.
>
> (Cajete, 1999, p. 8)

Cajete writes that hunting in the Indigenous mindset is both a spiritual and educational act, represented in the metaphor of the "hunter with a good heart." Cajete describes hunting as a 40,000-year course of study, involving humans from across the planet. "The hunter of good heart was a bringer of life to his people: he had to have not only a very intimate knowledge of the animals he hunted but also a deep and abiding respect for their nature, procreation and continuance as a species" (1999, p. 9). This respect was enacted in the rituals that took place both before and after the hunt, when communities came together to give thanks for the animals killed. This thanksgiving was ritually enacted by the telling of stories about the animals that were killed, relating the importance of the lives now being transformed to keep the people alive.

Harrod emphasizes that these traditions created specific understandings within communities about what it means to be human, and "required that one assume an appropriate relation with the other-than-human powers of the world, including the animals" (2000, p. 43). And further, definitions of what it meant to be human—a people's cultural identity and self-understanding—were specific to their relationships with particular animals within a place. Thus, for the Plains peoples, buffalo were more than simply a resource for food and shelter, they were members of a kinship system that extended beyond the bounds of human families, and constituted a part of their very being. The same was and is true of whales and other sea creatures for the Inuit, or the alpaca for the Quechua.

Recognizing this, we are confronted with the deep tragedies brought about by the loss of these animals for the spiritual and psychological stability of these peoples, especially as perpetrated by the colonizing mindset of European invaders and the subsequent modernist ways of life. And again, learning of the deep knowledge that Indigenous Peoples have had of animals as integral members of their communities and an interdependent world helps us to understand what our own culture has lost over the centuries of modernization. Pushing the rest of the living world metaphorically to the "outside" in order to define humans as superior to animals in modern consciousness has had disastrous effects worldwide. Indigenous cultures in North America have been experiencing the effects of the loss of biodiversity culturally, psychologically, and ecologically for over 500 years.

On Protecting Diversity: Subsistence in a "Pluriverse" of Communities Versus Universal Human Rights

Throughout this book, we have been calling your attention to the necessary—though mostly invisible (to the modern observer)—relationship among linguistic, cultural, and biological diversity. And here, in this chapter, we've been emphasizing the ways that Indigenous cultures organize knowledge and use oral traditions as a means of educating each other about and protecting the diverse communities of life around them. They do so in very diverse ways using diverse languages that emerged in relation to diverse bioregions. And, in the cultures that we've been telling you about, they do this by recognizing that their own survival as communities of people is absolutely dependent upon protecting this linguistic and cultural, as well as ecological, diversity.

One way that contemporary tribes are working to protect their knowledge and cultural ways is through language reclamation programs. Across Canada, for example, First Nations schools are realizing the importance of teaching native languages as a means of protecting their cultures.

Language reclamation has become an important priority among Elders who recognize that without it, their traditional values, ways of living, and knowledge of the world will be lost. Confronting the damaging effects that Eurocentric modes of education have had on Indigenous cultures, these efforts represent an important struggle to reclaim cultural and linguistic integrity in the face of enormous losses. As Marie Battiste and Jean Barman (1995) point out "Only 16% or 21 First Nations have flourishing languages; 21% or 28 First Nations have declining languages; 26% or 15 first Nations have critical languages" (p. xii). Thus, even while they face huge obstacles—lack of federal resources, understanding, and support, and major illiteracy in their own communities—there is a clear move to use education to protect the Aboriginal diversity represented in over 52 languages spoken among First Nations peoples in Canada.

Traditional Indigenous cultures see diversity as a necessary factor of community, and so they protect the inter-dependencies through which life is nurtured and flourishes. As we will explore in more depth in the next chapter, people living in modernist cultures protect community too, although the ways in which we do so is often devalued, and so hidden by an emphasis on individual merit and advancement.

While modern industrial societies emphasize that they are organized to maximize human "progress," offering "autonomous" individuals the "right" to compete with each other in the race to consume more and more, Indigenous cultures are traditionally subsistence-based, and survival depends on tight-knit community relationships. Esteva and Prakash (1998) discuss how this works in contemporary Mexican contexts via the ancient Mexican tradition of *comida*, or communal production and consumption of food. Not only is most food grown locally; the many local varieties of corn, cultivated over thousands of years, are part of the culture and are integrally tied to the preparation of meals.

> The fire is at the center of the warmest room of the house. And *Dona* Refugio is there, every day, at the very center, surrounded by her whole family, talking with her husband, children and grandchildren; discussing personal difficulties or the predicaments of the community. That fire and *Dona* Refugio are at the center of their conversations; and, in fact, at the very center of family life. And family life is the center of the community. The whole community's life is in fact organized around such fires, the center of kitchens, the source of *comida* . . . The essence of their "we," . . . is precisely here; around the communal fire, in the very heart of the family. To eat, to care for comida, to generate it, to cook it, to assimilate it: all these are the activities that do not belong to industrial eaters; to individual selves who define themselves with abstract "we's."
>
> (Esteva & Prakash, 1998, p. 58)

This is more than the family hanging out in the kitchen. It's a way of valuing the process of preparing food as much as the product, and of valuing the relationships that create community more than any individual. Here relationships both with the food and with each other are a key to survival, and to the simple pleasures of savoring a meal together.

Similarly, Luis Macas describes his Quechua culture (in Ecuador): "For us it's always important to include an idea of 'complementary duality.' We maintain in our community what we call reciprocity. Ours is a world not of individuals but of communities and living in reciprocity" (Macas, 2006, p. 44). As we have been pointing to throughout this chapter, community in the Indigenous mindset is not conceived as separate from the land, and the land is not separate from the animals and plants, or the rains, the sky, or the stars. An integral part of Quechua culture is the idea of "chacra," a word that means at once a general sense of nurturance and the actual plot of land that people tend to cultivate for the food they need to eat (Rivera, 1998). Again emphasizing the impossibility of separating this sense of nurturance from all relationships within a broad conception of community, Rivera writes:

> The *chacra* is the piece of land where the peasant lovingly and respectfully nurtures plants, soil, water, microclimates and animals. In a broad sense *chacra* is all that is nurtured, thus the peasants say that the llama is their *chacra* that walks and from which wool is harvested. We ourselves are the *chacra* of the huacas, the deities who care for, teach and accompany us.
>
> (Rivera, 1998, p. 57)

Similarly, Jeannette Armstrong, an Okanagan, says:

> I do know that people must come to community on the land. The transience of peoples criss-crossing the land must halt, and people must commune together on the land to protect it and all our future generations. Self-sustaining Indigenous Peoples still on the land are already doing this, and they are the only ones now standing between society and total self-destruction . . . Indigenous rights must be protected, for we are the protectors of Earth.
>
> (Armstrong, 2006, p. 39)

Or, as an Apache man told Keith Basso, "The land takes looks after us" (Martin, 1999, p. 10).

Importantly, these soil-based cultures create, within their own diverse traditions and languages, specific rules and processes of governance that are intended to protect what they need to survive. And, while there are commonalities in what they believe, there is what Esteva and Prakash

(1998) call a "pluriverse" of traditions arising from the deep knowledge that diverse peoples living within distinct biospheres have created over many centuries.

Community Traditions as Alternatives to Universal Human Rights

Thus, every culture has a system of moral teaching and a way of enacting justice. But where Western ideals present the idea of *human rights* as universal, and promote a one-approach-fits-all justice system that aims to protect the individual, most Indigenous cultures understand these systems of justice to be part of a diverse set of traditions, unique to each tribal group, and geared to protecting the community above all. Looking at this pluriverse of community-enhancing traditions helps us see what is often so hard for Westerners to see—that even something as widely accepted in the West as the concept of "universal" human rights is in fact one particular tradition of one particular culture rather than a self-evident creed.

For Indigenous People, even the idea of "rights" is quite different. As an Annishinaabeg Elder relayed to us at a recent teaching, his people are taught that humans have only two rights, which they share with all other living creatures: the right to be born, and the right to die. Everything else, he told us, is a privilege.

Indigenous communities have diverse sets of traditional practices that govern what they do on a day-to-day basis and which are woven through with their spiritual beliefs and their knowledge of the larger living systems in which they participate. Yet, these traditions are overridden by current state and federal laws. International adherence to "human rights" is often in conflict with native beliefs, practices, and forms of governance.

As modern Western ideas and discourses of individualism have been globalized, so has a dominant set of ideas that refer to universal human rights where justice is carried out by a neutral arbiter between opposing sides. But, say the Triqui people of Oaxaca, Mexico, "we want her with her eyes open, to fully appreciate what is happening" (Esteva & Prakash, 1998, p. 111). The open eyes, for example, may not look for punishment for violations that we moderns might take for granted as cause for a prison sentence or other legal sanction. Esteva and Prakash give the example of someone who burns part of the forest—for an Indigenous People, justice would be for the person to reforest it. Even for the crime of killing someone, for which Western justice demands severe punishment, Indigenous justice may instead expect the killer to care for the victim's family for the rest of their lives (Esteva & Prakash, 1998, p. 111).

However, where a Western justice system is installed, community members who do not like the penalty imposed by an Indigenous system will sometimes go to the Western system for a "fair" trial. This, of course, further undermines the authority and integrity of the community—which is exactly what is meant when Indigenous People say that the Western system is colonizing, even when it doesn't directly force out other forms of justice. And, on the other hand, where Indigenous "laws" may require community members to behave in one way, state or federal law may say otherwise.

A recent event in Point Hope, Alaska, helps make these conflicting systems clear. In January 2010, three Indigenous hunters were charged with leaving caribou carcasses "unharvested"; that is, left to decompose on the tundra contrary to state law. The following is a transcript of National Public Radio coverage of the story with Leann Hansen interviewing Jill Burke, a reporter from the *Alaska Dispatch*, a local newspaper.

Hansen: What was the hunters' defense?

Ms. Burke: The hunters basically said they felt they had no choice but to leave these animals behind. That one of them they encountered was sick and out of fear of the spread of disease, it's their traditional practice to leave it on the tundra, essentially quarantining the community. They attempted for more than an hour to salvage meat, but they said in the end, the only thing they were able to bring back was the tongue.

Hansen: Was this a big deal in Point Hope?

Ms. Burke: This was a huge deal. This was a very huge deal. People felt that this was an attack on their subsistence way of life, on their native culture. There are traditions that have been handed down from fathers and fathers before them, over generations—out of survival and custom. This trial really exposed this great fissure between some of those still ongoing traditional subsistence practices and the lives of the state. And in the case of the game laws, they're really orchestrated to prevent the waste of meat from trophy hunting—people that might want to just go out and get the horns and leave the meat behind. But there are laws everyone needs to follow.

(Retrieved on January 31, 2014 from www.npr.org/
templates/story/story.php?storyId=123463726)

In the sense of "human rights" these Indigenous men were given the right to a fair trial, and subjected to laws that were made to prevent trophy hunting that would harm the animal populations they depended upon. But according to whose conception of the law was it fair? Certainly not to the native people's notions of their responsibility to keep the community safe.

To offer another example of the colonizing aspect of human rights: every culture has concepts that demand respect for other beings. In Hindu culture, the concept of *ahimsa* expresses that all life is sacred and that we are to practice non-violence toward them. But international conferences about the treatment of women are always framed as conferences on Women's Rights. "Why not a conference that explores *ahimsa* towards women?" ask Esteva and Prakash (1998, p. 119). Or why not a conference that focused on the variety of Indigenous ways that women's lives are valued within a community?

But what about the cultures who oppress women? What about traditions such as *sati* (widow-burning) in India, or female genital mutilation (genital cutting) in some African cultures? Does supporting Indigenous traditions mean ignoring such horrendous practices? No, suggest Esteva and Prakash (1998). Oppressive actions can still be challenged, but they should be challenged from within the culture's own traditions rather than from outsiders who claim to be morally superior. Thus, *sati* can be challenged by the principle of *ahimsa*, and genital cutting can be challenged from within Islam's principle of avoiding damage to bodies.

It may seem odd or incongruous to question the idea of human rights—after all, isn't this one of the most important contributions of modern cultures? The issue lies in the notion of the "universal" nature of rights. In claiming such, we assume that what we consider to be just and correct applies to all people in all cultures, and thus we deny both the diverse ways of knowing among other cultures, and that they have the ability to determine for themselves what is good for their people. To say that certain ideas are absolutely more valuable than other ideas is inherently colonizing and dismissive, part of that same hierarchizing mentality that we've been analyzing, because it thus claims a right to replace one culture's way of making decisions with the Western way. It assumes that the West is somehow more "evolved" when it comes to understanding justice or community well-being, and thus it reproduces racism.

Conclusion

We share the ideas and stories in this chapter with you first as a way of recognizing the plurality of those cultures that have "an intimate understanding of the relationships between humans and the ecosystem, and of the need to maintain this balance" (LaDuke, 1992, p. 71). We share it as a means of recognizing what these groups have to teach us about how to honor and maintain living systems, and as another means of understanding our own culture. So what can we take away as members of modernist cultures?

First, the Indigenous "lifeways" that we have examined here serve as fundamental reminders that the Western ways of being that we may take for granted are by no means universal or natural. Whatever suggestions we may make in this book for how to live more sustainably, there have been many cultures around the world doing so in very diverse ways and with very complex knowledge systems for many hundreds of years. We owe them our respect for the wisdom they have to share, and we need to be open to learning from them. As the Elder said at the conference that we told you about in the opening story, we have a lot to learn.

Second, while we should certainly be open to the creation of technologies that can help us to live in simpler, more integrated, ways, sustainable ways of living do not need to be invented. The knowledge of how to live in interdependent relationships that do not overshoot the carrying capacity of the land already exists and in fact is quite diverse and ancient. There are already technologies that are capable of supporting living systems, though we may not identify them as such: Take the example from contemporary Cuba where they are currently using oxen—a very old practice—to plow a field rather than fossil fuel dependent tractors; or imagine using compost made from our daily food scraps and other vegetation for fertilizer rather than synthetic chemicals. Indeed, ancient farming practices that include a diversity of crops are great examples of how to provide food without destroying the soil required to grow it. Or, look at the ancient technology of using stone channels to bring water to the fields of Ladakh from the far-off glaciers, and the companion practice of sharing that water among the families in the community. These technologies require a different relation to time; using them wisely means that we must slow down, which also allows us to consider more carefully the consequences of our actions for the well-being of future generations. There are many people from many diverse cultures around the world who live this way already, and have been learning how to do so within communities that are bound to what Gary Snyder (1990) calls "mature cultures." These cultures have created spiritual systems that are integrated with very complex ecological knowledge and understanding that is passed on generation to generation. We should be open to thinking about the ways that science and technology can support what we already know, rather than assuming that knowledge develops in a straight developmental line.

Third, Indigenous education is not necessarily about schooling. In fact, most education about how to live sustainably is passed on in informal ways in intimate relationships and through oral traditions, stories passed down within the diverse cultures and in diverse languages. Thus, the preservation of Indigenous languages is one of the keys to preserving this essential knowledge across the planet. And, further, there is a growing body of scholarship that is beginning to uncover and analyze the ways in which Western education actually undermines the traditional knowledge about ways of being that do not interfere with the ability of the natural world to regenerate (Prakash & Esteva, 1998; Prakash, 2010). The languages associated with ancient land-based cultures are part of an important cultural commons in which knowledge about how to protect living systems is incorporated into patterns of belief, daily practices, ceremonies, and traditions. Understanding the links between language, knowledge, traditions, and the protection of the environment is an essential lesson that we can transfer to better understanding our own cultural commons.

As we will discuss more fully in the next chapter, the commons—those day-to-day practices and relationships passed on generation to generation and found in the very local spaces and places of our communities and local ecosystems—are the sources of important ecological wisdom that must be identified and preserved. This may be the most important lesson of all. Since we are not going to become Apache, or Quechua, or Ladakhi, we need to recognize and reclaim old patterns of relationship and practices that offer more sustainable ways of being. These may be patterns that our own Elders, our parents and grandparents, were taught to devalue and escape because they were seen as barriers to becoming successful and modern in an industrial society. Yet, they persist and are connected to ways of living that have long histories. As our Annishinaabeg teacher said to his white students, "You all have Indigenous roots! Back in Scotland, Germany, Italy, and other parts of Europe. They're old! Find out about them. You'll discover forms of wisdom about the land there too!" We cannot "become Indigenous" in the sense of taking on the stories and traditions of peoples whose ancestors lived on this North American continent for thousands of years, but we can look deeply into our own traditions for what remains of the practices that made life simpler and sustainable.

We don't need to go that far back, actually. Our own commons traditions have been transplanted and have roots that go very deep. They exist among us now in ways we are unaware of, waiting to be reclaimed as valuable alternatives to the damaging practices of our current hyperconsumerist, self-indulgent lifestyles. So, yes, we should look to the cultures with whom we share this North American continent for what they can teach us about this land (and all its important diversity). And, we should also be aware that we too have deeply-embedded ways of knowing that, while highly attenuated by the individualistic thinking and relationships of our current systems, are still at play and nurturing us. Make no mistake, our commons are complicated by modernist ways of thinking that exist simultaneously with more ancient land-conscious, community-supportive practices. This is a source of hope. We need to learn to identify and reclaim healthy traditions and relationships with trust and gusto—

and joy. For it is those practices that keep love alive and offer us hope for a simpler, healthier way of being together on this planet. Below you will find, as in chapters before, a list of resources including activities for your class and school, a Conceptual Toolbox, Suggested Readings, Films, Organizations, and Links. You will find more resources at our website at www.routledge.com/ textbooks/9780415872515.

What Schools and Teachers Can Do

Teach With Respect

In other words, when you read Indigenous stories or read about Indigenous cultures, treat them as products of living, breathing cultures, not as exotic or cute stories for entertainment.

Investigate Indigenous Cosmology Through Metaphor

Read Indigenous Creation Stories and discuss the different sorts of metaphors that they use to discuss the more-than-human world. Have a discussion of the elements of Indigenous spirituality as a starting point for analyzing anthropocentrism.

Contact Local Tribal Organizations

Many tribes have outreach programs to provide speakers or materials on their people and traditions. Giving the students the opportunity to hear from and talk with Indigenous People is an important way to break down stereotypes.

Include Indigenous Cultures

Include Indigenous People when you teach about a region or time, such as making sure that Indigenous history is always part of U.S. history or Canadian history. Don't avoid addressing the violence perpetrated against the tribal peoples who once lived in North and South America by colonizers, military, and educational organizations. Use this as a way to challenge students to a cultural ecological analysis of modernism.

Current Issues

Make sure to be aware of current issues for Indigenous Peoples in your area. Discuss these issues with your students. Whenever possible, talk to local tribal peoples themselves about the various perspectives on issues.

Conceptual Toolbox

Indigenous knowledge: Knowledge that has been passed down through generations regarding how to live successfully in a particular place. It is generally spiritually-based and includes a variety of interrelated dimensions: physical, biological, linguistic, spiritual, social, and economic.

Indigenous People: Those peoples who predate any other groups living in a particular region, and who define themselves through a "spiritual link to the land."

Oral traditions: The Indigenous practice of passing on knowledge and moral instruction through verbal modes such as storytelling.

Pluriverse: Rather than universe, the multiplicity of cultural perspectives, worldviews, traditions, and ways of being in the world.

Suggested Readings and Other Resources

Books and Essays

Cajete, G. (1994). *Look to the mountain: An ecology of Indigenous education.* Ashville, NC: Kivaki Press.

Esteva, G. & Prakash, M. S. (1998). People's power: Radical democracy for the autonomy of their commons. In *Grassroots post-modernism: Remaking the soil of cultures.* New York, NY: Zed Books.

Harrod, H. L. (2000). *The animals came dancing: Native American sacred ecology and animal kinship.* Tucson, AZ: The University of Arizona Press.

Lyons, O. (2008). Listening to natural law. In M. K. Nelson (Ed.), *Original instructions: Indigenous teachings for a sustainable future* (pp. 22–25). Rochester, VT: Bear & Company.

Mohawk, J. (2008). The art of thriving in place. In M. K. Nelson (Ed.), *Original instructions: Indigenous teachings for a sustainable future* (pp. 126–136). Rochester, VT: Bear & Company.

Films

Cullinham, J., & Raymont, P. (1993). *A long as the rivers flow film series.* Brooklyn, NY: Icarus Films.

Includes: Flooding in Job's Garden; The Learning Path; Starting Fire with Gunpowder; Tikinagan: Time Immemorial. This series of five videos addresses human rights questions while examining various aspects of the native struggle for self-determination.

Ferrero, P. (2008). *Hopi: Songs of the fourth world*. Harriman, NY: New Day Films.
A compelling study of the Hopi that captures their deep spirituality and reveals their integration of art and daily life.

Frankenstein, E. & Gmelch, E. (1992). *A matter of respect*. New York, NY: New Day Films.
Portrays a diverse group of Tlingit people expressing their culture and identity and honoring their ancestors' way of life through teaching language, harvesting and preparing traditional foods, restoring community cemeteries, and dancing, carving, and weaving.

Page, J., Beeman, C., Norberg-Hodge, H. & Walton, E. (1993). *Ancient futures: Learning from Ladakh*. Bristol, England: International Society for Ecology and Culture.
Examines the root causes of our environmental and social crises through a look at development processes currently occurring in Ladakh, India.

Walker, C. (1996). *Trinkets and beads*. Brooklyn, NY: Icarus Films.
The story of how the Huaorani struggle against "development" by a big oil company, attempting to survive the Petroleum Age on their own terms.

Organizations and Links

Cultural Survival (www.culturalsurvival.org)
An organization that does research and advocacy work to protect Indigenous Peoples.

Honor the Earth (www.honortheearth.org)
Creates awareness of and support for native environmental and cultural issues and develops innovative financial and political strategies for the survival of sustainable native communities.

ICC, Inuit Circumpolar Conference (www.inuitcircumpolar.com)
An international non-governmental organization formed to strengthen unity and promote rights among Inuit of the circumpolar region.

Indigenous Education Institute (www.indigenouseducation.org)
An organization to preserve, protect, and apply traditional Indigenous knowledge in a contemporary setting, that of Indigenous Peoples today, around the world.

Indigenous Peoples Council on Biocolonialism (ipcb.org)
Organized to assist Indigenous Peoples in the protection of their genetic resources.

ISEC, International Society for Ecology and Culture (www.isec.org.uk)
A non-profit organization concerned with the protection of both biological and cultural diversity, emphasizing education for action.

Notes

1 While we will use specific tribal names as much as possible in this chapter, we have chosen to use the term "Indigenous Peoples" to identify the cultures we wish to discuss, though there are many other ways of naming or categorizing these groups: In North America, for example, you may also see the use of

Native Americans, First Nations, and even Indians to refer to the people we'll be discussing here, depending on the authors on which we draw. You may also see the term "aboriginal" peoples used in some literature.

2 Trent University in Peterborough, Ontario, is home to one of the oldest Indigenous Studies programs in North America. They host an annual Elders Conference that offers the public a weekend of teachings by Elders from local Annishinaabeg and Haudenashuane tribes as well as others from across Canada. Johnny and Rebecca have had the privilege of learning from these teachings over several years.

Chapter 10

Teaching for the Commons

Educating for Diverse, Democratic, and Sustainable Communities

Introduction

In Chapter 8, we introduced you to the idea of the cultural and environmental commons, and in the previous chapter we explored how Indigenous Peoples from around the world—even while many may be living within modernist consumer cultures—work to organize their lives within diverse commons practices and relationships. As set forth by the EcoJustice Dictionary, "the commons represent both the natural systems (water, air, soil, forests, oceans, etc.), and the cultural patterns and traditions (intergenerational knowledge ranging from growing and preparing food, medicinal practices, arts, crafts, ceremonies, etc.) that are shared without cost by all members of the community" (Retrieved on June 13, 2010 from www.EcoJusticeeducation.org). In this chapter, we return to that concept to explore how communities and schools across North America and around the world are working to teach from an EcoJustice framework, in order to reclaim the commons as a means of learning to live more sustainably and build community.

One of the important messages in all of this work is that we do not have to reinvent the wheel or depend wholly on technological experts to show us how to make the changes we need. While modern technology has a lot to contribute, much of the knowledge we need has existed for many thousands of years all over the world, and indeed, still exists, even in our own highly consumerist society. This knowledge is often assumed to be "old hat" or "out of date"; this is part of our saturation with the discourse of "progress" that relies on the idea of "advancing" civilization through constant change fed by "newer and better" inventions. EcoJustice scholars and teachers recognize this modernist way of thinking as very limited, and assert the need to revalue and re-teach those forms of knowledge that offer a smaller ecological footprint and stronger communities. We recommend considering traditional practices and knowledge alongside newer scientific and technological knowledge and the social sciences as the best way to address the challenges that we are facing.

Three Stories From the Commons

To begin an exploration of what the commons looks like in our society, we offer three stories from our own lives as a mean of introducing you to how the commons function in day-to-day lives. These stories come from very different contexts: a white Anglo-Saxon rural working class commons; an Italian-American, urban working class commons; and a Jewish urban middle class context. We offer them to you realizing that there are many, many, diverse cultures with very unique commons experiences and practices even within modern industrial contexts. As you read our stories, think about some of the different experiences in your own families or neighborhoods.

Rebecca's Commons Story

I have a strong memory of my grandfather coming through the back door of our house at dinnertime with a creel-full of cleaned trout slung over his back and a milk can in his hands, stinking of the cows in his barns not a mile away. My mother would take the fish and the milk out of his hands, invite him to sit down, and proceed to cook the slim, beautiful fish, heads and all. Rainbow trout caught that very afternoon and cooked crispy were a favorite of my family. There would probably be potatoes, and some vegetable—corn or beans, perhaps—most likely something picked straight from our garden or a neighbor's, and then a pie for dessert, blackberry or rhubarb. My mother, who learned the art of pie-making from my father's mother, knew all the best woodland places to pick berries, and the rhubarb grew abundantly around my grandfather's barns. The trout were from a stream right across the road from the farm, along which I also rode horseback with friends on hot summer days.

I learned to fish from my brothers and my dad, and to ride, garden, and cook from my mother. She spent hours with me in our backyard teaching me how to hold the reins in my hands, the proper angle of my feet in the stirrups, how to send signals and understand what the horse was communicating, how to love the animal. "Watch his ears," she'd say, or "Run your hand over his neck, let him know you're pleased." She and my father had grown up in the small rural northern New York town, and knew every nook and cranny of its woods, the back roads, the streams and pastures. I ran and played and grew up in those woods and streams, with my brothers and neighborhood pals, and the horses and dogs. Thinking about that place, I know my body is still connected there: the shape of my legs whose muscles learned to grip the sides of a horse, the bottoms of feet that ran barefoot all summer and remain tough to this day, and now aging skin that browned in the sun. I am, to borrow a Native American term, "barefoot hearted." My flesh is connected to that land. I feel my throat constrict and tears burn as I remember those days and how much I learned. These were my commons: my family and friends' intimate relationships with and knowledge of the land, the streams, the wildlife, the domesticated animals at the farm and in our home, the food practices, the sharing of stories around the table in my grandfather's huge quiet presence.

Johnny's Commons Story

I can remember when I was a small boy growing up in Detroit, my mother, aunts, grandmother, and great grandmother hard at work to prepare large meals. The smell of freshly chopped garlic and stewing tomatoes permeated the small Detroit home. Despite the lack of space, the entire home was set up to function like a restaurant that could accommodate cooking and eating for many. The kitchen was barely large enough for two people, demanding the presence of a second stove in the basement. The living room was permanently a dining room, and the basement crowded by folding tables and chairs. Inside, the food cooked, while outside men drank, smoked, and shared stories.

Meals were planned and always required a variety of fresh ingredients. I would get excited weekly to venture to the Italian market with my mother and grandmothers to buy the things they needed to cook with and can remember how important it was to get those ingredients because they came from the "old country." At least once a week, we would wake up while it was still dark and drive my father to work, dropping him off at the factory and taking the station wagon to the market. We were off to what I referred to as "the Italian store," where my great grandmother would take her empty container to be filled with olive oil. Other days, we would walk a few blocks to my great grandparents' home where the entire yard consisted of a little stone patio with a statue of Mary "The Blessed Mother" and a large garden of tomatoes, peppers, herbs, eggplants, and cucumbers.

I can remember these meals beginning early in the day—sometimes days before, as my mom, grandmother, and aunts gathered ingredients and began preparing food. As they cooked, putting the final touches on the meal, the men—my father, uncles, grandfather, and a handful of "regulars" who were not kin but considered family—gathered in the front room or the porch to talk and smoke. There was so much food that Sunday dinner often lasted us throughout the week.

To this day, I have strong habits of mind associated with food and family that are the direct result of growing up in an Italian community. My family still gathers together on Sundays. My mother cooks big meals and sends us home with Sunday leftovers to eat for several days into the week.

Jeff's Commons Story

I came to one of my most valued commons traditions through marriage into a Jewish family. Though not particularly religious, I have found parts of Jewish tradition to be highly meaningful. In particular is the tradition of Shabbat—or the Sabbath—celebrated from Friday sundown to Saturday sundown. When time allows, my wife and I make challah, the traditional egg bread, which my wife learned to make from her mother, and her mother's mother, back into the distant generations. While the earthy smell of baking bread fills the house, we make dinner. When dinner is ready, we say the prayers of thanks over wine and the challah. These rituals help us note the gift we have received. We sit down for a leisurely family dinner, usually the longest meal of the week. We talk and share stories from the week and what's coming up for the weekend. Shabbat separates us from the rigors of the work-week and gives us time together. It ties us to a long chain of tradition. We think often of my wife's parents; when they were alive, we had Shabbat dinner at their house almost every week. Now we sometimes have friends over, or go to their houses for Shabbat—in which case we are always expected to bring some challah, since nobody makes it like we do.

These stories are shared as a way of beginning an exploration of what we mean by the commons and commons-based education, and to emphasize that community is built in powerful and often invisible ways in our daily lives. Paying attention to the day-to-day practices and relationships that offer us ways to flourish is an essential part of solving the social and ecological problems plaguing communities across the world. To review, the commons can be understood in two interrelated ways: The environmental commons refer to our shared and non-monetized relationship to the land, water, air, and all the creatures that exist within the living systems where we dwell. The cultural commons refer to the beliefs, practices, traditions, and relationships that we share without paying for them and which are generally used to help us live well together. The commons is often associated with all of those taken-for-granted ways of being and relating in which subsistence cultures—the world's "social majorities"— engage as a way of surviving (Esteva & Prakash, 1998). Note that all of us shared memories of practices that involve the ways our families prepared and shared meals, and the pleasures that these activities gave to our families. Many practices in our traditional food commons have been dislodged in industrial societies by the introduction of packaged foods, fast food restaurants, and other so-called "modern conveniences," so that many families no longer prepare or share meals together. Still, a food commons remains, albeit in ways much less visible than just a few years ago. For those still practicing, it may include the cultivation, harvest, preparation, and preservation of what we eat, requiring a whole range of knowledge, skill, and experience. It also includes things like conventions of table setting, manners, conversations, and so on. Because they have been practiced over time and have come to be understood as important to the general health and happiness of the group or family, the skills or traditions are very often taught across generations via our parents and grandparents, aunts, uncles, and other family members. How many of you (perhaps mostly women) remember learning how to set a table, where the knife, fork, and spoon should go? Ever learn to cook greens? Pickle beets? Bake a potato?

When considering cultivation practices, our food commons also generally require a relationship with and knowledge about the land—the soil, water, seeds, plants, bugs, seasons, weather, and so on. And, while all over the world people feed themselves and each other in widely diverse ways, there are also beautiful commonalities that have to do with our humanity, with the ways that communities nurture one another. Those who cultivate for food put seeds in the ground (often saved from the previous year's harvest), nurture seedlings, know when to harvest, and enjoy their bounty in celebrations and around communal tables. Those who hunt or fish develop and pass on important knowledge of the animals' habits and specific characteristics of the species they rely on. In this sense, the commons includes important ways of knowing—many hidden and devalued—that help us to survive and care for each other as well as the land and its creatures.

Note, too, that laced through each of the stories are other practices that support food practices or interweave with them. These include our relationships with animals and with each other. In Rebecca's story, her grandfather's farm and his work with the cows that graze on his fields factor into both her relationship with him, his aromatic presence at the table, and the milk her family drank. In Jeff's story, the tales shared at the table over Shabbat form an invaluable connection to loved ones no longer with them, and help to nurture current friendships, as well. Johnny's commons story includes memories of going to market, and of the house and household: the setting up of tables and the talk among men and women while food was prepared and shared. In all three examples, storytelling and language form essential parts of the commons just as it was in the previous chapter's discussion of Indigenous Peoples' commons.

"Economies of Affection" and the Gift of "Blessings" in Our Day-to-Day Lives

All these seemingly mundane practices and relationships form bonds that are made of very old knowledge of what it takes to keep our communities healthy, safe, and happy. The environmental commons are protected by specific practices in our cultural commons because our security and our children's futures depend on it. In the intersections of these practices, sustainable communities form deep relationships that keep them strong. When a culture emphasizes consumerism and, with it, individualism, these bonds are broken and communities begin to disintegrate.

On the other hand, when a neighbor walks across the street to talk to a woman cultivating tomatoes in her front yard, or a young man offers to shovel his elderly neighbor's driveway, they talk to each other, appreciate each other, share with each other. The neighbor may offer the use of a tool he has in his garage. In a friendly exchange, the gardener may offer a handful of Swiss chard—a particularly tasty and nutritious green leafy vegetable—explaining how to prepare it (this example just happened this morning in Rebecca's front garden!). Perhaps there will be an exchange of recipes, or a short conversation about their recent travels.

Geographers WinklerPrins and de Souza (2005) refer to this sort of exchange as an "economy of affection." They describe the networks of support, trust, and reciprocity that keep traditional communities alive. While their work focuses on home gardens in the Brazilian Amazon and people living "at the economic transition from subsistence peasant to commercial producer" (p. 118), the term "economy of affection" also works nicely as a concept describing non-monetized relationships of exchange that can develop among people in consumer cultures.

Ivan Illich (1992) calls these sorts of practices and relationships "blessings" because of the wealth of generosity they represent, and the mutual well-being that gets created as we engage in them. Illich uses the idea of "dwelling" to talk about the craft of living in a place; the shared meaning and relationships that have nothing at all to do with the monetary value of any act or object, but everything to do with the value of interwoven mutuality. The homes, the food, the work, the animals, the kinship ties, friendships, and intimate relationships, the celebrations: All these require attention, skills, and knowledge that, while usually unexamined, are ancient and passed down generation to generation, surviving because they help us to live well together. Rebecca and her neighbor didn't examine the knowledge and skills that were exchanged this morning, or even comment on the affection growing between them, and there was no money exchanged in the use of the tool or offering of chard. And yet the exchange was very valuable to both parties. A sense of trust and respect was nurtured.

Work in this sense is about doing what is necessary to produce what one needs to subsist and enjoy one's life in community with others. And, because it generally means that one has a much more direct relationship with the product of one's labor (the lush garden or the food, for example) and very often requires interactions with others, it generally creates a strong experience of self-determination, happiness, and mutual well-being.

In fundamental ways, to work towards dwelling creatively is to create a commons that is a basic requirement for peace and happiness. Think about how it feels when you make something, like a pie, or maybe a fort or a tree house when you were a kid, or a garden. Who did you share that with? Who taught you? Ever painted a room, or fixed something mechanical instead of paying someone to do it or throwing it out? It could be almost anything. The point is that there is a lot of personal satisfaction that can lead to an increased sense of self-worth and fulfillment while also benefitting others. Imagine that on a larger community-wide scale, and add in the ecological benefits that come with more awareness of the living systems around us, and decreased consumerism and waste, and you begin to get the idea.

The friendships that form when people interact around work or play become the "glue" of respect, compassion, and goodwill that communities need to support life. The bonds that form can help people to overcome the internalized violence within racist, sexist, ageist, and other modes of domination in our culture. In addition to increasing access and opportunity, is the simple need for people to make relationships with one another and what can grow from them. A story from Robert Putnam's book *Bowling Alone* (2000) makes this case beautifully.

Before October 29, 1997, John Lambert and Andy Boschma knew each other only through their local bowling league at the Ypsi-Arbor Lanes in Ypsilanti, Michigan. Lambert, a 64-year-old retired employee of the University of Michigan hospital, had been on a kidney transplant waiting list for three years when Boschma, a 33-year-old accountant, learned casually of Lambert's need and unexpectedly approached him to offer to donate one of his own kidneys.

> Andy saw something in me that others didn't." said Lambert. "When we were in the hospital Andy said to me, 'John, I really like you and have a lot of respect for you. I wouldn't hesitate to do this all over again.' I got choked up." Boshma returned the feeling: "I obviously feel a kinship [with Lambert]. I cared about him before, but now I'm really rooting for him." This moving story speaks for itself, but the photograph that accompanied this report in the Ann Arbor News reveals that in addition to their differences in profession and generation, Boshma is white and Lambert is African American.
>
> (Putnam, 2000, p. 28)

What Makes Us Happy?

Happiness and friendship may not be the concepts generally brought to bear on how to solve ecological and social problems, but they are exactly what we see as at the heart of strong, healthy communities. Happiness and friendship—and learning to care for others—grow out of relationships with others.

We believe strongly that the active engagement of practices that are more sustainable, while requiring us to consume a lot less, help us to be happier because they invite us to build strong collaborative relationships with each other. Strong relationships are the basis for generosity, compassion, caretaking, and authentic happiness. Working together to revitalize the commons generates and draws from a kind of systemic wisdom, or what Susan Griffin (1995) calls "collaborative intelligence." As Gregory Bateson (2000) taught us, collaborative intelligence or wisdom circulates through the complex communication patterns in all healthy living systems. When it fails, or when we see ourselves as outside of or superior to it, the system fails, causing death. In contrast, when it is allowed to flow freely, the system and the creatures within it flourish.

A recent study by political scientists James H. Fowler and Nicholas A. Christakis (2010) demonstrates that collaboration in social networks creates generosity that "cascades"; as people experience generous relationships, they are more apt to offer such gifts to others in ever increasing networks.

> The results [of the study] suggest that each additional contribution a subject makes to the public good in the first period is tripled over the course of the experiment by other subjects who are directly or indirectly influenced to contribute more as a consequence. These results show experimentally that cooperative behavior cascades in human social networks.
>
> (2010, p. 1)

This is another way of saying that working for the common good is a "blessing" that creates cascading blessings.

This way of thinking about living in community flies in the face of the now taken-for-granted notion of consumerism and enclosure-based economics that dominates our worldview, and the worldview of the "experts" who we must pay to manage the ever more complicated tasks needed (or believed to be needed) to live in a consumer culture. While we clearly need to meet basic material and social needs—food, water, health, housing, and so on—happiness is not dependent on accumulating more and more stuff. Yet we are constantly bombarded with that empty promise. Happiness is, in fact, only linked to satisfaction of material needs to a point, after which the whole principle of growth (in personal income, as well as Gross Domestic Product) as the source of human happiness begins to collapse. According to a study by Princeton economist Alan B. Krueger and psychologist and Nobel Laureate Daniel Kahnemann, and their colleagues:

The belief that high income is associated with good mood is widespread but mostly illusory. People with above-average income are relatively satisfied with their lives but are barely happier than others in moment-to-moment experience, tend to be more tense, and do not spend more time in particularly enjoyable activities. Moreover, the effect of income on life satisfaction seems to be transient. We argue that people exaggerate the contribution of income to happiness because they focus, in part, on conventional achievements when evaluating their life or the lives of others.

(Kahneman et al., 2006, p. 1908)

Recognizing these limits between income and happiness provides an important opportunity to think differently about "wealth," "success," and "well-being" as they manifest within relationships at the level of local communities. While our day-to-day commons-creating activity is often enacted in unconscious and undervalued ways, more and more people are becoming aware of how attending to local relationships—economic, social, educational, and ecological—can help us to create more sustainable communities. What we're interested in here are all the ways people in communities the world over are working to revitalize traditional social patterns as an intentional way of addressing serious social and ecological problems. In the process, they are slowing down, spending more time talking with one another, and creating important mentoring relationships that have deeply healthy consequences—for the individuals, for the groups, and for the planet.

The Commons in Modernist Cultures

Before we proceed, a word or two of caution. Because we live in a modern industrial culture with a very complicated history that includes institutionalized racism, sexism, homophobia, social inequality, and other deeply ingrained forms of social and ecological violence, it is very important not to romanticize or valorize everything that goes on at the local level or in the commons. It's important to remember that the commons—our shared beliefs, practices, and rituals—also includes many traditions and ways of living that undermine community and hasten environmental destruction. Our cultural commons are fraught with all kinds of contradictions that require vigilant exposure and eradication. In fact, all those modernist discourses that we have been discussing throughout this book—anthropocentrism, androcentrism, ethnocentrism, mechanism, and individualism, for example—are, by virtue of the ways they infiltrate our beliefs and behaviors, part of our cultural commons. A rather poignant example of what we mean here is the way racism continues to operate. It was one of the roots of the institution of slavery, a part of the commons, and, even though slavery ended nearly 150 years ago, racism continues to infiltrate our institutions and relationships with each other, often quite unintentionally. Sexism works in similarly unconscious but often institutionalized ways in our communities too. Many families are still quite dominated by patriarchal beliefs even though we are benefitting from feminists' challenges to those traditional relationships. Clearly, it is not to our mutual benefit to believe in the superiority of some people over others or some species over others, and yet we enact such hierarchized ways of thinking in myriad ways every day.

And, to make it even more complicated, very often these destructive traditions are interwoven with more sustainable traditions. For example, consider Rebecca's story from the beginning of the chapter about traditions that connected her to the earth and animals. While she learned early on to question anthropocentrism, an integral part of the patterns in her family is the patriarchy inherent in the division of labor between her mother and father. Similar patterns can be seen in Johnny's story, and probably, if we probe, could be discerned in some of Jeff's family relationships and traditions as well, even though we may be fundamentally unaware of how they work on us psychologically.

As we've been discussing throughout this book, we live in a culture that is organized around the naturalization of value hierarchies. So, even though the feminist movement has done a lot to name and interrupt the ways patriarchy plays out in our families, work contexts, and larger community relationships, androcentrism continues to weave its way into our patterns of belief and behavior. It is important to be aware and willing to identify how this and other forms of hierarchized thinking play out in our lives. Certainly, we have made clear how racism, heterosexism, anthropocentrism, and other destructive patterns create barriers to social and ecological justice, but this does not mean that there is no hope. The point is that we must be willing to teach each other how to identify what is useful and mutually beneficial in our commons and what is harmful. And we must be willing to work together to do so.

Guidelines for Successfully Working Together in the Commons

Up to this point, we've been discussing the cultural commons in terms of the informal day-to-day practices and relationships that are for the most part invisible. In most of these interactions, the "rules" governing the behavior in these interactions would be considered just "good manners." It is important to recognize such practices as part of the commons. C. A. Bowers (2006) has also pointed to the formal decision-making processes that get set up among people in sustainable communities to guide behavior and protect the commons. It is precisely these collectively agreed upon processes that protect against what Garrett Hardin (1968) called "the tragedy of the commons." Harden's mistake was to disregard the ways communities work together to set up guidelines against the selfish misuse of ecological resources.

In 2009, Elinor Ostrom was awarded the Nobel Memorial Prize in Economic Sciences for her work exposing the explicit ways people organize to cooperatively solve shared problems in their communities. In an interview with *Yes! Magazine* (Spring, 2010), she asserts that, "We have to think through how to choose a meaningful life where we're helping one another in ways that really help the Earth" (p. 14). Ostrom's research highlights eight elements for successfully collaborating for the commons. Successful collaborators will:

1. Define clear group boundaries.
2. Match rules governing use of common goods to local needs and conditions.
3. Ensure that those affected by the rules can participate in modifying the rules.
4. Make sure the rule-making rights of community members are respected by outside authorities.
5. Develop a system, carried out by community members, for monitoring members' behavior.
6. Use graduated sanctions for rule violators.
7. Provide accessible, low-cost means for dispute resolution.
8. Build responsibility for governing the common resource in nested tiers from the lowest level up to the entire interconnected system.

> (Ostrom, 1990, as adapted by Korten for
> *Yes! Magazine*, Spring 2010, p. 15)

"Choosing a meaningful life" that protects living systems requires working with others and is at the heart of Earth democracy as Shiva (2005) has taught us. What we are advocating here is that teachers recognize that these are skills that need to be taught as part of overcoming the harmful modernist assumptions crowding our beliefs and behaviors. This can best be accomplished in partnership with others in the community.

Educating for the Commons in Communities and Schools

Educating for the commons is a specific way of ensuring that communities flourish by emphasizing that an important knowledge base of skills, craft, tradition, relationship patterns, and decision-making practices that are more in balance with the needs and processes of our ecosystems will not be lost.

We are witnessing an important revitalization movement across the United States, Canada, and the world, where people in communities are educating each other about how to take care of one another without relying on conventional industrial mechanisms as the primary source of food, housing, work, or entertainment. In the sections that follow, we will share stories of the ways that communities—both urban and rural—are embracing the commons in both formal and informal educational relationships as a direct way of saying "no" to the damaging effects of industrialization and enclosure. We will also be focusing on what schools and teachers are doing with community partners in introducing and involving students in revitalization efforts in their communities.

While it would be impossible to document all the myriad informal and interpersonal ways that people work to reproduce their commons every day, there are many great examples of people organizing to support activities, skills, practices, and knowledge that they have explicitly identified as helping to support more sustainable communities. According to journalist and environmental activist Paul Hawken (2007), in fact, there are at least a million, and perhaps as many as two million non-profit organizations doing both social and ecological justice work all over the world in order to address the problems we have discussed in this book (p. 2), and many of them are working expressly with teachers and schools. As we write this, in fact, thousands of U.S. and Canadian grassroots activists and educators are converging over several days in Detroit, to learn from one another how to best address the social and ecological problems challenging our communities. This annual meeting is a subset of a much larger World Social Forum, whose anthem since its inception in January 2001 in Porto Alegre, Brazil, has been "Another World is Possible."

Commenting on both the scale and uniqueness of this phenomenon, Hawken (2007) writes:

> By any conventional definition, this vast collection of committed individuals does not constitute a movement. Movements have leaders and ideologies. People join movements, study their tracts, and identify themselves with a group. Movements, in short, have followers. This movement however doesn't fit the standard model. It is dispersed, inchoate, and fiercely independent. It has no manifesto or doctrine, no overriding authority to check with. It is taking shape in schoolrooms, farms, jungles, villages, companies, deserts, fisheries, slums—and yes, even fancy New York hotels.
>
> (Hawken, 2007, pp. 2–3)

We often hear from our students that the issues and problems we ask them to consider are overwhelmingly depressing, so much so that they cannot bear to pay attention. Their complaints are certainly understandable. We three authors know well how difficult it can be to face the despair that can come from thinking about such devastation. So, we offer practicing teachers and community activists—public intellectuals—all the following examples. We hope to inspire you to do what may feel impossible but is actually emerging as a global humanitarian ecological movement to turn around the life-threatening processes being perpetrated on the planet and in our communities. As Hawken wrote, "Inspiration is not garnered from the recitation of what is flawed; it resides, rather, in humanity's willingness to restore, redress, reform, rebuild, recover, reimagine, and reconsider" (2007, p. 4). The following examples are offered with this in mind. Take from them what makes sense in terms of your own specific situation.

Communities Revitalizing the Commons

In the examples that follow, we share some of the ways that non-profit organizations in our own communities are working to support informal educational relationships to revitalize the commons. Some of these are networking organizations whose primary contribution is to help connect existing organizations with each other; too often pitted against one another especially in competition for funding and clients, they collaborate and form coalitions. Others are great examples of commons-revitalizing movements that are supported by well-established, even nationally-based organizations. Still others are far less visible, operating primarily at the local level, but doing terrific work there. Many are working directly with schools, and all have very important educational functions at the community level. At the end of this chapter, we offer a list of websites to help you look into these organizations or use those sites to locate them in your own communities.

Peak Oil, Transition Towns, and the "Great Reskilling"

Facing the challenge brought on by the realization that the fossil fuels driving our economy as well as our day-to-day habits in modern Western societies will not last forever means looking squarely at alternatives. For some, "alternatives" means inventing new energy technologies to run the same system, but for others it means reconsidering the viability of the overall system for a sustainable relationship to the planet, and recognizing that there is a lot of existing wisdom about how to live much simpler, more sustainable lives.

In 2005, Rob Hopkins and Naresh Giangrande started a local organization in Totnes, UK, that they called Transition Town Totnes (TTT). They started by holding events designed to raise awareness about peak oil and climate change. And, they began thinking about the core elements needed by communities to respond to these problems and "transition" to a world with less and eventually no dependence on oil and coal-based energy, calling it the Transition Model. Five years later, this general vision and the Transition Model was being picked up and used as a general framework in cities, towns, and neighborhoods all around the world.

> A Transition Initiative (which could be a town, village, university or island, etc.) is a community-led response to the pressures of climate change, fossil fuel depletion and increasingly, economic contraction. There are thousands of initiatives around the world starting their journey to answer this crucial question: "for all those aspects of life that this community needs in order to sustain itself and thrive, how do we significantly rebuild resilience (to mitigate the effects of Peak Oil and economic contraction) and drastically reduce carbon emissions (to mitigate the effects of Climate Change)?"
> (Retrieved on July 2, 2010 from www.transitionnetwork.org)

The Transition movement relies on positive visioning of the future with the assumption that things can actually get better for us after oil. This affirmation gets us past the potentially incapacitating realities of climate change, etc. For example, many local Transition activities include some sort of collaborative future vision: newspapers with fake stories that imagine what is going on in the town after transition; or the construction of three-dimensional dioramas of a town's transition.

The basic idea is that communities have within them all the basic resources and wisdom needed to live secure, sustainable, and happy lives. We just need to tap into them, refresh our communal memories, teach each other the needed skills, and start to live more sustainable lives. All around the United States, including the cities where we live, people are using these very simple principles to refresh what it means to live well together in communities.

All over the world, reskilling workshops are being offered to educate folks interested in learning all sorts of things from how to plant and cultivate a garden for food and save the seeds for next year, to how to roof your own house, to how to repair small engines, keep bees, sew clothes, make cheese, brew beer, build furniture, knit sweaters, rebuild bicycles, capture rain water, hook rugs, preserve and cook nutritious food, "husband" animals, and on and on. As Transition organizers help to support these pluralistic workshops, identifying and drawing together both those with knowledge or skills to share and those who wish to learn, the process has been dubbed "the Great Reskilling."

Besides the great skills such workshops offer, the biggest outcome of such community-based work is the fun! Strong friendships can grow from focusing our attention on and giving value to what our neighbors know and can teach us. And, it is very satisfying to know that instead of buying something or paying to have it, it was created or repaired by oneself! It may be a slower way to get what we want or need, but slowing down is good, and absolutely necessary to real lasting relationships.

City Repair

In Portland, Oregon, an organization called City Repair is creatively working on ways to reclaim the cultural and environmental commons. Its mission statement says it best:

> City Repair is an organized group action that educates and inspires communities and individuals to creatively transform the places where they live. City Repair facilitates artistic and ecologically-oriented placemaking through projects that honor the interconnection of human communities and the natural world.
> (Retrieved on July 2, 2010 from http://cityrepair.org)

Among the original projects of City Repair was "intersection repair," which simply involved remaking neighborhood intersections to inspire more community gathering. Intersection repair can involve painting intersections, creating community spaces around intersections, and constructing small buildings that enhance community. Now City Repair organizes the Village Building Convergence, an annual event during which community spaces are built in several places around the city. The projects range from small shelters, gazebos, and benches made from cob (a straw/mud concoction), to gardens and composting sites.

An interesting recent project of City Repair is "Depave," which does just what it sounds like. Depave's goal is to reclaim land from pavement, by organizing groups to assist in removal of unnecessary pavement from schools, businesses, and homes, and reclaiming the land for community use as gardens or other public spaces. As Depave points out, "The removal of impervious pavements will reduce storm water pollution and increase the amount of land available for habitat restoration, urban farming, trees, native vegetation, and beauty, thus providing us with greater connections to the natural world" (Retrieved on July 2, 2010 from http://depave. org/blog/about).

Bartering, Time Banks, and Alternative Currency Systems

Across the United States, the recent economic crisis has brought with it an explosion of bartering. According to *The New York Times* (March 21, 2010), Craigslist is now listing over 200,000 advertisements per month for bartered goods and services: "Consumers can use their time, skills and possessions instead of money to obtain goods and services like piano lessons, dental work, and dog training—and to meet new people along the way."

A slightly more organized way of supporting bartering relationships in local economies, "time banks" are popping up all over the world: "For every hour you spend doing something for someone in your community, you earn one Time Dollar. Then you have a Time Dollar to spend on having someone do something for you" (www.timebanks.org). Alternative currencies (also referred to as "slow money") are similar. While there are variations for how it works, Ithaca Hours is typical. Founded in 1991 in Ithaca, New York, this community-organized system is the oldest sustained local currency in operation. Here's how it works: Participants sign up to become members. Once members, they can exchange goods and services by using the currency instead of Federal currency. Laboring for one hour in participating businesses, members earn one Ithaca Hour, a note that is worth $10, which they can use to buy food, services, and other goods in other participating businesses and individual members. For more information on how the system works, go to www.ithacahour. org. You can also find lots of information about other communities' systems by conducting an Internet search for "alternative currencies."

Back Alley Bikes

In Detroit, Michigan, an organization called Back Alley Bikes works to strengthen local skill sharing and reclaim transportation in a city with limited public transit. The shop was started in 2000 by a group of volunteers and employees working in Detroit Summer, a collective that has been providing community youth educational programming and activism since 1992. Youth and workers in the program were using bicycles as a means of getting themselves, their tools, and materials around town to various sites where they were working. Recognizing a vital need, Back Alley Bikes was born, in a tiny shop down a back alley off Cass Avenue in a neighborhood known as the Cass Corridor, to teach adults and youth in the local neighborhoods to build and repair bikes.

This organization offers a unique variety of educational programs for youth and adults including bike repair classes, bike art workshops, "Community Drop-In," and a "Mechanics in Training" program. All programs are offered to the public free of charge. The "Mechanics in Training" program is an excellent example of local intergenerational learning. The program involves funding apprenticeships for local youth to learn from a bike mechanic while working in the shop, and where they can earn a bike in exchange for their work. The "Community Drop-In" program, which more or less has become a regular concept in the shop, offers members of the community access to tools and assistance from a mechanic in order to build or repair a bike.

Back Alley Bikes is a solid example of programs in communities centered on reciprocity and strengthening non-monetized local exchanges of labor and knowledge and is well-known locally for creatively involving the local community in Bike Art Auctions, community dinners, and social gatherings. In recent years, they have been able to gift bikes to children in the neighborhood too young to earn a bike, while consistently engaging volunteers of all ages, races, and locations in the programs mentioned above. In response to a need to secure stable funding and a desire to expand their ability to serve the local community, Back Alley Bikes opened a local bike shop called the "Hub of Detroit," offering more than your typical bike-related retail. Check out the Hub of Detroit at www. hubofdetroit.org.

Detroit Dog Rescue

As is probably the case in many urban centers where poverty is severe, Detroit is home to many thousands of stray dogs. While there are those who counter this claim (Hall, 2014), some estimate that number to be as high as 50,000 dogs, many of whom were left behind as people were forced to move from their homes. Others are born on the street and are therefore feral. Whatever the case, these animals suffer from malnutrition, disease, and general neglect as they try to survive in an urban context. Some suffer from terrible injuries resulting from abuse inflicted by former owners.

In 2011, an organization called Detroit Dog Rescue was born after the city refused to grant access to a network television series interested in documenting the lives of these dogs. Daniel "Hush" Carlisle decided to do something about it.

> There is a stray dog epidemic in the city, just as there is in many cities across the United States that have had to deal with economic decline, dwindling populations and abandoned buildings. If other animal lovers around the world could see what we see on the streets of Detroit every day, we know that they would help us make a difference in this city, one dog at a time.
>
> (Retrieved from www.detroitdogrescue.com on January 26, 2014)

Their mission since organizing has been to create a "state of the art no-kill animal center in Detroit." As of January, 2014 DDR had rescued hundreds of dogs, providing them with veterinary care, fostering them, and eventually finding homes for many. They also take food and shelter (dog igloos) and provide education to residents who own dogs but have difficulty caring for them. The dream of a shelter got underway when an anonymous donation of a million dollars came into the organization. Renovation of a former veterinary clinic began in 2013 with plans for completion in early February, 2014. Detroit Dog Rescue is an example of what can happen when ordinary citizens decide that they will not allow other creatures to suffer.

Urban Farms and Community Gardens

As the detrimental effects of our conventional industrial-based food system become clearer and clearer—epidemic levels of diabetes, obesity, and malnutrition—people in all our major urban centers across the United States and Canada as well as across the world are turning toward the cultivation and preservation of their own food. We wrote about what has developed in Detroit in Chapter 8, where over 1,500 gardens have sprung up under the guidance and wisdom of organizations like Earth Works, the Black Community Food Security Network, and the Garden Resource Program within the Greening of Detroit.

In cities and towns across the United States and Canada, community organizations are partnering with local residents to revive and reclaim traditional agricultural knowledge. Mentoring relationships are being developed to teach people the skills needed to bring healthy food back to communities stressed by the lack of grocery stores and other sources of fresh produce. And, in the process, people in neighborhoods are coming together to work shoulder to shoulder to reclaim their local social, economic, and political lives, and the life of the soil. This is an especially important form of self-determination for communities devastated by the economic, social, and psychological consequences of racism.

Food Gardens on University Campuses

In universities, faculty and students are also beginning to see the community garden movement as an important tool for teaching about the necessity to revitalize the commons. At the University of British Columbia Okanagan, Professor Veronica Gaylie created the Learning Garden (http://learninggarden.blogspot.com) to introduce her pre-service teachers to the importance of getting outside to learn about the fundamentals of soil and water, and appreciating the sensual and aesthetic richness of the more-than-human world (Gaylie, 2009). In Ypsilanti, Lindsey Scalera, an alumnus of the Master's of Arts program in EcoJustice Education at Eastern Michigan University, helped to found the Giving Garden(http://givinggardenemu.blogspot.com) as a space for community members to come together to learn about both the fundamentals of gardening, but also where the cultural roots of the ecological crisis could be discussed. Ypsilanti community members join students and faculty learning together by cultivating "buddy plots" as well as a "fresh food donation plot" used to provide fresh produce to S.O.S. Community Services, a local organization that works on issues for homeless and low income families. The key idea is that college should be about learning fundamental skills needed by communities, and building strong relationships that lead to sustainability.

In the summer of 2009, Scalera and others involved with the garden worked with Growing Hope, a local community organization, to organize a summer program to educate local youth about the value of gardening for healthy communities. In addition to gaining skills related to cultivation, students also took their produce to the Ypsilanti farmers market, interacting with local farmers and residents and experiencing the power of localization firsthand.

Scalera used what she learned with her colleagues in that endeavor to help found the Michigan Young Farmers Coalition. This organization brings together youth from around the region who are interested and/or active in the practice of agriculture as a primary form of localizing the economy and creating a necessary response to the region's food security crisis. There is a strong focus on intergenerational learning, cooperative work share, and an emphasis on female leadership.

Chickens and Honeybees in the City

Many of the urban farmers who are raising food for their families have also successfully challenged city ordinances that have prevented keeping farm animals or bees within city limits. In Ypsilanti, Michigan, and neighboring Ann Arbor, city residents organized using localization principles from the Transition Model to argue for the introduction of laying hens for backyard residential egg production. This successful lobby was followed by an agreement for bringing beekeeping into the city. Substantial re-education about the safety of honeybees in city gardens was required as local people expressed fears of increased potential for bee stings. Honeybees are generally non-aggressive when left undisturbed to do their pollination work, and the local activists won City Council over. The first season for city bees in Ypsilanti was in 2011, and, as a gardener, Rebecca is thrilled to see a much larger number of honeybees pollinating and tending her plants. The local Ypsilanti Food Co-op, as well as a local organization called Growing Hope, and a host of individual families, are keeping hives and selling their honey at local markets.

These local efforts are directly addressing the severe public health issues plaguing urban areas as well as the social violence inherent in an economic system that leaves impoverished communities to starve, or exist on cheap processed sugar and fat. Further, this localization of the agricultural system directly addresses the adverse effects on the land and animals of conventional agriculture. It may not yet be enough to thoroughly change or stop the huge corporate power behind our current food system, but it is demonstrating that people can successfully say no to processed food, return to ancient methods of feeding themselves, their neighbors, and their families, and live much healthier and happier lives.

Community Art

Many of the organizations and initiatives we are calling attention to have a strong connection to the arts. Mural painting, found-art sculptures, gardening, politically charged ephemeral art, poetry, music, and theater are among the many mainstays of revitalizing the commons and strengthening communities around the world. Art, especially public art, brings people together and gives voice to underrepresented or silenced groups. Among the many examples of how the arts strengthen community, Public Art Workz and Matrix Theatre Company in Detroit stand out for the work they do to specifically address revitalizing the commons in partnership with teachers and students.

In many urban areas, murals play a major role in bringing both beauty and inspiration to local neighborhoods. In Detroit, Michigan, Public Art Workz (PAWZ), directed by artist Chazz Miller, works together with local volunteers to eliminate blight and emit positive images in neighborhoods through large murals on the sides of buildings.

In 2005, Miller and internationally-known poet-scholar Aurora Harris partnered with Rebecca to develop a Summer Arts Program for Detroit youth, combining poetry, mural painting, and community gardening as a means of responding to violence in their community. They painted murals and wrote poetry inspired by the local environment and what they wanted for their community. They learned about composting, and planted several small gardens of their own design. The art they produced was aimed specifically at challenging deep cultural assumptions about why Detroit suffers from poverty, racism, and blight, and the role of violence in the city's problems. Miller's words capture the Public Art Workz mission best:

> Public Art Workz is stimulating community growth, providing a cultural and artistically rich environment conducive to the needs of artists, local residents, and business owners in Northwest Detroit and its surrounding community. Our purpose is to foster social and emotional growth while educating students that art is in everything and should be used to achieve their highest academic performance and a mastery of skills necessary to become effective and productive members of society.
>
> (Retrieved on July 13, 2010 from www.publicartworkz.org)

Another strong example that combines the arts and activism with revitalizing the commons is the Matrix Theatre Company, located in Southwest Detroit. Their mission sums up why what they do is so important. The Matrix Theatre Company Mission reads:

> Matrix Theatre Company uses the transformative power of theatre to change lives, build community, and foster social justice. It creates opportunities for children, youth, adults and elders, especially those in isolated or challenged communities, to become creators, producers, and audience of original theatre.
> (Retrieved on July 13, 2010 from http://inwork.matrixtheatre.org)

Matrix Theatre Company involves teachers and students in schools, community organizations, local residents, and artists from all over the world in socially and ecologically engaged theatre with a specific goal of revitalizing the community. The company uses hand-crafted puppets and often performs on the streets. An example of this transformational theatre is their original show "Ghost Waters." This performance directly draws attention to the undermining of local water systems by modern culture while calling for the rise of lakes, streams, and marshes that were made invisible by industrialization in Detroit. In affiliation with the production of "Ghost Waters," the theatre company hosted a parade of over 100 participants featuring a variety of originally crafted puppets and costumes as part of the "River Resurgence Pageant" at the 2010 U.S. Social Forum held in Detroit.

These examples give just a taste of the sorts of organized commons-based activities beginning to spread throughout our communities. The key for teachers and schools is to join with these organizations in projects that teach our young people the value of reclaiming the commons and working for more sustainable communities. Imagine, for example, a teacher who uses bike repair to teach math, connecting with the organizers of Back Alley Bikes. Or think about the power of the folks from Matrix Theatre Company bringing their art to the construction of a rain barrel, beautifully decorated by the art of a group of youngsters and adults and placed in their own schoolyards. Or a farmer taking a group of students on to help him plant or harvest a field, all the while talking about the richness and life in a handful of soil.

What's Going on in Schools? Teaching for EcoJustice and Community-Based Learning

In fact, along with this explosion of community organizations and private individuals dedicated to revitalizing the commons, educators all over the world are also taking up the call. And, in the most powerful examples, we see community organizations partnering with teachers and students out in the community to identify and remediate problems, engage inquiry skills, and share information that is deeply relevant to their lives. Further, we are beginning to see the impact of our own work with teachers and students to address the deep cultural roots of social and ecological problems as they manifest in their own communities. While recognizing that there are excellent examples popping up all over the country, we share some of the best examples from our own work here, in order to demonstrate all the diverse ways that EcoJustice educators are beginning to help their students make a difference.

As we have throughout the book, we emphasize the importance of diversity here, and ask that, as you think about these examples, you recognize that no two schools or neighborhoods or communities are the same. They all have their own particular history, ecosystem, culture, and politics even while they may share important roots. The schools have their own structural realities, strengths, and weaknesses that will make each effort unique. Big or small, however, we hope these examples help you to see what is possible. Following the examples, we offer some general guiding principles that we think could help you get started with your own project, course, curriculum unit, lesson, community partnership, or whatever works as you move toward a commitment to teach for EcoJustice and community-based learning. What we encourage you to do is just get started! It all starts with that first determined effort!

Sunnyside Environmental School: A Full School Model for Sustainability Education

Sunnyside Environmental School is a K-8 public school in Portland, Oregon. Begun as a middle school in 1995, it expanded to K-8 several years later. The founding principles included putting the environment at the center of the curriculum, the importance of students spending time in nature, and a responsibility to the larger community. A Native American Elder was part of the founding group, and the school was also designed to meet the needs of Native students (Williams & Taylor, 1999).

In the middle school, students spend two days a week in community service projects, which may range from stream restoration, to working with elderly patients at a nursing home, to making bag lunches for social service organizations. Students also work in the school's garden, and at the partnered urban farm a few miles away. Indeed, gardening and food are central to SES. According to the school's website:

> Teachers at Sunnyside Environmental School integrate gardening and cooking activities throughout the curriculum in kindergarten through eighth grades. We study world cultures and create meals from them,

apply mathematical learning to baking, and eat our way through literature. We plant gardens and follow the process of growing food from seed to harvest to feast.

(Retrieved on July 1, 2010 from www.sesptsa.com/curriculum/kitchen/kitchen.php)

In addition, once per month, each middle school class prepares and hosts a community meal for the school. Parents and elders are welcomed for these meals, providing another opportunity for intergenerational communication.

The curriculum of SES is centered around the environment. Each term, subjects are all connected to a common theme, such as rivers, mountains, or forests. When students study rivers, for example, they look at novels about rivers and do math about water use, but also focus on the local watershed within which they live.

As two of the founders of the school summarize: "By moving environmental science from the margin to the center of education, and by grounding students' experiences in their own place, students at [the school] are provided with a framework that enables them to create context-based knowledge and to 'feel' their place" (Williams & Taylor, 1999, p. 99).

It should be noted that SES is not explicitly rooted in EcoJustice principles. There is little effort to examine the deep cultural assumptions of modernity or the language that carries those assumptions. Still, many of the practices reflect commons-oriented thinking.

Nsoroma Institute

Nsoroma Institute, a K-8 African-centered charter school in Detroit was organized with a school-wide focus on food security. The decision to establish a school with this focus was a direct response to food insecurity in Detroit especially among the African American population. Malik Yakini, the founder and principal for over 20 years, is also the founder and chairman of the Detroit Black Community Food Security Network:

We have an organic farm that we maintain in a city-owned park that we hope is creating a template for other groups who might want to utilize some of the under-utilized land owned by the city of Detroit . . . All members of a community should have access to affordable, nutritious, culturally appropriate food . . . As of 2007, the last major grocer left the city of Detroit, which was Farmer Jack. Now, I grew up in Detroit—I'm 53 years old—and when I was a child there were many national chains in Detroit . . . but now there are no major grocers in the city . . . we have a serious problem both in terms of access to fresh produce in the city of Detroit and we also have a problem in terms of the quality of food, because often the quality of food is markedly different in the city of Detroit than the quality of food that is available in the suburban rings that surround the city.

(Ecology Center, 2010)

Under Mr. Yakini's leadership, teachers from Nsoroma worked to design interdisciplinary curriculum materials around food security used throughout the school. Teachers from several grade levels—K-2 and sixth, seventh, and eighth graders—worked on community mapping with their students, looking at the characteristics of their immediate neighborhood. Younger students made drawings of what they saw, while older students posed questions about safety and the general condition of both the natural environment and residences. This project was used as a jumping off point to engage students in a discussion of what they would like their community to be like.

Expanding the raised beds established just outside the school doors, the teachers and principal got permission from the City government to establish a school garden in a local park about three blocks from the school. Students have helped to plant, cultivate, and maintain these gardens, learning about nutrition, preservation, and preparation of healthy food along the way. This garden also boasts a water catchment system that was built with the support of participants from the recent U.S. Social Forum.

Catherine Ferguson Academy: A High School for Pregnant and Parenting Girls

Once a public school and now a charter, CFA is located in downtown Detroit, not far from the Motor City Casino. This school features a fully functional farm complete with chickens, bees, rabbits, goats, two horses, and a cow, all tended by the students. There is also a beautiful orchard of fruit trees, a large vegetable garden on grounds once used as athletic fields, and a barn constructed by the young women.

CFA was founded by Principal Asenath Andrews to provide quality education for pregnant and parenting girls and to interrupt the cycle of pregnancy in the next generation of children. Not long after it was opened in 1985, biology teacher Paul Weertz realized that asking pregnant women to work with formaldehyde to study anatomy was dangerous. He decided to raise rabbits instead, and, as the principal says, "The rabbits turned into chickens, and the chickens turned into goats. Then the goats turned into horses. We even had a steer for a while" (Retrieved on July 7, 2010 from www.oprah.com/world/Gardening-in-the-City-Changing-Detroit).

The agri-science program at the farm offers important life skills for young parents, enhancing a sense of what it means to nurture and care for others, including non-human others, as well as fostering connectedness and purpose among the students. Partnering with several local community organizations including EarthWorks and the Greening of Detroit, the young women develop skills that range from the cultivation of gardens and beekeeping to raising baby goats and the other animals, lessons important to being mothers and nurturing their own children.

When they realized that they needed a barn to hold hay harvested by Weertz from vacant lots across the city, the women raised a barn. Realizing how important the resulting construction skills were to the students' overall sense of self-assurance, employability, and self-sufficiency, they soon took up a project to renovate several houses within a few blocks of the school. Now a construction program joins the biology classes as central to the curriculum offered at the school. This is place-based education at its most powerful, and while there is no direct integration of EcoJustice curriculum, issues of justice and eco-ethical responsibility permeate this school's approach, preparing these students to critically analyze the social, economic, and environmental contexts within which they are situated and will raise their children. And, students have free access to fresh produce, which, as we have pointed out, is extremely important in this food desert—and is essential to the health of their babies.

Blossom School and the Children's Wet Meadow Project

The Buhr Park Children's Wet Meadow project in Ann Arbor, Michigan, grew out of the interest of a group of young children at Blossom Pre-School in the early 1990s. They were worried about what was happening in a creek near their school. With their teacher, Jeannine Palms, they explored the creek and found many dying or deformed frogs. Investigating, the children learned that storm water run-off from parking lots in a park next to Jeannine's school was causing problems. They decided to do something about it! With the permission of the Ann Arbor Parks Commission and a lot of cooperation and hard work, the children, their parents, their teacher and other community members created a wet meadow ecosystem to catch the water before it reaches the stream, providing a habitat for native plants and animals, an attractive educational site for the children and their neighbors, and an environmental filter for storm water run-off from the park grounds.

> The original meadow was planted in September, 1997, and the plants have thrived and bloomed ever since. The project has expanded with a second set of three basins, called Wet Meadow II on the west side of the park. More than 150 volunteers helped plant [a second meadow] in June of 2004. The wet meadows are thriving beyond our wildest dreams.
>
> (Retrieved on January 26, 2014 from http://www.wetmeadow.org)

The children at Blossom formed a group called the Super Swampers. Each year they brainstorm what the next steps will be to improve the health of the stream. More than 20 years after they started, many adults who were part of the first group of children now support the school and the Wet Meadow Project with their families! And Jeannine continues to work with 3–5 year olds to develop gardens, an orchard, prairie, and wet meadows at Buhr Park.

"Food for Thought": A Senior Seminar at Souhegan High School, Amherst, New Hampshire

In the fall of 2006, three teachers from Souhegan High School in Amherst, New Hampshire, representing social studies, English/language arts, and science, launched an interdisciplinary seminar for 12th graders focused on food systems and sustainability. Gary Schnakenberg, Ken Boisselle, and Melissa Chapman, joined by Rebecca while on sabbatical, planned and implemented this course, and were supported by a faculty Committee on Sustainability that served in an advisory capacity. At Souhegan, students in their senior year receive English credit either through an Advanced Placement course (a minority take this route), or a two-credit interdisciplinary Senior Seminar where one credit is dedicated to English and one credit to another discipline, creating a specific elective course dedicated to a particular topic. These seminars are organized in a modified block scheduling structure, utilizing two back-to-back course periods every day, and as close to a two-course enrollment as possible. Each section enrolls between 30 and 45 students.

All seminars, including this course, are required to meet state mandates and benchmarks in all three disciplines, and serve a very heterogeneous group of students in terms of ability. While many of the Amherst students come from white professional affluent families, about one third of the students in this seminar the year it was launched came from lower socioeconomic segments of the community and upon graduation planned to move into the workforce rather than pursue higher education. This variety made for a very rich set of discussions, activities, and relationships that ultimately evolved into a strong community over the course of the year. The description for the Sustainability and Food Systems course reads as follows:

> This interdisciplinary course examines the various aspects of U.S. and global food production, allocation, and distribution. It draws on environmental, botanic, cultural, geographic, economic, civic, and ethical lenses of focus, utilizing fiction, poetry, and nonfiction literature to provide perspectives on place, nature, food, and agriculture.
>
> (Course syllabus, 2006)

The course intentionally utilized the primary elements of EcoJustice, offering students an analytic frame for understanding the processes and politics of food on both global and local scales. Students begin the year reading *Ishmael*, a novel by Daniel Quinn (1992), as an introduction to the idea that there are diverse cultural worldviews leading to very different ways of organizing societies and relating to the surrounding natural systems. Students are introduced to key concepts—individualism, ethnocentrism, anthropocentrism, "progress," and mechanism as tools for examining the workings of socio-linguistic systems on their own thinking and on Western industrial/consumer cultures more generally.

Exploring Quinn's example of a "Taker" worldview under the banner "The World Belongs to Us," Rebecca led a discussion, one day, on anthropocentrism. She asked the students to imagine and list out examples of the sorts of things they might see in a culture organized by anthropocentric ways of thinking. We defined the concept carefully and they thought a while, soon offering examples like "road kill," mountain-top mining, deforestation, animal abuse, zoos, and so on. After several examples were on the board, a young woman raised her hand. "I might be way off here," she started, "but I think in a culture where humans are defined as superior to animals, it would be a short leap to believing that some people are superior to others." There was quiet, and then we were swept up in a flurry of other examples of how value hierarchy works to structure our thinking. "There would be poverty!" "Men would think they're better than women!" "Yeah! It's why we had slavery! We thought they were 'like animals!'"

Later, using concepts from human geography, the students explored cultural points of view akin to Quinn's notion that "We belong to the world." They were introduced to Ladakh (Norberg-Hodge, 1991), then human geography concepts were introduced that enabled students to analyze in a non-deterministic way the manner in which the Ladakhis developed a "culture complex" that helped them to thrive in this physically harsh environment. Students were also exposed to Hopi, Quechua, and the local Abenaki First Nations peoples as a means of exploring diverse cultural patterns and belief systems, especially related to their relationships with the land and food production. Focusing closer to home, students study the history of these different worldviews in their own bioregion, reading William Cronon's *Changes in the Land* (1983). Cronon's work is a classic environmental history comparing land conservation practices and attitudes of native peoples versus commodification-based views of colonizing New Englanders and the effects of these differences. They also read Wendell Berry's novel *Jayber Crow* (2000b), a tale of how a Kentucky farming community was changed in tragic ways after World War II as the country shifted to an industrialized food production system. Alongside these explorations of diverse cultural perspectives and practices, students studied their own food commons. They learned to grow, preserve, and cook food themselves, building six raised-bed gardens (using lumber from a local sawmill that promotes "sustainable forestry" and has been operated by the same family for nearly 200 years!) where a wide range of vegetables and herbs were grown. The class harvested lettuces and other greens to supply the school salad bar for two weeks in the fall. With the science teacher they examined soil science and soil analysis, nutrients and nutrient cycling, soil conservation practices, and the ecological impact of synthetic fertilizers. A major research project and exhibition was organized around the science of composting, including the construction and implementation of a school composting system. They read most of Michael Pollan's *The Omnivore's Dilemma* (2006) and portions of Barbara Kingsolver's *Animal, Vegetable, Miracle* (2007).

Mixed in were lectures on physical geography: world soil-type distributions and classification systems, world climate, glaciers and glaciation, soil forming processes, and "agricultural revolutions." In a major project, teams of students studied the history of the town's food commons, interviewing descendants of some of Amherst's long-established farming families. This project was designed to connect the students to their community's not-too-distant past, examining the specific knowledge and memories of food production from elders who still live among them. They used the community library and town hall to access records and historical archives about the agricultural history of their now largely suburban community.

While space does not permit us to examine all the aspects of this course, we want to emphasize that these three disciplines were woven together to help students examine the multidimensionality of sustainability. All three teachers were often present in full class discussions of these topics, or outside with students working in the gardens. There was substantial effort by all three teachers to weave into their assignments the key aspects of the EcoJustice framework and to continually pose questions about the ecological effects of specific practices or policies. Students worked back and forth between projects that asked them to inquire into the policies of modernization and the effects of the industrialized food system on their own bioregional and community history and land-use patterns. A "commons" project engaged them in one-on-one mentoring relationships to learn about the value of particular non-monetized skills and traditional practices. All through these activities and assignments, students were reminded to use the EcoJustice analytic tools to think about the way that language operates to keep the market-based/consumerist systems functioning, as well as the existence of practices in their own and other cultures that leave a smaller ecological footprint. At the end of the first year, students were asked to write reflective essays examining their relationship to the course, what they had learned, what was difficult, and so on. It was an emotional experience for all, as student after student stood up and gave testimony the power of the course in changing the way they see the world, their future plans, and the experience of community with all members that had been created.

Rebecca's experiences in this seminar paved the way for the development of a major project currently underway in Michigan. Teams of teachers in partnership with non-profit community organizations are learning to use EcoJustice Education to frame authentic community-based learning projects with their students. The Southeast Michigan Stewardship Coalition (SEMIS) was founded largely as a result of what was learned in New Hampshire and is currently in its seventh year.

The Southeast Michigan Stewardship Coalition: A Coordinated Effort Among University, Schools, and Community Organizations

The Southeast Michigan Stewardship Coalition (SEMIS) at Eastern Michigan University is one of eight "hubs" established since 2007 by the Great Lakes Stewardship Initiative (GLSI) (www.glstewardship.org), which is funded largely by the Great Lakes Fisheries Trust, a private foundation. The primary goal of the SEMIS Coalition is to develop students as citizen stewards able to understand and promote healthy ecological and social systems affecting the Great Lakes basin and their communities. In southeastern Michigan, the center of which is Detroit, a steady decline in manufacturing jobs and sprawling suburban development has led to a declining tax base in the city and inner ring of suburbs, as well as loss of farmland, inadequate infrastructure, and negative environmental and public health impacts throughout the region.

Given this context, it is very important that teachers begin to introduce their students to the tools that they need to respond. Supported by the resources offered through SEMIS, students, teachers, and community members learn to work together effectively to address the intersecting social, economic, and ecological problems in their communities, and their underlying root causes. Working in schools and communities across southeastern Michigan, the Coalition's objectives are to (1) offer sustained professional development for teachers using a model of community-based education within an EcoJustice framework; (2) develop partnerships between schools and community organizations working on social and ecological problems; (3) promote collaboration among community organizations in the service of schools; and (4) help these school and community partners to develop community-based learning projects that engage students in addressing critical ecological and social problems in their own neighborhoods.

Working with 12 schools and over 25 non-profit grassroots community organizations in the region, the SEMIS Coalition is the only one of the GLSI hubs that emphasizes the intersection and inseparability between social and ecological justice and uses a cultural-ecological analytic approach for solving these problems. A major part of their work is dedicated to coalition building among non-profit organizations, helping them to build capacity for collaboration that reflects regional thinking and cooperation in order to best serve schools and communities. These organizations participate with the schools in all parts of the professional development workshops, as well as developing relationships with specific schools and helping to mentor individual teachers. Teachers are learning to focus on the specific social and ecological problems in the communities where their schools are located, while studying the larger economic, political, and socio-linguistic context in which these problems occur.

Even if a school's scheduling and programming does not explicitly create opportunities for school-wide reform, collaborative associations among teams of teachers with community organizations and with teachers from nearby schools can inspire the sorts of curriculum reform needed for student engagement. The work of three of our schools is described below.

Hope of Detroit Academy

Hope of Detroit was the first school to join SEMIS. At this K-8 charter school in Southwest Detroit, fourth through eighth grade students are learning to think about how they can contribute to making their community a safer, healthier, more sustainable place by studying the history of land use, water systems, blight, and brownfield remediation. This school serves about 400 students from a largely Latino community in a section of Detroit highly impacted by the ravages of industrialization, outsourcing, and immigration policies.

Working from the essential question "What is Community?" teachers and students from Hope of Detroit Academy have been working to clean up their surrounding neighborhood by partnering with the Southwest Detroit Environmental Vision and Cass Community Social Services in an annual Tire Sweep. It began in the spring of 2008 when a handful of sixth graders took a walk around their southwest Detroit neighborhood with several of their teachers and interested community members to "map" their neighborhood. The group walked about a square mile through a neighborhood of small clapboard houses and neat yards which was also plagued by abandoned lots and high levels of illegal dumping, toxic soil, and "tagging" by gangs. As they walked, the students pointed out where they lived, where they rode their bikes and played, which yards had gardens with fresh vegetables, and which had dogs to be wary of.

One ten-year-old boy, George, was particularly passionate about pointing out the piles of old tires and other debris in abandoned factory lots surrounding the school. He was upset and perplexed about these lots, asking questions about why those tires and piles of construction material got dumped in his neighborhood. "We need to do something, and soon! But (pointing to a tire in a storm drain), don't take those tires away! I put those there so my sister wouldn't fall in with her bike!" Many of the grates and manhole covers have been stolen, and sold as scrap metal.

In May 2009, supported by their teachers, members of SEMIS, and a truck provide by Detroit Public Works about 30 eighth graders participated in a neighborhood Tire Sweep, first mapping the location and then collecting a truckload of illegally dumped tires that were taken to Cass Community Social Services where homeless men are employed to turn the tires into mud mats. As one student told a local news station that first year, "anything can make a difference." As the Tire Sweep continues along with other efforts in this school, more and more students are learning what that means. Now the school partners with other elementary schools in SW Detroit, collaborating to help other students learn what it means to work for a sustainable community.

Ann Arbor Learning Community

This school in Ann Arbor, Michigan, was established as a public charter school whose mission is "to nurture independent learners as they acquire the tools they need to shape an environmentally and socially responsible future" (http://www.annarborlearningcommunity.org). Supported by SEMIS, teachers have established a school garden tended in various ways by all grade levels, but especially by one teacher and his students who learn the principles of permaculture in their science classes. One year, the art teacher collaborated with a dance teacher, using basic ideas about "value-hierarchized thinking" to get her students to see connections between social justice concerns and ecological problems and creating a public dance performance. Yet another teacher takes her fourth grade students to a nearby creek where they spend the year studying bank erosion and water quality in partnership with a local organization, the Huron River Watershed Council. These students spent the day teaching other teachers from the SEMIS Coalition all about their creek project during the 2013 SEMIS Summer Institute, and they presented at a statewide place-based education conference, sharing their studies with teachers and community organizations from all over Michigan.

Individual Teacher Efforts

While we believe strongly that working at the level of school reform through interdisciplinary collaborations among teachers and community partners is the most effective and powerful approach, not all our examples exist within fully developed organizations or schools. In fact, most of the success that we've had developing this approach has been with the individual teachers who take our courses and then go back to their schools, "close their doors" and teach. Rebecca teaches in a teacher certification program, as well as an EcoJustice Master's and Educational Studies Ph.D. program at Eastern Michigan University. Jeff is the Director of Master's degree programs in Education Studies at the University of Oregon, and Johnny now works as an Assistant Professor in Washington State University's Department of Teaching and Learning working with pre-service undergraduates, Master's students, and Ph.D. students. The pre-service and practicing teachers we work with would probably be the first to tell you of their own skepticism about the possibility of using this approach when they sat in our courses, but once they got started putting together lesson plans and units that utilized the concepts and general commitments and linking learning objectives to state standards, they realized it wasn't as difficult as they had imagined.

Mr. Bartz's World Studies Curriculum, Wylie Elementary School, Dexter, Michigan

Scott Bartz is one such teacher. Scott teaches third and fourth graders in a "specials" area course (in the same category as Physical Education, Music, Art, and Media) that his district offers called "World Cultures," at Wylie Elementary in Dexter, Michigan. Wylie houses all the third and fourth grade students enrolled in the Dexter Community Schools. The students attend "World Cultures" for one hour a week and receive instruction that is aligned with the Michigan social studies benchmarks. The program was originally designed to relieve the classroom teachers of some of the social studies benchmarks outlined in the Michigan Content Standards, as well as to provide students with more teacher contact hours. Scott uses this course to focus students' attention on concepts such as anthropocentrism, interdependence, the commons, and consumerism. In a series of lessons that introduce students to the Ladakhi and the Chipko (tree huggers) movement in India, Aboriginal Peoples in Australia and the effects of Western culture and world trade on traditional land-based cultures, he starts conceptually, by getting the students to think about all the non-human creatures that we depend upon and introducing the concept of "interdependence." Then he moves to a critical analysis of culture through a conversation about how anthropocentrism works and what its effects are. He shows students the film, *Ancient Futures: Learning from Ladakh* (Page, Beeman, Norberg-Hodge, & Walton, 1993) in two parts. First they witness how the traditional Ladakhi culture works, discussing how they think about wealth, happiness, and work. Then, returning to the concept anthropocentrism, he shows them the second part of the film, in which Ladakh is experiencing the effects of Westernization. The students are asked similar questions about the wealth and happiness of the people in the second part of the film and what they thought about as they witnessed the "development" of Leh, the capital of Ladakh.

This lesson is followed by a series of other lessons, where the students "visit" other non-Western countries and explore the diverse ways their commons are enacted and the overall effects of the people's lives on their environment as compared to their own community's ecological footprint. Scott has learned to directly introduce and translate complex concepts related to modernism to young students, teaching them to do a cultural-ecological analysis that children can relate to their own lives.

Ms. Shah's Classroom: The King Learning Garden

Neha Shah, at Martin Luther King, Jr. Elementary School in Ann Arbor, Michigan, is another example of a strong community educator. Ms. Shah's work in her classroom and community are not only inspiring, but also serve as models for how teachers can integrate curriculum around a school garden. A teacher of eight years, Ms. Shah refers to her fifth grade classroom as a "learning community." After years of working with partners in the community, she decided to expose her students to a broader ecological understanding of science, social studies, and language arts by starting her work on a school garden. Ms. Shah would be the first to admit that it didn't happen overnight, but with strong administrative and parent support, Shah was able to secure funding, working with local organizations and the school PTO. They started planning the garden in the fall of 2011 and broke ground in the spring of 2012. Ms. Shah and her fifth grade class—together with parents, teachers, other students, and members of the community—grow and learn in what has been named the King Learning Garden. Ms. Shah describes the garden as "a great place for students to learn academics, health, and life skills." An advocate for fresh and local organic food, as well as a strong supporter of social justice and sustainability, she explains that the "garden is more than just a place to grow vegetables and fruit. It is a place to grow community" (retrieved from http://shah5thgrade.blogspot.com/p/meet-ms-shah.html).

The King Learning Garden is now an accessible learning environment for the approximately 475 children from K-5 classrooms in the school. Calling this work ecologically responsive learning, Ms. Shah explains:

> The King Learning Garden acts as a sustainable model for local food production that includes ecological knowledge, cooperative school culture, and an immersion in hands-on learning through garden-based educational concepts. The program provides positive health benefits to our students through school garden programs that

promote physical activity, healthy eating habits, and expanded access to fresh, local, and organically grown food. It supports increased learner engagement through students' cognitive, social, and emotional needs of experiential, interdisciplinary, and cross-cultural learning. The King Learning Garden is designed to represent a cultural and practical shift in priorities towards the earth by engaging students to utilize the garden during and outside of the school day. Our organic garden is a place to learn about sustainability and the biodiversity that exists in our backyard. Ultimately, the King Learning Garden provides a source of local food for our school community and offers a connection to the earth that inspires new ways to think, learn, and live.

(Shah, 2014, p. 1)

An example from Ms. Shah's learning community that illustrates the cross-content, cross-grade-level connections that emerge from having the garden at the school is a lesson involving Native American popcorn. In the fall of 2014, the students in Ms. Shah's class harvested native popcorn. Many of the children were thrilled because they had never seen colors like that in corn. In fact, most of her students had never pulled corn off a stalk. While harvesting the corn and removing the kernels, she connected the experience to a history lesson in the social studies curriculum on Native American culture. The second grade classes examined and removed kernels from harvested cobs of corn as part of a science lesson in a unit on plants. Possibly most exciting to the students at M.L.K. Elementary is that, after the harvest, the entire student body gets to eat the popcorn produced in the garden on what they call the King Learning Garden Popcorn Fridays.

This collaborative project is testimony to what a teacher can do to grow a movement in the school that spreads throughout the building and beyond—to engage children not only in learning the content in the district and school curriculum but also in learning to live together in responsible and healthy ways—to provide opportunities for these powerful objectives to supplement and strengthen the curriculum.

Dr. Schnakenberg's Human Geography and World Studies Classes

As we mentioned earlier, Gary was a social studies teacher in New Hampshire for about 20 years. He now holds a Ph.D. in Geography and works for Michigan State University in their Geography Department, focusing on a field known as "political ecology." He also happens to be married to Rebecca, so the two of them talk a lot about issues and concepts related to EcoJustice. That's how he was introduced to the framework and began to use it in his high school classes about eight years ago. It started slowly, but once he began learning about the concepts of EcoJustice, he suddenly found himself asking particular sorts of questions of his students, encouraging them to look critically at the ways value hierarchies and a logic of domination operate to create specific cultural patterns. Geography is a particularly useful field to apply this framework since it examines the intersections and interactions of humans with the land they occupy. The content units in his 11th /12th grade elective in Advanced Placement (AP) Human Geography (and now his undergraduate geography courses) were fairly well prescribed by the AP framework, but Gary was free to determine how the concepts and content in those topic areas should be addressed. Specific EcoJustice concepts included anthropocentrism, Eurocentrism, and the complicating of Western notions of "progress" and "development." The units on cultural and linguistic geography, economic geography, urban geography, and rural geography were especially useful for applying these EcoJustice concepts to issues of globalization, marginalization, flows of capital, patterns of health and mortality, species and habitat loss, suburbanization, and conversion of farmland to residential construction.

In his 11th grade World Studies curriculum, which he taught paired with an English teacher (this double-class-size, double-block-long course is the required social studies and English credit vehicle for juniors), examinations of colonialism and resource extraction in Latin America and Africa served as effective entry points for the introduction of EcoJustice concepts. Gary's English teaching partner "came on board" as well, and so examples of EcoJustice-related themes or incidents that occurred in literature read in class could be named as such in discussion and writing assignments, reinforcing students' abilities to apply them. Despite their own immersion in a "hyper-consumerist" culture, students often strongly identified with these ideas. In multiple cases, Gary's students chose to examine EcoJustice-linked topics for their "Junior Research Project," a graduation requirement completed within their World Studies/World Literature courses. Student choices of writing topics were entirely self-generated, and included examinations of tropical deforestation, language extinction, biopiracy, Indigenous Peoples' rights, and problems with mainstream "development" projects.

Dr. Lupinacci's High School Math Class

When he was teaching high school math, Johnny used EcoJustice Education as a way to structure and frame the learning. So, with Bateson in mind, the math content itself was taught as a set of patterns in a language. Whatever the specific subject—algebra, geometry—it was presented as a language system created and applied to explain phenomena in the natural world. While studying geometry, for example, his students spent time outside with Johnny journaling about what sorts of shapes they noticed in nature, and what sorts of shapes occurred because of human effects. Becoming aware of the socio-symbolic system of Western society, students almost immediately recognized the obsession our culture has with right angles. Students struggled with the limits of our language to fully describe the world. They asked questions like, "What shape is this? How would you describe this leaf?" "Well," Johnny responds, "using a set of metaphors in mathematics, there are several ways to describe that leaf." His objective was to use EcoJustice as an overall approach to get students to recognize the power and limits of language. And, as he did that, students began to articulate the limits, strengths, and the potential to use math in support of living systems or in support of killing systems.

We hope that these examples have been helpful in giving you a sense that this approach to teaching is not only possible, but happening in a variety of ways. In the next section, we give you some guidelines for how to get going in your own school or classroom.

Conclusion

Helping teachers and students to examine the cultural roots of social and ecological problems in their own communities, and working side by side with other community members to address those problems, is extremely satisfying and important work. To be sure, it has its challenges, but those of us who teach this way know how inspiring it is to see students' enthusiasm and sense of empowerment bubble over as they identify problems, link them to problematic ways of seeing and being in the world, and then step up to do something about it. As Lori Thorp (2006) has written, working in this way responds to the question, "Where am I going to declare my loyalty? Where am I going to exercise my citizenship? Where is the place I belong?"

These are essential questions for creating sustainable and democratic communities. Answering them as educators and students to claim our communities makes it clear that we will not stand by while others make the decisions that impact our lives in some far-off place. We will not stand by while our homeplaces—the people and creatures that live there—are degraded or destroyed. We will not give away democracy to a global marketplace.

We will see students move from apathetic unawareness to dawning understanding to full-out activism if we are careful to lay out paths of learning that help them develop the values, skills, and attitudes they need. It is essential that we engage their hearts, minds, and hands. As Thorp (2006) writes, "Once you stake your claim and dig in, this act, this conscious choice, will set off a chain reaction" (p. 2).

Youth of today know very well the crises that face us all, and too often are left in a morass of depression and helplessness. Getting them outside the confines of school walls and taken-for-granted assumptions and into mentoring relationships with the elders in their communities, to do real work that matters to them, creates the physical, intellectual, and interpersonal skills needed to reclaim our communities. And, as David Sobel (2004), Amy Powers (2004), and others are demonstrating, approaches that involve students directly in their communities work "simultaneously . . . to boost student achievement and improve a community's environmental quality and social and economic vitality" (Powers, 2004, p. 17).

In an era of "No Child Left Behind" and "Race to the Top," those teachers who recognize the value of "no child left inside" (Louv, 2006) are ironically likely to be most effective. In an educational environment in which "achievement" has come to be defined narrowly by test scores, "covering all the material" on which students could potentially be assessed is a fool's mission. On the other hand, engaging students' minds and hearts, inspiring students to be active participants in local, regional, and world affairs, and giving them the analytical tools that enable them to think about issues and problems may actually result in increased test scores. At the same time, these all contribute more fully and effectively to the realization of an idea of "education" that got us all into this business anyway.

Seriously, beyond this current obsession with "achievement," we are asking you all to stake your claim in the places that matter most and work hard to make them healthy, happy places for the generations who come after us. This means that you have to be willing to look carefully and critically at the ways harm is being perpetuated, and trace its roots to the cultural causes still circulating to make it seem natural or "just the way it is." Teach to interrupt ways of thinking that continue to do harm, with assertions and actions, questions and activities that refuse to accept the normalization of violence. This means recognizing the richness of cultural, linguistic, and ecological diversity, and working to protect that diversity as the source of all living systems. We offer you this book to honor all teachers' capacity to do exactly this work.

What Schools and Teachers Can Do

Tips for Getting Started

How might you get going and do something like these teachers are doing? As you may have noticed through these examples, good EcoJustice Education has two essential characteristics: (1) it examines the cultural roots of social and environmental degradation; and (2) it emphasizes community, looks toward revitalizing the commons, and is place-based. This means that there will be both common and diverse elements in any given EcoJustice pedagogy. Not everyone gets to all of this all at once, but, in its fullest form, the common elements have to do with examining the deeply rooted modernist discourses and their effects on our beliefs and behaviors, and focusing on how to get students involved in revitalizing their commons. It is oriented toward effecting a conscious change in beliefs and behaviors that will lead to becoming citizens able to create more sustainable and healthy communities. The diverse elements have to do with place and situation. As we have emphasized throughout this book, diversity of context is essential to the specific character of any particular project. So, the first thing to remember is that there is no one right way to do this work. It will look different depending on where you live, what the opportunities and resources available are, and where you are in your own development toward becoming an EcoJustice educator. So, be patient and creative! We have no exact recipe. However, there are important things to keep in mind or work toward as you begin:

1. Start small: If you are working as an individual teacher, begin with a lesson or two that gets kids engaged and from which you can feel successful. For example, choose one of the Modernist discourses—say, anthropocentrism, or individualism, or consumerism—and create a lesson or lessons that ask your students to examine their relevance and effects in their own lives. As you develop confidence, you can build from this beginning point.

2. Work with others: Whenever possible, even at the smallest scale (like an activity or lesson versus a unit), work with other teachers, or community members. The collaborative process may seem more difficult, but will also prove richer in the end for all involved. This is not always possible, of course, but we always recommend collaboration over trying to do something alone. It really helps alleviate the despair factor, too, when you have someone to work with on issues that are difficult.

3. Utilize a cultural-ecological analysis: Remember that EcoJustice requires us to learn to think differently (more ethically) and deeply about the cultural foundations of the problems we face, and the effects of the interaction of humans with the more-than-human world. Teaching a cultural-ecological analysis includes introducing students to the primary modernist discourses and asking them to use these as conceptual tools to help them expose and "see" how our culture works. So, think carefully about what concepts will help your students to do that. Powerful concepts are an essential tool of your pedagogy, and the stuff of all critical thinking. It is great but not enough to get your students outside doing stream studies or soil sampling if they can't think deeply about the underlying cultural reasons for the problems we are facing.

4. Get out in the community: While guideline number three is something we feel strongly about, it isn't enough either! Get your students

outside and engaged with the community as much as you can! A focus on the social and ecological conditions within our communities is also essential to the relevance of the lessons you are teaching and to keeping the students engaged. Use the community as much as you can to situate the learning, and draw on community members as resources, too. Getting folks from local organizations in to help students identify and examine particular problems is a key to successful community-based learning projects. You can find many ecologically-oriented organizations by using an Internet search engine and typing in your city or region, and "environmental organizations." This is a way to start. Another way is to type in "bioneers" and your city. Bioneers is a networking organization that operates at the national and regional levels. They are a great source for lots of people and organizations who do this work. Transition Towns is, too. Doing an Internet search for either of these will get you started. Or try keywords like "non-profit," "environment," "gardens," "Detroit" (or your city's name).

5. Encourage student questions: Invite your students to ask questions and look for answers. The lesson will always be more powerful if it is generated from what they want to know. While you may not be accustomed to giving over the reins this way, you'll find out that it generally leads to very interesting paths of learning, many that you may not have thought of.

6. Ask powerful questions: While student questions and experience are important, you are the teacher and they need your help to frame and guide the inquiry. So, don't be afraid to ask them questions and push them to use the concepts you are introducing to them. That is your job!

7. Plan backward: It helps to start by imagining what the final activity or product might be, even if you don't know exactly what the students might come up with. For example, you may know that there is a debate brewing in your community about some specific environmental issue and you want your students to study the issue and provide potential solutions. Start there, imagining that they will create a final project based on that issue, and then back up: (1) What do the students need to know in order to begin to inquire about the issue? (2) What learning objectives can you come up with to help guide the inquiry while allowing them to pose their own questions? (3) What concepts might help them to think through the problem? (4) What community members might they need to contact to learn more or get help? As you create the sequence of lessons needed, what state standards or benchmarks will your lessons be attending to? Knowing that will help you to facilitate any sorts of permissions you need from administration or parents, and help to legitimate what may appear to

be unusual teaching. (5) Get administration and parental permissions for any out of school visits or activities. Knowing this as much ahead as possible will help!

Conceptual Toolbox

Barter: The exchange of goods or services for goods or services in return. This process cuts out the exchange of money. Barter is a strong practice that revitalizes the commons and strengthens local communities.

EcoJustice Education: Educational efforts of students, teachers, and members of the local community learning collaboratively while engaged in revitalizing the local commons. EcoJustice Education is shaped by an understanding that local and global ecosystems are essential to all life; challenging the deep cultural assumptions underlying modern thinking that undermine those systems; and the recognition of the need to restore the cultural and environmental commons.

Educating for the Commons: Curriculum and pedagogical relationships that support the local community. Education that specifically engages in the steps defined in the previous concept.

Revitalizing the Commons: Acting in collaborative local democratic efforts to strengthen local decision-making in ways that ensure the continuation of healthy sustainable aspects of the local commons and which revitalize aspects that have been enclosed. This process is a key step in taking sustained action in strengthening community. The process can be broken into steps: (1) identify aspects of the commons in our daily lives; (2) evaluate those aspects of the commons as to whether they support living systems or support killing systems; and (3) take action to strengthen those aspects that support living systems.

Suggested Readings and Other Resources

Books and Essays

Berry, W. (2002). People, land and community. In N. Wirzba (Ed.), *The art of the commonplace: The agragrian essays of Wendell Berry*. Washington, DC: Shoemaker and Hoard.

Berry, W. (2005). Local knowledge in the age of information. In *The way of ignorance and other essays* (pp. 113–126). Washington, DC: Shoemaker and Hoard.

Bowers, C. A. (2006). Community-centered approaches to revitalizing the commons. In *Revitalizing the Commons: Cultural and educational sites of resistance and affirmation* (pp. 85–106). Lanham, MD: Lexington Books.

Ecologist, The. (1994). Whose common future: Reclaiming the commons. *Environment and Urbanization*, 6, 106–130.

Prakash, M. S. (2010). Commons, common sense, and community collaboration in hard times. *PowerPlay: A Journal of Educational Justice*, 2(2). Online at www.emich.edu/coe/powerplay.

Films

Norberg-Hodge, H., Gorelick, S., & Page, J. (2011). *The economics of happiness.* UK: International Society for Ecology and Culture.

Offers not only a big-picture analysis of globalization, but a powerful message of hope for the future: a systemic shift—away from globalizing economic activity and towards the local—allows us to reduce our ecological footprint while increasing human well-being.

Poppenk, M. & Poppenk, M. (2009). *Grown in Detroit.* Netherlands/United States: filmmij.

Focuses on the urban gardening efforts managed by a public school of 300, mainly African American, pregnant and parenting teenagers.

Organizations and Links

Bioneers (www.bioneers.org)

Non-profit providing solutions-based education and social connectivity through national and local conferences and programs.

Center for Ecoliteracy (www.ecoliteracy.org)

Focuses on education for sustainability, and particularly on food: school gardens, school lunches; has a wealth of information on related projects.

Creative Change Educational Solutions (www.creativechange.net)

Non-profit offering curriculum and professional development portfolio support to cultivate deep instructional change for social justice and sustainability in K-12 classrooms, after-school programs, college courses, and adult educational settings.

Natural Capital Institute (www.naturalcapital.org)

A team of researchers, teachers, students, activists, scholars, writers, social entrepreneurs, artists, and volunteers committed to the restoration of the Earth and the healing of human culture; they create tools for connecting the individuals, information, and organizations that create change.

U.S. Social Forum (www.ussf2010.org)

The U.S. Social Forum (USSF) is a movement-building process. It is a space to come up with the peoples' solutions to the economic and ecological crisis.

Yes!: The Magazine of Positive Futures (www.yesmagazine.org)
This magazine has an excellent website offering concrete examples of people exploring ways of living differently. Magazine is available free for one year to teachers.

Note

1 Not his real name. We have used a pseudonym to protect his identity and anonymity.

References

AAUW. (2008). *Where the girls are: The facts about gender equity and education.* Washington, DC: AAUW Educational Foundation.

Abram, D. (1996). *The spell of the sensuous: Perceptions in a more-than-human world.* New York, NY: Pantheon Books.

Abram, D. (1999). A more-than-human world. In A. Weston (Ed.), *An invitation to environmental philosophy* (pp. 17–42). New York, NY: Oxford University Press.

Achebe, C. (1958). *Things fall apart: A novel.* London, UK: Heinemann.

ACLU. (October 2, 2007). U.S. Supreme Court weighs 100-to-1 disparity in crack/powder cocaine sentencing. Retrieved September 13, 2010, from ACLU http://www.aclu.org/drug-law-reform/us-supreme-court-weighs-100-1-disparity-crackpowder-cocaine-sentencing

Adams, D. (1995). *Education for extinction.* Lawrence, KS: University Press of Kansas.

Adamson, R. (2008). First nations survival and the future of the earth. In M. K. Nelson (Ed.), *Original instructions: Indigenous teachings for a sustainable future* (pp. 27–35). Rochester, VT: Bear & Company.

Adelman, L. (Writer). (2003). *Race: The power of an illusion* [film]. USA: California Newsreel.

Allen, T. W. (1994). *The invention of the white race (Vol. 1: Racial oppression and the social control).* Brooklyn, NY: Verso.

American Academy of Pediatrics. (2005). Lead exposure in children: Prevention, detection, and management. *Policy Statement, 116*(4), 1036–1046.

Animal Enterprise Terrorism Act 2006. Washington DC: U.S. Government Printing Office.

Ankele, J., & Macksoud, A. (Writers). (2001). *The global banquet: Politics of food.* Maryknoll World Productions.

Anquandah, K. (1999). *Castles and forts of Ghana.* Accra, Ghana: Ghana Museums and Monuments Board.

Anyon, J. (1989). Social class and the hidden curriculum of work. In J. Ballantine (Ed.), *Schools and society: A unified reader* (pp. 257–279). Mountain View, CA: Mayfield Publishing.

Anyon, J. (2005). *Radical possibilities: Public policy, urban education, and a new social movement.* New York, NY: Taylor & Francis.

Apffel-Marglin, F., & PRATEC. (1998). *The spirit of regeneration: Andean culture confronting Western notions of development*. New York, NY: Zed Books.

Armstrong, J. (2006). Community: "Sharing one skin." In J. Mander & V. Tauli-Corpuz (Eds.), *Paradigm wars: Indigenous people's resistance to globalization* (pp. 35–40). San Francisco, CA: Sierra Club Books.

Atwood, W. (1922). *Civic and economic biology*. Philadelphia, PA: Blackiston's Son and Company.

Au, W. (2000). Teaching about WTO. *Rethinking Schools, 14*(3), 4–5.

Ayers, W., & Ford, P. (1996). *City kids, city teachers: Reports from the front row*. New York, NY: The New Press.

Bank, B. J., Delamont, S., & Marshall, C. (2007). *Gender and education: An encyclopedia*. Westport, CT: Praeger Publishers.

Banks, R. (2008). *Dreaming up America*. New York, NY: Seven Stories Press.

Barber, B. (1989). Public talk and civic action: Education for participation in a strong democracy. *Social Education*, Oct, 355–356.

Barber, B. R. (2003). *Strong democracy: Participatory politics for a new age* (20th anniversary ed.). Berkeley, CA: University of California Press.

Barlow, Z., & Stone, M. K. (2005). *Ecological literacy: Educating our children for a sustainable world*. San Francisco, CA: Sierra Club Books.

Barnhardt, R., & Kawagley, A. (1999). Education indigenous to place: Western science meets indigenous reality. In G. Smith & D. R. Williams (Eds.) *Ecological education in action* (pp. 117–140). Albany, NY: SUNY Press.

Bartky, S. (1996). The pedagogy of shame. In C. Luke (Ed.), *Feminisms and pedagogies of everyday life* (pp. 225–241). Albany, NY: State University of New York Press.

Basso, K. H. (1996). *Wisdom sits in places: Landscape and language among the Western Apache*. Albuquerque, NM: University of New Mexico Press.

Bateson, G. (1987). Men are grass: Metaphor and the world of mental process. In W. I. Thompson (Ed.) *Gaia: A way of knowing. Political implications of the new biology*. (pp. 37–47). Great Barrington, MA: Lindisfarne Press.

Bateson, G. (2000). *Steps to an ecology of mind* (University of Chicago Press ed.). Chicago, IL: University of Chicago Press.

Bateson, G., & Donaldson, R. E. (1991). *A sacred unity: Further steps to an ecology of mind* (1st ed.). San Francisco, CA: HarperCollins.

Battiste, M., & Barman, J. (1995). *First Nations education in Canada: The circle unfolds*. Vancouver, BC: UBC Press.

Bello, W. (2013). Twenty-sex countries ban GMO: Why won't the US? *The Nation*. Retrieved from: http://www.thenation.com/blog/176863/twenty-six-countries-ban-gmos-why-wont-us#

Berger, J. (1979). *Pig earth*. New York, NY: Pantheon Books.

Berger, P., & Luckmann, T. (1966). *The social construction of reality: A treatise in the sociology of knowledge*. New York, NY: Anchor Books.

Bernard, J. (1964). *Academic women*. University Park, PA: Pennsylvania State University Press.

Berry, W. (1995). *Another turn of the crank: Essays*. Washington, DC: Counterpoint.

Berry, W. (1996). Conserving communities. In J. Mander & E. Goldsmith (Eds.), *The case against the global economy: And a turn toward the local* (pp. 407–417). San Francisco, CA: Sierra Club Books.

Berry, W. (2000a). *Life is a miracle: An essay against modern superstition*. Washington, D.C.: Counterpoint.

Berry, W. (2000b). *Jayber Crow*. Washington, DC: Counterpoint.

Berry, W. (2001). The idea of a local economy. In *In the presence of fear* (pp. 11–33). Great Barrington, MA: Orion Society.

Berry, W. (2002). People, land, and community. In N. Wirzba (Ed.), *The art of the commonplace: The agrarian essays of Wendell Berry* (pp. 182–194). Washington, DC: Shoemaker and Hoard.

Berry, W. (2005). Local knowledge in the age of information. In *The way of ignorance and other essays* (pp. 113–126). Washington, DC: Shoemaker and Hoard Publishers.

Berry, W. (2010). *The hidden wound*. Berkeley, CA: Counterpoint.

Best, S. & Nocella, A., Eds. (2004). Behind the mask: Uncovering the Animal Liberation Front. In *Terrorists or freedom fighters? Reflections on the liberation of animals* (pp. 9–64). New York, NY: Lantern Books.

Bigelow, B., & Peterson, B. (2002). *Rethinking globalization: Teaching for justice in an unjust world*. Milwaukee, WI: Rethinking Schools Press.

Bigelow, W., & Diamond, N. (1988). *The power in our hands: A curriculum on the history of work and workers in the United States*. New York, NY: Monthly Review Press.

Blackburn, M., Clark, C., Kenney, L., & Smith, J. (Eds.), (2010). *Acting Out! Combating homophobia through teacher activism*. New York, NY: Teachers College Press.

Blount, J., & Anahita, S. (2004). The historical regulation of sexuality and gender of students and teachers: An intertwined legacy. In M. Rasmussen, E. Rofes, and S. Talburt (Eds). *Youth and sexualities: Pleasure, subversion and insubordination in and out of schools* (pp. 63–84). New York, NY: Palgrave Macmillan.

Boer, J. T., Pastor, M., Sadd, J., & Snyder, L. (1997). Is there environmental racism? The demographics of hazardous waste in Los Angeles County. *Social Science Quarterly*, 78(4).

Bohn, A. (2006). A framework for understanding poverty. *Rethinking Schools, Winter*.

Bowers, C., & Flinders, D. (1990). *Responsive teaching: An ecological approach to classroom patterns of language, culture, and thought*. New York, NY: Teachers College Press.

Bowers, C. A. (1993). *Education, cultural myths, and the ecological crisis toward deep changes*. Albany, NY: State University of New York Press.

Bowers, C. A. (1995). *Educating for an ecologically sustainable culture: Rethinking moral education, creativity, intelligence, and other modern orthodoxies*. Albany, NY: State University of New York Press.

Bowers, C. A. (1997). *The culture of denial: Why the environmental movement needs a strategy for reforming universities and public schools*. Albany, NY: State University of New York Press.

Bowers, C. A. (2001a). How language limits our understanding of environmental education. *Environmental Education Research*, 7(2), 141–151.

Bowers, C. A. (2001b). *Educating for eco-justice and community*. Athens, GA: University of Georgia Press.

Bowers, C. A. (2003). *Mindful conservatism: Rethinking the ideological and educational basis of an ecologically sustainable future.* Lanham, MD: Rowman & Littlefield Publishers.

Bowers, C. A. (2006). *Revitalizing the commons: Cultural and educational sites of resistance and affirmation.* Lanham, MD: Lexington Books.

Bowers, C. A. (2012). *The way forward: Educational reforms that focus on the cultural commons and the linguistic roots of the ecological/cultural crises.* Eugene, OR: Eco-Justice Press, LLC.

Bowers, C. A. (2013). *In the grip of the past: Educational reforms that address what should be changed and what should be conserved.* Eugene, OR: Eco-Justice Press, LLC.

Bowers, C. A., & Martusewicz, R. (2006). Revitalizing the commons of the African-American communities in Detroit. In C. A. Bowers (Ed.), *Revitalizing the commons: cultural and educational sites of resistance and affirmation* (pp. 47–84). Lanham, MD: Lexington Books.

Bowles, S., & Gintis, H. (1976). *Schooling in capitalist America: Educational reform and the contradictions of economic life.* New York, NY: Basic Books.

Bradshaw, G. A., Schore, A. N., Brown, J. L., Poole, J. H., & Moss, C. J. (2005). Elephant breakdown: Social trauma: Early disruption of attachment can affect the physiology, behaviour and culture of animals and humans over generations. *Nature, 433,* 807.

Brantlinger, E. (2003). *Dividing classes: How the middle class negotiates and rationalizes school advantage.* New York, NY: Routledge Falmer.

Brenner, E. D., Stahlberg, R. Mancuso, S. Vivanco, J. Baluska, F., & Van Voldenberg, E. (2006). Plant neurobiology: an integrated view of plant signaling. *Trends in Plant Science, 11*(6): 413–419.

Brod, H., & Kaufman, M. (1994). *Theorizing masculinities.* Thousand Oaks, CA: Sage.

Brosio, R. A. (1994). *A radical democratic critique of capitalist education.* New York, NY: Peter Lang.

Brunson, J. M., & Rashidi, R. (1992). The Moors in antiquity. In I. Van Sertima (Ed.), *The Golden Age of the Moors.* Piscataway, NJ: Transaction Publishers.

Bullard, R. D. (2000). *Dumping in Dixie.* Boulder, CO: Westview.

Bullard, R. D. (July 2 2002). *Poverty, pollution and environmental racism: Strategies for building healthy and sustainable communities.* Paper presented at the NBEJN Environmental Racism Forum World Summit on Sustainable Development Global Forum, Johannesburg, South Africa.

Cajete, G. (1994). *Look to the mountain: An ecology of indigenous education.* Ashville, NC: Kivaki Press.

Cajete, G. (1999). *A people's ecology: Explorations in sustainable living.* Santa Fe, NM: Clear Light Publishers.

Cajete, G. (2000). *Native science: Natural laws of interdependence.* Santa Fe, NM: Clear Light Publishers.

Carter, P. L. (2009). Geography, race, and quantification. *The Professional Geographer, 61*(4), 465–480.

Cavalcanti, O. B. (Writer). (1992). *Life and debt* [Film]. Oley, PA: Bullfrog Films.

Cavanagh, J., & Mander, J. (2002). *Alternatives to economic globalization: A better world is possible.* San Francisco, CA: Berrett-Koehler Publishers, Inc.

Cavanagh, J., & Mander, J. (2004). *Alternatives to economic globalization: A better world is possible*. San Francisco, CA: Berrett-Koehler Publishers.

Center for Food Safety. (2005). Monsanto vs. U.S. Farmers. Washington DC: Center for Food Safety.

Chamovitz, D. (2012). *What a plant knows: A field guide to the senses*. New York, NY: Scientific American/Farrar, Straus and Giroux.

Chasnoff, D., & Cohen, H. (Writers). (1996/2007). *It's elementary: Talking about gay issues in schools* [film]. USA: New Day Films.

Children's Defense Fund (CDF). (2007). *America's cradle to prison pipeline*. Washington, DC: Children's Defense Fund.

Clarke, E. (1875). *Sex in education: Or, a fair chance for girls*. Boston, MA: J. R. Osgood and Co.

Coates, P. (1998). *Nature: Western attitudes since ancient times*. Berkley, CA: University of California Press.

Coetzee, J. M. (1999). *The lives of animals*. Princeton, NJ: Princeton University Press.

CollegeBoard. (2005). *2005 College-bound Seniors: Total group profile report*. New York, NY: CollegeBoard.

CollegeBoard. (2009). *2009 College-bound Seniors: Total group profile report*. New York, NY: CollegeBoard.

Connell, R., & Messerschmidt, J. (2005). Hegemonic masculinity: Rethinking the concept. *Gender & Society, 19*(6), 829.

Conners, N. (Writer). (2008). *The 11th Hour* [film]. USA: Warner Home Video.

Cook, G. (2012). Do plants think? An interview with Daniel Chamovitz. *Scientific American*. Retrieved on October 26, 2013 from http://www.scientificamerican.com/article.cfm?id=do-plants-think-daniel-chamovitz

Corbett, C., Hill, C., & St. Rose, C. (2008). *Where the girls are: The facts about gender equity in education*. Washington, DC: American Association of University Women.

Cowperthwaite, G. (Writer). (2013). *Blackfish*. USA: Magnolia Home Entertainment.

Crittenden, J. (2002). *Democracy's midwife: An education in deliberation*. Lanham, MD: Lexington Books.

Cronon, W. (1983). *Changes in the land: Indians, colonists, and the ecology of New England* (1st ed.). New York, NY: Hill and Wang.

Cronon, W. (2003). *Changes in the land: Indians, colonists, and the ecology of New England* (1st rev. ed.). New York, NY: Hill and Wang.

Cullinham, J., & Raymont, P. (1993). *A long as the rivers flow film series*. Brooklyn, NY: Icarus Films.

Curry, M. (Writer). (2011). *If a tree falls: A story of the Earth Liberation Front*. USA: Oscilloscope Laboratories.

Danaher, K. (1994). *50 years is enough: The case against the World Bank and the International Monetary Fund*. Boston, MA: South End Press.

Darwin, C. (1859). *On the origin of species by means of natural selection, or, The preservation of favored races in the struggle for life*. London, UK: J. Murray.

Davenport, F. G. (1917). *European treaties bearing on the history of the United States and its dependencies to 1648*. Washington DC: Carnegie Institute of Washington.

DeCosta, M. (1974). The portrayal of Blacks in a Spanish medieval manuscript. *Negro History Bulletin, 74*(1), 193–196.

Dell'Amore, C. (December 14, 2009). Ten climate change "flagship" species named. Retrieved August 15, 2010, from National Geographic News http://news.nationalgeographic.com/news/2009/12/091214-copenhagen-climate-talks-species-list.html

DeMott, B. (1990). *The imperial middle: Why Americans can't think straight about class.* New York, NY: William Morrow & Co.

Descombs, V. (1980). *Modern French philosophy.* Cambridge, UK: Cambridge University Press.

Duncan, I. J. H. (2004). Welfare problems in poultry. In G. J. Benson, & B. E. Rollin (Eds.), *The well-being of farm animals: Problems and solutions.* Oxford, UK: Blackwell Publishing (307–324).

Eckholm, E. (2010). School suspensions lead to legal challenge. Retrieved September 14, 2010, from *The New York Times,* http://www.nytimes.com/2010/03/19/education/19suspend.html?_r

Ecologist, The. (1994). Whose common future: Reclaiming the commons. *Environment and Urbanization, 6,* 106–130.

Ecology Center, The (Producer). (Retrieved on July 8, 2010). Interview with Malik Yakini, Chairman, Detroit Black Community Food Security Network. Retrieved from http://www.channels.com/episodes/show/6349233/Malik-Yakini-Chairman-Detroit-Black-Community-Food-Security-Network#/ajax/feeds/show/16954/Ecology-Center

Edmundson, J. (1998). *A culture of reproduction.* Portland State University. Portland, OR.

Edmundson, J. and Martusewicz, R. A. (2013). "Putting our lives in order": Wendell Berry, EcoJustice, and a pedagogy of responsibility. In A. Kulnieks, K. Young, & D. Longboat (Eds.), *Contemporary studies in environmental and indigenous pedagogies: A curricula of stories and place* (pp. 171–184). Rotterdam, Netherlands: Sense Publishers.

Elsbree, W. (1939). *The American teacher: Evolution of a profession in a democracy.* Santa Barbara, CA: Greenwood Press.

Else, J. (Writer). (1992). *Eyes on the prize: America's civil rights years.* [television series]. Alexandria, VA: PBS.

Emecheta, B. (1976). *The bride price: A novel.* New York, NY: George Braziller.

Esteva, G., & Prakash, M. S. (1998). *Grassroots post-modernism: Remaking the soil of cultures.* New York, NY: Zed Books.

Everhart, R. (1983). *Reading, writing, and resistance: Adolescence and labor in a junior high school.* New York, NY: Routledge and Kegan Paul.

Fausto-Sterling, A. (2001). Gender, race, and nation: The comparative anatomy of "Hottentot" women in Europe, 1815–1817. In M. Ledermann, & I. Bartsch (Eds.), *The gender and science reader* (pp. 343–366). New York, NY: Routledge.

Ferrero, P. (2008). *Hopi: Songs of the fourth world.* Harriman, NY: New Day Films.

Fien, J. (1995). Teaching for a sustainable world: The environmental and development education project for teacher education. *Environmental Education Research, 1*(1), 21–33.

Fitzgerald, F. S. (1995). *The great Gatsby*. New York, NY: Scribner.

Fordham, S. (1996). *Blacked out: Dilemmas of race identity, and success at Capital High*. Chicago, IL: University of Chicago Press.

Fordham, S., & Ogbu, J. (1986). Black students' school success: Coping with the burden of acting white. *The Urban Review, 18*(3), 176–206.

Fowler, J. H., & Christakis, N. A. (2010). *Cooperative behavior cascades in human social networks*. Paper presented at the National Academy of Sciences of the United States of America (PNAS).

Frankenstein, E. & Gmelch, E. (1992). *A matter of respect*. New York, NY: New Day Films.

Fraser, N. (1997). *Justice Interruptus: Critical reflections on the "postsocialist" condition*. New York, NY: Routledge.

Friedman, T. L. (2005). *The world is flat: A brief history of the twenty-first century*. New York, NY: Farrar Straus & Giroux.

Fuson, R. (1992). *The logbook of Christopher Columbus*. Camden, ME: International Marine Publishing.

Garcia, D. K., & Butler, C. L. (Writers). (2004). *The future of food* [film]. Mill Valley, CA: Lily Films.

Gay, G. (2000). *Culturally responsive teaching: Theory, research, and practice*. New York, NY: Teachers College Press.

Gaylie, V. (2009). *The learning garden: Ecology, teaching, and transformation*. New York, NY: Peter Lang.

Goleman, D., Bennet, L., & Barlow, Z. (2012). *Ecoliterate: How educators are cultivating emotional, social, and ecological intelligence*. San Francisco, CA: Jossey-Bass.

Gonick, M. (2004). The mean girl crisis: Problematizing representations of girls' friendships. *Feminism & Psychology, 14*(3), 395.

Goodman, J. (1989). Education for a critical democracy. *Journal of Education*, 88–117.

Gould, S. J. (1996). *The mismeasure of man*. New York, NY: W.W. Norton.

Gould, S. J. (1998). On mental and visual geometry: Reply to Thomas Junker, Blumenbach's racial geometry. *Isis, 89*, 498–501.

Green, A., Carney, D., Pallin, D. J., Ngo, L. H., Raymond, K. L., Iezzoni, L. I., et al. (2003). Implicit bias among physicians and its prediction of thrombolysis decisions for black and white patients. *Journal of Experimental Social Psychology, 39*(4), 399–405.

Greenhouse, S. (2008). *The big squeeze: Tough times for the American worker*. New York, NY: Random House, Inc.

Greenwald, A. G., Oakes, M. A., & Hoffman, H. G. (2003). Targets of discrimination: Effects of race on responses to weapons holders. *Journal of Experimental Social Psychology, 39*, 399–405.

Griffen, S. (1995). *The eros of everyday life: Essays on ecology, gender, and society*. New York, NY: Doubleday.

Grim, J. A. (2001). *Indigenous traditions and ecology*. Cambridge, MA: Harvard University Press.

Gruenewald, D., & Smith, G. (2008). *Place-based education in the global age: Local diversity*. New York, NY: Lawrence Erlbaum Associates, Taylor & Francis Group.

Guggenheim, D. (Writer), Guggenheim, D., Weyermann, D., Skoll, J., Ivers, J. D., & Lennard, L. (Producers). (2006). *An inconvenient truth* [film]. USA: Paramount Vantage.

Guinier, L. (1995). *The tyranny of the majority: Fundamental fairness in representative democracy*. New York, NY: Free Press.

Haberman, M. (1994). The pedagogy of poverty versus good teaching. *Phi Delta Kappan, 73*(4), 75–90.

Hall, C. (2014). Survey: Detroit's stray dog problem not as bad as rescue group claims. *Detroit Free Press*, January 20, 2014.

Hansen, J. (2009). *Storms of my grandchildren: The truth about the coming climate catastrophe and our last chance to save humanity*. New York, NY: Bloomsbury.

Hardin, G. (1968). The tragedy of the commons. *Science, 162*, 1243–1248.

Harris, S., Iossa, G., & Soulsbury, C. D. (2006). *A review of the welfare of wild animals in circus*. Bristol, England: School of Biological Sciences, University of Bristol.

Harrod, H. L. (2000). *The animals came dancing: Native American sacred ecology and animal kinship*. Tucson, AZ: The University of Arizona Press.

Harvey, D. (2005). *A brief history of neoliberalism*. New York, NY: Oxford University Press.

Hawken, P. (2007). *Blessed unrest: How the largest movement in the world came into being, and why no one saw it coming*. New York, NY: Viking.

Hayden, J. (Writer). (1998). *Children in America's schools*. Columbia, SC: ETV Network.

Henderson, J., & Hursh, D. (2014). Economics and education for human flourishing: Wendell Berry and the oikonomic alternative to neoliberalism. *Educational Studies, 50*(2), 167–186.

Herrnstein, R. J., & Murray, C. (1994). *The bell curve: Intelligence and class structure in American life*. New York, NY: Free Press.

Hoffman, N. (1981). *Woman's "true" profession: Voices from the history of teaching*. New York, NY: McGraw Hill.

hooks, b. (2000). *Where we stand: Class matters*. New York, NY: Routledge.

Hribal, J. (2008). The story and Ken Allen and Kumang: Orangutans, resistance and the zoo. *Counterpunch*. Retrieved on January 12, 2014 from http://www.counterpunch.org/2008/12/16/orangutans-resistance-and-the-zoo/

Hribal, J. (2010). *Fear of the animal planet: The hidden history of animal resistance*. Petrolia, CA: CounterPunch.

Huntington, E. (1912). Geographic environment and the Japanese character. *Journal of Race and Development, 2*(3), 256–281.

Hursh, D. (2007). Assessing No Child Left Behind and the rise of neoliberal education policies. *American Educational Research Journal, 44*, 493–518.

Hursh, D. (2008). *High-stakes testing and the decline of teaching and learning: The real crisis in education*. Lanham, MD: Rowman & Littlefield.

IFG. (2003). The World Trade Organization vs. the environment, public health and human rights. Retrieved September 13, 2010, from International Forum on Globalization www.ifg.org/pdf/cancun/issues-WTOvsEnv.pdf

Ignatiev, N. (1995). *How the Irish became white*. New York, NY: Routledge.

Illich, I. (1992). *In the mirror of the past: Lectures and addresses 1978–1990*. New York, NY: Marion Boyars.

Imhoff, D. (2010). *CAFO: The tragedy of industrial animal factories*. San Rafael, CA: Earth Aware Press.

Irvine, J. J. (2003). *Educating teachers for diversity: Seeing with a cultural eye*. New York, NY: Teachers College Press.

IPPC. (2007). *IPCC Fourth Assessment Report: Climate Change 2007*. Retrieved September 20, 2013, from Intergovernmental Panel on Climate Change http://www.ipcc.ch/publications_and_data/ar4/syr/en/contents.html

IPPC. (2013). *IPCC Fifth Assessment Report: Climate Change 2013*. Retrieved January 9, 2014, from Intergovernmental Panel on Climate http://www.climatechange2013.org/images/report/WG1AR5_ALL_FINAL.pdf

IUCN. (2009). *Red list: Species and climate change: More than just the polar bear*. Gland, Switzerland: IUCN.

Jensen, D. (2006a). *Endgame, volume I: The problem of civilization*. New York, NY: Seven Stories Press.

Jensen, D. (2006b). *Endgame, volume II: Resistance*. New York, NY: Seven Stories Press.

Jensen, D. (2009). Forget shorter showers: Why personal change does not equal political change. *Orion Magazine*. Retrieved from: http://www.orionmagazine.org/index.php/articles/article/4801/

Jensen, D., & Tweedy-Holmes, K. (2007). *Thought to exist in the wild: Awakening from the nightmare of zoos*. Santa Cruz, CA: No Voice Unheard.

Jhally, S. (Director), Katz, J., & Earp, K. (Writers). (2002). *Tough guise: Violence, media, and the crisis in masculinity*. Northampton, MA: Media Education Foundation.

Kahn, R. (2010). *Critical pedagogy, ecoliteracy and planetary crisis: The ecopedagogy movement*. New York, NY: Peter Lang.

Kahneman, D., Krueger, A., Schkade, D., Schwartz, N., & Stone, A. (2006). Would you be happier if you were richer? A focusing illusion. *Science, 312*(5782), 1908–1910.

Katz, J. (2006). *The macho paradox: Why some men hurt women and how all men can help*. Naperville, IL: Sourcebooks.

Kaufman, A. (2013). 'Blackfish' gives Pixar second thoughts on 'Finding Dory' plot. *Los Angeles Times*. Retrieved on January 10, 2013 from http://www.latimes.com/entertainment/movies/moviesnow/la-et-mn-blackfish-seaworld-finding-dory-pixar-20130808,0,7662071.story#axzz2qcyHHNLH

Kaufman, M. (1994a). *Cracking the armour: Power, pain and the lives of men*. New York, NY: Penguin.

Kaufman, M. (1994b). Men, feminism, and men's contradictory experiences of power. In H. Brod & M. Kaufman (Eds.), *Theorizing masculinities* (pp. 142–163). Thousand Oaks, CA: Sage.

Kenmmerer, L. (Ed). (2011). *Sister species: Women, animals and social justice*. Urbana, IL: University of Illinois Press.

Kenward, B., Rutz, C., Weir, A., & Kacelnik, A. (2006). Development of tool use in New Caledonian crows: Inherited action patterns and social influence. *Animal Behaviour, 72*, 1329–1343.

Khor, M. (2002). Commentary: Conflicting paradigms. In J. Cavanagh & J. Mander (Eds.), *Alternatives to economic globalization: A better world is possible* (pp. 13–14). San Francisco, CA: Berrett-Koehler Publishers, Inc.

Khor, M. (2009). Martin Khor on the global economic meltdown (Interview). Retrieved September 14, 2010, from DemocracyNOW! http://www.democracynow.org/2009/2/17/martin_khor_on_the_global_economic

Kimmel, M. S. (2000). *The gendered society.* New York, NY: Oxford University Press.

Kingsolver, B. (2007). *Animal, vegetable, miracle.* New York, NY: HarperCollins Publishers.

Klipp, G. (unpublished). *The price of bigotry in school: PreK-12. Glossary of terms.* Ann Arbor, MI: Office of Equity and Diversity Services, HR/AA, University of Michigan.

Korten, F. (2010). Common(s) sense wins one. *Yes! Magazine*, Spring, 12–15.

Kozol, J. (1991). *Savage inequalities: Children in America's schools.* New York, NY: Harper Perennial.

Kuhn, A. (1947). *The mother's role in childhood education: New England concepts, 1830–1860.* New Haven, CT: Yale University Press.

Ladson-Billings, G. (1994). *The dreamkeepers: Successful teachers of African American children.* San Francisco, CA: Jossey-Bass.

Ladson-Billings, G. (2004). Landing on the wrong note: The price we paid for *Brown. Educational Researcher, 33*(7), 3–13.

LaDuke, W. (1992). Minobimaatisiiwin: The good life. *Cultural Survival Quarterly, 4*(Winter), 6–71.

LaDuke, W. (2008). Protecting the culture and genetics of wild rice. In M. K. Nelson (Ed.), *Original instructions: Indigenous teachings for a sustainable future* (pp. 126–136). Rochester, VT: Bear & Company.

Lakoff, G., & Johnson, M. (2003). *Metaphors we live by.* Chicago, IL: University of Chicago Press.

Latour, B. (1987). *Science in action: How to follow scientists and engineers through society.* Milton Keynes, UK: Open University Press.

Lawrence, C. (1980). One more river to cross. Recognizing the real injury in *Brown*: A prerequisite to shaping new remedies. In D. Bell (Ed.), *Shades of Brown: New perspectives on school desegregation* (pp. 48–68). New York, NY: Teachers College Press.

Le Quéré, C., et al. (2013). Global carbon budget 2013. *Earth System Science Data, 6*(2), 689–760.

Lee, V., & Burkam, D. (2002). *Inequality at the starting gate: Social background differences in achievement as children begin school.* Washington, DC: Economic Policy Institute.

Leonhardt, D. (2007). Income Inequality. Retrieved July 5, 2009, from *The New York Times* http://topics.nytimes.com/top/reference/timestopics/subjects/i/income/income_inequality/index.html

Lesiak, C. (Writer). (1992). *In the white man's image* [film]. USA: PBS.

Lipkin, A. (2004). *Beyond Diversity Day: A Q & A on gay and lesbian issues in schools.* Lanham, MD: Rowman and Littlefield.

Lipschutz, M. & Rosenblatt R. (2005). *The education of Shelby Knox: Sex, lies and education.* New York, NY: Cine Qua Non InCite Pictures.

Louv, R. (2006). *Last child left in the woods: Saving our children from nature-deficit disorder.* Chapel Hill, NC: Algonquin Books of Chapel Hill.

Lydersen, K. (2003). Bottled water blues: Battling Nestle in Michigan. Retrieved January 31, 2010, from AlterNet http://www.alternet.org/story/16044

Lyons, O. (2008). Listening to natural law. In M. K. Nelson (Ed.), *Original instructions: Indigenous teachings for a sustainable future* (pp. 22–25). Rochester, VT: Bear & Company.

Mac an Ghaill, M. (1994). *The making of men: Masculinities, sexualities and schooling.* Philadelphia, PA: Open University Press Buckingham.

Macas, L. (2006). Amautawasi Quechuan University. In J. Mander & V. Tauli-Corpuz (Eds.), *Paradigm wars: Indigenous people's resistance to globalization* (pp. 41–45). San Francisco, CA: Sierra Club Books.

Mahaffy, J. P. (2005). *Decartes* (Elibron Classics Replica Edition). Boston, MA: Adamant Media Corporation.

Mancuso, S. (July 2010). TED talk: *The roots of plant intelligence.* http://www.ted.com/talks/stefano_mancuso_the_roots_of_plant_intelligence.html

Mander, J. (1996). Technologies of globalization. In J. Mander & E. Goldsmith (Eds.), *The case against the global economy: And for a turn toward the local.* (pp. 344–359) San Francisco, CA: Sierra Club Books.

Mander, J., & Goldsmith, E. (1996). *The case against the global economy: And for a turn toward the local.* San Francisco, CA: Sierra Club Books.

Mander, J., & Tauli-Corpuz, V. (2006). *Paradigm wars: Indigenous people's resistance to globalization.* San Francisco, CA: Sierra Club Books.

Marcos, S. (2001). The fourth world war has begun. *Nepantla: Views from the South, 2*(3), 559–572.

Martin, J. W. (1999). *The land looks after us: A history of Native American religion.* New York, NY: Oxford University Press.

Martusewicz, R. (1994). Guardians of childhood. In R. Martusewicz & W. Reynolds (Eds.), *Inside out: Contemporary critical perspectives in education* (pp. 168–182). Mahwah, NJ: Lawrence Erlbaum.

Martusewicz, R. (2009). Toward a "collaborative intelligence": Revitalizing cultural and ecological commons in Detroit. In M. McKenzie, P. Hart, H. Bai, & B. Jickling (Eds.), *Fields of green: Restorying culture, environment, and education* (pp. 253–270). Creskill, NJ: Hampton Press, Inc.

Martusewicz, R. (2013). Toward an anti-centric ecological culture: Bringing a critical ecofeminist analysis to ecojustice education. In A. Kulnieks, K. Young, & D. Longboat (Eds.), *Contemporary studies in environmental and Indigenous pedagogies: A curricula of stories and place* (pp. 259–272). Rotterdam, Netherlands: Sense Publishers.

Martusewicz, R., & Edmundson, J. (2005). Social foundations as pedagogies of responsibility and eco-ethical commitment. In D. W. Butin (Ed.), *Teaching social foundations of education: Contexts, theories, and issues* (pp. 71–92). Mahwah, NJ: Lawrence Erlbaum.

McAnallen, S. (Writer/Director). (2012). *The superior human?* [film]. Australia: Ultraventus.

McBay, A., Keith, L., & Jensen, D. (2011). *Deep green resistance: Strategy to save the planet.* New York, NY: Seven Stories Press.

McIntosh, P. (1988). *White privilege and male privilege: A personal account of coming to see correspondences through work in women's studies.* Wellesley, MA: Wellesley College Center for Research on Women.

McIntosh, P. (1998) White privilege: Unpacking the invisible knapsack. In P. S. Rothenberg (Ed.), *Race, class, and gender in the United States: An integrated study.* New York, NY: St Martin's Press.

McCormick, T. (2007). Strong women teachers: Their struggles and strategies for gender equity. In D. Sadker & E Silber, (Eds.), *Gender in the classroom* (pp. 1–32). Mahwah, NJ: Lawrence Erlbaum.

McKechnie, J. L. (1983). *Webster's unabridged dictionary*. Cleveland, OH: Dorset & Baber.

McKibben, B. (2007). *Deep economy: The wealth of communities and the durable future* (1st ed.). New York, NY: Times Books.

Menendez, R., Musca, T., & Olmos, E. (Writers). (1988). *Stand and deliver* [film]. USA: Warner Brothers.

Merchant, C. (1983). *The death of nature: Women, ecology, and the scientific revolution*. San Francisco, CA: Harper Collins.

Merchant, C. (1990). *The death of nature: Women, ecology, and the scientific revolution*. San Francisco, CA: Harper Collins.

Merchant, C. (1998) The death of nature. In M. E. Zimmerman, J. Baird Callicott et al. (Eds.), *Environmental philosophy: From animal rights to radical ecology* (pp. 325–344). Upper Saddle River, NJ: Prentice Hall.

Merton, L., & Dater, A. (2008). *Taking root: The vision of Wangari Maathai*. Marlboro, VT: Marlboro Productions.

Meyer, E. (2010). *Gender and diversity in schools*. New York, NY: Springer

Miller, R. (1991). *New directions in education: Selections from Holistic Education Review*. Brandon, VT: Holistic Education Press.

Mohawk, J. (2008). The art of thriving in place. In M. K. Nelson (Ed.), *Original instructions: Indigenous teachings for a sustainable future* (pp. 126–136). Rochester, VT: Bear & Company.

Monroe, M. (Writer), Psihoyos, L. (Director), Hambleton, C., Stevens, F., Clark, J., Ahnemann, O., & Pesemn, P. D. (Producer). (2009). *The cove*. USA: Lions Gate.

Monson, S. (Writer), Harrelson, B., Raz, B. C., Visram, N., Q, M., & White, P. (Producers). (2005). *Earthlings*. USA: Nation Earth.

Moore, M. (2010). *Capitalism: A love story*. Beverly Hills, CA: Anchor Bay Entertainment.

Morgan, F., Murphy, E. P., & Quinn, M. (Writers). (2006). *The power of community: How Cuba survived peak oil* [film]. Yellow Springs, OH: Community Service, Inc.

Muska, S., & Olafsdottir, G. (Writers), Muska, S., &. Dekrone, J. (Producers) (2000). *The Brandon Teena Story* [film]. USA: Docurama.

Nasaw, D. (1979). *Schooled to order: A social history of public schooling in the United States*. New York, NY: Oxford University Press.

National Geographic News. (July 14 2007). Global warming fast facts. Retrieved September 12, 2010 from National Geographic http://news.nationalgeographic.com/news/pf/73625218.html

NCES. (2009). Table A-28-1. Number and percentage of students who were suspended and expelled from public elementary and secondary schools, by sex, and race/ethnicity: 2002, 2004, and 2006. Retrieved September 14, 2010 from http://nces.ed.gov/programs/coe/2009/section4/table-sdi-1.asp.

NCES. (2009). Table 16-1. White–Black and White–Hispanic gaps in average reading and mathematics scores, by grade: various years, 1990–2007. Retrieved September 15, 2010, from National Center for Educational Statistics http://nces.ed.gov/programs/coe/2008/section2/table.asp?tableID=884.

NCES. (2009). Table A-10-2. Average reading scale scores of 8th-grade students, by selected student characteristics: selected years, 1992–2009. Retrieved September 14, 2010, from National Center for Educational Statistics http://nces.ed.gov/programs/coe/2010/section2/table-rgp-2.asp.

NCES. (2009). Table A-10-1. Average reading scale scores of 4th-grade students, by selected student characteristics: selected years, 1992–2009. Retrieved September 14, 2010, from National Center for Educational Statistics http://nces.ed.gov/programs/coe/2010/section2/table-rgp-1.asp.

NCES. (2009). Table A-12-2. Average mathematics scale scores of 8th-grade students, by selected student characteristics: selected years, 1990–2009. Retrieved September 15, 2010, from National Center for Educational Statistics http://nces.ed.gov/programs/coe/2010/section2/table-mgp-2.asp.

NCES. (2009). Table A-12-1. Average mathematics scale scores of 4th-grade students, by selected student characteristics: selected years, 1990–2009. Retrieved September 14, 2010, from National Center for Educational Statistics http://nces.ed.gov/programs/coe/2010/section2/table-mgp-1.asp.

Nelson, M. K. (2008). *Original Instructions: Indigenous teachings for a sustainable future*. Rochester, VT: Bear & Company.

Nettle, D., & Romaine, S. (2000). *Vanishing voices: The extinction of the world's languages*. New York, NY: Oxford University Press.

New York Times, The. (March 21, 2010). No wallet necessary. *New York Times, Business section*. Retrieved on September 12, 2010 from *The New York Times*, http://www.nytimes.com/slideshow/2010/03/21/business/20100321_BACK-DROP_index.html

Newcomb, S. (2008). *Pagans in the promised land: Decoding the doctrine of Christian discovery*. Golden, CO: Fulcrum Publishing.

Nieto, S. (1996). *Affirming diversity: The sociopolitical context of multicultural education*. White Plains, NY: Longman Publishers.

Noguera, P. (2008). *The trouble with Black boys: And other reflections on race, equity, and the future of public education*. San Francisco, CA: Jossey-Bass Inc Pub.

Norberg-Hodge, H. (1991). *Ancient futures: Learning from Ladakh*. San Francisco, CA: Sierra Club Books.

Norberg-Hodge, H., Gorelick, S., & Page, J. (Writers). (forthcoming). *The economics of happiness* [film]. UK: International Society for Ecology and Culture.

Norberg-Hodge, H., Merrifield, T., Gorelick, S., & ISEC. (2002). Cuban organic agriculture. In J. Cavanagh & J. Mander (Eds.), *Alternatives to economic globalization: A better world is possible* (pp. 186–187). San Francisco, CA: Berrett-Koehler Publishers, Inc.

Oakes, J. (1985). *Keeping track: How schools structure inequality*. New Haven, CT: Yale University Press.

Oakes, J. (2005). *Keeping track: How schools structure inequality* (2nd edn.). New Haven, CT: Yale University Press.

O'Connor, J. (2013). Canada's fur trade is booming again—thanks to demand from China's new capitalists. *National Post*, June 25, 2013.

Orenstein, P. (1994). *Schoolgirls: Young women, self-esteem, and the confidence gap* (1st ed.). New York, NY: Doubleday.

Orzechowski, S., & Sepielli, P. (2003). Net worth and asset ownership of households: 1998 and 2000. Washington, DC: U.S. Census Bureau.

Owen, D. (1985). *None of the above: Behind the myth of scholastic aptitude*. Boston, MA: Houghton Mifflin.

Page, J., Beeman, C., Norberg-Hodge, H., & Walton, E. (Writers). (1993). *Ancient futures: Learning from Ladakh.* UK: International Society for Ecology and Culture.

Painter, N. I. (2003). *Why white people are called "Caucasian."* Paper presented at the Slavery and the Construction of Race at the Fifth Annual Gilder Lehrman Center International Conference, New Have, CT.

Pascoe, C. J. (2007). *Dude, you're a fag.* Berkeley, CA: University of California Press.

Payne, R. (2001). *A framework for understanding poverty.* Highlands, TX: aha! Process, Inc.

PBS. (2004). Slavery and the making of America: Education, arts, and culture. In *Slavery and the making of America* [series]. Retrieved August 3, 2009, from http://www.pbs.org/wnet/slavery/experience/education/history2.html

Pelo, A. (2008). *Rethinking early childhood education.* Milwaukee, WI: Rethinking Schools.

Person-Lynn, K. (2006). Afrikan involvement in the Atlantic slave trade. Retrieved July 29, 2010, from Africa Within http://www.africawithin.com/kwaku/afrikan_involvement.htm

Petrini, C. (2007). *Slow food nation: Why our food should be good, clean, and fair.* New York, NY: Rizzoli.

Phang, J. (2013). Concentrated animal feeding operations. South Orange, NJ: Seton Hall Law School eRepository. Student Scholarship, 5-1-2013.

Plumwood, V. (1993). *Feminism and the mastery of nature.* New York, NY: Routledge.

Plumwood, V. (1996). Being prey. *Terra Nova, 1*(3).

Plumwood, V. (2002). *Environmental culture: The ecological crisis of reason.* New York, NY: Routledge.

Polakow, V. (2000). *The public assault on America's children: Poverty, violence, and juvenile injustice.* New York, NY: Teachers College Press.

Pollan, M. (2006). *The omnivore's dilemma: A natural history of four meals.* New York, NY: Penguin Press.

Poppenk, M., & Poppenk, M. (Writers). (2009). *Grown in Detroit* [film]. Netherlands/USA: filmmij.

Powers, A. (2004). An evaluation of four place-based education programs. *Journal of Environmental Education, 35*(4).

Prakash, M. S. (1994). What are people for? Wendell Berry on education, ecology, culture. *Educational Theory*, Spring, 135–157.

Prakash, M. S. (2010). Commons, common sense, and community collaboration in hard times. *PowerPlay: A Journal of Educational Justice, 2, 2.*

Prakash, M. S., & Esteva, G. (1998). *Escaping education: Living as learning within grassroots cultures.* New York, NY: Peter Lang.

Putnam, R. D. (2000). *Bowling alone: The collapse and revival of American community.* New York, NY: Simon & Schuster.

Quinn, D. (1992). *Ishmael.* New York, NY: Bantam/Turner Book.

Ramsey, P. (2010). *Bilingual public schooling in the United States: A history of America's "polyglot boardinghouse."* New York, NY: Palgrave/Macmillan.

Ramsey, P. (2012). *The bilingual school in the United States: A documentary history.* Charlotte, NC: Information Age Publishing.

Regan, T. & Rowe, M. (2003). What the Nobel committee also failed to note. December 19, 2003.

Remafedi, G. (1994). *Death by denial: A study of suicide in gay and lesbian teenagers*. Boston, MA: Alyson Publications.

Rich, A. (1980). Compulsory heterosexuality and lesbian existence. *Signs, 5*(4), 631–660.

Rivera, J. V. (1998). Andean peasant agriculture: Nurturing a diversity of life in the Chacra. In F. Apffel-Marglin & PRATEC (Eds.), *The spirit of regeneration: Andean culture confronting Western notions of development* (pp. 51–88). New York, NY: Zed Books Ltd.

Rivera, J. V. (2008). Dancing for the Apus: Andean food and farming. In M. K. Nelson (Ed.), *Original instructions: Indigenous teachings for a sustainable future* (pp. 196–200). Rochester, VT: Bear & Company.

Robbins, C. (2005). Zero tolerance and the politics of racial injustice. *The Journal of Negro Education, 74*(1), 2–17.

Robbins, C. (2010). Tased and confused: From social exclusion to shock in the war on youth. In K. J. Saltman & D. A. Gabbard (Eds.), *Education as enforcement: The militarization and corporatization of schools* (pp. 114–129). New York, NY: Routledge.

Rosset, P., & Borque, M. (2002). Lessons of Cuban resistance. In F. Funes, L. Garcia, M. Bourque, N. Perez, & P. Rosset (Eds.), *Sustainable agriculture and resistance: Transforming food production in Cuba*. Oakland, CA: Food First Books.

Ryan, W. (1976). *Blaming the victim*. New York, NY: Vintage Books.

Ryder, R. (2000). *Animal revolution: Changing attitudes toward speciesism*. New York, NY: Bloomsbury Academic.

Sachs, W. (1992). *The Development dictionary: A guide to knowledge as power*. Atlantic Highlands, NJ: Zed Books.

Sadasivan, L. (2001). A mother speaks out *Rethinking our classroom: Teaching for equity and justice* (Vol. 2). Milwaukee, WI: Rethinking Schools Ltd.

Sadker, D., Sadker, M., & Zittleman, K. (2009). *Still failing at fairness: How gender bias cheats boys and girls in school and what we can do about it*. New York, NY: Scribners.

Sadker, M., & Sadker, D. (1989). Sexism in the schoolroom of the 80s. In J. Ballantine (Ed.), *Schools and society* (pp. 358–362). Palo Alto, CA: Mayfield Publishing.

Sadker, M., & Sadker, D. M. (1994). *Failing at fairness: How America's schools cheat girls*. New York, NY: C. Scribner's Sons.

Scientific Veterinary Committee Report, Animal Welfare Section (1997). *The welfare of intensively kept pigs*. European Commission, 95, 1997, retrieved on December 2, 2013, from http://ec.europa.eu/food/fs/sc/oldcomm4/out17_en.html.

Scott, J., & Leonhardt, D. (2005). Shadowy lines that still divide. Retrieved on July 7, 2014 from http://isite.lps.org/akabour/web/documents/ShadowyLines ThatStillDivide-NewYorkTimes.pdf.

Segura-Mora, A. (2008). What color is beautiful? In A. Pelo (Ed.), *Rethinking early childhood education*. Milwaukee, WI: Rethinking Schools.

Sennett, R., & Cobb, J. (1972). *The hidden injuries of class*. New York, NY: Vintage Books.

Shah, N. (2014). *The King Learning Garden: Starting and sustaining an ecologically responsive school garden.* Paper presented at the 3rd Annual EcoJustice and Activism Conference. Ypsilanti, Michigan.

Shiva, V. (1993). *Monocultures of the mind: Perspectives on biodiversity and biotechnology.* Atlantic Highlands, NJ: Zed Books.

Shiva, V. (1997). *Biopiracy.* Cambridge, MA: South End Press.

Shiva, V. (2002). *Water wars: Pollution, profits and privatization.* Cambridge, MA: South End Press.

Shiva, V. (2005). *Earth democracy: Justice, sustainability, and peace.* Cambridge, MA: South End Press.

Shiva, V., & Holla-Bhar, R. (1996). Piracy by patent: The case of the Neem tree. In J. Mander & E. Goldsmith (Eds.), *The case against the global economy: And for a turn toward the local* (pp. 146–159). San Francisco, CA: Sierra Club Books.

Shor, I. (1986). *Culture wars: School and society in the conservative restoration, 1969–1984.* New York, NY: Routledge & Kegan Paul Books Ltd.

Shorrocks, A., & Davies, J. (2013). Credit Suisse Global Wealth Report 2013. Retrieved on December 10, 2013, from Credit Suisse https://publications.credit-suisse.com/

Siddle-Walker, V. (1996). *Their highest potential: An African American school community in the segregated South.* Chapel Hill, NC: The University of North Carolina Press.

Slobodchikoff, C. N., Perla, B., & Verdoli, J. (2009). *Prairie dogs: Communication and community in an animal society.* Cambridge, MA: Harvard University Press.

Smith, L. T. (1999). *Decolonizing methodologies: Research and indigenous peoples.* New York, NY: Zed books.

Smith, P. K. (2011). The prom as a spectacle of heteronormativity. In D. Carlson & D. L. Roseboro (Eds.), *The sexuality curriculum: Youth culture, popular culture, and democratic sexuality in education* (pp. 156–170). New York, NY: Peter Lang.

Snyder, G. (1990). *The practice of the wild: Essays.* San Francisco, CA: North Point Press.

Sobel, D. (2004). *Place-based education: Connecting classrooms & communities.* Great Barrington, MA: The Orion Society.

Socha, K. & Blum, S. (2013). *Confronting animal exploitation: Grassroots essays on liberation and veganism.* Jefferson, NC: McFarland and Company.

Spring, J. (1994a). *American school, 1642–1990.* New York, NY: McGraw Hill.

Spring, J. (1994b). *Deculturalization and the struggle for equality: A brief history of the education of dominated cultures.* Boston, MA: McGraw Hill Higher Education.

Spring, J. (2002). *American education.* New York, NY: McGraw-Hill Companies.

Spring, J. (2009). *Globalization of education: An introduction.* New York, NY: Routledge.

Spring, J. (2010). *American education.* New York, NY: MacGraw-Hill Companies.

Spring, J. H. (1989). *The sorting machine revisted: National educational policy since 1945.* New York, NY: Longman.

Stamets, P. (2005). *Mycelium running: How mushrooms can help save the world.* Berkeley, CA: Ten Speed Press.

Stein, N., & Sjostrom, L. (1994). Flirting vs. sexual harassment: Teaching the difference. In B. Bigelow, L. Christianson, S. Karp, B. Miner & B. Peterson (Eds.), *Rethinking our classrooms* (Vol. 1, pp. 106–107). Milwaukee, WI: Rethinking Schools.

Sterling, S. (2001). *Sustainable education: Re-visioning learning and change.* Schumacher briefings. Bristol, UK: Schumacher CREATE Environment Centre.

Sue, D. W., Capodilupo, C. M., Torino, G., Bucceri, J., Holder, A., Nadal, K., et al. (2007). Racial microaggressions in everday life. *American Psychologist, 62*(4), 271–286.

Sugg, R. (1978). *Motherteacher: The feminization of American education.* Charolottesville, VA: University Press of Virginia.

Sugrue, T. J. (2005). *The origins of the urban crisis: Race and inequality in post-war Detroit.* Princteton, NJ: Princeton University Press.

Suicide Prevention Resource Center. (2008). *Suicide risk and prevention for lesbian, gay, bisexual, and transgender youth.* Newton, MA: Suicide Prevention Resource Center Education Development Center.

Sundberg, A., & Stern, R. (2008). *The end of America.* United States: IndiePix Films.

Takaki, R. (1993). *A different mirror: A History of multicultural America.* Boston, MA: Little, Brown.

Tanenbaum, L. (1999). *Slut!: Growing up female with a bad reputation.* New York, NY: Seven Stories Press.

Tannock, G. W. (1995). *Normal microflora: An introduction to microbes inhabiting the human body.* London, UK: Chapman and Hall.

Taylor, S. (1991). *Tacquamenon country: A look at its past.* Ann Arbor, MI: Historical Society of Michigan.

Tenorio, R. (2008). Raising issues of race with young children. In A. Pelo (Ed.), *Rethinking early childhood education* (pp. 17–22). Milwaukee, WI: Rethinking Schools.

Thomas, M. C. (1908). Present tendencies in women's college and university education. *Publications of the Association of Collegiate Alumnae, Series III, 17*(February), 45–62.

Thorp, L. (2006). *The pull of the Earth: Participatory ethnography in the school garden.* Lanham, MD: Rowman & Littlefield Publishers, Inc.

Tunde, O. (2000). Slave trade as root of contemporary African crises. From Africa Economic Analysis, http://www.afbis.com/analysis/slave.htm

Tuso, P. J., Ismail, M. H., Ha, B. P., & Bartolotto, C. (2013). Nutritional update for physicians: Plant-based diets. *The Pemanente Journal, 17*(2), 61–66.

Twine, R. (2010). *Animals as biotechnology: Ethics, sustainability and critical animal studies.* London, UK: Earthscan Ltd.

Twine, R. (2012). Revealing the "animal-industrial complex"—A concept & method for critical animal studies? *Journal for Critical Animal Studies, 10*(1), 12–39.

UN. (2005). *Human development report 2005: International cooperation at a crossroads.* New York, NY: United Nations.

UNDP. (2005). *The state of human development.* New York, NY: United Nations.

Unks, G. (1995). Thinking about the gay teen. In G. Unks (Ed.), *The gay teen* (pp. 3–12). New York, NY: Routledge.

U.S. Department of Energy Office of Science. (August 31 2007). Human genome project information: Minorities, race, and genomics. Washington, DC: U.S. Department of Energy.

Valencia, R. R. (1997). *The evolution of deficit thinking: Educational thought and practice.* London: Falmer Press.

Valli, L. (1986). *Becoming clerical workers.* New York, NY: Routledge.

Van Gelder, S. R., & Shiva, V. (2003). Earth democracy: An interview with Vandana Shiva. *Yes! Magazine,* Winter.

Vanneman, A., Hamilton, L., Anderson, J. B., & Rahman, T. (2009). Achievement gaps: How black and white students in public schools perform in mathematics and reading on the national assessment of educational progress. Washington, DC: National Center for Education Statistics.

Walker, C. (1996). *Trinkets and beads.* Brooklyn, NY: Icarus Films.

Walsh, M. (1977). *"Doctors wanted, no women need apply": Sexual barriers in the medical profession, 1835–1975.* New Haven, CT: Yale University Press.

Warren, K. (1998). The power and the promise of ecological feminism. In M. E. Zimmerman, J. Baird Callicott et al. (Eds.), *Environmental philosophy: From animal rights to radical ecology* (pp. 325–344). Upper Saddle River, NJ: Prentice Hall.

Wasilevich, E. A., Lyon-Callo, S., Rafferty, A., & Dombkowski, K. (2008). Detroit—The epicenter of asthma burden. In *Epidemiology of Asthma in Michigan.* Bureau of Epidemiology, Michigan Department of Community Health.

Watson, C. (2003). Sell the rain: How the privatization of water caused riots in Cochabamba, Bolivia. Retrieved January 31, 2010, from CBC Radio.

Weis, L. (1990). *Working class without work: High school students in a de-industrializing economy.* New York, NY: Routledge.

Weis, L. (2004). *Class reunion: The remaking of the American white working class.* New York, NY: Routledge.

West, C. (1993). *Keeping faith: Philosophy and race in America.* New York, NY: Routledge.

Williams, D. R., & Taylor, S. (1999). From margin to center: Initiation and development of an environmental school from the ground up. In G. Smith & D. R. Williams (Eds.), *Ecological education in action* (pp. 79–102). Albany, NY: SUNY Press.

Williams, R. (1983). *Culture and society, 1780–1950.* New York, NY: Columbia University Press.

Willis, P. (1977). *Learning to labor: How working class lads get working class jobs.* New York, NY: Columbia University Press.

WinklerPrins, A. M. G. A., & de Souza, P. (2005). Surviving the city: Home gardens and the economy of affection in the Brazilian Amazon. *Journal of Latin American Geography,* 4(1), 107–126.

Woody, T. (1929). *A history of women's education in the United States.* New York, NY: The Science Press.

Zimmerman, M.E., Callicott, J. B., et al. (Eds.), *Environmental philosophy: From animal rights to radical ecology.* Upper Saddle River, NJ: Prentice Hall.

Zinn, H. (1980). *A people's history of the United States.* New York, NY: Harper.

Index

Note: Page entries in *italics* refer to boxes and illustrations